Learning Science
A Singular Plural Perspective

NEW DIRECTIONS IN MATHEMATICS AND SCIENCE EDUCATION
Volume 1

Series Editors
Wolff-Michael Roth
University of Victoria, Canada
Lieven Verschaffel
University of Leuven, Belgium

Editorial Board
Angie Calabrese-Barton, Teachers College, New York, USA
Pauline Chinn, University of Hawaii, USA
Brian Greer, Portland State University, USA
Giyoo Hatano, University of the Air, Chiba, Japan
Terezinha Nunes, University of Oxford, UK
Peter Taylor, Curtin University, Perth, Australia
Dina Tirosh, Tel Aviv University, Israel
Manuela Welzel, University of Education, Heidelberg, Germany

Scope

Mathematics and science education are in a state of change. Received models of teaching, curriculum, and researching in the two fields are adopting and developing new ways of thinking about how people of all ages know, learn, and develop. The recent literature in both fields includes contributions focusing on issues and using theoretical frames that were unthinkable a decade ago. For example, we see an increase in the use of conceptual and methodological tools from anthropology and semiotics to understand how different forms of knowledge are interconnected, how students learn, how textbooks are written, etcetera. Science and mathematics educators also have turned to issues such as identity and emotion as salient to the way in which people of all ages display and develop knowledge and skills. And they use dialectical or phenomenological approaches to answer ever arising questions about learning and development in science and mathematics.

The purpose of this series is to encourage the publication of books that are close to the cutting edge of both fields. The series aims at becoming a leader in providing refreshing and bold new work—rather than out-of-date reproductions of past states of the art—shaping both fields more than reproducing them, thereby closing the traditional gap that exists between journal articles and books in terms of their salience about what is new. The series is intended not only to foster books concerned with knowing, learning, and teaching in school but also with doing and learning mathematics and science across the whole lifespan (e.g., science in kindergarten; mathematics at work); and it is to be a vehicle for publishing books that fall between the two domains—such as when scientists learn about graphs and graphing as part of their work.

Learning Science
A Singular Plural Perspective

Wolff-Michael Roth

Applied Cognitive Science, University of Victoria, Canada

SENSE PUBLISHERS
ROTTERDAM / TAIPEI

A C.I.P. record for this book is available from the Library of Congress.

Paperback ISBN: 90-77874-25-9
Hardback ISBN: 90-77874-26-7

Published by: Sense Publishers,
P.O. Box 21858, 3001 AW
Rotterdam, The Netherlands

Printed on acid-free paper

CONTENTS

PREFACE

Every book is the result of a historical process that authors both produce and are subjected to. This is also the case for this book, which has long been coming. Or, to express it differently, I have wanted to write this book for a long time, ever since I engaged in extended investigations aimed at better understanding what it means to learn from the perspective of the learner. For a considerable time now, I have had a sense that the fundamental problem of learning theories is their failure to explain why I do one thing rather than another and how learning arises from my engagement with the world in the way it is given to me rather than to someone else. For reasons that I exemplify, discuss, and theorize in the course of the book—especially in chapter 3—learners forget characteristic aspects of the learning process at the moment they come to know. This may not be a problem generally, but it becomes a problem when these learners become teachers: unless they remember what it means not to know and about the aporia of learning, they expect from their students the impossible: to intend the unknown learning object. There is a process of amnesis, whereby the newfound understanding obliterates how human beings perceived and understood the world just minutes before their new knowledge has taken hold. Although I began to become aware of the problems most theories have in describing learning from the perspective of the learner in 1995 during two extended research stays abroad, I never found the time to investigate the relevant issues in depth.

In 1999, following an invitation that Manuela Welzel and Stefan von Aufschnaiter (then at the University of Bremen) extended to me, accompanied by a successful application to the section cognitive neurosciences of the *Hanse Institute for Advanced Studies*, Delmenhorst, I decided to spend three months in that part of northern Germany where the *Institute* and the university are located. Manuela provided me with access to an extended database featuring tenth-grade students in the process of learning (*about*) static electricity in a class that she and Stefan had co-taught. My explicit goal was to take a first-person perspective on learning. I was reading Maurice Merleau-Ponty's book on the phenomenology of perception at the time and had long been interested in Martin Heidegger's work on how the world is experienced during everyday activity (*Being and Time*).

Every day at the *Institute*, I watched the videotapes, attempting to understand how these students perceived the world, *why* they were doing what they were doing, and how to infer from their conversations and actions just what it was they attended to, which things in the setting they were conscious off, and which things they took for granted without consciously being aware of these. To support my interpretive work, I had requested from Manuela the curriculum materials that she had used with the students. So from early on, the desk in my apartment at the *Institute* was littered not only with the normal implements of research—books, videotapes, computer, and transcripts—but also with the materials that I could use to produce and reproduce electrostatic phenomena.

It was while I attempted to reproduce something I was seeing students do that I noticed myself perceiving or not perceiving in the same way students did. For example, it was after watching one of the teachers interact with students about testing static electricity that I began to notice the fact that the lamp I was using was glowing differently depending on the materials I was using at the moment. That is, much like the students I had not attended to the fact that the lamp reacted differently when testing positive versus negative charges. This realization hit home hard. If I—a trained physicist with a masters degree and with a good part of the coursework toward a Ph.D. in physical chemistry—do not see something that is crucial for understanding a physical phenomenon and therefore do not act toward or use as resource in my own thinking some specific feature that the teachers take for granted and as shared, how much more difficult must be the situation for the students with considerably less experience? At the time, this realization provides me with the impetus to engage in an extended study of learning from a first-person perspective. In this endeavor, I am not interested in the traditional lore of scientific concepts and conceptual change or (radical, social) constructivism—from experience I know that these theories do not work well when I try to understand learning in real time, real contexts, surrounded by real people. Rather, I decide at the time to experience knowing from a learner perspective and to re-experience what it means to learn in a domain that I do not know; and I decide to do this in the most rigorous way. As a trained physicist, however, there is a possible danger that I am already looking with a conditioned lens, though there are many situations where I act just like the students I observe, that is, in terms of a discourse of negativity that many in the discipline of science education use.

For this reason, I decided to engage also in an extended inquiry of my own learning, taking note of events whenever it strikes me that I have learned something about learning. In one case, I decide to take a bicycle ride along an unfamiliar route (unfamiliar at least the first time) for number of times, which turns out to be twenty days in a row, and to note everything that I came to know, remember, anticipate, and so forth.

In this way, I created a large database of original observations and interpretations in the course of my stay at the *Institute* and following the stay to this day. However, even during my stay I got sidetracked with an emerging interest concerning gestures, which pre-occupied me over the next several years and let me come to understand how gestures function as a communicative precursor of verbal scientific language. In fact, today I know that these studies have not been on a sidetrack at all but central to my present-day understanding of how human beings come to know. Gestures are central to my ways of taking up position in the world and they, just as my actions, directly connect me with my environment. They are central to understanding why my everyday actions, including thinking and communication, are so efficient: I do not have to make present again the things I am connected to, as long as I can expect to be connected to the world and the situations I find myself in. I do not need to memorize the functions and pull-down windows on my computers, because I know that I can find these windows and their contents whenever I need them. I know that I have not memorized them as soon as someone asks me how to do something on the computer when there is none present. I cannot respond and will seek a computer to show the person how to do what he or she is asking me about. But this case is not interesting, as my knowing always is relevant only in specific settings. Incidentally, however, science educators and science teachers have students to do a variety of things disconnected from any relevant context that everybody else uses and under almost every other situation that is relevant. There always are resources that I can draw on to accomplish my goals.

Since my stay at the *Institute*, I have also become deeply familiar with dialectical theories of activity, such as those that are framed in terms of an agency|structure dialectic (e.g., Sewell, 1992) or as a cultural-historical activity theory (Leont'ev, 1978). Dialectical theories have their origin in a lineage of philosophical and social psychological work that began with Georg W.F. Hegel and Karl Marx and subsequently has become central to the sociocultural and cultural-historical schools of Soviet psychologists, most notably Lev Vygotsky and his student Alexei Leont'ev. Klaus Holzkamp, a German Critical Psychologist, has taken this latter person's theory furthest in his own work on learning from a subject's perspective, resulting in what he calls *Subjektwissenschaft*, science of the subject.

After having written a section in my *Doing Qualitative Research: Praxis of Method* (Roth, 2005a) about how to do cognitive phenomenology, I have felt ready and in the position to tackle the contents of the present book. I can now say that although the book has long been coming, the intervening years have been important for my own learning about learning and for developing suitable theoretical resources that today allow me to think about the aporias of learning. It turns out that I also have become familiar with an area of continental philosophy that has taken its leads both from dialectics and phenomenology, overcoming the weaknesses of both. The philosophers include Jacques Derrida, Paul Ricœur, Emmanuel Levinas, Jean-Luc Nancy, and Didier Franck. Through reading these philosophers, I have been able to integrate many heretofore-separate domains in my understanding.

A book such as the present does not emerge from thin air but is itself the result of a historical process that includes writing in general. Other pieces of writing with direct relevance to one or the other chapter often precede a book, though they may have undergone substantial transformation, sometimes required by the new context in which they appear. This also is the case here. I have written about student learning from a phenomenological perspective: Two articles on the topic, which appeared in *Learning and Instruction* (Roth, McRobbie, Lucas, & Boutonné, 1997a) and the *Journal of Research in Science Teaching* (Roth, McRobbie, Lucas, & Boutonné, 1997b) have been integrated into chapters 1 and 2, respectively, because they constituted the starting point for the present inquiry. Some of the material on perception in chapters 3 and 4 has figured in an article on the phenomenology of perception that has been published by the editors of *FQS: Forum Qualitative Sozi-*

alforschung / Forum Qualitative Social Research. However, the context for the data—and therefore my arguments generally—has changed substantially: context, data, and arguments have become an integral aspect of a more general, dialectical theory of culture, knowing, and learning. Aspects of chapter 7 and 9 have been developed and used in an article that was published by *Cognition & Pragmatics.* The ideas articulated in chapters 6 and 7 have their origin in a variety of papers normally using very different data, published in *Discourse Processes, Journal of Pragmatics, Learning and Instruction, Language in Society, Science Education, Journal of Research in Science Education,* and *Semiotica.*

A project such as this never succeeds without the support of those close to the author, the agencies that provide grants, the institutions that give authors leave, and everybody else who contributes to making society what it is and thereby provides the author with the space to do research and write books. But there are also some organizations and individuals who contribute more directly and immediately to making a project possible; and I want to thank those specifically relevant to my work on the current book. The first two chapters derive from data that I collected together with Cam McRobbie, Keith Lucas, and Sylvie Boutonné in a high school in Brisbane, Australia, supported both by the *Center for Science and Mathematics Education* at Queensland University of Technology and by the Social Sciences and Humanities Research Council of Canada. I am grateful to the teacher and students, who willingly hosted us. I am particularly grateful to Manuela Welzel (University of Education, Heidelberg, Germany) and Stefan von Aufschnaiter (professor emeritus, University of Bremen) for their generosity of hosting me. They have provided me with the required connection to receive the funding from the *Hanse Institute of Advanced Studies* and who provided me with access to the videotapes of the physics course they had taught and for the extensive discussions they engaged me in concerning knowing and learning. These discussions allowed me to evolve a better understanding especially because both Manuela and Stefan and their graduate students were taking a perspective on knowing and learning that differed from my own. My thanks go to Gerhard Roth, the director of the *Hanse Institute,* which funded my stay and provided for an opportunity to do nothing but research in an environment conducive to research and writing. Finally and most importantly, I thank my wife Sylvie Boutonné for her continued support, which allows me to engage in such time consuming efforts as writing books.

Victoria, Canada
January 2006

TOWARD A SINGULAR PLURAL PERSPECTIVE ON SCIENCE LEARNING

The natural sciences have a strong experimental character. In schools, this aspect of science is reflected in laboratory work. It therefore comes as no surprise that for a long time now science educators have suggested that there are many benefits from using laboratory activities as part of instruction. Traditionally, this laboratory work consists of exercises in which students verify textbook equations or are asked to observe phenomena relevant to their current topic of study. These laboratory exercises generally are well planned ahead of time and students usually are given step-by-step instructions. Although there is a sense that understanding science and about science requires understanding its experimental nature, many questions have been raised about the real benefits of laboratory investigations to students' scientific understanding. All too often, teachers find that their students do not learn or come to understand the science in intended ways—leading them to use laboratory tasks only as ancillary activities and frequently to introduce some "fun" into the subject.

A central reason for engaging in laboratory tasks is to prepare and see in action phenomena that otherwise may not exist or may not be accessible but that nevertheless are the phenomena as theorized in science. That is, science teachers frequently ask students to conduct laboratory activities designed to show specific scientific principles in action. However, there are some problems with this practice. It is widely accepted that all observation is interpretation. This contention, initially brought forth on philosophical grounds, has recently found support in research on the physiology of perception and on the interaction of discursive practices and "seeing." Because interpretation arises from the interplay of existing understandings and experienced world, what I observe depends on what I already know. This means that students who do not yet know the scientific principles associated with a particular laboratory experiment or demonstration probably will not see just what their investigation is to show, for the very principles (laws, concepts, theories) that are to be exhibited are prerequisite to seeing the phenomenon. As a result, students perceive different worlds than teachers, making science learning through discovery next to impossible. It does not surprise then that many science teachers do not trust learning through laboratory activities and prefer to stick to lecturing, doing word problems, and teaching how to respond to questions about concepts on exams ("teaching to exams").

Despite the shortcomings of laboratory tasks, teachers still use them; some even use it in the discovery mode. Discovery learning, which had its heydays during the 1960s and 70s, still underlies much of students' practical activities in school science and mathematics. When students do more open ended laboratories, the learning situation is exacerbated in that scientific phenomena require not only observation but also the preparation of materials; that is, embodied laboratory skills are prerequisite to setting up nature in such a way that it exhibits the phenomena of interest to scientists. This leads to two sources of problems why students do not make the observations, or discoveries, that teachers—working from a traditional paradigm—want them to make. First, because of their different theoretical lenses, students are likely to perceive and interpret any situation differently than their teachers do. Second, because of their different competencies in laboratory practices, students frequently prepare events that, do not illustrate the concepts at hand even within the teacher's framework; that is, there is a gap between the instructions students receive for doing the investigations and what they actually enact when they manipulate the materials.

Few studies in science education have investigated at a micro-level and in a minute-by-minute fashion what students do and learn through traditional laboratory exercises in science. But there are some indications that students learn to follow instructions rather than developing a scientific understanding of the observed phenomena (Amerine & Bilmes, 1990). One sociological study showed that doing an experiment successfully according to the instructions given by another person is not a self-evident event but requires considerable situated interpretation. In that study, a sociology student volunteered to execute the instructions of a quadriplegic student enrolled in a chemistry course (Lynch, Livingston, &, Garfinkel, 1983). The authors suggest that the relationship between instructions and students' actions is quite precarious and ambiguous. While indispensable for the students, the adequacy of formal instructions cannot be determined through reading them:

> These written instructions were simply not adequately descriptive of the work of doing an experiment since they omitted the embodied engagement of the students with the table-equipment. And since the students did not yet know these embodied practices, it was up to them to discover them. (p. 211)

The cited study has been conducted within an ethnomethodological framework. In the science education literature, however, assumptions about laboratory work remain largely unexamined. There are studies indicating that laboratory activities are largely auxiliary and, from the teachers' perspectives largely dispensable aspects of science classes; but fine-grained analyses of traditional laboratory work are lacking. There are no empirical studies that show how doing something with the hand brings about *conceptual* and *discursive* practices, for example, how opening and closing the tap on a burette leads to an understanding of acid–base titrations and how to write balanced chemical equations for these. Therefore, definitive answers to questions about the pedagogic value of laboratory work are unlikely to exist until the moment when science educators focus on what students actually do in the laboratory tasks that they are assigned to do. This requires researchers to study why students do what they do, based on what they actually perceive as objects in and opportunities for action.

Claims about the value of laboratory activities are largely unexamined and constitute a powerful, myth-making rhetoric; and school laboratory activities are largely ill-conceived, confused, and unproductive in that many students learn little of or about science and do not engage in doing science at all but take the tasks as a diversion from listening to teacher lectures. To understand why students appear to learn so little from laboratory tasks, researchers need to take the students' points of view; that is, researchers need to view classroom events from the perspective of someone who does not yet know what he or she is expected to learn and who therefore cannot *intentionally* learn what it is to be learned. That is, the thing to be learned cannot be the goal of actions or the motive of activity, because in both cases, the object has to be given, which is exactly not the case in learning. What I-student will learn by engaging in some task is beyond the horizon of what I currently know and therefore I cannot intend to know what I am supposed to know through engaging in the task. Yet students are evaluated on what they do in the laboratory, how they do it, and what their outcomes are. Thus, students engage in tasks that they have little control over because they cannot evaluate what they do, yet they are graded in all phases on how well they do what they do. It is not surprising then to have a considerable number of students continually asking, "Am I right so far?"

Students cannot know the object of learning, because it is the intended outcome of the unit of study. Students therefore are better understood as groping in the dark, attempting to bring light to what it is that they are to know; or, to use a different metaphor, students are to be seen as travelers who decide to go beyond the horizons of their familiar territory so that they cannot intentionally go somewhere specific, as they do not know what lies beyond, much like Columbus could not go to a specific place as he did not know what was beyond. But what do I do in such a situation and how do I deal with the aporia that the thing to be learned cannot be intended but has to be welcomed whenever it knocks at my (the learner's) doors? Taking the learner's perspective on learning is a methodological move characteristic of phenomenology and first-person approaches in social psychology.

Some of the basic assumptions underlying phenomenological thought that also figure in much of the current work in situated cognition and ethnomethodological analyses of everyday practices are: (a) Beliefs and assumptions implicit in everyday practices cannot all be made explicit and are discursively constituted for the purposes at hand; (b) practical understanding, which is observable in the spontaneous activity of people acting in their everyday worlds, is more fundamental than detached theoretical understanding; (c) my primary relationship to the objects and events of my activities is not through having representations of them; (d) sense is fundamentally social and cannot be reduced to the meaning-giving activity of individual subjects and social activity is the foundation of intelligibility and existence; and (e) in a first-person framework, it makes little sense to speak of things that bear individual properties independently of acts of perception.

In a first-person approach, my world, a world that consists of objects with properties and events, is considered to arise through my involved, purposive, and goal-directed activities. The thinginess of objects and events that are relevant to what I do emerge from my active engagement with the world as it is given to me in my perception. In many circumstances, I act without a need to represent the context in my mind; I live in a transparent world, where I can take much for granted, where a lot goes without saying, and a world to which I do *not* have to attend consciously. However, because the verbal articulation of the unspoken is a never-ending process, new articulations and interpretations of an object or event are always possible. Such interpretations are always from within my horizon that is constituted by my past experiences, assumptions implicit in everyday discursive and material practices ("common sense"), and my familiarity with the current situation. For my interpretations to be similar to those of someone else, I have to share with him or her a great deal of this horizon: even an instruction for operating a photocopier can lead to considerably different actions if the operator is a designer of such a machine—and thus a participant in a community with a common worldview—or not. A second important way for aspects and features of things to emerge into my consciousness is when the inconspicuous, unobtrusive and inoffensive nature of my everyday world and its transparency disappear. At this moment, a moment I denote by the term *breakdown*, objects and events take on properties and aspects.

THE EVERYDAY WORLD

Human beings primarily are embedded in the material world because of their bodies; and because of this, they have a primary contact with this world. My body is body among bodies; as a person, I am person among persons. Being, therefore, is *being singular plural* (Nancy, 2000), in a material and a social sense. Before the world can be reflected upon, before experiences and different parts of the world can be talked about, human beings always already have gained experience and have developed some knowledge about it through this bodily inclusion in the world. This corporeal experience of the physical and social world cannot be fully recovered in the use of language; it remains implicit in human actions but constitutes a background and horizon that "biases" any future experiences. Reflection and speaking about this embeddedness in the world is always delayed with respect to practical understanding; human beings can never totally explicate what they already have experienced, particularly not in any approximation of a totality.

What I know defines the ground for what I can learn. Given that I—as a concrete realization of general human possibilities and being singular plural—am endowed with common sense because of my participation in society from my very beginning and because of my use of a common language, one critical question is: "How can I know science given that in the final recourse, my 'prior knowledge' always is common sense?" That is, science education presupposes that during instruction, I have to appeal to and build on common sense to overcome common sense. That is, common sense constitutes a fundamental lens through which I perceive and act toward the world; what is given to me in perception is not divided into real and "perceived," but is always real to me. This perceived world is characterized by articulations or segmentations at different levels. The most prominent organizing principles of the commonsense world are parts, wholes, and their relations, part to part within a single whole, identity, overlapping, and discreteness. Entities are three-dimensional, have two-dimensional closed surfaces, and are attributed qualities (color, temperature, hardness) and properties (mass, weight, size).

Research on the processes involved in learning science seldom if ever focuses on more fundamental questions of how people can learn from *their* experiences—as distinct from an objective world—and what they learn during this experience of something really new. Science educators and science teachers simply assume that their students encounter a world cut up—i.e., articulated—in particular ways and that they are more or less successful in copying to appropriate the theories humankind has developed for understanding this world. Rarely does research focus on more basic questions such as what, why, and how students should learn anything from laboratory experiences, and what these experiences are like.

An important aspect of this book therefore deals with the world and things as these are given to students in their perception—mainly touch and sight—and with the fundamental conditions that this provides for their learning of science. I sometimes use the term *ontology*, which denotes a theory or conception of being, that is, the ensemble of things that surround a person, which constitutes the world of my experience, and which I experience as objectively present. Here the pun arising from the double meaning of "objectively" is intended: The objects of my experience truly are *objectively* present, *as* objects; these objects, in the way they are present, constitute resources for me to make plans, to formulate goals, and to act. It is only when there is reason to doubt my perception that I begin asking whether there are other ways of looking at the situation. This is the case for entities and processes: Common-sense notions take substances to exist continuously and identically through time, existing in their totality at every moment; processes unfold in time existing at no one moment in time in their totality.

In this book, I use classroom examples where high school students come to experiment with and use simple devices that sometimes are used with much younger and even elementary students. The investigations include simple tubular and solid cylinders and spheres that are made to roll down an inclined plane or they include a variety of materials that are rubbed against each other to create static electricity and subsequently are tested using a glow lamp, Styrofoam ball, or an electroscope. A major question I attempt to answer is, "How do students perceive these materials and devices?" For example, they charge and discharge an electroscope (Figure i.1) in particular ways. I provide answers to questions such as "How do students possible experience and encounter this instrument?" "What structures do they attend to?" "What whole and part relations do their actions and talk reveal?" The questions are pertinent, as the world is never given to me, the learner, as a whole, but, as shown here, is revealed to me in my making connections between my actions and perceptions. Tools in particular—such as the instruments for detecting static electricity (Figure i.1)—are encountered not as assemblies of material parts, but as integral wholes that are useful because one can do things with them. Thus, in chapter 11 students first encounter the electroscope as a whole, as one connected thing. My case materials exhibit how some plastic insulation between the central suspension and the outer ring comes into being as students engage with the instrument,

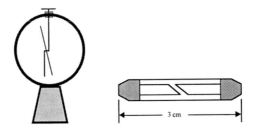

Figure i.1. Electroscope (left) and neon glow lamp are instruments used to test for the presence of electrical charges.

and sometimes only after a teacher asks some questions. Similarly, in chapter 4 I describe and theorize how the different elements of a neon glow lamp (Figure i.1) come into being in the course of students' extended inquiries and as a result of their need to understand why the lamp does or does not glow—especially in situations where a presumably charged object has been brought close.

In this book, students' learning is articulated as a positive phenomenon, that is, in its own terms rather than in terms of an external framework in respect to which students' knowledgeability is judged as deficient and in need to be improved. In a positive perspective, I ask how students' action possibilities and the worlds given to them in their perception change; in a negative approach, I would make statements about what students do not know and what they do incorrectly. Most current research reports on science learning reads as if students do something wrong within the standard frame intentionally or because of something missing. Instead, I take the position that to understand why students do ("wrong") what they do I need to understand the world they live in and that is apparent to them in their perception. I assume that at every point, students make the most reasonable decision and take the most reasonable action. Because it is reasonable, all I need to understand what they do is to find out the grounds that allow what they do to be reasonable. If what students do is different from what I might have done, it may be because the world looks different from their position. This position, I take to be constitutive of their *dis-position* (Nancy, 2000), that is, the position as different from my own. This dis-position arises from our being singular plural, that is, body among bodies, which cannot be at the same place at the same time, forcing them to be positioned differently. Because I am dis-positioned, I also make different suppositions and embody different (pre-) suppositions, that is, dispositions. To understand the positions ("where they are"), dispositions ("what the world looks like from there"), and (pre-) suppositions that characterize students in science learning tasks is the principal goal of this book. My own fundamental presupposition is that learners do what they do because it is the most plausible thing to do or because it is the most promising thing to do to expand their action possibilities with respect to realizing the goals of the task they are working on.

AGENCY|STRUCTURE

Most theories of acting, knowing, and learning are deterministic. It is only within a deterministic approach to science teaching practice that curriculum objectives—often stated in terms such as, *At the end of this lesson, students will know [be able to] . . .*—make any sense at all. Wherein theories differ is the source of the forces or causes. In psychological theories, including (radical, social) constructivism, the causes for our actions are located in the individual—in the epilogue I articulate reasons why (radical, social) constructivism certainly is a wrong theory of learning, one that is internally contradictory and inconsistent. Thus, for example, young students are said to say that the earth is flat *because* they "have" a "misconception." The misconception, which is depicted as a structure in or of the individual mind, is theorized to be the *cause* of the sentences in which the misconception is expressed—and this independent of the interaction that elicits the sentence, the problematic and perhaps aporetic nature of the relationship between thinking and language. On the other side is environmental (social) determinism, according to which students are said, for example, to do poorly in schools and on tests *because* they come from a low-income family, *because* they are of African American or First Nation origin, or *because* they are male or female, depending on the context. Social constructivism posits some group (society, community, class), which is said to construct knowledge, without providing for theoretical mechanisms that would allow this knowledge to be appropriated into the actions of individuals.

In contrast to deterministic approaches, theories based on dialectical relations emphasize the emergent, indeterminate character of actions, and therefore also of knowing and learning. Depending on their particular cultural-historical origins dialectical theories—e.g., structuration theories in the West, cultural-historical activity theory in the former Soviet Union—provide different sets of concepts. All concepts, however, emphasize the dialectic relationship between the human subject and the object of its conscious attention, which is *sublated* (mediated) in activity, where the verb "to sublate" simultaneously has the sense of "to destroy" and "to preserve" (Hegel, 1977). In other words, subject and object are like two, one-sided expressions of the same phenomenon that transcends and integrates both, including the contradiction they constitute. The phenomenon itself is concrete human praxis, which Marxian psychologists—such as Lev Vygotsky (1989)—attempt to research and understand by conducting *concrete human psychology*. The notion of a dialectical relation is foreign to most Western scholarship and thought; the following analogy is offered to assist readers unfamiliar with dialectics in understanding its nature.

The two faces of a Canadian one-dollar depict Queen Elizabeth II and a loon, respectively. The two sides are clearly different, but in their difference, they are also the same—namely literally "one-sided" expressions of the same one-dollar coin. In purchasing something, however, it does not matter which side is up and recognized; the purchasing value is the same for both customer and salesperson. To express the dialectical relation, the fundamental concept relating subject and object is expressed in the form of *subject|object*; here, the "|" denotes a "not and" opera-

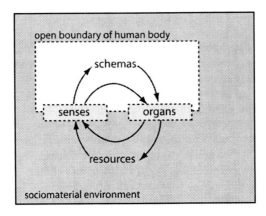

Figure i.2. Schematic of the agency\structure dialectic.

tion in logic so that the expression is true if and only if it contains a contradiction (Roth, Hwang, Lee, & Goulart, 2005). I use this way of writing throughout this book, wherever there is a need to overcome received dichotomies. In using a dialectical approach, I also draw on another way of thinking about knowing and learning based on a structure|agency dialectic. It, too, allows me to deal with dichotomous concepts and, to me, constitutes a way of highlighting different aspects of concrete human praxis.

Diagrammatically, the structure|agency dialectic is represented in Figure i.2. Fundamentally the dialectic expresses that when I study social-psychological phenomena, *agency\sensibility* (my organs, which allow me to act and my senses) and *structure* (embodied schema, external resources) mutually constitute and presuppose each other. But they are opposite faces of the same coin—and this in a double sense. First, what I can do with my *organs* arises from the *schemas* I embody—built up over the course of my biography—and the *resources* I find in the world outside of my bodily surface. (This is where radical constructivists get it wrong: without a boundary in the material world, there could not be an "I" that experiences itself as different from the remaining material world, an "I" that can make the difference between self-touching and touching-the-other.) The knowledge exists in the form of bodily *schemas*, which come in sensorimotor (including articulatory) varieties and, as shown here, are not independent of each other. Practical actions therefore arise *indeterminately* from the schemas|resources relation (Figure i.2). This relation is dialectic, because schemas and resources are both different, therefore non-identical, and the same, identical, because the schemas mediate my perceptions of the resources.

Second, the schemas|resources dialectic arises in the course of experiences in the world, which is itself the product of my experiences or rather, my agency|sensibility. A frequently cited experiment in support of this dialectical relation is that involving pairs of kittens (Held & Hein, 1963). For a few weeks, one kitten of each pair pulls a cart in which the other is placed. Both sets of kittens therefore have perceptual access to the same material setting, but only the kitten pulling the cart actually moves about in it. When the pairs of kittens are tested at the end of the experiment, only the one that has pulled the cart recognizes edges and walls, that is, the structured resources in the setting, and therefore behaves normally as any other kitten would. The one that has been pulled around for all of that time, however, behaves like a blind kitten, bumping into walls and falling over edges; in the worlds of the kittens that have been carried around, the walls and edges do not to exist. As a consequence, any organism perceives the material world because it has developed specific schemas; but it develops these schemas because it perceives the equivalent material structures (i.e., resources) in and of the material world.

When the researchers open up the kitten brains, they find ten times the amount of myelination in the kittens that have moved about compared to those that have been pulled around. The conclusion with respect to the present discussion is that the structures—embodied schema and external resources—both come into being as a product of the kittens' agency; but, of course, without the structured material world, walls, edges, and the kittens' material bodies with their specific articulations (length of bones, nature of joints and body parts), the agency would not have been possible in the first place. That is, the senses, which constitute the interface between the world that I experience as lying outside myself and my inside, are "tuned" by my previous experiences so that what I can experience at any one point in time is mediated by the traces that all prior experiences have left in my body. Similarly, what we can do in the world (by means of "organs" [Figure i.2], hands, feet, mouth, body in general) is mediated by what I objectively perceive to be the case, the possibilities for action and the resources available to me.

To reiterate, agency and structure are dialectically related. More so, because structures of the world have arisen from the kittens' experiences that correspond to their bodily structures, the schemas they have formed are more typical for cats than for human beings or flies. The kittens experience the world as having very different resources for action than newborn children or recently hatched flies. The structure of an organism's body and the actions and perceptions it mediates (affords and constrains) the schemas it develops (Uexküll, 1928/1972). And finally, because the kittens are not identical to start with, they have different experiences; this leads them to have different structures (schemas and perceived resources) and therefore to individually different worlds. But although each kitten differs from others in the particular schemas it evolves, these schemas are more similar than when each is compared to the schemas that a human being or a fly develops moving about in the same material setting.

These results lead to an aporia (perplexing and possibly unsolvable difficulty): *How can I learn, then, which means, build new schemas that are associated with new resources available to me?* In this book, I provide answers to this question.

The original agency|structure dialectic as found in the literature has limitations in the sense that it does not make thematic the fact that to perceive anything at all, living beings—flies, cats, and humans—have to be endowed with *sensibility*. It is sensibility that together with agency affords understanding the evolutionary and cultural-historical nature of the human psyche (Holzkamp, 1983). Sensibility is foundational to intentional life, seeking food, satisfaction of needs, and so forth. It is only because of my sensibility that the world can enter and affect me, as an impression on my skin, a sensation of heat or cold, a fleeting image on my retina, or a smell. The nature of structure given by the schema|resource dialectic presupposes the agency|sensibility dialectic, paradigmatically exemplified in the phenomenon of *touching* (Derrida, 2005), which sublates agency (reaching out) and sensibility (sensing). The intention to touch implies abandoning to being affected by the (re-) action of the touched on the person touching. It is this sensibility that opens my body to experience, allows me to be affected, underlies my openness to experience as such, and therefore the formation of anything like the dialectical relation between the structures of the sociomaterial world and personal schemas. Although I can intend to sense I cannot intend the contents of what my senses will offer to me. There therefore is a fundamental passivity involved in the very (intentional) act of sensing, finding out about the world by allowing it to impress itself upon me. This passivity, or rather, the passivity of passivity is antecedent to all being, is *otherwise than being* and therefore *beyond essence* (Levinas, 1978a/1998).

LIFEWORLD

The world characteristic for species and individuals is denoted variously depending on discipline; pertaining to human beings it generally is referred to by the term *lifeworld*. My *lifeworld* is the world given to me in my experience in the way it provides me with resources for actions. I act toward the things and events that perceive. Thus, if I perceive ghosts, then I act in a world populated with ghosts. To understand my actions—why and how I do what I do—others have to take the ghosts into account. If they do not do so, then my actions no longer are logically connected, irrational, and illogical. Similarly with learners: when I, researcher, observe them, I need to understand *their* lifeworld to understand what they perceive, what they do, how they do it, and why they do it. Alternatively, I have no recourse other than saying that their actions are wrong—where I have to assume that they act toward the structures available to me—or, worse, that the actions are unintelligible and incomprehensible. But such an approach is untenable because actions are inherently social phenomena, for each individual "sees the *other* do the same as it does; each does itself what it demands of the other, and therefore also does what it does only in so far as the other does the same" (Hegel, 1977, p. 112). The frame for understanding actions in this way is the societally mediated activity in and for which they are produced—more on this in the subsequent section.

My lifeworld is a dwelling that welcomes me; but it is a dwelling of my making. All intentionality therefore also is hospitality, where I, the host, offer welcome to the other, material entity or person (Derrida, 1999). But I am host only because I already have been welcome in my own dwelling, which is not completely mine. The lifeworld predates my (conscious) *being* in the world; it is itself associated with a third, the society into which I have been born. Therefore, even the most phenomenological inquiry leads me to articulate structures of knowing and learning that are not inherently mine but always already possibilities (acting, knowing, learning) that also consist for others. This, too, derives from the singular plural being of the world.

The fact that a specific material setting constitutes different lifeworlds—constitutes a different dwelling (disposition) for different individuals—is immediately evident when considering the following example. My kitchen provides me with specific possibilities for action; I act in specific ways because of the opportunities and constraints that the kitchen provides me with. Any other person inherently has a different disposition and therefore does not perceive the same possibilities and exhibits different actions to some outside observer. Yet both sets of actions also share similarities, which arise out of the material constraints of the kitchen, limiting, for example, what can be cooked and where. When I visit others and cook in their kitchen, I am confronted with a different set of possibilities, opportunities and constraints: the kitchen is not only materially different, having a different layout, different stoves, and knives of different quality, but also I experience it differently. That is, the Michael-in-another-kitchen corresponds to a different person–lifeworld ensemble. And yet there are similarities between other kitchens and my own, in layout, collocation of knives, forks, and spoons in a common cutlery tray, placement of particular foods in the fridge (milk, vegetables), and so on. My previous involvement in and with such places as kitchens has left (i.e., inscribed) in me traces that mediate the possibilities and constraints I perceive and therefore the actions I produce in the pursuit of the goals I have framed.

The upshot of these considerations is that to understand what I do, a researcher needs to know how the world looks like to me, what my lifeworld is at the time, and what the opportunities and resources are that I perceive. It does not help a bit to consider a physicist's description of the kitchen (using, e.g., Cartesian coordinates) and the materials that fill it in the attempt to understand the actions of a person, why and how she does something. *This* is among the core concern of this book: understanding the world through the eyes of learners, the possibilities and constraints they objectively experience in particular settings, and how any knowing and learning unfolds from that.

The problem of many theories of knowing and learning is their presupposition (i.e., pre-sup-*position*) that the world is entirely represented in the mind. Human beings, however, do not have full and therefore monolithic internal mental models of the world. As implied in Figure i.2, I am bound up with and *organically* (senses, organs) connected to my lifeworld. I am an integral and constitutive part of my lifeworld; my lifeworld and I always go together. Because the material world is structured, there are opportunities and constraints for *my* acting and sensing; and these opportunities and constraints, I *find* in the world. I do not have to carry them around in my mind. Human beings tend to minimize the thinking tasks and the internal representation of the world; I am not and do not have to be a robot that keeps track of things in terms of physical coordinates and extensions but I take the world as it is. Whatever I perceive as entity, I can use as a resource in my actions. Rather than keeping a full model of some scene that I am looking at in its entirety, I can leave much of the information in the world until the moment that some information is required in my task. Thus, for example, I do not need to memorize all or any of the features and tools of my word processor because I know I have every-thing available and can find it when needed as I am working along in producing this manuscript. This is not to deny that there are undoubtedly some things in my brain that can be attributed to human reasoning and decision-making. But relevant to my behavior are those structures in my material environment that I experience as objectively given and that I use in (non-) conscious ways. (*Non-conscious* means that they can become or be made conscious.)

In this sense, the social world, too, has to be understood as objectively given to me in my experience. It, too, is needed in phenomenal accounts of my lifeworld, because it is toward it that I orient and act. If I experience another person as power-ful then I will act in ways—e.g., deferentially—that produces and reproduces a power differential.

Perhaps the most obvious and most overlooked (with the exception of the phe-nomenological literature) aspect of human knowing is that it is embodied: I am continuously coupled with my material and social environments (Figure i.2) be-cause I am (material, social) body among (material, social) bodies. In fact, it is difficult to draw the boundary between the material setting and myself: From the perspective of an oxygen molecule, does my body start at the lips, in the larynx, lungs, or bronchi? Or does it start when the molecules come to be attached to a blood cell? Does the boundary between my finger and the thing I touch belong to the inside or outside of my body? I develop some of these ideas with respect to knowing and learning in chapter 5, which deals with the relationship of parts and wholes, the boundaries that separate them, and how the maps so prepared consti-tute specific lenses.

Embodiment and material coupling allow humans to use the material world, including their own bodies, as a tool that mediates the organization and manipula-tion of knowledge (Nancy, 1992). Through my body, the multifarious ways of coupling with my lifeworld are brought about and integrated into mutually consti-tutive (e.g., motor and perceptual components) and supportive (e.g., auditory and visual) relations. This coupling decreases the demands on any cognitive effort I have to spend to cope with the demands of navigating the world. Recent work in robotics shows how systems that capitalize in the way humans do on their situated nature develop much more robust behaviors all the while being computationally less complex because certain constraints are already built into real worlds for agents to use—such constraints include forces such as gravity and friction and in-teractions with others from the same and other species. Thus again, because know-ing is embodied, the very existence of the body integrates sensibility and agency, which decrease what I have to process in thinking and reflecting.

Viewing knowing and learning in a dynamical way, in terms of being connected to the places (i.e., positions) I inhabit comes with advantages. Dynamical systems theories converge with phenomenological insights about the central role of the body and with the body, the central role time and temporality in our knowing and learning—these issues are taken up in chapter 9. Rather than understanding know-ing as occurring *over* time, a dynamical perspective allows me to view knowing as occurring *in* time and therefore as an entirely temporal phenomenon. Details of timing are essential aspects of knowing rather than incidental details; knowing is not a sequential and cyclic process but a process of continuous coevolution. Doing therefore simultaneously *is knowing and learning*; in doing, I exhibit knowing and because agency is connected dialectically with sensibility, doing implies sensing and learning. Subtlety and complexity of human knowing and learning are found not at some specified time in elaborate static structure, but rather *in* time, in the flux of change itself (van Gelder, 1998).

SINGULAR PLURAL NATURE OF ACTION

In this book, I articulate and elaborate a perspective of learning through the eyes of the learner, that is, a first-person perspective. Such a perspective, sometimes and often falsely denoted by the adjective "phenomenological," frequently is taken as a reduction of knowing and learning to the individual subject. That is, knowing and learning phenomena are theorized beginning with the individual subject as the unit of analysis. A typical aporia then arises: "How can intersubjectivity arise when all communicative activity already presupposes intersubjectivity?" Some respond to this aporia by suggesting built-in mechanisms, such as a genetically wired-in basic grammar that allows humans to generate language. The aporia is even more poignant when theories begin with mind independent of bodily existence in the world, because in this case an explanation is needed for how knowledge, which is a matter of mind (consciousness), relates to anything material at all. In the artificial intelligence and cognitive science community, this aporia is referred to as the "grounding problem." The disconnect between ideas, on the one hand, and the "real" material world, on the other, has been a long-standing problem in philosophy, ever since ancient Greek philosophers first articulated it.

The reverse aporia arises when I begin to theorize knowing and learning from a social perspective (e.g., social constructivism). Typical theoretical terms in related discourses are *reproduction, inculcation, appropriation, enculturation*, and *apprenticeship*. The collective entity (i.e., culture, society, group) is thought of as a box into which new individuals (i.e., children, students) enter; this box is said to shape the newcomers until they are acceptable and accepted core members. The collective entity is (inappropriately) presupposed to antedate the individual being. Formulated in this way, learning is a deterministic process, whereby the individual is a dope, who does what he or she is *determined* to do.

Neither approach is very productive; both only lead into theoretical cul-de-sacs. To understand learning through the eyes of the learner, a simultaneous account is needed of how my actions always are actions that are also recognized by others as intelligible actions, that is, actions that they could have produced. Every sentence uttered presupposes its own intelligibility because otherwise it would make no sense uttering it. At the same time everything I do, even without someone else present, is not a completely singular act. I am *singular plural*, because what I do and who I am are possibilities that *immediately* (both instantly and without mediation) exist for and are intelligible by others. What I say and do is always and already intelligible not only to me but also to others because I am held accountable for my acts. I do what I do for reasons that are always reasons I can articulate and explain to others; consequently, these actions and their reasons are intelligible to others and, therefore, inherently not just mine but already reasons and actions of the other. They are reasons and actions for the other, of the other, and reasons and actions that therefore return to me from the other so that I can deploy them in turn.

Each act, whether it is a perceptive, discursive, or manipulative act, always is both singular and not singular, individually produced but also reproducing a collective (cultural) possibility. In any one actions, one therefore can identify cultural possibilities; in my singular experience, I can always identify *ways* of experiencing that transcend the singularity of my own acts. The phenomenological method employed throughout this book is directed at this possibility of transcending the individual toward the culture; and any effort of doing so is itself already grounded in its intelligibility, and therefore constitutes a cultural possibility.

OVERVIEW

This book is divided into four parts, each of which deals with what I have come to consider as a major dimension of learning that past research and teaching praxis in the field of science education have not addressed. In Part I, I present some of the aporias (unsolved and unsolvable problems) of learning science through hands-on investigations and demonstrations. In this part, I revisit some data sources that I assembled in a study conducted in an Australian twelfth-grade physics classroom. Having redeveloped an interest in phenomenological issues of knowing and learning, my personal interests during the study were concerned with better understanding the events through the eyes of the learners. At the time, I wanted to understand why students were saying what they did, their reasons for acting, and *what* they perceived, which, as I thought, would mediate what they said. I assumed that students are not voluntarily and mischievously inconsistent or irrational but rather that they acted in ways that made sense from their position. My program was this: *To do justice to student actions that others—teachers, researchers—might characterize as irrational or as defective, I needed to enter and understand the lifeworld of these students, that is, I needed to see the world in their ways.* In this first part of the book, learning from perceptual experience and the nature of perceptual experience itself arises as a fundamental aporia: To know what the teacher wants me-learner to perceive in an experiment or a demonstration, I need to know the phenomena that I am asked to look for; but to know the phenomena I am asked to look for, I need to be able to perceive them. This aporia is taken up and at the center of the second part of this book.

In part II, I present three chapters dealing with the aporia of perception. The materials for this and the subsequent parts III and IV have been assembled during a three-month stay as a fellow in the cognitive neurosciences section of the *Hanse Institute for Advanced Study*. I used this stay, among others, to do an extensive and extended analysis of perceptual experience and how I, being singular plural, come to see in and through experience. In addition to closely watching a set of videotapes featuring tenth-grade students in the process of learning about static electricity through hands-on explorations in small groups, I equally closely attended to and recorded my own perceptual experiences. These experiences came about while I attempted to understand what was happening in the tapes, while I conducted investigations using the same materials that students had available while taking the class, and while I cycled to the university or while I went on a bicycle trip designed to provoke perception in an unfamiliar environment. In this second section, I therefore show how I (we, students) come to perceive, how my (our, students') lifeworld unfolds and becomes increasingly articulated, and how I (we, students) develop maps for perceiving and understanding the world, maps that actually constitute disciplinary lenses.

Part III of this book is devoted to the relationship of world, lifeworld, and language. The latter has received very special treatment by science educators, as if it had an ontological status apart, that is, as if it was different from other things that humans use to communicate, such as hand gestures, pointing, head nods, and things in the setting people are attuned to. Rather than beginning to think about communication in terms of language, subordinating the former to the latter, I begin with communication and subordinate patterned sounds to communication generally. I show how sounds are part of taking up position and orienting in the world and how they exist side-by-side with other communicative forms. The special status of language derives from the fact that it often better serves to talk reflexively about bygone situations and communicative exchanges than other communicative forms do. Taking this position also gives me a better handle on how discourse emerges from hands-on investigations and how language is related to other communicative forms in the process of the evolution of understanding and theory, especially the split between the material body of the signifier and the sense that is signified. Finally, I am concerned in this part III with the reverse relationship between language and manipulation when I investigate how instructions are followed and implemented, or rather, how actions are related to instructions in such a way that I can say that the latter have been followed.

In part IV, I deal with time and temporality in learning through engagement with material things, including the experience of flow and the temporal constitution of objects, tools, and knowledge. In chapter 9, I show how time and temporality are central aspects of the experience of knowing and learning and result from experiences in and of the world. In the subsequent chapter, I describe an instance of learning where I, an individual who has previously received a M.Sc. degree in physics, learn some new things about static electricity and how to understand the specific phenomenon of charging a metallic object by induction. In the final chapter of part IV, I show how a tool comes to be known theoretically not through its use, but in a variety of situations that make its aspect the *object* of intentional activity, including moments of breakdown or moments in which the unanticipated nature of an observation becomes salient.

Throughout this book, I draw on materials that come from either a twelfth-grade (chapters 1 and 2) or a tenth-grade (chapters 4–7, 9, 11) physics classroom. However, the investigations in which students engage in are not esoteric. Rather, these are so simple that they can be conducted at home; and I have found descriptions of them in elementary school curricula. Thus, in the twelfth-grade class, students investigate, for example, objects rolling down an inclined plane; or the students observe someone sitting on a rotating stool spinning a bicycle wheel. In the tenth-grade classroom, students investigate the electrostatic charging of objects. Charging objects can be done at home using different types of materials, woolen cloth, transparency sheets, combs, and so on; tests for the presence of charges can be conducted using bits of Styrofoam, paper snippets, or simple electroscopes made from the silver paper found in cigarette boxes or chocolate bars—paper part removed. Throughout the book I also use drawings to make available what students and teachers have seen or might have seen, thereby providing readers with a way of seeing for themselves.

METHODOLOGICAL REFLECTION

This book is the result of my attempt to provide a learner's perspective on learning in science. Whereas it is easy to talk and write about what one perceives and to provide reasons for one's own actions, it is more difficult to note what someone else perceives and to know why they do what they do, unless they explicitly articulate and thereby make available to others their reasons in the course of action. To deal with the inevitable constraints in writing about learning from a learner's perspective all the while writing about the learning of others, I draw in this book on my own perceptual experiences and learning as well as on my observation of others. Here, I am not interested in *my* experience per se, but in what I can learn about learning more generally, that is, about aspects of learning pertinent to the plural in being singular plural. To reiterate, I am not interested in *my* perspective or position, but in the structures that make this perspective possible in the first place and how another perspective could have easily replaced it. I am interested in articulating *why* there are different forms of experience rather than merely describing them.

Although *my* perspective is not at issue, I nevertheless use the first person pronouns "I" and "me" and the reflexive pronoun "myself" in places where other texts might use "our," "you," "one," and so on. I chose this form because of the general intent to present a first person perspective on learning; I could have equally used the first-person plural forms "we," "us," and "ourselves." I am not interested in portraying a specific person's position but rather emphasize the fact that the perceptions of all human beings are *their own* all the while recognizing that each perceptual act and the verbal articulation of its contents is a possibility that also exists for other human beings. That is, each individual action is singular plural, both inescapably individual *and* radically sociocultural and cultural historical.

With respect to students who learn science, I cannot make the assumption that what I am seeing while observing the tapes—for example, that a lamp glows or a pointer moves (Figure i.1)—is exactly the same as that what they have observed. Perceptual experience always is singular. In fact, I show in chapter 1 that even within the student body, the same material event is perceived in very different ways. It is difficult to say based on watching a lesson whether or not some material that students are currently using "really has been charged" and, if so, a student "really" perceives it as such unless he or she *articulates* the perception. The video-tape cannot provide evidence for that. The video only shows that a person has rubbed one material against another. Whether it is in fact charged can not be established until an electroscope pointer begins to move, a lamp when brought close begins to glow, another piece of material is attracted, and so on. But when none of this happens, I still cannot be certain that the material was not charged. That is, to be able to make a statement about what is the case in any one situation, I (researcher) have to look for evidence: to say something about what a student perceives I have to provide evidence that this is the case. For example, when a student says in surprise, "Oh, this thing is not connected" after having attempted to use some tool for some time without success, I have supportive evidence for a claim about her not having seen the lacking connection—which may in fact be the way the tool is built so that two wires do not connect. Surprise, statements about noticing something for the first time, and discovering (presumed) causes of material breakdowns all are events that hint at what is currently salient in someone's perception.

Throughout this book I use pseudonyms, even though it is nearly impossible to track down the original schools and classrooms where the data sources have been constructed initially. To make it easier to distinguish students and teachers, the first names of the latter always begin with the letter "T," whereas the first names of the former begin with letters other than "T." Throughout the book, I use drawings rather than photographs because they allow me to reduce the amount of unnecessary, gratuitous detail, thereby making it easier for readers to perceive what I intend them to perceive.

PART I

APORIAS OF LEARNING SCIENCE

Aporias are perplexing difficulties or problems that may not have any solution. Thus, the inner contradictions of dialectical notions and the corresponding resistance in the material phenomena they denote constitute aporias: they are irremediable and unsolvable. Learners are exposed to a number of fundamental aporias that make us wonder how anyone can learn any science. The most fundamental aporias include: (a) How can I learn science if it requires my prior experience, which, in the final analysis always is everyday, mundane, and non-scientific? (b) If observation is theory-driven, how can I, who always already comes with a mundane understanding of the world, a *disposition*, make observations that support a fundamentally different pre-scientific ontology (collection of worldly things) and non-scientific theory? How can I know that what I see is what I am supposed to see? How can I know that what I do in laboratory task is what I am supposed to do?

The answers to all of these questions require me to deal with the fact that teaching science presupposes the perceptual experiences and explanations that they are supposed to teach. For me, a learner of science, the fundamental aporia therefore exists in the fact that I have to intentionally aim at learning something that I do not know what it is. This is an aporia, as an intention is always object-directed. Thus, if there is no object, for example, because it is unknown, I cannot have an intention directed toward it. It is as if I had to be able to provide a roadmap to get to an unknown place in an unknown country prior to having roamed it for some time to become familiar with it. Christopher Columbus could not intentionally go to the Americas, as he did not know about the Americas. Asking students to learn something they do not yet know is like asking Columbus to discover Cuba without being able to give him descriptions of what it may be like to face this island. And yet, in my search for what it is I am to learn, the things I am in the dark about, I always already bring some light, my existing practical understanding of how the world works. Columbus had some hunch about the shape of the earth, which would get him to India if only he kept on sailing westward. It is with this light, or, as presented in chapter 5, with a particular lens that I begin all learning in a chicken-and-egg situation: to overcome my everyday mundane discourse and appropriate a new, more scientific discourse, I have to rely on the former. To change my disposition, I have to change my position (dis-position), which always is a change from the position (dis-position) I am currently in: to "overcome" my everyday, mundane way of seeing the world to develop a scientific perspective, I nevertheless have to rely on and ground new perceptions in, my current non-scientific ways of seeing.

In this part I, I revisit and reinterpret my observations made during a study of physics learning in an Australian classroom, taught by an experienced, highly knowledgeable, very willing physics teacher whom I refer to as Toby Mory. In the first chapter, I focus on possible reasons that might mediate what students actually perceive and why they do not agree among themselves and with their teacher about what it is that can be seen in a demonstration. My analysis reveals six dimensions that may have prevented students from perceiving a demonstration in the way Toby had intended it and therefore what they could learn from a demonstration. These dimensions include (a) students theoretical framework that did not yet separate signals—the phenomena—from noise, (b) interactions with discourses learned in other contexts of the physics course, (c) interactions with traces of other demonstrations and images that had some surface resemblance, (d) students' difficulties in piecing together coherent representational frameworks from the information given, (e) low salience of demonstrations on tests, and (f) lack of opportunities for students to test their descriptions and explanations.

In chapter 2, I provide a fine-grained description of students' discursive and material actions in the same traditional senior physics class. From a first-person perspective, I focus on the processes by means of which students bring order to their observations and material practices. In the process of their ordering work, the phenomena students articulate in the laboratory arise from an intertwining of embodied material and discursive practices, the possibilities and constraints of the material world, and their relations with other people. They evaluate the adequacy of any action by means of an interpretation of its outcomes and not by means of an assessment of the actions themselves, which leads them to a contradictory situation: To know that they have seen what the teacher intended them to see, they need to know that what they have done is what they are supposed to do; but to know that what they are doing, students need to know that what they are seeing is exactly what they are supposed to see.

APORIAS OF PERCEPTION IN SCIENCE

The focus in this book is on laboratory investigations in which students learn and learn about science in and through their own investigations. However, laboratory tasks require students not only to observe but also to prepare the phenomena that are of interest to scientists and that in fact constitute the world that scientific formula, concepts, and theories really describe. There therefore is the potential that students do not see a phenomenon because they have prepared something very different. Thus, to get a handle on perception first, I focus in this chapter on teacher-presented demonstrations, in which those phenomena are present that the teacher uses as basis for his or her explanations of concepts and theories.

In chapter 2, I describe high school physics students who do not generate the phenomena that the teacher wants them to generate and therefore they do not see what he wants them to see. I take a quick look ahead to properly contextualize the concerns in this first chapter. In chapter 2, my descriptions highlight that students are coping with instructions that pose them with an aporia, an unsolvable problem:

1. to know whether they do what they are supposed to do, they need to know what they see is what they are supposed to see; but
2. to know that what they see is what they are supposed to see, they need to know that what they have done is what they were supposed to do.

This aporia constitutes a serious situation for any teacher who wants students to learn legitimized and legitimizing science knowledge through discovery and inductive reasoning. Some science teachers perhaps want to suggest that the time in the laboratory might be better spent looking at demonstrations, which the teacher can set up such that the scientifically relevant phenomena rather than any other can be seen. This would then be the equivalent of what Michael Faraday had done when he sent equipment to his scientific peers so that they would reproduce *his* experiment and therefore arrive at *his* observation descriptions and observation categoricals rather than their own. One may ask, however, whether producing demonstrations will solve another aporia: If I need to know a phenomenon to perceive it, then how can students perceive a demonstration scientifically given that they come with their own everyday, mundane ways of seeing things? They come with dispositions that do not overlap with scientific dispositions required to perceive the phenomena scientifically. What will they perceive given a particular demonstration? These are the questions I track in the present chapter. But let me begin by taking a look at the classroom episodes from an Australian twelfth-grade physics course; here, the teacher Toby Mory, who loved to design demonstrations, frequently used them not only because he could illustrate scientific concepts but also because he thought these demonstrations might motivate students.

A DEMONSTRATION OF ROTATIONAL MOMENTUM

Toby picks up a bicycle wheel and sits down on his rotating stool, which is hidden from view for all but the students in the first row (Figure 1.1). He invites students to observe, "So alright now there are a few other ideas we can put together with this, I got the bicycle wheel, some kind child donated it. Now just watch very carefully, at least you can see the part you need to see, that is the top of my body and the wheel. Right, watch carefully." He rapidly spins the wheel with its axis vertical, that is, parallel to the axis of the turning stool. This is associated with an almost unnoticeable opposite spin in his body. Toby comments, "This chair isn't very good I'll try that again." This time, the chair makes about an eighth of a turn. "Did you just see it? Look again," he urges, "look at my body mainly. What was my angular momentum just now? Zero, I'm isolated sitting in this awkward looking position. When I spin it what do you notice?" Norm calls out, "Opposite to the wheel." "Yes I'm going the opposite way to the wheel. When we are looking at these vectors, to start with L was zero wasn't it? That's my angular momentum. It's made up of two things: My angular momentum and the wheel's both zero to kick off with."

Toby walks to the chalkboard and writes

$$\underline{L} = 0 = \underline{L}_{me} + \underline{L}_{wheel} \tag{1}$$

Figure 1.1. While sitting on the rotating chair, the teacher spins the bicycle wheel. When the axis of the wheel is parallel to that of the chair, the latter rotates in the opposite direction of the chair. When the axis of the wheel is perpendicular to that of the chair, no movement should be observed.

Figure 1.2. The teacher illustrates the "right-hand rule," which is used to determine the direction of the rotational momentum (direction of thumb) given an entity rotates in a specific direction (curled fingers).

where he uses the convention of underlining the letters that denote vector quantities (i.e., variables that have magnitude and direction and therefore can also be represented by arrows). He continues, "The angular momentum is the vector and has direction, this is how we measure the direction of angular momentum. You see when I spin that, when it spins, if I put my fingers in the direction of the spin my thumb comes out the axle." He curls the fingers of his right hand in the direction of the turning wheel, while sticking out his thumb (as in Figure 1.2). "So that was taken as a vector representing angular momentum. That vector," he says while moving his hand a bit thereby attracting attention to the thumb sticking out, "it's a radial vector. If I spin it that way that's the vector; if I spin it reverse, my fingers that way, the vector would be going down." He repeats the curling of the hand with the thumb pointing along the bicycle wheel's axis every time he talks about direction and vector. "It's not a *real* vector like linear ones. It's called a *radial* vector or an axial vector. It's the direction of the axis using a right-hand grip rule. All right? Now when I'm down here and spin it that way, it now has a value of L vector pointing upwards of so much magnitude. How long that arrow is, depends upon— I'd have to do an *I-omega-squared* for the wheel ((angular momentum: $\underline{L} = I\underline{\omega}$; angular kinetic energy: $E_{kin} = \frac{1}{2} I\omega^2$)). My body went the other way, didn't it? How did I spin the wheel? The wheel was going that way, my body rotated the other way, my body had a vector thus, so it was a positive vector, a positive angular momentum, so my body would be that." He gestures with his thumb upwards, and by gesturing drawing attention to it. He continues, "So this takes on positive; my body took on negative [angular momentum]. When I stop it ((he stops the wheel)), the reverse happens doesn't it?"

At this point, Toby sits on the chair (Figure 1.1). "So alright, have a look at this one. I'm going to spin it this way and nothing will happen because there's no way I'm going to let my body rotate." He spins the wheel with the axis at a right angle to the axis of the stool. "Hang on, I've just got to turn that up," and turns the wheel's axis 90 degrees. The stool rotates about one quarter turn. "Did you see that? I'm going to stop it." He stops the wheel, and the stool returns into its original position. He explains, "See what happened to me? This was going in that way, rotating that way, vector upwards." Again, he curls his hand in the direction of the wheel's motion while sticking out his thumb. "When I stopped it my body took it on and my body took on that angular momentum see."

After repeating the demonstration twice, he is about to move to the next demonstration, when Andy calls out a question, "When you turn this ((points to the wheel)) over will that do it in the opposite direction which will also help you stop? When you turn that over one-eighty degrees?" Toby responds, "That's what I want you to think about; why, when I turn it [wheel] over did I reverse. Now I should keep spinning if it wasn't for the darn friction in this chair." Andy is not satisfied, "But now, the chair's, the wheel is pulling a force which is stopping you if you turn it over one-eighty degrees." Toby replies, "I'm not even mentioning forces here, I'm an isolated system, by turning it over, at all times all I know is *big* L for this whole system is zero." Andy insists, "Just turn it ninety degrees." Andy goes on further to ask if Toby has the same qualities as the bicycle wheel, would he spin at the same speed. Toby says, "What's that? Comparably but the other way, yes" and moves on to demonstrate another example of the conservation of angular momentum.

This is a typical example for the many demonstrations Toby presents to his students during this and other lessons on angular momentum. It is typical in that he is doing most of the talking most of the time. He interacts little with students, especially in the way one can see in this episode where a student insists on pursuing some issue. In fact during my six-week stay in this classroom, there only are two such interactions, the second one involving Christina as described in chapter 2. At the same time, all observers in the classroom agree that the numerous demonstrations are skillfully performed and a rich source of applications of angular momentum. The posttest results, which included interviews with ten students, then come as a little surprise: in a demonstration of the same phenomenon using a low friction turntable rather than a stool, four students show the direction of the vector representing angular momentum as shown by the teacher (Figure 1.2); and of these, three also know how to indicate angular velocity by means of an arrow (vector). These are the only students who draw on the conservation of angular momentum as a resource to explain why there is little or no movement when the axes of the wheel and turntable are (nearly) perpendicular, but a considerable rotation of the turntable in a direction opposite to that of the wheel when the axes are parallel.

The videotapes of this classroom exhibit similar issues in the context of other demonstrations. Toby likes to develop demonstrations, spends much time in developing and building demonstrations that he uses to illustrate the standard principles students are to learn. In some sense, he earnestly tries to provide his students with a rich and varied experience. But all data sources collected in the classroom provide evidence for the claim that most students in this classroom fail to understand many of his demonstrations and the physics lessons to be learned in them. Although the demonstrations are technically well prepared, and although Toby talks about the major concepts involved, students learn little from these demonstrations. This raises the question, "Why do these students learn so little from Toby's demonstrations?" In this chapter, I articulate some of the features of the lessons that may mediate students' failure to learn the intended lessons. My interest here is not to blame the teacher but to highlight those features of the most well intended lessons that interfere with student learning. I feature those aspects of demonstrations that constitute a fundamental aporia for learning in this mode.

DEMONSTRATIONS AND OBSERVATIONS

Science teachers often employ demonstrations to exhibit scientific principles in action. However, there may be some problems with this practice. It is widely accepted that all observation is interpretation. Because interpretation arises from the interplay of existing understandings (prior experience) and the world, what I (in being singular plural) observe depends on what I already know, on my present disposition. It is unlikely therefore that students who do not yet know the relevant scientific principles will see just what the demonstration is to show, for the very principles that are to be exhibited are prerequisite to seeing the intended phenomenon. That is, students perceive science demonstrations differently from teachers and scientists, a fact that mediates what they can perceive and how they can articulate it in observational language. As I show in chapter 3, not only students but also experienced scientists reveal a relevant world in and through their individual interactions rather than comprehending this world in its entirety when they first lay their eyes or hands onto it. That is, even in the demonstrations learners are faced with the fundamental aporia that to perceive what they are supposed to perceive they need to know and understand the phenomena; but they are presented with these demonstrations because they are supposed to learn to perceive and explicate them. The upshot of this is: more than simple exposure to some event through a demonstration is required if students are to learn.

Most research regarding learning assumes the existence of an inherently structured world with clearly identifiable phenomena. Phenomenological and pragmatist philosophers consider this assumption problematic and even untenable. It is easy to show that perceiving the world around me with specific objects and properties is not a self-evident process—I explore this in subsequent chapters—and, as seen in the next chapter, students structure the world differently from their teachers and the community they represent. To understand students' talk and manipulations in science classrooms, it is therefore helpful to model the presumed ontology (i.e., ensemble of objects and events perceived) of the lived world as ambiguous and undetermined before the act of interpretation. Through the interpretation of perceptual experience, objects become the things I know of together with their specific attributes. Specific interpretations arise from the interaction of the horizons (presuppositions, dispositions) I bring to a situation and the material world. That is, my interpretive horizon has formed in previous experience and is embodied in the practical competence of seeing something as something. Recent neurophysiological and neuropsychological evidence supports this: all signals—e.g., from the eye to the brain—are filtered, modulated, and shaped by signals from the brain to the eye. What hits my retina is not what is available to my consciousness—but this issue has to await a description of novel perceptual experiences as I articulate these has to await a description of novel perceptual experiences as I articulate these in chapter 3.

There are other descriptions of knowing and learning that question traditional conceptions of demonstrations. Etymologically, the word *demonstration* derives from the Latin *monstrare,* to show, point out; and *de-* is a reinforcing device. To be able to recognize that which is strongly made explicit and pointed out, I already must be able to perceive it. But *perceiving it* requires that I master the theoretical framework, that is, the observation sentences and observation categoricals that the demonstration is intended to facilitate my learning of them. That is, a demonstration works for those who already know; it is an inherent aporia for the learner familiar neither with phenomenon nor with the theoretical frame that supports it.

A new relationship between descriptive and explanatory language and visibility of phenomena has been suggested in recent work in the history and philosophy of science (e.g., Pickering, 1995). Accordingly, discourses—or rather and more poignantly, observation categoricals and the theories issuing from them—and the world I perceive are mutually constitutive: they presuppose each other. They are and do so, but not in any simple fashion; rather, their relation is dialectical and indeterminate. Material practices (manipulating objects, artifacts, tools) and discursive practices (observation sentences, observation categoricals, theoretical explanations) coevolve and reify each other. There is historical evidence that initially, Galileo Galilei could not see motion on the inclined plane as I see it today. His understanding of velocity and the linear relationship between instantaneous velocity and time came about only after he changed his notion of *velocita* (average velocity) to the present day notion of instantaneous velocity. In his days, two accepted pieces of knowledge mediated his seeing and understanding. First, ratios could only exist between like things (four stones and two stones), not of two unequal things (e.g., distance and time) as is required for the modern notion of velocity. He therefore could not conceive of the ratio of distance traveled and the time it took to cover this distance. Second, he could not conceive of an instantaneous velocity, the distance an object covers in the course of a time interval that approaches zero seconds in the limit. Without a theoretical discourse about velocity, there is no phenomenon; and without the phenomenon, a discourse that describes and explains it is of little use.

To understand this relation between the things perceived and my descriptions of them, the philosopher Martin Heidegger (1977/1996) uses the notion of *articulation,* both in the senses of *utterance* and *joint.* I articulate, that is, tell the world into wholes and parts exactly where it has its joints, *articulations.* Words and language therefore have no other use than helping human beings to point out what is and can be articulated, perceptually. That is, I can articulate something *as* something only when I perceive it as different from everything else. In other words, observation sentences require corresponding things perceived; entities and processes in the world and the sentences that describe them presuppose each other in as far as they are relevant to my actions. By analogy, I can also talk about (articulate) things that are not available perceptually but nevertheless constitute jointed wholes and parts.

SEEING AND EXPLAINING DEMONSTRATIONS

As I conducted research in this Australian science classroom, I formulated an assertion stating that students learn very little from the many demonstrations performed by Toby. To test this assertion, I constructed a posttest task that was very similar to one of the demonstrations differing only in the object that permitted the person to spin: Toby sat on a rotating stool during the lesson (Figure 1.1) whereas my fellow researcher doing the demonstration during the posttest stood on a rotating table. The drawings accompanying the test questions have high epistemic fidelity: the naturalistic drawings of objects, direction of motion, verbal descriptions of motion and objects, and perspectives are as they can be perceived them from the students seats (positions).

A standard explanation of the situation in Figure 1.1 runs as follows (Figure 1.3). The rotating chair or table (and person sitting/standing on it) with an axis in the vertical direction has an angular momentum of zero ($L = 0$). As long as the bicycle wheel's axis of rotation, and with it its angular momentum (L_2) is perpendicular to that of the rotating table with the person (L_1), it remains at rest because the angular momentum of the bicycle wheel does not carry over (Figure 1.3a). If the bicycle wheel is turned so that its axle has a component parallel to that of the turntable, the latter begins to rotate in the opposite direction (Figure 1.3b). Taken together, the momentums of the bicycle wheel and that of the rotating chair or table cancel out so that total angular momentum is conserved ($L = 0 = L_1 + L_2$), that is, has a value of zero.

On the posttest, only three students provide the answer that Toby Mory expected. In two of these instances, the direction is inconsistent with that of angular velocity, although the students invoke the relationship according to which angular velocity and angular momentum have to point in the same direction. Eight students

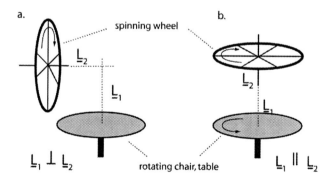

Figure 1.3. The standard explanation of the experiment depicted in Figure 1.1 is based on the concept of conservation of momentum. The rotational momentum in the direction of the rotating chair or table initially is zero. a. As long as the axle of the spinning wheel is perpendicular to that of the chair or table, nothing is observed. b. When the two axles are parallel, the chair or table moves in the direction opposite to the wheel so that the momentums of the two taken together cancel out.

29

use arrows either parallel to the axes, or curved and parallel to the trajectory of the rims of wheel and chair or table, as I have drawn them in Figure 1.3. Twelve students do not respond at all or indicate, "don't know." Even Sean, one of the highest achieving students in this course, does not infer the direction of the angular momentum vector:

> Angular velocity. It's like the momentum. Not sure about the direction of it. Mr. Mory hasn't told us yet or I probably didn't think or couldn't remember it. I wasn't sure what the actual direction was that the arrow represented so. . . . Well I obviously had an idea on vectors, and they have magnitude and direction. I couldn't recall the direction, so I just gave the magnitude value.

When asked to explain why the person on the low friction table spins when the wheel is turned as indicated, four students provide explanations that the teacher accepted as correct. These explanations invoke the law of conservation of angular momentum. Three students provide explanations in which the direction of the table's and the wheel's axis is the central feature. Seven students explain the situation by drawing on forces and torques or action–reaction systems. For example, Allan suggests:

> It is a closed system. The force of the wheel caused his body to turn. Every action has an equal and opposite reaction. Therefore his body turned in the opposite direction to the spinning wheel.

Like many of his peers, Jon brings his prior understanding from Newtonian mechanics into play to interpret what he has seen:

> Instead of talking of the momentum I was talking about the forces and direction and so I think I was talking about the forces activating the wheel, like friction and stuff like that instead of actually momentum.

Nine students suggest that the total angular momentum changes (although the system is to be considered closed from a physics perspective). Ten students provide no explanation at all.

In this situation, Toby, a well-intentioned teacher has presented a classical demonstration couched in the typical discourse about the topic. From his point of view (position, dis-position, and disposition), he has provided all the requisite knowledge pieces to "construct" an understanding of the phenomenon. Students observe and, despite all the explaining, gesturing, and writing on the chalkboard Toby performs, exhibit little if any understanding of the theory that the demonstration is to exhibit. Readers can already imagine that there are a number of mediating elements that make it difficult for students to learn. For example, if they perceive no movement in a demonstration but the teacher's explanation is intended to explain why an object moves, then students have difficulties integrating the contradictions. Or they hear only selected aspects of the explanation and fit it to their observation, which is different though neither they nor the teacher realize this. In the following section, I provide an account of mediating circumstances that may have interfered with students' understandings.

MEDIATING CIRCUMSTANCES

Based on my observations, I identified a number of influences that mediate students' observation sentences and explanatory discourse relative to the demonstration. The influences, however, cannot all be separated entirely because they interact. For example, in this course, students use force talk to explain why the stool rotates. At the same time, their force talk also fits with force talk related to the phenomenon of precession (the circular motion a spinning top undergoes because of the gravitational pull). In the data sources assembled as part of the research, one can identify a number of influences that mediate what and how students learn from demonstrations. These include: (a) students have difficulties separating signals from noise, that is, they do not know which aspects of the display they need to focus on to understand the teacher's accompanying or following theory talk; (b) when students come to see a particular demonstration, they bring with them different discourses that frame their descriptions and explanations, which may be inappropriate for and mediate the development of a discourse suitable for the situation at hand; (c) other demonstrations students have seen mediate their development of a discourse because of superficial similarities in images and discourse; (d) students may not be able to connect the different representations that are implicit in the teacher's theory talk to other aspects of their knowledge about physical systems; (e) the low priority given to constructing and understanding phenomena compared to being able to get the correct results on numerical tasks affects students' engagement with the demonstrations; and (f) a lack of opportunity for students to engage in a discourse about the demonstration to test the appropriateness and suitability for describing, constructing, and explaining phenomena. In the following subsections, I articulate issues and aporias concerning each of these mediating influences.

Separating Signal from Noise

For demonstrations to work at all, students need to perceive what the teacher intends them to see so that his presumably correct explanation provides a plausible account for what the students actually perceive. However, the videotapes show that there are frequent situations in which it is not clear to students just what Toby wants them to see. Nor is it clear whether what they have actually seen is to be taken as a relevant signal or as an irrelevant noise. Here I use the terms *signal* and *noise*, which are the standard concepts for people concerned with information and information transfer. They are appropriate here, because they make crucial distinctions that are at the heart of the problem with which scientists and our students have to wrestle. In one situation, for example, Toby throws a beach ball repeatedly to students and instructs them to throw it back in a certain way. The observers in the room find out only long after the demonstration that it has not shown what Toby wanted it to show: An object that experiences a force away from its center of mass will exhibit both translational and rotational motion (see also the investigation with the baton described in chapter 2). Whereas Toby knows that the demonstration is not working as intended, the students do not and cannot know if they are observing a signal or noise.

In their explanations for what they have seen in the posttest demonstration with the spinning bicycle wheel, students' notes indicate that they are divided in their observation. During the demonstration, a slight movement of the person on the turntable can be observed, which is possibly due to the axis of the wheel not being completely horizontal. In this case, physicists would explain that there is a component momentum parallel to the axis of the turntable (a position of the bicycle wheel between the two extremes shown in Figure 1.3), which reacts by turning so that the overall momentum remains zero. The analysis of the posttest shows that five students—all normally high or very high achieving—do not observe any movement—three students have predicted this, while two have changed between prediction and observation. They consider the wiggles as noise on top of the real signal, no motion. Eighteen students state on their posttest that the demonstrator–table system has moved—eight of them adding that the movement has been "little" or "slight." These students maintain that the person has moved, even when this experiment is contrasted right away with a situation where the axis of the spinning wheel is parallel to the turning table's axis, which gives rise to several complete rotations of the turntable in the direction opposite to the bicycle wheel. For these students, the wiggles are the real signal: they have observed significant motion. The uncertainty whether what she has observed is to be interpreted as motion or stationary state is apparent in Karen's account of the situation: "The wheel that he was turning, spinning, and that he was fairly much stationary but he moved slightly and I wasn't quite sure what the actual movement was."

After the fact and by closely watching the videotape, I-analyst can say that the stool has moved about one-eighth of a turn. From the perspective of the uninitiated students, it is not clear whether this is actually noise or signal. After the lesson during a moment when he reviews this demonstration on video, Toby shows awareness of the small size of the movement but notes that he has told students about the friction that has slowed him down. In reaction to the test item, where the angular momentum of the wheel is perpendicular to the table's axis, Toby suggests that some students may predict to observe rotation. However, he suggests that all students should be able observe that there is no rotation and he expects students to use an explanation of the type, "The axis of the wheel was *horizontal*; hence the man did not spin about a *vertical* axis."

During interviews, I later ask those students who have seen and described the movement as insignificant how they might defend their claim in the face of the fact that so many of their peers have seen the demonstrator move. In all cases, the students continue to maintain their description of the motion as negligible. For example, Jon contrasts the two situations, with the wheel's axis perpendicular and parallel to the stool's axis. In the light of the movement with axes of bicycle wheel and turntable parallel, he interprets the other movement as non-significant.

An explanation drawing on students' inexperience in separating signals from noise, or worse, invoking "low ability," cannot be satisfactory as I show especially in chapter 3 concerned with a phenomenology of perception. Developing the competence to separate signals from noise constitutes the daily work of scientists and engineers alike. They, too, struggle with separating signal from noise prior to being thoroughly familiar with the phenomena under study, at which point they make rapid assessments of what there is to see or not to see; it may take weeks or months before they get to this point (Roth, 2003). Such interpretations are impossible to make out of context, for signals of the same order are significant in one, but simply noise in another context. That is, the nature of a data point—signal, noise—is not given in any absolute sense but depends on the theory. That is, any demonstration risks not being perceived in some intended way that supports and is explained by, some specific concept or theory.

Mediating Discourses

Students always already bring to the classroom ways of talking from different, out-of-school and in-school contexts. These everyday, mundane ways of talking enable, envelope, and ground any new ways of talking, that is, scientific discourse. I-learner never only talk one language; and talk about any physics topic will involve words, sentence structure, topical organization, and so forth that also have currency in mundane language. Given that Toby's demonstrations and the posttest have been in the context of a physics course, students might be expected to draw on discursive resources appropriated in this course for explaining what they have seen during the demonstrations. This is evident during the demonstration featured in the opening vignette when Andy invokes forces. During the test situation, seven students explicitly draw on the terms *force*, *torque*, and *action–reaction* systems to articulate an explication for what they have seen. The results on the test suggest that many students bring into play previously appropriated language concerning Newtonian mechanics for interpreting what they saw. The very fact that they find themselves in a physics course makes it likely that they inappropriately find relevance in other physics discourse involving phenomena with some external similarities (Roth & Duit, 2003). For example, Jon says:

> Because if you use the rule, the acceleration and momentum is going through him and it's perpendicular to where he's standing. So a force is not applied in this vertical axis but it is applied in the x-axis, so if there's not force applied in that direction you wouldn't expect him to move.

Jon also invokes Newton's third law according to which every action is associated with an equal but opposite reaction to explain his observation. Such explanations appear especially appropriate because there usually is some movement whenever the wheel is accelerated so that the acceleration of the wheel and the beginning of the person's motion coincide. Aubrey suggests, "Because it is a closed system. The force of the wheel caused his body to turn. Every action has an equal and opposite reaction. Therefore his body turned in the opposite direction to the spinning wheel." Others combined discourses from other domains including torques and their magnitude as a function of an angle.

Mediating Observations

During the posttest, students predict and interpret events on the basis of prior experience. They used "mental images" as resources in their predictions, interpretations, and explanations. However, these images and the predictions students derived from them often are inappropriate in the context of the posttest questions. For example, both Christina and Karen suggest that the person on the frictionless table should turn although the axis of the spinning wheel is perpendicular to that of the table. Asked to explain, Christina responds, "Partly because I have seen Toby and partly because of my own experience with my study chair. . . . Mainly knowledge, that I had seen it before." Karen explains,

> I thought there would be some movement, because I had seen it before but I couldn't remember what the movement was. I sort of missed it a little bit because the movement was so slight, so I wasn't quite sure what was going on, so I couldn't really explain it.

Students' explanations of the phenomenon are mediated by a number of other demonstrations with surface similarities even if these other demonstrations occurred at a later point in time. One mediating effect is produced by a rather spectacular demonstration during which a spinning bicycle wheel is suspended from one side of its axle without falling to the ground, precessing around the rope that suspended it (Figure 1.4). On the surface, the situations in Figures 1.1 and 1.4 appear similar: a bicycle wheel is held parallel to the ground. However, whereas in Figure 1.4 the wheel is free to pivot vertically about the point of suspension, which leads to the precession producing torque; the bicycle wheel in Figure 1.1 is fixed and is not allowed to move downward. Structurally these are different situations so that a different explication has to be chosen. These images and Toby's associated

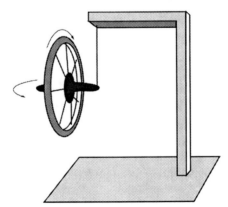

Figure 1.4. Prior to the posttest, students had seen this spectacular demonstration, in which a spinning bicycle wheel is hung from one side of its axle. Rather than falling down, as people unfamiliar with the demonstration predict, the bicycle wheel will precess, *that is, slowly revolve in a horizontal plane around the string by means of which it is suspended.*

talk provide students with resources for explaining the demonstration they have seen earlier and which reappears during the posttest. Thus, students explain, "The two torsional forces acting on him caused a resulting force which turned him to the left" [Andy], "The torque on the spinning wheel forced the man's body around with enough force to rotate it" [Allison]," "He moved in this direction because of precession" [Brett], and "Precession only occurs when something is rotated around two axes at right angles. The wheel is only rotating around one axis, so no other movement occurs" [Dean]. Karen's explanation is exemplary in one sense. She draws on the discourse that the teacher previously has employed during the precession demonstration and invokes the existence of two forces, the different directions these forces need to have relative to each other, and the resulting movement of the system.

Students also make explicit reference to a sketch that has been provided with the test item. Dean derives his explanation from the teacher's talk, his perception of the wheel, and the arrows the teacher has drawn on the blackboard as part of his explanation of the precessing bicycle wheel:

> I took a lot of it just from what Mr. Mory said and what he showed us with the three axes joined at right angles, so with the wheel being rotated in front which is one axis and then also round the second one. So the third one is straight up and down so you're spinning around that way, so you have to spin one way or the other and I didn't know which way. So, yes, from what he said there's a force somewhere that tends to make it turn around a third axis.

Switching Representations

From Toby's perspective, students should have been able to show the direction of angular momentum by means of an arrow in a pencil drawing. Students already have been familiarized with the right-hand rule and repeatedly have been exposed to Toby's explanations using it: when an object moves in the direction of the curled fingers of the right hand, the thumb points in the direction of the vector that physicists use to represent angular momentum, angular velocity, and so on (Figure 1.2). In these situations, the videotape features Toby showing students the direction of the vector using the right-hand rule, and writing the algebraic equation from which the equality of magnitude can be taken. Toby even says, "This was going in that way, rotating that way. Let me see, vector upwards." He accompanies this statement by a hand movement showing the direction of the "that way" with his curled fingers, followed by the thumb pointing upwards into the air.

But Toby does not draw on a standard convention for representing vectors: that is, draw arrows whose lengths are expressions of magnitude and whose orientation indicates the direction of vector quantities. Without the actual drawings, however, "vectors" may be just another term that has no or little meaning; that is, students might use the notion for their own intention or might fail to integrate it into their discourse about the situation.

Toby's discourse (see opening vignette) is composed of many elements from different domains; they provide, as I show in chapter 5, different maps or lenses. Here, because the elements of the different lenses appear together as if they are part of one and the same lens, they lead to confusion. There are descriptions of: events happening before the students' and teacher's eyes; how to find the direction of the angular momentum vector from the observation (right-hand rule according to which the thumb shows the direction of the vector when the fingers are curled in the direction of the wheel's motion); a vector as radial rather than a "real" one; intentions normally absent from physics discourse ("there's no way that I'm going to let my body rotate"); and of the "darn friction in that chair" which interferes with his presentation of the ideal world of physics. These descriptions refer to different positions in and dispositions toward the world. The right-hand rule (depicted in Figure 1.2) integrates these dispositions. The physical experience that can be observed, measured, and manipulated constitutes one of these worlds. The curled fingers pictorially represent the rim of the wheel—pointing in the direction in which the wheel turns—denote an aspect of this world. The thumb stands for an object in a very different world. It is part of a discourse physicists use to describe and explain phenomena. The thumb stands for a vector, a mathematical quantity which itself can be depicted and represented in a number of ways, some pictorial (arrow of specified length and direction) others in what seems more abstract ways as letters, matrices and so forth. Whereas teachers exchangeably use these different ways of presenting, they constitute different pieces of knowledge for the students. These ways of denoting the theoretical expressions do not make sense to students because the expressions do not fit into the already everyday language patterns they are familiar with and therefore do not fit into the inherently meaningful lifeworlds that the students inhabit. The posttest and the associated interviews show that students do not integrate these worlds and their descriptions to an internally consistent framework.

Mediating Context

The events in which students participate and constitute make sense in their nature as socially and societally organized. I participate in lessons as teacher or as student, and *what* I hear, I hear through the lens of participating as I-student or as I-teacher. That is, although my actions are embodied in the sense that only through them I can act—even talk requires work—they also are mediated by the nature of the current activity. An action presupposes the nature of the activity; but it is only through concrete actions that the activity (e.g., *schooling*) is realized. Therefore, the ongoing event and specifically the currently relevant entities in and aspects of the setting mediate the production and "consumption" of an action. This activity, involves others; even my (material, discursive) actions are such that I can always provide reasons for them, which means that their intelligibility is inherently oriented toward others. First and foremost, students participate in schooling, which provides them with resources to go on to university or with constraints that prevent them from being accepted in some program of their choice. *This* rather than questions of knowledge mediates what students do as part of their physics course, including note-taking during demonstration, studying without paying attention to demonstrations they have seen, and so on.

Even the shortest excerpt from a classroom videotape serves to illustrate how (discursive) actions both mediate and are mediated by the context; that is, in each situation is produced in its singularity but also reproduced as a type of situation. In the following excerpt from the introductory episode, Andy asks what will happen if the teacher holds the bicycle wheel over. Toby responds suggesting that he wants the student or students think about (turn 02).

01 Andy: When you turn this ((points to the wheel)) over will that do it in the opposite direction, which will also help you stop? When you turn that over one-eighty degrees?

02 Toby: That's what I want you to think about, *why*, when I turn it over, did I reverse? Now I should keep spinning if it wasn't for the darn friction in this chair.

In this situation, one person asks a question, but the other person turns the question around, which suggests that the person who has asked also is made responsible to provide an answer. Immediately afterwards, Toby moves on to attend to and talk about something else without waiting for an answer. Looking at this exchange without knowing the two individuals but only have the utterances available, I-analyst might not immediately discover that the person asking the initial question is a student. But the response provides me with resources for hearing it as the response of a teacher—just imagine a student answering the teacher question "Why are you late?" or "What is the answer to this question?" by responding, "That's what I want you to think about." Thus, in acting as they do, Andy and Toby also reproduce a typical teacher–student interaction (which researchers then often describe and explicate in terms of power relationships). Other aspects of the setting also mediate what students hear, how they hear it, and how they attend to what they hear.

In the videotapes from the classroom, many demonstrations are flagged and prefaced with some remark, which suggests that students would not be accountable for them on tests. Toby wants to raise interest and wonderment. However, over the six weeks in this classroom, I arrived at the conclusion that there is a very low priority on understanding from demonstrations. Toby and his students appear to assume that they remember the events in the case of a test or exam (e.g., "I just watch and soak it all in," "We just observe what happened"). In such instances, many students diminish their active engagement (e.g., "I mean you immediately don't write any notes down or anything, we will just listen to this and have a bit of enjoyment"). As to the importance of demonstrations flagged by Toby as being for interest, Rhonda's response is indicative and representative of many I receive: "I probably wouldn't concentrate on that as much, like I would take notes on what he was doing but then go back to, maybe just use the other stuff if I wanted to know how something worked. Some of it I don't think I really need to know."

Students' notebooks make no reference to any of the demonstrations, as if these are not useful resources for doing well in this course ("Examples were good there didn't seem to be enough behind them they were just examples of like, of what it relates to"). Where there are any records of students' note-taking during demonstrations, these are always formulas, equations, and calculations that Toby notes on the chalkboard; I cannot find in these notebooks descriptions or other forms of representation of what Toby shows or the explanations he gives. Problems that require the calculation of missing quantities, and any information that might pertain to these activities, are the few things students always copy down from the chalkboard. In the recorded interviews, some students lament the fact that demonstrations do not lead to better understanding; thus Christina says, "We didn't sort of work out exactly the physics behind what was happening and why it was. I think it would have been better to do that."

In this class, there are few discussions, which, from a sociocultural perspective, provide students with opportunities to talk, and in talking, to test their own understanding. But neither students nor Toby appear to be willing to create such situations, that is, exchanges during which alternative explanations and discourses are evident. Toby is quite happy to present his demonstrations without interruptions. He repeatedly tells me that his own interests are the primary determinants of what he does in his physics class. As a result, he is so engrossed in demonstrations that he forgets about student learning: "It's only when sometime down the track I get a wrong answer in a test or I get a wrong comment somewhere that I realize that what was clear to me, wasn't clear to them."

When students do ask questions, Toby frequently does not take the time to assess what might motivate the student to ask this particular question at this time (Toby always is willing to listen and talk to students after class, or to be called at home by students when they experienced difficulties with their textbook problems.) The exchange with Andy is typical. Andy provides an alternate description and explanation for the system, including talk about forces. Toby, however, simply turns the question around and then shrugs Andy's comment off, "I am not even mentioning forces." During the posttest—which features the same phenomenon— nine students employ force to explain the phenomenon. The episode with Andy illustrates that an important opportunity may have been missed: for students to know and know about physics, for Toby to know about student knowing. The test results show that his comment, "I'm not even talking about forces" is insufficient for students to abandon force talk in the context of this demonstration. It is not far-fetched to think that an open discussion may have encouraged more students to join Andy, and therefore may have provided Toby with an opportunity to recognize the extent of this inappropriate discourse.

As I-author sit with the students in the course listening to Toby, they appear to to be content that Toby does not ask them to talk about the phenomena. During the six weeks I spend in the classroom, there are few moments when students engage Toby, and when someone actually asks a question, then he or she always comes from a small subsample of the class (Andy, Christina). Some students also want to avoid embarrassment. They do not ask questions because it might be about something they ought to know. They fear Toby interprets such questions as obstinate behavior and may become unkind ("I think everyone kind of gets scared that if they ask Mr. Mory, he is going to yell at them or something like you sort of think maybe it is something that you're supposed to know"). Another student cites specific instances where Toby had called on her, and each time she felt it was to embarrass her ("he wanted to embarrass me or something").

GAP BETWEEN DEMONSTRATING AND PERCEIVING

Toby Mory is typical of many teachers in his view of learning and teaching as involving the process of transmission. He is atypical in so far as—based on the views of his peers and some observers—he is very skilled in conducting demonstrations and that he commands a large repertoire of demonstrations. He is very well intending, but—bringing to this teaching technique an epistemological stance according to which the world is inherently mathematical and knowledge matches this structure—overestimates what physics neophytes can see in and learn from demonstrations. Thus, he expects students to see conservation of angular momentum in his demonstration, separate noise from real signals, reconstruct the equivalence of signs across representational systems, and so forth. But Toby's assumptions—and likely those of many other science educators—are unwarranted. Despite his efforts and skill, the students in this class do not come to understand this and other demonstrations, the conservation of momentum, or the vector representations associated with the various quantities involved.

Teaching and Students' Learning Aporia

My intent here is not to criticize Toby or any other teacher using demonstrations. Rather, I attempt to understand how a very common teaching practice—the demonstration of events that are suitable to make scientific discourse intelligible and plausible—under certain circumstances fails to lead to student learning. I am interested in finding out about and understanding these circumstances. In the present context, there are six important aspects of the situation that mediate the experience in such a way that student learning of the target concepts does not come about: (a) without a theory, students have difficulty in separating noise from signal, (b) previously appropriated discourses interfere with the development of a new, situationally appropriate one, (c) the image traces of other demonstrations and everyday phenomena lead students to alternate explanations, (d) students do not construct on their own the equivalence of signs from different representational systems, (e) the overall context is such that many students did not consider demonstrations as something of importance, and (f) students have no opportunities to test whether their descriptions and explanations of the event are viable. I cannot know whether these aspects in fact *caused* students not to learn, nor does it permit me to say which of the aspects contributed to a larger extent. The available evidence only permits the hunch that the order of these aspects differs among students.

To know what the teacher wants them to learn from a demonstration, students need to be able to separate signals from noise: Is a wiggle in the body of the experimenter a significant motion or simply an artifact of his preparation? How can students make such a decision? My ethnographic studies among scientists show that they often spend a lot of time differentiating "blotches and wiggles" from "real signals." Their work consists of coming to perceive the "real signals" from a sea of blips and blotches in rationally accountable and defensible ways. Thus, the decision whether a peak in a spectrum is signal or noise usually is based on theory. But if the theory does not yet exist, scientists may proceed by evolving tentative descriptions and embodied laboratory skills until a local theory emerges.

Students who watch demonstrations, however, neither have the scientific theory that the demonstration is to provide evidence for—this is what they are to learn from the lesson—nor the opportunity (or competence) to make the necessary distinctions. The students also do not have the opportunity to ascertain whether they can achieve agreement as to what they observed. Furthermore, students face similar problems when they are to learn specific scientific concepts from the laboratory activities Toby has asked them to complete. As I show in chapter 2, in these laboratory activities, it is virtually impossible to isolate what the real signals were without some notion of the theory to be learned. Thus, from the posttest data I know that for the "same" event the observations ranged from no motion to significant motion; that is, the same event really constituted two events, the event seen by different bodies in different positions and therefore dispositions. It is clear that such discrepancies can be used as topics of debates in which the teacher raises the signal versus noise issue on a metatheoretical (nature of science) level.

A traditional problem of school knowledge is that symbolic systems (numbers, vectors, diagrams) remain isolated and have no referent or relevance to anything else students know. Students learn to manipulate symbolic structures without referential content and are not provided with opportunities to integrate those symbolic structures that can be used alternatively to describe the same system. Students in this study know that vectors are quantities with magnitude and direction, have had previous experience in writing vector quantities as underlined letters (e.g., $\underline{v}$ for velocity), using arrows to represent vectors, and using fingers to represent directions ("right-hand rule" to find the direction of a magnetic field generated by an electric current in a wire loop). But I assume that all this knowledge exists in the form of separate pieces of memorized information—it is not surprising that some science educators talk about "knowledge in pieces" (which I think to be nothing but an artifact of schooling). Toby has used two of these representational forms, vectors (e.g., "$\underline{L}$"), gestures (e.g., Figure 1.2), and words (e.g., "right-hand rule"), but when asked, students do not use arrows to indicate the direction of angular momentum including the normally highest achieving among them. Toby, though, has behaved in an ordinary way for scientists. Scientific discourse does not referentially isolate but integrates different forms of representation in situationally appropriate ways; as I show in chapter 5, science works because it layers perspectives and maps. The present students do not have opportunities to participate in science talk that uses multiple modalities in the way their teacher, in the taken-to-be-appropriate ways, practiced it. Consequently, they fail to provide appropriate responses, namely those that the teacher expects them to give. Using different forms of making an investigation present again and developing ways of communicating what can be articulated is the topic of chapters 6 and 7.

The students do not develop the competence to talk about the phenomenon of interest in a way compatible with scientific canon. From the perspective of many students in this class, there is no real need to carefully watch demonstrations and to attempt to understand them. In this course, word problems are the main evaluative tool. Students can get these problems right, or at least garner enough partial credit to get a reasonable grade without understanding what the problem is about, or whether it refers to anything at all. Students describe strategies for achieving good marks without conceptual understanding. In this context, students have little incentive to see what the demonstration is to show and to develop competence in the associated physics talk (i.e., to develop an understanding). But even if students try to make their own frequently alternative descriptions the topic of conversation, Toby does not engage them and brushes off any comments that do not fit into his plans. Students therefore have no means or opportunities to assess in which way their talk is inappropriate because, from a language perspective of knowing, competence in "talking science" requires participation in scientific discourse.

Toward a Social Praxis of Science Learning

My concern in this chapter lies with understanding how a specific teaching practice is mediated by particulars of the setting. My ultimate goal is to arrive at one or a series of recommendations that could be a starting point for an action research project. A (social) praxis view of knowledge provides teachers with a new referent that entails changes in actions and classroom climate more conducive to learning from demonstrations.

From a received perspective on science teaching, Toby has done many things appropriately. A received perspective of knowledge treats it in modular form. Words (concepts) "have" "meaning" and refer to real objects. Looking at real objects and events provides a direct view of the concepts. Through observations individual students are enabled to see the underlying structure. The teacher only has to provide the correct labels (we note that this is also a central part of other teaching strategies such as the learning cycle). For example, in a classical perspective, a reasonably intelligent student should be able to "put together" the idea of the thumb up into an arrow and the content knowledge required on the test, given the knowledge that vectors have magnitude and direction. From a discourse perspective, any one of the three ways could be appropriate as part of the discourse about angular momentum of the bicycle wheel and replace the other two. The important difference is that the alternate signs and symbols can only be learned in praxis, for whatever sense is attributed to them is always mediated by the activity of which they are part. The thumbs-up gesture and utterance are aspects of an *in-joke*, inherently a joke that only insiders understand; but I am an insider in my lifeworld, culture, or familiar settings. If I do not get the joke then it is perhaps because I am not inside the group that defines through its practices what is in and what is not. Teachers therefore may take a perspective in which all activities, doing experiments, talking about design, explaining phenomena, constructing re-presentations, and so forth are considered social practices; these practices are realized in concrete human praxis. These are shared, developed, and negotiated within specific communities of knowing.

A social praxis perspective might help Toby to view learning as one of participating in the production and reproduction of perception, manipulations of the world, separation of signals from noise, talk about phenomena, constitution of phenomena through adjustment of discourse, representation of phenomena in terms of vectors, and construal of invariants (not finding or discovery of invariants). A social praxis perspective might help Toby to recognize that to make sense together, students have to engage in and develop practices together, be able to negotiate understandings, and repair discursive trouble (misunderstandings, errors). It might help him to recognize that in his classroom, and especially around the demonstrations, there were a lack of opportunities: (a) for discussion in which he, Toby, comes to understand students' understanding (or lack thereof); (b) for the students to check whether their own talk about the phenomena is shared with others, is viable and fruitful, or whether it needs to be changed; and (c) for checks whether what students construct as a phenomenon is from a scientific perspective, the phenomenon to be of interest or simply noise.

When teachers adopt a social praxis perspective, their learning environments changes. These are then no longer considered places where experts transfer their knowledge and products to less knowledgeable others. Rather, learning environments become places where all participants engage in developing new and common social practices (doing practical things, describing events, talking theory, etc.). These new social practices develop out of previously existing ones if they are to be robust and connected instead of piecemeal. There is evidence that such an approach works. I have read about how Swedish designers of a computer program to be used in a printing shop got together with the workers. Rather than imposing their computer-based work places on users, these design engineers of the new generation begin their work with mockups to establish a common discourse between professional designers and future "users"; they establish common ways of looking at, interacting with, describing, and theorizing a world that they make and take to be in common. In the process of talking about relevant artifacts, this common discourse begin to change as the artifacts evolved; and with the evolving artifact, designers' and future users' mutual understandings changes so that in the end, an intelligible and functional workplace emerges.

One of the things teachers like Toby may want to try is to present a demonstration, followed by student discussion, and presentation of a received framework with vector representations both in parallel and in orthogonal orientations. Keeping the different representations (in chapter 5, I suggest the analogy of *lenses* and *maps*) separate and show how science means to coordinate them may assist students in developing more consistent discourses about specific phenomena. This may help students in the present context develop explanations in which the conser-

Figure 1.5. A researcher gives a thumbs-up to students after a test, which required the right-hand rule. To get the joke, a person needs to perceive the similarity with the right-hand rule (Figure 1.2) and its relation to the test.

vation of angular momentum, the relationship between the relative angular veloci-ties (moments of inertia), and the influence of friction on the system are important resources—there is evidence that such an approach works. I have experienced first-hand how seventh-grade students engage in a lengthy argument about the outcome of a tug-of-war between themselves and the teacher (me) who was assisted by a block-and-tackle. In this case, students and teacher move from talking about the event and the actual block-and-tackle to the chalkboard where their discussions evolve around representations, both simpler and more convincing than the actual artifacts.

Teachers can learn by adopting a social praxis perspective of teaching and learn-ing physics, as captured in the following episode. After the posttest on rotational motion, one of my researcher colleagues says to a group of students, "thumbs up" and gives them a thumbs-up gesture (Figure 1.5). The students looked at him in a perplexed way, evidently not understanding what his comment can or shall mean; they did not get the intended joke. Although a joke explained no longer is a joke, here is how my colleague intended it: Because the right-hand rule can be used to answer most of the questions on the posttest, he finds this everyday expression humorous. The thumbs-up gesture resembles the gesture that embodies and articu-lates the right-hand rule (Figure 1.2), so that it can be understood as making an oblique reference to the answers on the test. However, what the speaker did not realized is that to understand this humor, one has to be part of the particular dis-course community in which the relationship between the gesture and the phenome-non is taken in a very particular way. This in-joke is comprehensible only to those who are already competent participants *in* the community (fluent speakers). And it requires seeing the thumbs-up *as* denoting the right-hand rule rather than a thumbs-up. That is, the joke resides in the crossover from the everyday domain to the spe-cialized physics domain, where it has a second, very different signified.

When teachers understand that knowing means knowledgeably participating in such conversations rather than carrying around stuff in the head that can be regur-gitated when requested—on tests—then they have made a big step toward a social praxis perspective. It is then easier for teachers to engage students in conversations and active exchanges, because this is where knowledgeability comes to be enacted. Most importantly, teachers no longer ought to think in terms of knowledge as something stable that is in and can be transferred to students' minds. Knowing is doing, and in doing I articulate knowledgeability for others. Equivalently, it is in and through their actions that others make their knowledgeability available to me. That is, perceiving others' actions is all that we ever have available, never any knowledge, conception, or conceptual structure. Participation in praxis, therefore, means participating in exhibiting my own knowledgeability and being confronted with that of the other. I do not have to go one in deeper, below the skin, and even less into the brain case of others.

CHAPTER 2

APORIAS OF ORDER PRODUCTION

In chapter 1, I articulate what students expect to perceive, how they articulate their perception, and how they explain what they have seen after observing an event. There are a number of situational factors that mediate how students orient themselves to a demonstration and what and how they can see in it. In the case of demonstrations, someone else (here the teacher) produces some spectacle and the audience is asked to observe and perceive the spectacle in an often-unspecified specific way. Chapter 1 shows that the student audience does not see what it is supposed to see, which requires knowledge of the knowledge to be learned, and therefore does not learn from the demonstration. Perhaps students learn when they produce the spectacle themselves? To find an answer, I studied all the videotapes taken while students engaged in investigations. The following narrative exemplifies what I can see when students engage in laboratory tasks.

To assist in learning about moment of inertia, Toby Mory, the experienced physics teacher from chapter 1, instructs his twenty-four students in his twelfth-grade physics class to conduct an investigation. "We have here an assemblage of various cylinders and ball bearings of two sizes. We'll be rolling these on your benches and you don't need to have a great slant, two diameter ball bearings. Solid, solid cylinders, we got at least two diameters; hollow cylinders, we have a couple of different diameters and each of those will roll." He shows each of the objects as he instructs students what to do and adds, "I really want you to compare something moving down the bench without rolling. It seemed to me and I haven't tried that before, that if I can make a trolley light enough of a bit of balsa and I bought a few little toy cars from K-Mart." He shows to his students the chassis of a toy car and then continues, "We won't take into account the turning of the wheels because they are insignificantly puny. This would give us the cylinder sliding, frictionless in effect, as compared to rolling, cylinder and solid. I really want you to tabulate what observations and conclusions you get. It will be mostly of a qualitative nature, hardly quantitative. Don't measure, don't stopwatch. Okay? And you are making comparisons, and you are looking for patterns and ideas, and I don't think that any of you will get all of the patterns and ideas that you could get out of this. That is up to you to prove me wrong." Subsequent to these instructions, Jon, Rhonda and Sean—much like the other five groups in the class—collect their materials, raise up one side of a desk by placing books under its legs on one side, and begin their investigation (Figure 2.1).

Sean places a medium solid cylinder on the chassis, releases it down the inclined plane, and describes the motion as "slow acceleration, slow velocity." He

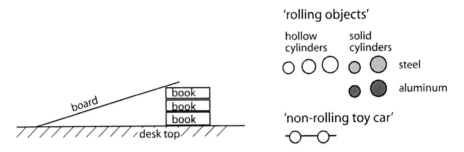

Figure 2.1. Set-up and materials used by the students in the exploration of various rolling cylinders and a 'sliding' object.

takes the cylinder off the trolley, rolls it down the incline and describes the resulting motion, "That would have been parabolic, the acceleration, not acceleration but the displacement." Rhonda, speaking at the same time, corrects, "You mean the distance?" After rolling the large solid cylinder, Sean concludes, "It has constant velocity when it is not rolling." Sean and Jon roll several other objects alone and on the chassis, commenting "It's much the same" and "they are all pretty much the same when they are rolling."

To the outside observer, the three appear to have "discovered" their phenomenon. They become playful and begin to interact with other students. Although the outside observer sees (and hears) that the trolley with the cylinder accelerates down the inclined surface, contrary to Sean's claim, the three students do not appear to perceive the motion in the same way. After twenty trials, Sean is ready to draw some final conclusion. He selects the very first set up again and utters, "This is at constant velocity." But then comments on the outcome of the experiment, "What happened there, mate?" Jon responds, "It accelerates?" Sean repeats the experiment and, after observing the same outcome: "What happened to my first theory?" "What theory?," Rhonda questions, and Jon responds, "Let's see what happened to it." After another trial, Sean suggests, "They all accelerated, it's probably the wheels." "They're a bit crooked," Rhonda adds and Jon chimes in, "The wheels always are on these little carts, they never used to work in primary school."

At this point, Toby announces that he wants students to arrive at a conclusion within the next minute. The three students quickly run a few more tests. At first they test Sean's proposal that the mass of the objects makes a difference by following Jon's suggestion to race two objects at a time. The results of two different combinations of solid cylinders do not yield the significant difference they are expecting. Before the teacher stops the activity, the three get in two more runs with different combinations of a solid cylinder against a hollow cylinder while holding the radius constant. Sitting down they agree: "the solid accelerated faster."

This episode points out at least four important aspects relevant to the question, "What do students learn from laboratory activities?" First, the three students had constructed a phenomenon after the initial few runs: *Sliding objects move down an incline at constant velocity, while rolling objects accelerate all the way down.* It is only much later that they deconstruct this phenomenon (Sean's "first theory") as an artifact attributable to the wheels of the trolley. Second, the three students have constructed a phenomenon that is incompatible with that which the teacher wants them to "discover." Although the three manage to deconstruct their phenomenon before Toby calls an end to the activity, I observe many instances where students construct phenomena that are incompatible with a legitimized legitimizing perspective—e.g., Christina has collected data that disproves Toby's theory about rolling objects. Third, the construction of a phenomenon appears to be bound up with students' embodied material practices and language. Students' descriptions, manipulation of material and the phenomena they construct are mutually constitutive and depended on each other. And fourth, the students do not see what the outside observer sees when the chassis is loaded with the medium hollow cylinder accelerated down the incline. My interpretations of the laboratory activities in this twelfth-grade physics class lead me to *order production* as the core issue in understanding just what students learn from laboratory activities.

In this chapter I provide first answers to the questions, "How do students construct a phenomenon?" "What is the relationship between phenomena and students' material and discursive practices?" "What is the relationship between the teacher's instructions and students' actions?" and "How do students know that what they have seen and done is what the teacher wanted them to see and do?" This articulates a first understanding of the relationship between what students see when they do laboratory experiments and what teachers want them to see, and the relationship between laboratory instructions (written or spoken) and students' actions in laboratory activities. These are the central themes of this book, which I further articulate and explicate in subsequent chapters.

The central purpose of laboratory activities is the collection of data from which, through ordering and making inferences, students are to construct knowledge. Ordering objects and events in the field of vision is not a unique and unambiguous process: it can be done in different ways, leading to different phenomena, which themselves can be interpreted in a variety of ways. Although the context of the activity in my opening narrative is constrained—Toby has selected the objects of investigation, has suggested the inclined plane, and has suggested that students look for differences—students do not discover automatically what he wants them to discover. From his perspective, watching objects roll or slide down the inclined plane should make it easy to construct this series of inferences: As an object moves down a plane, its potential energy changes into translational kinetic energy and rotational kinetic energy, which is a function of the shape, which influences the inertia.

Out of six groups doing this investigation, only one independently arrives at a result consistent with what the teacher wants them to find out; another group arrives there with his help. The other four groups do not construct a phenomenon at all or do construct one inconsistent with what he has wanted—for example, Christine claims during the whole-class debriefing to have data that disprove Toby's theory and that radius does make a difference. The situation is exacerbated by Toby's tendency to reject all those student-produced phenomena that did not fit his intention and to admit only those where spheres showed a greater acceleration than solid cylinders, which in turn displayed a greater acceleration than the hollow cylinders (for more on this tendency, see chapter 1). It is left to students to re-interpret their prior actions and observations and to construe one of them as artifacts.

It is apparent from my account that the group quickly derives the two descriptions that constituted their first phenomenon. Accordingly, the medium-sized solid cylinder moves with a constant velocity when it slides but accelerates when it is rolled. (Although Sean's utterance is "slow acceleration, slow velocity," his later actions and utterances in the lab and his statements during stimulated recall lead me to the conclusion that he probably has meant to say "zero acceleration, constant velocity." But for the moment, because of lack of evidence from the data sources, I have to leave the interpretation open.) These two observations are generalized to become the tentative observation categoricals "It has constant velocity when it is sliding" and "They are all pretty much the same when they are rolling." Because these observations are novel and the two construals are the result of generalizing observation categoricals, the activities constitute moments of learning.

Much ordering activity and learning is evident during the second part of the investigation. The group makes a new and discrepant observation, which disconfirms Sean's earlier theory that sliding objects move at constant velocity, and the students evolve hypotheses that account for the artefactual nature of the observations that has led to the first theory. In the last section of the experimentation, the students generate two new hypotheses: one is disconfirmed, the other one confirmed. This resulted in an observation categorical: "solid cylinders accelerate faster than hollow cylinders." In the section, I am concerned with how students produce order—i.e., phenomena—and how this order arises from students' embodied practices (e.g., what is the function of the loops of repeated action).

LOOKING AT, OBSERVING AND SEEING AS

In my effort to understand students' laboratory activity, I have found it necessary to refine the notion of "observation" when applied to students' activities of learning from laboratory activity. I distinguish here between *looking (gazing, staring) at*, *observing*, and *seeing as*. When students *look (gaze, stare) at* some material, they do not engage in structuring activity. That is, there is no intentional articulation (carving up) of the world into things with specific aspects and properties, and no commitment to a viewpoint about the part of the material world of interest in the lesson. *Observing* is the active ordering and thus structuring of the world, the search for possibilities to carve the world into singularities, things (phenomena) characterized by specific aspects and properties. Through observing, a way of framing new experience in terms of previous and newly developed language, world becomes expressible and accountable (i.e., it can be accounted for). *Seeing as*— e.g., seeing a spinning ice skater as an instance of conservation of angular momentum—requires a particular lens and recognizing an object or event as something that is part of the shared world, recognizing the object as such. In chapter 5, I specifically deal with the constitution of such lenses, and how they interact with the contents given to students in their primary perception.

Looking (Gazing, Staring) At

In the videotaped materials, I see many instances where students merely look (gaze, stare) *at* the events they produced. There are indications that learning is occurring. Following the initial observations and discovery, the three students roll a number of objects without giving any indication of whether they are in fact *observing* or *seeing as*. The video shows the three students only partially engaged in further data collection, rolling the objects while attending to other events in the classroom. This may be an indication that they merely *look at* the rolling objects. Interesting cases are two observations when the cart accelerates, which is inconsistent with the initial observation Sean has made. Nobody takes note of this, yet during a stimulated recall session, Jon and Sean instantly recognize that their fifth and sixth observations contradict their initial ones. The students appear to *look at* rather than *observe* in this instance. Another possibility is that they see later outcomes as instances of earlier observations, that is, as replications.

In another recorded episode, students are to investigate the motion of a loaded pipe (called "the baton," which consists of pipe half of which is filled with metal so that the geometric center and center of mass did not coincide). Without saying a word, Arlene and Ellen strike the pipe three times, but differently, with the ruler and then sit down while their peers engage in longer but equally unsuccessful attempts at making sense of instructions and structuring events. I interpret this as occasions of *looking at* rather than *observing*. Arlene and Ellen make no attempt to frame the motion in one or another way. Their concerns hold back from producing any structured way of seeing, from *making* a phenomenon. The videotapes show the same behavior in two groups after they have overheard Toby commenting about a student experiment: "It is not doing as I want." Playful behavior observable on video and re-presented in the vertical orientation of the activity maps replete with broken squares are different but interrelated ways in which *looking at* took expression.

When students are asked afterward what has happened and what they have observed during these moments in their experimental work, some suggest that they have been simply looking, others (among these Sean, one of the very high achieving students) that they "are pretty much soaking it all in." Subsequent interviews further reveal that in some instances, students refrain from committing themselves to observations until they find out "what [they] are supposed to see" (Rhonda). The videotapes show that in these situations, they talk to other students to find out what they have observed or students wait until the teacher indicates what they should have observed. For a variety of reasons related to the classroom environment and especially the teacher's reactions to their findings (see section "Students' Fundamental Dilemma" below) students do not commit to observations anywhere in the videotapes and ultimately refrain from producing phenomena. In this case, they engage in what one might call a mode of being in which I just tarry alongside, that is, to linger in expectation of an occurrence until something is done or happens.

Parenthetically, it has to be noted that asking students after an event what happened and what they have been thinking is laden with all the problems of events that take on a different sense when they are discursively made present again for different purposes and events. On one of the videotapes, there is a situation in which Sean clearly predicts the outcome of an event. Later, in the interview, he claims that he could not have known the outcome because "the [cart] didn't always go straight or the wheels would get jammed." However, the videotape shows that the group frames the problem with the cart's wheel only much later. It is for this reason that researchers interested in the everyday mundane and work practices, rely on videotapes and interaction analysis rather than on stimulated recall of the participants. Their statements have to be taken very much with a grain of salt. It is entirely possible that the students do not describe aloud their framing so that I might draw an incorrect conclusion. However, because the activity structure is such that students are to come to a common description and agree upon a phenomenon, they have to communicate to each other what they observe. As soon as one student utters a description, others can voice their disagreement. If no one disagrees, agreement can be assumed.

Observing

In the experiment with the rolling objects, Toby expects students to make any one of a number of discoveries that show canonical physics in action. Students have to prepare the materials in some appropriate way to create events that appear significant and worthy of being reported in the subsequent whole-class debriefing. However, observation may not lead to the structuring of the material world such as to reveal the teacher-intended structure; students may in fact produce order but an order that differs from the teacher's own. In the videotapes, the three students featured in the introductory episode (and Sean in particular) frame the first event as an instance of constant velocity, whereas they structure the second as an instance of accelerated motion. A first utterance such as "constant velocity" or "that would have been parabolic" is a tentative observation sentence, describing an evidently vague something that only with time and through processes of reification becomes a more-or-less certain object. In the context of the lesson concerned with motion, the difference between the first two observations is significant, leading to a specific finding within Sean's group. In the same way, Andy describes and thus frames observations while observing rolling objects. It is especially clear that at this point, his first four descriptions are still apparatus bound: The fact that he describes the outcomes in different ways indicates a strong possibility for their artefactual nature.

Observing therefore is an active process by means of which an agent structures a field of experience into figure and ground; observing *seeks to* structure that which is not yet structured structure and if which I am aware only in an inarticulate way. The verbal description of an event then already constitutes an interpretation.

Prior to an act of observation, the field of experience is transparent, unnoticed, inconspicuous and unobtrusive. Students may look at the scene and "soak it all in" in a mode of "just tarrying alongside." But it is through the act of observation that students separate this field into objects with properties and surrounding context. Because of the diversity of their experience, deriving from their dispositions, students' perceptions of objects and events are likely to be different from those of the teacher (or any other representative of standard physics).

Science educators often assume that students need to state hypotheses explicitly and then test these to learn from their observations. To do this, students would need to confront their own ideas, which have therefore to be elicited and become object before they make their observations. But hypotheses require variables, and variables are exactly the desired outcomes of the activity in which Sean and his mates are engaged. This process would mean making hypotheses and therefore commitments before observations are made. Observations of scientists at work and scientists' own self reports, have not confirmed the necessity of such explicit stating of hypotheses. Frequently, scientists pursue experimental variations to bring out some effect; these variations contain hypotheses implicitly. They discover co-variations subsequently and then investigate these in ways that holds up in their community of practice. My videotapes contain many similar situations where students construct new phenomena by means of processes where hypotheses are initially implicit in experimental variations. For example, choosing the hollow and solid cylinders for configuration, Sean and his teammates can be said to test a specific hypothesis, although they never state one in the traditional sense of the concept. The hypothesis is embedded in the design of the apparatus and therefore was enacted in the course of the inquiry. Because it is embedded though not salient, it is already part of the familiar practically understood world—which, in as a result of the figure|ground dialectics described in chapter 3, allows the hypothesis to become figure (salient structure). But to lead to learning, it eventually has to be articulated—as I show particularly in chapters 3 and 4 and again in chapters 10 and 11.

Seeing As

Seeing as denotes the activity of a person looking at a situation and perceiving a particular order. As pointed out, for students to perceive the order that the teacher expects them to see, they have to share his tacit understanding and explicit framework. It therefore comes as little surprise that, if students see an event in the way he wants them to it is only during the occasional follow-up activity. For example, regarding the rolling and sliding objects, students are asked to verify the relationship between moment of inertia and speed when objects moved on an inclined plane. They can see the material phenomenon, though not necessarily understand it in the way scientists do, because the derivation of the relationship is rather difficult. This is exactly the point that I elaborate first regarding my own perceptual experience (chapter 3) and then regarding those of students studying static electricity in a German physics class (chapter 4). Similar instances of *seeing as* can be observed in the tapes, for example, after the teacher makes clear that when an object is struck at its center of mass, no rotational motion should be observed. After students return to their laboratory tables to strike a loaded pipe, they see the event in just this way. Similarly, in the previous chapter I show how students observe different phenomena in teacher's presentations of events as demonstrations. There I suggest that with the competence to talk about events students also come to see them in these specific terms, the *see* them *as* something.

In the same vein, once students perceive a phenomenon, they see subsequent events in terms of their observation sentences. Sean's observation "it's much the same," and his observation sentence about rolling objects that accelerate in the same way have to be interpreted as instances where he *sees* events *as* something, even if he eventually abandons the previously articulated phenomenon. In the videotapes, there also are examples of students who see an event as one of a class of entities. When Andy describes the outcome during the fourth observation in the same terms as the first observation, he orders it in the same class of events. Also, the fifth observation, "the same," constitutes *seeing as*, the ascription of a specific event to a class of events. This then constitutes an organization of observations under observation categoricals: "This cylinder accelerates" to "all cylinders accelerate if . . ."

REPETITION, REPLICATION, REIFICATION

A phenomenon constitutes, by definition, order, regularity, a repeatable and repeatedly observable event. Regularity cannot emerge from a single observation. To produce a phenomenon, the same actions—if there are such—have to be repeated on the same objects. Students who roll an object only once cannot be sure that what they see (e.g., the winner in a competition) is actually a phenomenon, for phenomena arise from repeated observation of something. An initially fuzzy and undetermined something is produced as the phenomenon when students reproduce it consistently—prior to that moment, as I show in chapter 4, no real observation categorical can be articulated and therefore no theoretical framework. So when Karen rolls a hollow cylinder with a solid cylinder only once and then continues with another object, she cannot produce an orderly phenomenon.

In the production of order, students frequently repeat sequences of actions. However, not all of these sequences have the same purpose so that there are different kinds of replication efforts. Jon, Rhonda, and Sean attempt to replicate the sequence between their first action A_1 and their sixth observation O_6, because the last observation contradicts the first observation O_1. An exact replication would indicate whether the first or second observation O_2 of the investigation with the first object is artefactual. Here, the artifact likely is an artifact of preparation; that is, the series of events really are not an exact replication. A problem emerges for students when the same objects are used but what they perceive does not turn out to be the same and hence is taken to be different. At this time, there is not a phenomenon and order cannot yet be produced with a set of actions students consider to be the same. In the present videotapes, they frequently interpret their own actions as constant but the outcome of their actions as different and possibly random. Repetition, then, may be used to produce order at another level. Repetition inherently means repetition of singularities, and therefore embodies difference (Deleuze, 1968/1994); order arises when similarity is recognized despite the differences.

In the following excerpt, Carl, Ellen, and Karen attempt to make sense of their investigation in which they compare the movement of a rolling solid cylinder and a solid cylinder on the cart. Turns 01 to 03 indicate that they have difficulties making sense because the outcomes of the experiment are inconsistent.

Episode 2.1
01	Carl:	This one ((toy car)) is larger and faster ((a solid cylinder)). Okay ((repeats the same experiment.))
02	Karen:	So, which one goes faster?
03	Ellen:	I don't think they are different.
	∷∷∷	
04	Carl:	It goes faster, the roller one
05	Karen:	But before, the other one was
06	Ellen:	But before, it went the same.
07	Karen:	I think we should maybe take an average the best of five anyway.

In this episode, Carl proposes that the toy car is faster, Karen questions her peers as to which of the two objects they should consider as being faster and Ellen suggests that one should interpret the contradictory outcomes as evidence that the two objects are equally fast. After completing a few more comparisons (a total of 8), the three still are unsure about how to interpret the outcomes (turns 04–06). Karen proposes a way out of their dilemma. By suggesting to "do *it* five times and take the average," she brings into play the scientific practice of multiple data point measurement and, implicitly, averaging (turn 07). Here, order is produced at two levels. First, there are different kinds of possible outcomes, that is, there is order at a lower level. Then, order at a higher level is produced, generated through statistical inference. In this case, the phenomenon itself is statistical rather than deterministic. They decide to repeat the experiment and select that outcome which occurs most frequently. They assume that their preparations and the observation process are identical to previous ones but the outcome statistical. After repeating the experiment a number of times, the most frequent observation (mode) is going to constitute the phenomenon. Below I show that the teacher undercuts this attempt without explanation by indicating that the event does not show what he has expected.

The videotapes show that replication with variation in the objects is infrequent in this classroom. Few groups arrange their set-ups in such a way that the phenomenon comes to be observed in an independent test that rules out some possibilities of being an artifact. One example can be seen in Jon, Sean, and Rhonda's experiments in which they first discard mass ("the heavier it is") as a significant variable (set up A_{15} and A_{16}, observation O_8) and then construct the shape (solid versus hollow) as significantly determining the rate of descent (set up A_{17} and A_{18}, observation O_9). Here, the students replicate the experiment but with a different combination of objects. In the first case, the fact that they make the same observation (observation O_8) despite the variation lends support to observation O_{8a}, "same velocity" and leads them to abandon their third hypothesis H_3. This third hypothesis has not been framed as such but implicitly is contained in the choice of materials, A'_2 (different types of cylinders with equal radius). Here, replication with variation results in a confirmation of the observation of difference, lending support to observation sentence O_{9a}. The teacher stops the investigations before these students get to the point of explicitly stating an observation categorical. They do so during the whole-class debriefing where Sean states, "hollow cylinders accelerate faster at constant radius."

These latter processes of independent replication, which lead to reification of scientific objects (phenomena), are those in which scientists have most experience and competence. Although there is little that distinguishes individuals in science and technology from ordinary people not working in these fields, the systematic use of repetition and independent replication in the construction of phenomena is clearly different from the often-reported confirmatory bias in everyday situations. In the present tapes, one can observe such systematic attempts of independent tests only in the case of Jon, Sean and Rhonda at the end of their investigation with rolling cylinders (observations $O_{8a,b}$ and $O_{9a,b}$). A different light is thrown on the students' work by more recent research on scientific thinking (Tweney & Chitwood, 1995), which requires researchers to take a more positive stance regarding human use of confirmatory evidence. In contrast to the usual focus on confirmation bias as a reflection of the limits of human cognition, the evidence suggests that a confirmation heuristic is one of the highly functional means by which knowledge is made possible.

VARIATIONS: ARE THEY SIGNIFICANT?

The work of differentiating blotches and wiggles from relevant signals constitutes much of scientists' situated inquiry. Their socially and materially situated, cultural historically mediated work consists in producing "real signals" from a sea of "blips" and "blotches" in rationally accountable and defensible ways. This is almost never made clear in science education (teaching or research). Why is variation important? At what point do I become aware of a variation as variation?

It is evident now—based on the results of the phenomenology of perception and neurophysiological experiments—that *my own* mobility and change are essential aspects of the material objects I know. Fixing the image of an object to a specific area on my retina makes the object disappear; it no longer exist form me (Roth, 2005a). Movement and change establish things in their environment and allow them to appear in their variant and invariant nature given the differences of the conditions that are brought about by my voluntary and involuntary movements. It is only because of variations, brought about voluntarily and involuntarily (e.g., the saccades of my eyes), that I actually can perceive the world and therefore learn and know anything at all.

The production of order (phenomena, observation categoricals, construal) often requires that students make some commitment as to whether small variations are relevant and significant or whether these are random errors. In the rolling, Jon and his mates interpret the difference between the first observation O_1 and the second observation O_2 as significant, leading to a construal, that is, the perceptual and verbal articulation of a phenomenon. Students in another group sometimes repeat an experiment but fail to replicate the observations because they interpret small differences as significant. Rather than interpreting the outcome of the races between a large and a medium solid cylinder as essentially the same with small differences as artifacts due to differences in the preparations, they interpret the sequence of actions that constitutes their preparation as essentially replicated but the outcome as different. They do not arrive at a consistent result but pursue another avenue ("What else affected it?") and decide to investigate the effect of radius on the motion. At another table, students interpret similar differences as negligible, which permits them to construct the outcomes of experiments A_{15} and A_{16} as "the same" (O_{8a}) and "equal velocity" (O_{8b}).

Most students in this class do not evaluate the significance of variations. Even within the same group, small variations are found to constitute significant differences at one moment, while only minutes later, the same difference is interpreted as not significant. These observations contrast those of sometimes much younger students in a variety of open-inquiry learning environments where there are many opportunities for students to familiarize themselves with the objects of their inquiry to assess whether qualitative and quantitative variations are significant or not. That is, extended investigation within a particular context, and repetition and replication of investigations allow students to develop an understanding of variations that is acceptable and permissible, and those that are significant and constitute differences to be accounted for. Such familiarity is important for scientists and engineers, for without having experienced a particular setting even experienced individuals in these fields cannot assess the significance of a particular variation. Thus, my ethnographic research among scientists suggests that when they work in a new context, new variables emerge for them in the process of becoming familiar.

ORDERING MANIPULATIONS: FOLLOWING INSTRUCTIONS

Teachers often provide students with written or verbal laboratory instructions. It is generally assumed that the relationship between a good instruction and the action it describes is simple: Good instructions are unambiguous and lead agents to do exactly what the instructions indicate. However, it is a well known fact that even the simplest instruction can be ambiguous unless I share the background assumptions and theoretical framework with those who have written the instruction—therefore the difficulties experienced in programming a VCR, in cooking a new dish following an unfamiliar recipe (see chapter 8), or in pruning trees based on the explanations that appear in a gardening book. As teachers are interested in students' production of specific phenomena, the question therefore has to be posed, "How do students know that what they have done is what they were supposed to do?" The

a.   b.

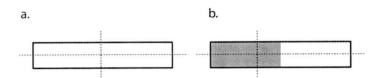

Figure 2.2. a. From the outside, the metal pipe looks symmetrical; its geometrical center is in the center, at the intersection of the lines. b. On the inside, the metal pipe is filled on one side so that the mass is unevenly distributed, shifting the center of mass with respect to the geometric center.

following episode illustrates the relationship between a teacher instruction and the observed student actions in one group consisting of Brenda, Jon, Rhonda, and Sean.

Toby has shown students a metal pipe, one-half of which is filled with a substance so that the center of mass (Figure 2.2b) is not in the geometric center of the object (Figure 2.2a); he calls this metal pipe a "baton." He has asked students to "mark dead center of the baton and give it a strike with, perhaps, a meter ruler. I just want you to comment later about the motion of the body." Rhonda tries to predict what they will observe in this activity, "may be the mass, the center of mass stays in one path, it doesn't move, like the center of gravity." Sean looks up, "A bit like what Jim said (earlier in the lesson)." "Strike it with a ruler," he continues and provides slight blows from the top to the pipe. Brenda, Jon, and Rhonda watch Sean change the blows' directions, now from the side so that the loaded pipe rolls to the left and to the right, a movement that Rhonda renders in descriptive terms, "It rolls around in a circle, it's like a fish."

Jon picks up the pipe and rolls it down the inclined table. Sean comments, "It rolls straight." Rhonda countered, "But if you push it, with a ruler it is not going straight" but acknowledges the straight movement Sean has brought about by gently pushing, which he comments upon by saying, "Yes it does." Sean follows Brenda's suggestion and hits the pipe in the middle (i.e., as I articulate it in chapter 8, he hits it in a way that he can be said to have followed her suggestion). Rhonda greets the resulting motion, "You see" and Jon comments, "It's changing on an angle." The teacher passes by and tells the students, "What I'd like you to do is just mark the center of strike and give me your comments." Sean strikes the pipe and engages Toby to check if what he is doing is what he is supposed to do. "Is that working?" "You just make a short sharp shot, just as in billiards," replies Toby. Sean obliges and makes the further observation, "It is not working," but Toby has already moved to another group. Jon then suggests, "I s'ppose. But that's what we are s'pposed to do." A few seconds later, Toby interrupts the activity and calls the class to order.

If this were an isolated episode or an episode involving so-called "low achieving students," many teachers and researchers might dismiss the problems it raises suggesting, perhaps, that the students have a problem because they cannot follow instructions. (In chapter 8, I analyze the difficulties of following instructions and the aporias inherent in the process through a phenomenological analysis of my own experiences.) However, the other five groups in this class have similar experiences. Some are spinning the loaded pipe ("baton"), some roll it on the table, and some strike it from above. In fact, one might say that this group has come closest to observing what Toby has wanted them to observe. Other observers might be tempted to blame Toby for giving poor instructions. Again, this would miss the mark for one can find on the videotapes similar student behavior in situations where they have detailed written instructions in their hands.

To the observers of the episode, the four students—who represent a cross section of the class in terms of their achievement in Toby's class—appear baffled. The four seem to be wrestling with many questions, "What does Toby want us to do? What could it mean, 'dead center,' 'give it a strike,' and 'perhaps with a meter ruler'?" "Were they to mark the geometric center or the center of mass?," "Which of these possible 'dead centers' were they asked to strike?," "What sort of strike?," "From which direction?," and "What has the meter ruler got to do with the strike?" Before answering this multitude of questions, students have to begin a situated inquiry from which, because something is significant, they can elaborate just what it is that the teacher has asked them to do.

In the course of my analysis, however, this question does not seem to be independent of another one, "What is it that Toby wants us to see?" The two questions are interrelated and in fact interdependent, for, to assess what they have to do, students need to be able to assess what they have seen. The four students need to know whether what they observe is in fact what they have been supposed to observe. Somehow, students have to interpret the outcome of their actions as significant. They have to produce and articulate a phenomenon. When they come to the conclusion that they have no phenomenon, they cannot know if the problem lies in the preparation of their investigation, or in their observation. It is the outcome on the basis of which the appropriateness of an action is determined or an assessment can be made whether an instruction has been followed.

At the moment Sean and his mates predict and produce the motion of the loaded pipe, they do not know if this is the intended phenomenon any more than they know if all the other phenomena they observe are the ones they have seen. Other groups, such as the one including Arlene and Ellen, move on to other tasks, although their striking of the pipe has not produced the phenomenon that the teacher has intended them to produce and understand. Towards the end of the lesson, the teacher indicates that he wants students to verify that the loaded pipes move in straight lines when the center of mass is struck. Arlene and Ellen strike the pipe at the center of mass once, produce and thus reproduce the desired phenomenon and return to their seats. They do not appear to be impressed and take the result of their experiment as a matter of course. Although they have not produced the desired motion previously, they are now satisfied that striking the cylinder at its center of mass produces straight-line motion. At this point they are certain that what they observe is what they are supposed to observe.

Rule following implies a competence that is described in ethnomethodological studies as an "ad hoc" elaboration of rules in use (Suchman & Trigg, 1993). Accordingly, the maintenance of "any rule of action requires the local elaboration by participants of just what the rule could mean in relation to specific circumstances of its application" (p. 167). Students in this physics laboratory tentatively elaborate, in very situated and contingent ways, what the instructions received from the teacher could mean relative to the specific context (including such things as the current curriculum, teacher's talk prior to the activity, the conversations and activities emerging against an open horizon of possible events). If it is not clear whether what students observe is significant, that is, matches events as they would be seen by the teacher (who in an ideal situation is the representative of canonical physics), students repeatedly change their actions to produce a variety of responses from the objects under study. They "fiddle" with and adjust objects and instructions to make them fit the contingencies of the setting. They then assess whether what they observe and describe makes the event significant relative to the present context. For example, Sean interprets his actions as inappropriate ("It doesn't work") possibly against the teacher's comment, "just as in billiards." Jon's comment, "But that's what we are s'pposed to do" opens the possibility that what they have seen is what they are supposed to see, a consequence of their appropriate prior actions. When the possibility opens for a response to be interpreted as significant, students are enabled to engage in *repetition* by means of which order arises through the consistency of a system's response.

Some readers may be tempted to argue that students do not understand how to produce and observe phenomena because of ineptitude, lack of skill, or simply lack of interest. Such an approach might be a reasonable explanation if failure to produce and observe phenomena is isolated to students. However, scientists are subject to the same phenomenon when they work at the limit of what they know, or attempt to reproduce a procedure that they are not familiar with in their own laboratory (e.g., Collins, 2001). The problem with the reproduction of phenomena and its dependence on embodied laboratory practices has been demonstrated for highly trained university researchers using the polymerase chain reaction and constructing lasers. There are reports that investigators in different laboratories could not reconstruct phenomena in spite of elaborate instructions and information about the setups. In these cases, not seeing a phenomenon was tied up with the associated embodied laboratory practices. Michael Faraday already knew about the problems of realizing an experiment in another lab and therefore, as described in chapter 1, sent copies of his apparatus with instructions of what to do and what to look for to colleagues around Europe.

STUDENTS' FUNDAMENTAL DILEMMA

The microanalysis of students ordering activities in a traditional physics laboratory shows how most students do produce and articulate phenomena and make sense even in this example of a traditionally taught physics laboratory. They observe, structure their field of experience and come up with reasonable results from their perspective; they also turn instructions into embodied actions through situated inquiries into possible matches between them. However, a few students who tried to refrain from making commitments necessary to construct order and thus phenomena. The above analysis cannot yield the motive or goal for such student behavior. Here, the analysis has to go to a different level and investigate the larger context in which students conduct their inquiries. At this new level, the students' fundamental dilemma emerges as shown by the following transcript extracted from a conversation recorded during the investigation with the rolling objects.

As mentioned above, Carl, Ellen, Karen, and their frequently silent partner Arlene have produced the outcomes of their races between a sliding cylinder (simulated by putting a cylinder on a toy car) and a rolling cylinder. Therefore, they decide to think about the phenomenon in statistical terms. Toby approaches the group just as the students conduct one run and observe that the rolling cylinder has a greater acceleration than the "sliding" equivalent.

Episode 2.2

01 Toby: I am a little disappointed keep going, keep going.
02 Karen: We are doing the best of five.
03 Ellen: It's a little slow.
04 Toby: Try it again! Put that ((points to a weight)) right in the middle. ((Karen obliges)) Yeah, right. But I know what I'm expecting and I haven't tried the trolleys. ((Karen conducts a race between the trolley loaded with a large hollow cylinder and a rolling large hollow cylinder.))
05 Toby: It is not doing as I want, so I'll have to . . .
06 Ellen: What is it meant to be?
07 Toby: Well, I tell you later.
08 Karen: It's a surprise!
09 Toby: Yeah, it's a surprise but it's not quite living up to expectations.

In this conversation, Toby exhibits his disappointment such as for everyone to overhear and perceive. Why does the teacher request me to "Try it again!"? Does what I have done not correspond to what I should have done?" Toby articulates that there is something he *expects* students to see without telling them that it is this: the objects accelerate faster when they are "sliding" than when they are rolling; instead he says that he has not tried the investigation himself (turn 04). He knows that a frictionless sliding object translates all energy into translational motion, whereas a rolling object translates some of its energy into rotational energy so that ultimately it accelerates less. The students, however, have no means to judge the outcome in the same way; they have to take events as they see them. From this perspective, "doing the best of five" (turn 02) is not unreasonable. The students' dilemma is made salient in Toby's assessment that the experiment is "not doing as [he] wants" and what "[he] is expecting." He shows students that he already knows what is still concealed and withheld from them. Toby does not want to tell students what the problem is (turn 07) and they are left on their own to make sense of the objects and events before them.

Students know that the correctness of the knowable in their laboratory exercises is prefigured in advance. They are not asked to produce an order helpful to understand a part of *their* lifeworld but to produce an order that they know the teacher is hiding from them. In other words, independently of students' material and interpretive actions, outcomes are to be assessed against a normative order that, depending on the teacher's own understanding, is more or less compatible with standard physics. Whereas the students have to work before an open horizon of possible positions and dispositions concerning the objects and events, they are asked to disclose the one yet-unknown possibility (dis-position, disposition) against which students' work is judged. This form of inquiry is closed and distinctly different from the ordinary situation of scientific research, where the search for an answer to a question can arise within an open horizon of investigation.

It is here that one can situate the fundamental dilemma and difference of students' work. While their inquiries can be within an open horizon—leading to results often quite different from those of standard science—the frame that situates their laboratory work forces them to search for a hidden order, which, to be discovered, requires students already to be a part of the legitimized and legitimizing worldview into which the activities are designed to introduce them. Such dilemmas exist even in the most well-meaning, student-centered instruction. Teachers still shape the format and content of lessons and produce fine-grained definitions of what is to be done, said, and understood. As a result, the forms of inquiry are closed and lessons are geared to the acquisition of one "right" way of seeing and explaining phenomena.

LEARNING FROM TRADITIONAL SCIENCE ACTIVITIES

Science educators sometimes claim that students' ability to relate the scientific theory they are to learn to the phenomenon observed is constrained by differences in perception. The problem with such research is that it models phenomena as independent of human observers. From a phenomenological perspective, however, there are no "things" that are bearers of individual properties (aspects) independent of acts of perception; the thinginess of objects and of the world emerges from *concerned* observation and action of the human agents and the breakdown of their tools and ways of seeing. But observation is always a function of the subject's current horizon, always occurs through a lens developed during past experiences; that is, the perceptions and interpretations are always from within a tradition, always positioned and reflecting a disposition. The presented analyses explicitly take a phenomenological perspective to eschew these problems in prior research.

Despite a lot of research and development efforts, traditional laboratory exercises have shown only limited promise: teachers use them to "motivate" students, and researchers find that students often do not develop an understanding of the phenomena that they create as part of their engagement. In the present chapter students *do* produce order (phenomena) during such tasks. The problem why these activities do not lead to the kind of understandings desired by science educators may lie in the teachers' failure to use students' understandings (whatever they are) within a sociocultural and cultural historical framework of learning. In such frameworks, differences in understanding are used in whole-class discussion to come to grips with the variations of material actions, framing of "phenomena" through descriptions and interpretations. Teachers' views could then be some of the many to be deliberated, as singular plural dispositions. Teachers not only would have to present that a particular view is accepted and shared by scientists, but also to students intelligible arguments for ruling out all the other views.

The events described here show that learning standard physics from laboratories is not self-evident and what students actually get from looking at a scene does not necessarily yield what the teacher intends students to see and learn. Further, following instructions is not self-evident, but requires an interaction of situated search for a match between instruction and action, whereby what one is doing is established only after the fact. Students' assessment as to whether what they have done is what they are supposed to do, the matching of instructions to actions, has to be done a posteriori. In some cases, this may span quite some time and distance. The students' real work therefore is this: Their praxis becomes progressively witnessable and tell-able as an orderly phenomenon, that is, in the form of practices. But what they do not know is whether their situated action, though repeatable, has produced *the* phenomenon that relates to the context from the teacher's perspective. Though they have produced order, they cannot know whether this is the order that makes sense and is analyzed in the legitimized and legitimizing framework. Their actions brought about by a reading of instructions emerge from a horizon constituted, among others, by the purposes of the embedding school and classroom situation, the present curricular context, and students' previous experience. Thus, there cannot be one literal meaning of an instruction like "striking the baton in the center," for all students take it as literal and they do what it literally means to them. Their work consists in interpreting the instruction, and enacting their interpretation. But then they also have to interpret the outcome of their action and assess whether this outcome corresponds to what they think they are supposed to see.

Teachers frequently misjudge the relationship between observation, theory and experiment; they see in theory generation little more than the collection of objective experimental and observational facts. The events in this and the previous chapter underscore the problematic nature of such assumptions. The order different students produce and articulate as they look at the "same" object varies; different orders are expected because of students fundamental dis-positions that are grounded in the singularity of their bodies. If there are no opportunities for the students to discuss the origin of these variations, they simply have to accept the teacher's evaluation of being wrong. In some situations, this has led students to refrain from generating any observation categoricals and thus phenomena. They completed a few token actions (e.g., Arlene, Ellen) or did not participate at all (e.g., Norm).

Many of those who critique traditional laboratories assume that there are phenomena and events that students should explore to construct episodic experience. However, my observations reported here suggest that it is not useful to think of phenomena in science classrooms as existing prior to students' engagement. Rather, it is through the students' agency|sensibility that phenomena come about. Because of their varied background, implicit theories and embodied experiences,

61

these phenomena more likely vary than are the same; and these phenomena are even less likely identical to those that the teacher intends them to see. Such an identity can come about only when all students and the teacher share background and experiences and above all, the same lenses (i.e., theoretical commitments). However, helping students develop theoretical commitments similar to those of the teacher is the very goal of the present lesson and not its premise.

"HANDS-ON, MINDS-ON?"

Some teachers and science educators use the expression "hands-on, minds-on" to distinguish simple hands-on activities from presumably better hands-on activities that bring about learning of standard science. The events described question this notion: Although I can find in the videotapes a considerable number of students who are genuinely interested in making sense of the phenomenon the teacher wants them to observe, so that "hands-on, minds-on" is an appropriate descriptor, they do not observe or understand the scientific phenomenon the teacher wants them to observe. From a phenomenological perspective, every interpretation emerges from the interaction of the *horizon* individuals bring to the situation and the *horizon* of the text and thing. In this interaction, world is divided into figure and ground. This figure brings out the *aspects* of the thing, the particular understanding of the text the individual looks at. Because students "put their minds on" to make sense of observations the order they perceive in most cases is not that of scientists. That is, in many situations students *cannot* perceive what they are to perceive because of their prior experiences and because the thing to be seen is not salient at all—but I return to these issues in greater depth in chapter 3.

Whereas the expression "hands-on, minds-on" suggests the interrelation of intellectual practices ("mind") and the manipulable material world, it does not go far enough. Students' conceptual objects that emerge from the intertwining of their lifeworlds, embodied practices, and social interactions frequently are not those of standard science. By itself, this outcome is not a problem: one can use such situations to engage students in exchanges where the different results would be discussed, critiqued, and researched. The phenomenon might arise as a (social) construction of the class. Problems arise when teaching is conceived of as the transmission of ideas. Students will feel rebuked when they evolve observation categoricals that the teacher does not expect. They may then begin to refrain from contributing at all. The videotapes exhibit that Christina is the only student to cite an experiment that disproves the teacher's theory. But again, Toby does not capitalize on the situation but says that the events observed are due to unevenness of the table or the objects themselves without even investigating whether his suggestions make sense in the context of the young woman's investigation.

The presented events therefore provide empirical evidence in support of the claim that it is unlikely that students will rediscover scientific knowledge in laboratory work in the absence of guidance and deep theoretical understanding. Many experiments yield unanticipated results so that students tend to "discover" an "alternative" explanatory scheme. In the tension between assessment and discovery, students consequently focus on what ought to happen and are preoccupied with right answers.

WEAK AND STRONG ORDERLINESS

In the empirical examples, students constitute phenomena through their discursive (interpretive) and material practices. Students construct order in laboratory activities through modification and repetition of actions, observation sentences, and tentative observation categoricals. In this, they face the challenges of ordering the world of their experience that are little different from those of scientists whose task it is to impose order on the apparent disorder. The orderliness of the phenomena literally is in the investigator's hands, and this orderliness offers itself in elaborating details of attempts, repairs, and discards locally motivated and locally occasioned modifications of any material shape. I can identify at least one major difference between the activities of the students in this Australian classroom and those that scientists enact. I may speak of a strong orderliness produced by the activities of scientists. This strong orderliness lies in the scientists' practices to make their actions and therefore the phenomena they construe, accountable in ways that the students are not yet familiar with. The latter have little experience in repeating particular sets of actions such as to reproduce an outcome, making it difficult at times to produce a phenomenon in the first place and to produce accounts that withstand critique or are powerful enough to question other accounts. They lack the quality of agency that brings material manipulations and observation categoricals onto such a convergent path that sufficiently stable interpretations emerge. Students' interpretations need to remain open in a classroom because what they think they observe may in many cases have to be revised as the artifact of their material actions and interpretations. So unless they are to experience failure or if they do not seem to mind to running the risk of "being wrong" (like Christina for whom this is a part of learning), they avoid making firm commitments in the form of phenomena they constructed on their own.

One can therefore speak of weak orderliness produced by students. Their phenomena and the associated accounts are subject to revision and deconstruction. In many instances, the final judgment about students' phenomena has been made by the teacher; in others, he decides that "data that disproves a theory" generated by students are artifacts. Here, the orderliness students produce easily can be destroyed and renounced. However, this weak orderliness can also change into strong orderliness when positively evaluated by the teacher's comments; then, the orderliness becomes detached from students' actions and something that belongs in the realm of scientific objects and events. Students' orderly phenomena become ratified and thereby reified as phenomena.

AGENCY IN SCIENCE LABORATORY

In my ethnographic research of scientists at work, I can see how their actions and the facts and explanations they produce become irremediably fused; it is only through rhetorical efforts and the linguistic dissociation between objects and scientific agent that scientific objects become independent. The present episodes show that the orderliness students produce—especially when, from a scientific point of view, they are artifacts such as Jon, Rhonda, and Sean's observation categorical "sliding objects move with a constant velocity"—and their actions are inseparable. For the purposes at hand and until further notice, tentative observation categoricals form the basis for future observations (often in the form of confirmatory bias) or tests. Actions and objects are discursively separated when students are certain that the resulting events are reproducible, subject only to insignificant variation. (I show in chapters 6 and 7 how the split between material world making a sign and the sense it signifies comes about.) However, when it eventually turns out that a phenomenon should be considered artefactual—Sean and his mates who deconstruct their phenomenon, Christina who abandons her phenomenon that contradicts the teacher's theory because he said so—the interdependence of action and phenomenon is reintroduced. For, one of the ways a phenomenon can be deconstructed is through a declaration that the preparation was artefactual.

My descriptions retain this unity of action and objects: any description, observation sentence, and observation categorical always is an outcome of, and visibly connected to, some prior action or action sequence. Furthermore, models and implicit hypotheses (and theories) that integrate mental and material objects are made explicit. By also indexing actions to singular individuals, my descriptions show how worldly objects, embodied practices, and social structure come to be intertwined to form the world of students' experience. This approach to representing human agency allows me to eschew the reductionism of other approaches that only focus on mental or physical actions, social or technological dimensions of laboratory work, and content or contexts; it is a symmetric anthropology that integrates all these dichotomies. This approach is thus appropriate for analysts who view knowledgeability as emerging from the interaction of the task, the individual, and the (physical, social, and cultural) setting; and it is appropriate for analyses that recognize (a) the heterogeneity of actions, goals, motives and activity and (b) the seamless way learning arises from situated activity.

The sample events show that the phenomena students produce emerge from the intertwining of discursive and practical activity, interactions with others and the material world that is the focus of their tasks. Seen thus, it is not surprising that students' phenomena often do not correspond to those the teacher wants them to perceive and explain; furthermore, students cannot even assess which of their actions do not conform to the teacher's instructions because to do so they already need to perceive the phenomenon with scientific eyes and know the theory from a scientific perspective. These results have considerable implications for science instruction through laboratory activities. To see what a teacher wants students to see and to do what the teacher wants students to do, students already need to know what they are supposed to learn. My microanalyses cannot be directly translated to provide recommendations for appropriate actions. To escape from this dilemma one needs to look at the context in which laboratory tasks are situated. In the present videotapes, the teacher simply labels those results "wrong" that do not fit into his explanations and there is evidence in the data sources that some students felt ridiculed by his remarks in these situations.

Toby has missed many opportunities that can facilitate student learning and he does not capitalize on the possibilities that arise from students' constructions of different phenomena. He tells students what they should observe or talk about the legitimized description (in terms of equations) of the system of objects they observe. On the other hand, he may ask students to argue the different outcomes of their activities, make their material and interpretive activities accountable, test alternative outcomes and explanations, and work on consensual explanations. By not engaging with students to discuss their observations, he too misses opportunities for learning. By listening to students and by engaging with them in a truly symmetric conversation, he can learn much about students' knowledge, their way of perceiving the objects and events of the laboratory, and so on. By discussing any differences in their observations, students are provided with the opportunity to experience an important aspect of science: the temporally emergent construction of phenomena (facts, objects, events) that arises from the interaction of individuals with material, social, and cultural worlds. By reflecting on their own constructive processes and products as the result of such interactions, they may come to understand standard scientific facts and explanation as outcomes of similar situated processes; and they have opportunities to wrestle with the question, "How does science manage to get facts out of the messiness, the confusion, the hunches, the subjective judgments, the broken test tube, the leaps of faith that are inherent in the experiment?"

An appropriate approach may begin with the assumption that the phenomena and observations students produce are diverse, different from, and incompatible with, legitimated and legitimate views. Rather than suppressing these phenomena (and with them the students who constructed them) teachers need to establish forums in which this diversity can be discussed and contrasted with standard views (which the teacher may need to contribute). In this way, teachers may answer the question, "Could you design hands-on experiments that raise doubts about the conclusions that were historically drawn from them instead of experiments or demonstrations that make the conclusion seem obvious or inevitable?" However, details of how this is to be done and how students learn under these new and different conditions are still open questions to be addressed by future research.

Another consequence of the present observations is that the capacity of traditional laboratory tests to do what they are designed to do has to be questioned. In the physics classroom under investigation, the teacher provides students with an instruction sheet intended to guide them through an investigation during which they collected data that were to be interpreted. These interpretations are the products used as evidence for an evaluation. However, such a practice is questionable when students have no indication of what their investigation is to yield. In this case, they have no means to assess whether their individual steps are situationally appropriate to collect those data needed to get to the answer that the teacher normatively established as the reference against which to judge students' answers. As an alternative, one might imagine that students choose their own problem to which they seek a solution. The evaluation might then assess the degree to which students' processes and products are convincing. As part of their efforts, students may establish a portfolio that documents their efforts including videos and written artifacts. Of course, students themselves also need to be asked about the degree that they think they achieved their initial goals. Again, future research needs to evaluate the suitability of such an approach for assessing students' laboratory competence.

PART II

SCIENTIFIC PERCEPTION

When you get sudden flashes of perception, it is just the brain working faster than usual. But you've been getting ready to know it for a
long time, and when it comes, you feel you've known it always.
Katherine Anne Porter

In the two chapters of part I, I present descriptions of participation in traditional
teacher demonstrations and laboratory exercises. The descriptions exhibit one of
the key aspects involved in learning science: what learners perceive and how they
perceive them plays a crucial role in what and how learners learn. A simplistic
response to the question of perception would be the suggestion that the world is out
there to be perceived and as soon as I lay my eyes on the world, it is given to me in
its entirety. That is, as soon as something falls onto my eyeballs in general and on
my retina in particular, I am supposed to see nature as it is in all its structural detail
and whole|parts configurations. But being is being singular plural, implying multi-
plicity, multiple positions, and dispositions. Even for the radical constructivist,
there has to be something that human beings interpret, and this something has
some structure, because both within and across human cultures there are interpretive preferences rather than willy-nilly articulations of the world. The self-
organizing human being, too, has to be structured, because without structuring
structure, no new structure could emerge.

Human beings act in the world even without interpreting it, but make themselves home in everyday situations much faster than any interpretive process allows this to do. The question then is, how is this possible? As I show in part II, this
is the case because I do not perceive the world in its entirety; rather, the world I
inhabit is disclosed to me over time and as needed. Without a frame, however,
there are differences in the ways in which the world appears to different individuals. The differences are the result of the singularity of human beings (rather than
singularity being due to difference). Chapters 1 and 2 already show that students
produce very different observation descriptions and, subsequently, of observation
categoricals, the basic pillars of any commonsense (naïve) or sophisticated theory.
Yet at the same time, I also know that when I analyze data together with my graduate students for a considerable length of time, we end up categorizing new tapes
nearly identically even if we work in separate rooms. That is, in collective activity
we converge on perceiving situations in ways that we recognize and agree upon as
being the same.

Once I accept that even the best intended learners do not inherently see nature as
it really is then there is the question about how the learner-I comes to perceive and
what it is that the learner-I perceives. In this section, I address the question of per-

69

ception, how it changes, the difference between *noticing* and *perceiving* or *seeing as*. In the course of the three chapters that comprise part II, I provide many examples, both from my own experience and from a set of materials from German tenth-grade physics classroom.

In the first of the three chapters in this section, I practice *cognitive phenomenology* (Roth, 2005a) as method for getting at the nature of perceptual experiences. This praxis strives to uncover and articulate the conditions mediating or determining experiences rather than descriptions of these experiences. That is, I engage in the phenomenological project to find out how human beings generally and I particularly can have different perceptual experiences, which is a question that transcends my personal experience and constitutes an inquiry into experience generally. I continue to use a first-person account not only to describe the experiences but also to write the analytic text, hoping that my readers join me in taking a look at perceptual experiences as I am conscious of them *during* the learning process. When I use the personal pronoun "I," it is to encourage readers to put themselves into the position of the experiencing person. My "I" therefore is a plural singular "I," which I could have easily exchanged for a singular plural "we." My analysis of my perception is useful to the extent that it highlights perception as such not merely my personal perceptions; the approach is legitimate because each human being (noun) is in a state of being (verb) singular plural (Nancy, 2000), lives one life in an immeasurable and unlimited realm of possible lives, concretely realizes an identity among possible identities, and always already acts in a way that others experience as a possibility of acting and being that is, if not accessible then at least intelligible.

There is a long philosophical tradition and epistemological commitment in research and practice to regard visual perception in particular and cognition more generally as mirrors of the material world. The descriptions of perception in chapter 4, as those provided in the chapter 3, challenge assumptions not only made every day in the teaching of science but also in the study of knowing and learning more generally: directing our eyes in some direction or at something, I am or should be aware of everything that meets my eyes. The teacher in chapter 1 expects students to see something specific in his demonstrations, which is an expectation that simply is not justified, as shown in chapter 3. Drawing on a first-person method for improving the validity of findings, I show that there is more to visual perception than meets the eye, much more than is assumed in the everyday practices of science teaching and of research on knowing and learning.

Across chapters 3 and 4, I articulate six important aspects of perception that educators need to be aware of but that they generally do not currently consider in their day-to-day practice. First, perception of a particular segment of the world is indeterminate. Second, as individuals actively explore the relevant segment, their perceptual fields become articulated into figure|ground relations that give rise to more specific objects, themselves subject to future (verbal) articulation into figure|ground and whole|parts relations. Perception is a historical, experientially conditioned and mediated process making available different worlds rather than a transparent window on a singular, stable world. Third, although I am visually attuned to my surroundings, I only perceive when something that I track is behaviorally relevant, that is, when this something is integrated with my capacities for thought and action-guidance. Fourth, articulation of the perceptual field and behavioral relevance often emerge in moments of breakdown. Fifth, in collective laboratory activity, contradictory observations have the function of, and solicit the same processes as (equipmental) breakdown. Sixth, when some feature emerges into my awareness for the first time, this something immediately changes its nature: from being immanently present to being transcendentally present. Perceptual amnesis is the process by means of which we forget that the world given to us in conscious perception is the result of a learning process.

In chapter 5, I propose a way of viewing the different ways in which scientific phenomena are represented and explained. Using the analogy of map and lens, I show how various scientific explanations can be viewed as perspectives that depend on the lens or map I use and how theses lenses and maps interact with what I see. These maps produce certain things as figure. When I layer such an explanatory map over my most basic map—the world as I experience it—and correlate features that appear in both of them, I arrive at explanations (layer 2, 3, etc.) of perceptions and experience (layer 1). I also suggest that the layers are not independent, but mutually presuppose each other: My conceptual lenses allow me to perceive certain objects and events, my perceptions drive which lens or lenses I choose to explain what I see; and my lenses are the result of my experiences.

PHENOMENOLOGY OF PERCEPTION

In the two preceding chapters, I introduce several aporias of learning. These aporias hinge in part on the problematic issues arising from perception. To articulate the aporetic nature of perception with greater precision, I have conducted many inquiries over the past decade. Here, I provide a first-person account of how I, as I-learner, become perceptually aware of things in the world that have not existed for me before, that is, how I become aware of a multiplicity of singular plurals that surround me. First, I move about (walk, drive, ride a bicycle) without being aware of most of my surroundings. Even if I am attuned to and visually track the surroundings, I am not consciously *aware* of most features that I could be aware of: I may drive somewhere talking to the person sitting next to me; and then, after a while, I realize that I have not been aware of my surroundings. At times, this experience can be so strong that I find myself at some location completely unaware of what has happened between here and where I have been before. Second, when I look at a particular scene for the first time, my perceptual field is not automatically and self-evidently articulated; I may look at a wristwatch but, because I am interested in the second hand remain completely unaware of the current chronological time. Third, although I seem to perceive "everything" when I look somewhere, I continually become aware of new entities during subsequent moments of experience. Relevant figure separates from the diffuse and indeterminate ground in and through extended experience, familiarity with the situation, and because of issues that have behavioral relevance. Perception is *articulated* in the course of moving about in the world (experience). *Articulation*, here, has a double sense. On the one hand, an articulation is the location where two things meet and are separated from an indeterminate perceptual field, that is, an articulation is the joint where a determinate perceptual figure separates from an indeterminate ground leading to the emergence of a figure|ground dialectic. This separation is associated with my active experience: with my actions, things separate out, I notice objects and their features, and a lifeworld aspect comes forth. On the other hand, articulation refers to the verbal naming of the perceptual figure (gestalt). Those entities that perceptually appear before the *indeterminate* ground and have become figure can be named, pointed out, talked about, and described in propositional form (observation sentences); that is, I can verbally articulate them so that others can become attuned to the same figure. Here indeterminate means that the ground, the field of my experience, does not determine the figures that will spring forth. Figure comes to stand before ground through my embodied, intentional|non-intentional taking care.

My first experiences with the strangeness of perception date to my childhood. But for the longest time, these experiences and my knowledge associated with them have not mediated how I looked at and understood learning in science especially during hands-on activities. I remember taking public transportation from my village to the city to attend grammar school, which I did over a nine-year period until I finished two years of college level. The bus always was so crowded that I had to stand on the front steps back against the door. I looked ahead, watching the road and the environs. One day I notice that I am perceiving new things, new (old) houses, and new perspectives even after having stood on the same steps every morning for several years—taking the same route and watching the same landscapes and cityscapes pass by. It was not that I "interpreted" the environs in a new way. I remember the strong impressions and strange feeling that I am *seeing* these things *for the first time*. That is, although at the time I have been looking out of the same windshield for years, I was still coming to perceive new things and aspects, which, upon reflection, I know not to have been introduced there during that period: these things and aspects I "discovered" and was becoming aware off must have existed all along. This allows me to understand that looking at the environs does not reveal them to me in their entirety, although one can show—using simple physics—that the light rays from these things and aspects must have been on my retina for quite some time. Because I have not perceived them, the fact of not noticing them is not a question of conscious interpretation. Rather, one has to look for an understanding of the phenomenon elsewhere. In this chapter, I interrogate the nature of perception for the purpose of providing science educators with an appreciation of perceptual processes while learning from experience—such as watching teacher demonstrations or doing laboratory tasks. Understanding these processes will allow a better comprehension of the reasons why students do not seem to learn from watching demonstrations and doing investigations in the way I describe these aporia in chapters 1 and 2.

For years, I have kept notes about the unfolding of critical problem-solving events in my life, paying particular attention to avoid after-the-fact rationalizations while describing and explaining events. I have been interested not in the description of my experiences but in the conditions that make them possible and how, in varying the conditions, my experiences would change. (Readers will find more on this method in *Doing Qualitative Research: Praxis of Method* [Roth, 2005a]). Sometimes I make a video recording of such an event, precipitated by an experimental attitude to learn about learning, and I save (digital) photographs of the materials involved. The purpose of these records generally and of the written notes particularly is to capture—to the extent that this is possible—the first-time-through nature of problem solving and particularly the perceptual processes involved. The database used in this chapter has been generated during my three-month fellowship at the *Hanse Institute of Advanced Studies,* where I (a) conducted the initial analyses of videotapes from a tenth-grade physics course and (b) recorded my own perceptual processes during "experiments" and during the data analysis. As I analyzed the videotapes, it became evident to me that students faced some fundamental aporias, "What is it that I-learner am supposed to see?" and "Do I-learner see what I am supposed to see?" To better understand the students' experience of learning about static electricity by producing new and unfamiliar phenomena in laboratory investigations, and primed by the work reported in investigations, and primed by the work reported in chapters 1 and 2, I conducted several "experiments" involving myself as the subject. I put myself into controlled situations of perceiving something for the first time. One of these experiments required me to take the same, initially unfamiliar thirty-kilometer route repeatedly, which turned out to be twenty times. During and after each daily bicycle trip along this route, I recorded perceptions, salient entities, and striking realizations, that is, anything that appeared to pertain to perceptual phenomena. On the next day, prior to taking the trip again, I noted everything I expected to see.

FIGURE: ARTICULATION OF THE FIELD

In chapter 1, the students in a twelfth-grade physics class see *the same event* in very different ways: in the same demonstration, some students see movement and others do not see movement. This ought to raise questions for science educators: "How can this be?" "What are the reasons and conditions for such experiences?" and "How do we need to design classroom environments so that these conditions for learning from experience are taken into account?" The episode from riding the bus already intimates that the perceptual field is indeterminate (not only on the periphery but also in the center of vision) in that it is not given to me at once but that I can discover new entities and processes over time. Whereas the world leaves traces on my retina, I never experience it in its totality: Specific things and features only emerge into consciousness with extended experience and as needed. The world is not given once and for all, in a unique way, but unfolds, continuously changing figure|ground and whole|parts relations as I become capable to structure the field before me to make it behaviorally relevant. My world—that which is taken into account in my thoughts and behavior—is brought forth through my experience of moving (eyes, hands, body) and moving about. These dimensions of learning from perceptual experience feature in the following excerpts from my notes, each of which has been written within minutes after returning from my trip.

> Day 1. As I am riding along, I am aware of my surroundings (trees, flowers, and so forth) without really focusing on anything in particular. Although I am aware at the moment, here at home, I remember few things in particular, few stretches of the trip. But those things I do remember are associated with a particular type of experience. There are things, like a particular house or a sign naming some street (e.g., "Landwehr") that has been *pulling* my gaze to take a closer look. As I focus, sometimes with considerable delay, a memory surfaces—the house looks *like* the one I had lived in forty years earlier; and "Landwehr" is the name of a professor and of a street in the city where I attended university.
>
> Day 2. As I am riding along, there are features in the environment that I have not remembered yesterday at home after the trip, but which I nevertheless re-cognize (cognize again) the moment I approach them. As I come around the Y-fork, I re-member that yesterday I had seen from here the child on the bike and with the dog ahead of me. They then turned into the farm some 200 meters further on. I re-member (re-articulate, articulate

again) the field with the freshly sprouting grain plants though I have not remembered them yesterday after I arrived from the trip at home. Thus there are things that despite the complexity of the experience, I recognized even before I reach the place, that I start to anticipate when I get within reach. But then there are other farms, other signs, and other features that I seem to see for the first time although I have come past this place yesterday.

Day 5. Today, I notice for the first time the little plates, inscribed with numbers that increase by 0.1 about every 100 meters. I infer that these are distance indicators with reference to some starting point. ((Comment: I subsequently found the starting point during an explicitly planned trip.))

Day 7. Today, I notice for the first time the upper parts of two gigantic towers that are visible above the treetops right next to the road. ((Comment: From then on, I not only saw the towers each time I came by this place, but I was expecting them to show up even before I got to the place.))

These notes show that in this situation I am perceptually tuned to my surroundings, which enables me to move about, yet my perception is indeterminate: Initially, few features come to stand as figures against the ground, to be remembered subsequently. Before I, my awareness, grasp and grab hold of detailed features, the physical world appears to exist, indistinct, and as invitation to be articulated. I remember few concrete things after the first and even subsequent trips along the same route. However, in the course of the repeated experience, new features emerge into my consciousness: I see the sign with the "Landwehr" inscription, the distance signs, and the gigantic twin towers for the first time.

Despite my self-awareness that the experiment is about recalling the maximum number of features and despite an extended effort to recall as much as possible, I perceive one or more new features "for the first time," each time I travel. Consequently, the world becomes more and more (perceptually) articulated, a whole consisting of parts, allowing me to articulate it (verbally) in my notes. In fact, the whole and its parts stand in a mutually constitutive whole|parts relation: the whole is made of parts, which are parts only because they make up *this* whole. At the same time, certain entities (e.g., the house looking like the one I have lived in, the "Landwehr" sign) have a certain "grabbiness," do not allow my regard to simply pass by. This turns out to be related to (and is articulated in terms of) previous experience. These things and features *draw* my attention for a reason I do not know *until* I find out that there has been something in my past that resembles them. The thing, though initially not even consciously perceived *as* thing, mediates the resurfacing of a memory; but my attention would not have been drawn had it not been for the strange familiarity of the things and features, the nature of which became evident to me only after the fact. These things, figures, *members* (parts) of the world, came to be *re*-membered, remembered in and through the dialectic of their likeness in difference. Encountering these entities brings forth an experience of *déjà vu*, including specific details (features) that come to stand as salient figure against an indeterminate ground. Here, the descriptive articulation follows the perceptual articulation because I can only describe what I see when I see it.

When I first perceive the twin towers, it is not as if they slowly emerged into my consciousness. Suddenly they are there. I am surprised by the violence of this experience. These towers are so gigantic. Yet I have failed to perceive them on the preceding trips. The violence of the experience is related to the surprise that something so gigantic has been able to appear *within* my perceptual field. It is as if a veil had been lifted that had covered my eyes, *un*covering part of the world and thereby allowing me to make this *dis*covery. I begin to wonder why I have not seen them on the six previous trips. How can it be that something so prominent has not come to my consciousness before? What does this tell me about students observing science demonstrations? Might students not have the same type of experiences, where they attend to a demonstration repeatedly only to discover some salient element at a much later point in time?

From that point on, these twin towers are so obvious to me. I begin to treat them as having been there all along. In fact, I remember how struck I have been at that moment by the fact that something I have begun to accept them as objectively given in the instant they appeared; and I have begun to extend this existence backward in time, though I have not perceived it until that moment. Yet in my experiential world, they have not existed and therefore would not have shown up in assessments of my knowing and learning. That is, at the moment the twin towers enter my awareness, I go through an experience of radical forgetting, where my previous lifeworld in which the towers did not exist comes to be obliterated. Subsequently, I am seeing these twin towers every time that I pass this particular part of the road only on and subsequent to the seventh trip. That is, from this point on, the two towers exist *immanently*, as things that I can reflect upon whenever I direct my attention toward them; the towers also have become something that exist *transcendentally*, outside of myself, as concrete singularities in the plurality of the material world. The difference between immanent and transcendent perception corresponds to the difference between "beings as experienced" and "beings as things"; things as they exist in themselves can be perceived only transcendently. Today I know that in fact, all variants of dialectical social theories posit a dialectical relation between these immanent and transcendent aspects of the object in consciousness: In cultural-historical activity theory, for example, objects are said to appear twice in activity, once materially, once as reflection in consciousness.

As individual entities increasingly burst into my consciousness, the experienced landscape as a whole grows proportionally with the sum of these bursts. But these entities are all over the landscape, literally and metaphorically; bits and pieces come to stand out against and held together by the indeterminate ground. Although I am perceptually coupled with this environment from the beginning of my experiment—I am staying on the path or road even though they are not reflected in my consciousness in any great detail—it is only over time that I become perceptually aware of, and focus attention on, particular *things*. My perceptual engagement with the environment constitutes the ground of perceptual awareness; but my perceptual awareness is possible only if this perceptual engagement with particulars of the environment is controlled.

In this first episode, I point out the sense of *déjà vu* that comes with some experiences. Whereas I may have had an awareness of something, it has not influenced my conscious thought or practical action. It is only a vague awareness, something I notice and yet do not notice. This something is diffusely noticed but is of no behavioral relevance. It is a difference that does not make a difference, as Gregory Bateson (e.g., 1972) used to say. I therefore cannot talk about having seen something, for this would imply not only that I track some environmental feature and exercise mastery of sensorimotor capabilities, but also that I integrate these with my capacities for thought and action-guidance. The episode also shows that full, conscious awareness is not necessary to cope with the world in which I find myself. Readers certainly will have had the experience of walking, riding a bicycle, or driving from some place A to another place B only to become aware later that they actually have not been consciously aware of our surrounding. I have arrived at B and cannot say how I have been able to stay on the sidewalk, bicycle trail, or road, as I do not remember at all how I got to B.

PROGRESSIVE DISCLOSURE AND ACTION-GUIDANCE

My experiences show that the world discloses itself progressively, mediated by my actions and intentions. My surroundings take on shape where there had not been shape before. They are both present—as ground against which my experiences take shape—and not present—as salient figure that I consciously take into account in my goal-directed actions. Latent awareness does not enter decision-making and therefore thinking in the way learning scientists write about it.

> I am cycling along a trail that was signed as a joint cycling/pedestrian path. Then, all of a sudden, I see cyclist to my left on another path. I have not noticed that there is a junction where the two paths had separated, but it must have been something like ((Figure 3.1)).

This episode shows that in my objective experience there has not been a branch prior to my noticing it. I have been riding in a world where there is but one trail. To understand my actions, a researcher studying me needs to understand what I have perceived and thus, my world. Thus, for example, it does not help the researcher to wonder why I have taken the right rather than the left trail, for I have not made a decision; the second trail has not existed for me. My being on the right trail therefore is the simple consequence of my perceiving only this one rather than

Figure 3.1. Drawing constructed after finding out that there was a pedestrian/bicycle path next to my own, without that I noticed a branching point.

two and the point where the two branch. For, if an analyst begins the analysis of knowing and learning with some outside world, he or she needs to assume that somehow I have been defective while passing the branch in the path. In fact, however, the branch does not exist for me *until after the* experience, when I construct the possibility of the branching point after the fact in the manner of Figure 3.1. On subsequent trips along this part of the world, I perceive the branch and am conscious of which one I take; the branch is both perceived and mediates/guides my actions. Thus, what is most crucial for understanding my actions of the learning and knowing person (organism) is the world from my perspective. I have been on the path the first time not because of conscious choice but because this is all there has been in my perceptual experience. There has not been another option requiring my decision-making. Therefore, to understand what I have done—taking the particular path, analysts need to know what my lifeworld is, both tacit in my actions and conscious in my considerations, lest they want to operate with models in which human experience is always in some negative mode, incomplete, to be bettered.

> I now vaguely remember having been on the bicycle trail one time before. At that time, then, my world has included either the bicycle trail only, or in fact a branching point, which I have taken in favor of the bicycle trail.

In this instance, I have a vague memory. I do not re-member exactly what has been the case before. All I remember is an impression that I have had the first time I passed this point. But *then*, I had been riding differently. While realizing during the second trip that there are two trails, I begin to objectify this experience. The existence of two trails forces itself upon me: I have no choice but to accept the reality and its nature as being given to me as *objects* of my consciousness, that is, *objectively*. The next time I pass this part of the world (third trip), I am consciously aware of the branching point. I perceive the branching point consciously. This part of the world has become differentiated; there exists a fine structure in my lifeworld and to what and how I experience it.

When I am riding my bicycle along the trail one day but find myself on the pedestrian path next to it on the subsequent day, my world in each case offers one possibility to act only. I have done what my lifeworld affords me to do. But when I notice that another cyclist rides to my left, on a trail that I have not been consciously aware, I am puzzled. There is a difference between where the other cyclist rides and where I find myself to be.

> Having become curious, I ride across the grass onto the other trail ((between the two in Figure 3.1)) that I recognize as such immediately. When I come this way the next time, I re-cognize the situation and perceive the branching point that I have not seen as such on previous occasions. The branching point is at hand, present, and cognized; from now on, I am able to make it present again, re-present it, even when I am not in that place. I can make it again in the present; I can make it present to me vividly, even though I am not in the situation. The image of the branching point has left a trace, which I can re-call and I can re-live my passing the branching

point and the moment of my astonishment while I realizing that I have been on the pedestrian trail.

What can science educators learn from this? What can I learn from this especially about learning physics? Here, the first and second time I pass the branch, I am experiencing a particular world; the particular resource, the branching point, is not salient to me in consciousness. There is no fine structure in this part of the world, not the fine structure that is salient to the teacher, but I find myself one day on one branch and on the next day on the other. What I have perceived is not the same (life-) world that I subsequently perceive, which is a lifeworld that includes a branching point in the bicycle path. In my previous lifeworld there has been no branching point. But right at the moment when I see cyclists to my left on another trail, I *am startled*. At this moment of being startled, I begin to objectify my experience, my presence on the trail. Being startled allows a new figure|ground and whole|parts configuration to emerge.

There is a contradiction in my experience. There is something relevant to what I am doing that I have not noticed previously; but immediately after taking note of the other cyclist, I have an explication. However, whereas I am already objectifying my experience in terms of a branching point that I have not noticed before, the Australian high school students in chapter 2 do not and perhaps cannot know (insufficient experience and more possibilities for make them arrive at where they are) why what they expected to achieve has not yet been achieved.

Knowledgeability, the philosopher Martin Heidegger says, is a fundamental mode of our *being-there* ("Dasein"), which inherently constitutes a position and therefore disposition. Explicit knowledge, on the other hand, is not the precondition of our interaction with the world. Explicit knowledge does not *create* the possibilities a subject finds in the world and interactions do not *originate* from an effect of the world on a subject. Rather, a world already known in and through practical experience—I have been riding both paths without accident before—allows itself to be disclosed and discovered. That is, I can look at my experiences as the alignment of conscious experience and my non-conscious, practical understanding of how the world works. The non-conscious constituted the very condition of consciousness. I navigate this world, my lifeworld, without having to know it in detail, that is, in the way a physicist might now it, objectively given by the coordinates in space-time. Rather, I inhabit a world that by and large I am not conscious of but that discloses itself to my consciousness in an unfolding way.

BREAKDOWN AND RESISTANCE

In the previous episodes, I show how things apparently entirely new to me emerge into my conscious experience (the twin towers, white distance markers, branch in the bicycle path) or how some things appear to be latently present in consciousness—at least after the fact. That is, there are phenomena in my experience that I know after the fact to have been at least vaguely aware of but that have not made a difference in my decision-making, as if they had not existed at all. The question then arises, how those things that only are latently present make it into my awareness where they then can be integrated with other aspects of my conscious life. *Being startled* is one starting point for many new things that make it into my conscious awareness. Such awareness and integration of new environmental, lifeworld features with thought is often triggered, as in this next episode, by situations of *breakdown* or *resistance*.

Breakdown occurs when something I normally presuppose—and expect even when I am not consciously aware of them, for example, when I eat dinner, I do not consciously think about the table, which nevertheless makes it possible for dishes, cutlery, and meal to be at a certain height—no longer exists or happens or happens only with difficulty (resistance). Thus, while writing this book, I do not think about the keyboard or monitor, at least as long as everything works. If hitting a key does not produce the expected results (as when earlier today I spilled some water over my keyboard), if the monitor does not show the expected image, then I experience breakdown of the usual ways of going about my daily business. At this point, I am startled; and in being startled, I realize that something does not work, has broken down, or resists the intended action. This breakdown (resistance) mediates my next steps—likely consisting in finding out how to remedy the situation that interferes with what I am doing. In the process, to find out *why* my tools do not work in the way they are supposed to work, I often learn a lot about the structure of the device that currently does not work. Breakdown or resistance normally is identified and analyzed in the context of using instruments, tools, and other forms of technology. However, the notion of breakdown is useful, too, for theorizing situations that do not involve material structures but that are discursive in nature. I may ask, for example, what mediates the breakdown in a conversation, and then begin to analyze the apparent lack of intersubjectivity concerning the topic of talk or form of interaction.

In the following situation, the breakdown is of material nature; it leads to *resistance*, which interferes with what I am doing at the moment. Because something goes wrong, I cannot continue my trip, which forces me to inquire what the problem is. Initially, however, the nature of the breakdown is not clear. Rather, what is wrong and what has to be done emerges at the moment when something that has been present latently in my consciousness now becomes a salient issue.

> I ride a long the road and jump with my bike off the bicycle path and onto the road. As I land, my rear tire explodes and is flat faster than I can come to a halt so that I roll on the rim for a while. I take the wheel off, remove the tire, remove the inner tube and inspect it. It has a long tear, about eight centimeters in length. I cannot fix it with my emergency kit and I have left my spare inner tube at home. I leave the inner tube in the correct orientation removing it without removing the valve. I inspect whether there are spokes coming through the lining in the region of the tear, for the tear seems toward the center, on the inner part of the tube.
>
> I walk back to town and get a new inner tube. While placing it, I am vaguely aware that some of the tire wall is detached from the wire that goes under the rim. I wonder whether I should return to the department

store and get a new tire. But I decide to buy one in the big specialty store in the nearby city where I might get something that is just like the one I have—I do not experience buying a new tire as a pressing issue. I mount the inner tube and inflate by hand it enough to ride comfortably. I ride the four kilometers to the next gas station that I know to be on my way to the university. There, as I inflate the tire, it explodes. I am startled. When I inspect the tire, I notice that it has a tear. All of a sudden, I expect the inner tube to be torn at that place.

"I put the pieces together." The inner tube had protruded through the place where the wall had come off the tire and exploded when I jumped off the bicycle path. It exploded again when I put a lot of air into the inner tube that made it protrude.

In this situation, the tear in the tire wall becomes salient as tear and therefore behaviorally relevant only after the second blowout. Exactly then I am startled, and being startled and realizing the tear as a tear and cause of my blowout occur at the same time. Initially, there merely is a *diffuse noticing*. In fact, that I have "diffusely noticed" becomes evident to me only at the gas station when the inner tube blows out for the second time. It is exactly then that I am aware of my earlier diffuse noticing. The second time, the tear is salient to me: in being startled, I re-cognize it. That is, there is evidence that I already have perceptually tracked the tire; but I have not integrated the perceptual capacities with those for thought and action-guidance. The tear initially does not exist as a fact in my conscious awareness, and therefore does not affect or mediate my decision-making. I act as if the tear does not exist and has no behavioral relevance. I ride the bicycle to the next gas station and then use the automatic pump to inflate the tire until it blows out. That is, I do not perceive (see) the tear *as* tear. If anything, I find it interesting that the metal wire has detached itself from the rubber walls of the tire. Even the question whether to buy a new tire at that instance or some time later is but a fleeting, indeterminate non-idea rather than a concrete deliberation of alternatives.

Today I know that the tear existed immanently, as something possibly to be grasped. It is at this moment that the tear becomes salient as a tear, a figure against the indeterminate ground of everything else. Simultaneously with being startled, an association between explosion and tear appears to me—I passively receive it. It is at this point that the thought "I should have known it" arises; I take the tear as *transcendentally* existing before I become consciously aware of it. The question of whether an impression or an initial noticing is something that I need to focus on and attend to arises from its covariation with other aspects in my perceptual field. This covariation is intimately tied to my sensorimotor activity (at minimum, eye movement to focus on one than on another aspect). My initial experience, while leading to an impression, is not a difference that really makes a difference.

The analysis of the episodes makes salient three key features of visual perception. First, perception is intimately tied to exploration; without inspecting the tire I have no way of finding out about the tear. But a theoretical look alone does not suffice; I begin to look with intent when I experience the second blow out, that is, when the breakdown interferes with my actions. Second, perception requires mas-

tery of sensorimotor contingencies (at a minimum, exercise of eye muscle for focusing and changing orientation); without active inspection, I cannot find out anything about why the tire may have blown out for a second time. Third, seeing
something *as* something requires an integration of visually tracking the surroundings with my capacities for thought and action-guidance. The tear alone does not
make a difference. It is the tear in the face of a blown inner tube and an unusable
bicycle that the relevance of the tear becomes salient in the contextual particulars
that mediate its presence. The tear *as* tear orients me to the situation of which I
then *take care* in a concernful way. It is from the orientation (see also chapter 6)
and my taking care that the actions I take spring forth.

These investigation of my perceptual experiences while riding a bicycle through
initially unfamiliar surroundings and discovering the tear in my tire *as* tear show
that the world is not given to me at the instant that I first lay my eyes on it. Rather,
following extended experience, different figure|ground relations (e.g., "Landwehr,"
towers, and distance signs) manifest themselves in time, as they emerge from an
indeterminate ground. They mark and make time in and as change. This result is
further underscored by the second episode, which shows that I might vaguely be
aware of something without being simultaneously aware of it in such a way that it
could become a behaviorally relevant entity. The tear does not exist as a reportable
and relevant "fact" in my lifeworld until the second blow out. I therefore could not
articulate it, that is, I could not have stated an observation sentence and even less
an observation categorical (generalization of observation sentences). If an all-
knowing science teacher had set up the tear (or the towers, distance signs, etc.), I
would have failed to demonstrate knowledge or failed to learn from the experience,
for during the first (and until the n-th) encounter, the entities are not salient to me. I
do not attend to these entities that the teacher expects me to see. As a result, I cannot understand whatever explanation the teacher provides for what I should have
(but have not actually) seen in the same way the Australian students in chapter 1
integrate what the teacher says with their own perceptions, which radically differs
from what the teacher sees and expects students to see.

These episodes therefore exemplify how a salient figure over indeterminate
ground is an emergent feature that comes with experience. Sometimes, resistance
provokes this emergence (as in the tire example); being startled leads to the recognition of a breakdown. That is, I discover a thing (fact, object, tool) and its features
not by looking and ascertaining properties but by taking note of co-varying figures
(tear, explosion) in the course of use and experience. To take note of covariation
requires orienting to and focusing on a minimum of two figures, that is, it requires
repeated sensorimotor activity. When I discover that the object (tire) can no longer
be used or that some fact does not fit my expectation, the entity (tear) becomes
conspicuous. Conspicuity, visual awareness, means that thought (expectation) is
integrated with conscious visual tracking of my surrounding.

In the writing of this section, I explicitly attend to the way in which agency is
represented. It is important to the understanding of perception that I do not "construct" the towers, the distance and *Landwehr* signs, or the tear. These things are
thrust into my awareness. I do not "construct" the relationship (covariation) be-

tween tear and explosion; these salient figures and their relationships emerge, without my (conscious) doing: and then are there, all of a sudden, violently. These figures can emerge because I am open, willing to be impressed, marked by my encounter with the world that I experience as outside of myself. Such sensibility also is vulnerability, because I cannot know beforehand what I will come to perceive and how it will change everything else I am knowledgeable about. This also means that I have no conscious control over the things that appear and become conscious. Opening myself to learning therefore constitutes a risk, as I have to engage in learning something that I do not know what it is; it is like being a host for strangers, which I do accept and do have to accept because I am a *host*. But because I have to accept, I am also hostage to the situation. Being a host to the unfamiliar also means being *hostage* to it. Learning in general and learning from perceptual experience in particular has an aporetic nature in the sense that I am asked to intend to learn something that I do not know what it is, so that in a strong sense, I cannot intend to know it by taking particular steps to get there. As host to strangers, I do not know who will come and cannot intend who will come unless I refuse to be a host to strangers—which means I refuse learning anything new at all.

These points underscore that the concept of agency—even in its dialectical formulation with structure—is limited, as it focuses my attention on the intentional aspects of human experience. However, there is more to learning than the intentional aspects embodied in the notion of agency. If I want to learn from experience, I not only have to act but also have to open myself to the world so it can touch me. I have to be willing to be a host to strangers, for this is what the unknown constitutes to me. I have to be endowed with sensibility (I return to this notion below), which mediates what and how I can experience phenomena that are outside myself, the world that I share with others. *Sensibility* is the frequently overlooked partner of agency; from an ontological perspective, it precedes agency as intent (Levinas, 1978a/1998). Because the notion of intending intent leads to infinite regress, intent itself is something that I accept in the way a host accepts a stranger. I am a host to my intent, the origin of which I do not intend and therefore have no control over. This passivity is absent, among others, in constructivism, all forms of which emphasize the transitivity of constructive actions.

POINTING OUT

When science teachers and science educators ask students to engage in experimenting, in reproducing some procedure, or in simply watching a demonstration, they presuppose—based on a pre-sup-position, inherently a position and disposition—that there are objective structures in the world, which can be apprehended irrespective of the formative experiences that brings a person to the present situation. This, as the everyday, mundane examples in this chapter show, is not the case. That is, while I talk about experiences as objectively giving me a world, it is not the same world objectively given to everybody in the same way: Exactly because I have a body, I have a position that others cannot simultaneously take, and therefore I am dispositioned differently to others, who, in turn, are dispositioned differently than

I. While material, the specific way in which the world becomes objectively present depends on practical activity, which mediates consciousness, among others through the intentional object/motive that characterizes it. Sometimes I notice things for a first time although I have spent a long time in a particular context, repeatedly taken a route, experienced a kind of breakdown that made a thing evident *as* the specific thing I encounter. But such presence does not always involve specific intentions: Engaging in a leisurely walk along a path likely leads to very different fig-ure|ground relations than if I am looking for something I presume to have lost while taking the walk. More so, I may not notice something even though somebody else may want to point it out to me. In this case, I do not perceive the pointing out *as* a pointing out, as a de-monstrating. In chapter 1, there is a moment when a re-searcher holds his thumb up and comments "thumbs up" after students have com-pleted a test in which the right-hand rule was required to solve many of the items. In this situation, the thumbs-up gesture and the utterance are signifiers that point to and point out a specific signified: the theoretically relevant right-hand rule. The students look incredulous, which leads me to the conclusion that what the re-searcher intended as a pointing out has not been perceived as such. The thumbs-up gesture is perceived for itself rather than as an index to something else. The sense of the gesture has not yet split from its material body—in the way I describe this phenomenon in chapter 7.

Thinking about the conditions that make *pointing out* possible, I come to realize that I already have to see what there is to see so that pointing out can do its job. For pointing out to work, I need to perceive the pointing—gesture or indexical (this, that, etc.)—*as* pointing, I need to perceive a thing possibly being pointed out, and I need to make the relation between the two so that the pointing points out does the work it is intended to do. In a strong sense, then, pointing out can never be the pointing out of something entirely new. The thing pointed out and the (vocal, hand, facial) gesture doing the pointing have to exist as possibilities within me. Thus, *communication never transmits something new but merely* highlights *what is already shared.* That pointing does not always point out, especially when we do not know or are not aware of what the pointing is to point out, becomes clear in the following episode.

While I was a fellow at the *Hanse Institute*, I not only rode my bicycle but also thoroughly cleaned its frame and parts on a regular basis. After one of these events, I recorded the following description in my research notebook.

> I sit outside my apartment, talking to a colleague while cleaning the chain of my bike. As I spin the chain to hear whether there is more of the noise from the ball bearings that have led me to do a cleaning job, a colleague remarks that the wheel wobbles. I do not think much about his comment at the time. Only later do I check, when the wheel appears to stick at the brake shoes at one point of its movement. I have a strange sensation and attempt to resituate the wheel, thinking that the axle has shifted out of alignment with the frame while I was fastening it to the latter. Later this afternoon, still cleaning the bike, I touch the wheel by accident and think to have noticed a "soft spoke." An idea slowly forms itself in my con-

scious awareness: perhaps one or two spokes might have come loose, which would have led to a warp in the wheel and make it stick. I cannot see the "soft" spoke off-hand; but when I check every spoke, I find one that is torn.

Similar to the previous episodes, I come to perceive the broken spoke *in the course of* the afternoon and while cleaning the bicycle. After the fact I might be tempted to reconstruct its existence as having predated my knowledge of it. Behaviorally, however, it has not mediated what I have been doing. That is, although the light rays from the spoke certainly hit my retina all afternoon, I do not notice the spoke as torn. Even though at one point my colleague points to the wheel and its wobble, I do not think about a loose or broken spoke. I do not interpret my perception either: I do not perceive the spoke. I do not perceive it even after my colleague notices that the wheel wobbles, which, after the fact, can be interpreted as the noticing of trouble. I do not notice and record his comment as a pointing-out trouble, although after the fact I remember having heard him make this comment (as evidenced in the fact that I recorded having heard him say what he has said). That is, even though I must have heard him make the comment, it apparently has not struck me as such. His description becomes salient only after the fact when I already perceive the wheel as wobbling. The sounds that made his words are part of the indeterminate ground. That is, once I perceive the wobble and once I linked it to the comment, that is, once the correlation between the two exists, the pointing has become a pointing out. In fact, therefore, the three aspects—pointing, perceptual isolation of some thing pointed out, and their relation irremediably are part of the same phenomenon: the process (seeing) and products of perception (seen).

The real search for a possible trouble spot began when I noticed that the wheel slightly sticks in regular intervals while spinning. This led to my being startled; or rather, in being startled I find the wheel to be sticking. The first possibility I pursue is to check whether I have aligned the axle and wheel properly with the frame while tightening the screws—I vaguely remember that as a kid I have had the problem of properly aligning bicycle wheels with the frame so that the axle was not always perfectly perpendicular to the main dimension of the frame. But in the present situation, I find that the alignment is all right and I turn to attend to different aspects of the cleaning work until the moment when I find myself startled.

Now I can see that there already are two occasions, two pieces of evidence that could have suggested trouble with the wheel itself, but these pieces of evidence have not been evidence for me at the time. That is, despite further evidence that there might be some trouble, I still do not see it as such. Another incident a little later in the afternoon—my being startled during the accidental noticing that there appears to be a soft spoke and the search for the spoke that follows—leads to the discovery of a problem: a spoke has torn.

In this situation, repeated possible hints initially are insufficient to make salient a broken spoke. That is, perception is not automatic, even in the situation that someone cares about something and even though trouble is highly relevant—the bicycle is my only means of locomotion and also my favorite pastime. One of the conclusions I draw from this episode is that even in the face of multiple evidence and even though somebody tries to point something out to me, I may not perceive this something that nevertheless later becomes a fact for me too. My colleague to me has been like a science teacher to students who wants to point something out, demonstrate some phenomenon. Yet although intended as a demonstration, a pointing out, the action does not have this effect and therefore cannot be considered to constitute a pointing out (demonstration). The action of pointing out, the de-monstration, is only complete when the pointing, its object, and their correlation have become salient to the learner. More strongly, the supposed evidence is not evidence but becomes evidence only with the perception of the fact (e.g., broken spoke). That is, evidence and fact are linked, and the salience of the two as fact and evidence emerges rather than being given to me at the very moment that I lay eyes on something or the moment that light rays from this something strike my eyes.

REMEMBERING: MAKING SENSE

Remember, to rememorate, to bring to memory again also is to *re*-member, put together again that has been articulated, taken apart at its joints. A member is a constituent part of a complex structure; to re-member also has the sense of supplying a new member. Making sense of something means making a space in what I already know to include a new member, which requires me to remember, rememorate the relevance relations in which the new member finds its place. Here, I use the term *articulate* in its sense to both describe and perceptually slice the world. Re-membering gives it, what has been articulated, the body again, in memory, a body that it has had at some different moment in time. That is, representing means to make present again, to re-presence an experience, which also is rememorate the original experience, to make it a part (member) of my current relevance relations. Re-present as making present again, re-presences. What does it mean, then, to re-member? Why do I not remember having been somewhere or done something? Why do I find students and myself repeating actions in the laboratory that we have already engaged in, as if we did not remember having done this before?

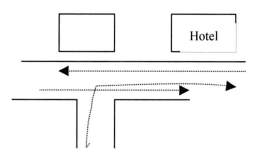

Figure 3.2. I have come this way repeatedly. Though when I return for the first time, I do not recognize the hotel. It is only after I had seen it multiple times from multiple angles that it becomes an aspect of my lifeworld and inherently makes sense.

> I am riding to the university taking a particular set of roads. After work, I take what I know to be the same roads, but I do not recognize them as such; I do not recognize the houses that I am certain I should have seen when I came the other way. Upon reflection, I know I have been here before, but I do not recognize it. After repeatedly going back and forth to the university via this set of roads, I see a sign, a house, sometimes just a detail such as a house number that I remember having seen, noticed before. After having done the trip repeatedly, I begin to notice on the way back a hotel, which I had been aware of only on the way to the university ((Figure 3.2)).

Why and how is it possible that such details come back into my mind? I possibly make inferences on the basis of such forgotten experiences that resurface at some later point in time. It is from such re-surfacing, re-membering, and remembering that I am able later to make the experience of the trip an object of my inquiry, to objectify it. A particular hotel, a particular bent in the road, even just a house number that "sticks out" and that I recognize when I pass it the next time become objects of thought. As I come by day upon day, the number of details I remember about the house and intersection increase. My world along this road to work is becoming increasingly differentiated, articulated and articulable. I begin to envision how to go to a place or what instructions I have to give to someone else to go there. I can recognizably communicate how to get to my favorite bicycle store so that locals can deduce which of the shops they know I am referring to.

> I have passed the intersection of *Remberti Ring* and *Rembert Strasse* multiple times in the north–south direction. Yet on the first time going west to east across the intersection—where I came to the assessment that it was the same intersection only after the fact—I notice only at the last minute that this is an intersection that I already know, alerted by a nearby underpass and a construction site I remember having seen, and a particular not-yet-filled-in pothole. This sense that I already know an aspect of this part of the city first arises from the *startling* way the bicycle path crosses a pedestrian path. Being startled becomes an occasion, the intersection a resource for me to look around intentionally; only then do I recognize the construction site and underpass. However, on this way back, I do not recognize this place as "this place again" until the very last moment, just as I am leaving the intersection again. Until that moment, I ride along as if riding in an unfamiliar part of the world. I have already passed the intersection when I the sense that I know it arises within me, again taking the underpass as a somewhat familiar point. And then, re-cognizing a bump in the sidewalk, I rapidly turn around and recognize the intersection for what I know it to be. From this moment on, this intersection has become the *intersection* of a number of different experiences, which are evoked every time I cross it on my habitual way of cycling in north–south direction. I know the intersection because I know what it means to approach and cross it from different directions. The intersection *as* intersection, that is, as ob-

ject, emerges from my multiple and different experiences. Its objective nature is the result of multiple and different experiences rather than the result of a first-time encounter.

Over the course of my three-month stay, I have the same type of experiences with other intersections (e.g., Figure 3.2), which I come to know in a more abstract sense—from different sides, so to speak, literally and metaphorically—after riding through them on many different occasions. In all of these cases, my knowing is mediated by the experience of having come across some place multiple times and in multiple directions. It is with my body, my senses, that I integrate the different experiences into *one and the same intersection* and come to see the particular place in an integrated way. *I come to know the place* as *place, because I know how it looks like from wherever I come and because I know how it will look differently when I come from another direction.* Any intersection, as an object of knowledge, arises from the totality and "intersection" of multiple experiences, which provide me with sufficient ground for anticipating what I perceive and experience from whichever direction I approach. Now the intersection *makes sense*: it is connected into a thick and extended web of experiences of traveling the city. Sense derives from the way something (object, word, gesture) is connected to other things; sense is not a property of some thing (object, word, gesture). But until such point, I come past a location where I have been before as if it is a new place and I know only after the fact that it is a position that I know coming from a different position and having a different perspective (disposition). That is, although I have come to some place (position) before—which I know after the fact that I have been there before—I come to it again for a first time. I do not have the experience that I have been here before.

These analyses show that I come to know an object (hotel, intersection) through repeated interactions that make the object appear in different ways, for example, under different light, from a different position, and therefore always from a different "angle" of the relation between the thing and its setting, always dispositioned. My movement with respect to the thing and its relation to other things establishes the very nature of the thing; my mobility therefore is central to the essence of the things, because it allows me to sense what comes to be a thing in different ways. The nature of an object as one and the same thing arises from my experiences that establish the correlations between my agency and my sensibility.

Such experiences allow me to understand when I see students (myself) doing "the same thing" over and over again, apparently without being aware of it. The problem with characterizing students as "doing the same over and over" is that this and similar assessments are made by an outside observer, whereas the learner does not recall having had the experience before. As the present account shows, I may have crossed the same intersection many times but when I come to it from a different direction, it is as if I am facing a new intersection. That is, it is a new experience to me rather than one I already have had and now re-experience. It takes more than simply experiencing something for it to leave a trace as and of something already known or completely new. How are such experiences to be understood?

In these experiences, my body has been a central element. Without it, I cannot move about and perceive. The materiality of my body provides me with the potentiality of an expression. In it, the visual, aural, kinesthetic, or gustatory find their expressiveness in a nonthetic and ante-predicated unity of the perceived world (Merleau-Ponty, 1945/1962). My bodily integration of these senses is the very foundation of verbal expressions in general and that of signification more specifically. My body is

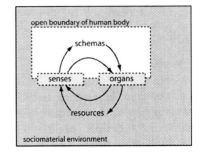

Figure i.2 repeated.

the common underlying texture of the experienced world; it is the condition and instrument of my comprehension.

My body not only provides me with a sense not only of the physical world, but also of the sociocultural world constituted by all those other bodies that I recognize as resembling my own, animated by the same sort of consciousness that I experience myself. From a phenomenological perspective, there then is no ontological difference between the way I am shaped by the physical or by the social world. Both are constitutive of our ways of making sense of the world. My perceptions themselves are shaped by these worlds such that there is a constitutive loop between individual and world. World and my experience of it (through sensual perception) mutually imply each other (Figure i.2).

My perceptual actions alone do not achieve the integration (synthesis) into a singular world from the multitudes of different sensorial experiences. My perception always already is made possible because of previous actions of synthesis that allow me to experience the world in the way I do. These previous experiences are traces that mediate my integration of new experiences into an existing, coherent world, which provides the foundation for later experience. *This existing network of experiences constitutes my implicit knowledgeability, sedimented experiences that form a thick foundational layer that constitutes the ground from which any figure can emerge. In other words, indeterminate ground is both known and not known; it offers possibilities to me despite its non-conscious nature.* My body therefore is the determining and formative precondition of my rationality. That is, the unity of the subject and world can be found in the pre-reflexive (pre-conscious) experience. Because of the special position of the material body both as instrument of perception and as location of the reflexive cogito (and its necessary individual situated perspective), I always and already presuppose what I find in the things.

The things I know—such as when a house brings about the memory of a house I have lived in, or when I see a house in terms of another house I know—allow me to make connections. It is a re-membering, a weaving together of the new and something already existing, a new member in a rememorated network of members, and *seeing* the new member *as* something, a perception in terms of, a likeness with the old. Re-membering is re-articulation. But there also is a difference between the old and the new, for it is the new seen in terms of the old rather than the other way around that comes to be integrated. However, such cases in which the old is seen in terms of the new are perfectly thinkable and possibly the case when I revise what I have seen based on new perceptual experiences. In this sense, re-membering is always re-cognition. Learning is an articulation of possibilities that I already embody. In learning I become consciously aware of something I already know practically, something that is already cast as possibility in my understanding prior to the learning event. Thus, re-cognition is an again, but also an again that—at least I— see differently than the first time. Perhaps, this is a reflexive component: In ordinary situations, when I do not reflect, and simply "see" forces in a relationship, I thereby re-cognize without making topic that which I have done so before. In this way, when I do not recognize the *re-* in the cognize, then I also do not reflect. Ultimately then, I do not recognize that my cognition is mostly re-cognition.

GROUND

In the previous sections I comment on perception. However, although I write about the things that become salient to me and therefore about the content of my perception, I so far have omitted something else—in fact, literally *everything* else that nevertheless is of equal importance and, perhaps, even constitutes the very condition for perception. That is, whenever and whatever I perceive, I do so against a *ground*. I do not perceive a house as if it were in an empty space, in the way houses might appear in some avant-garde paintings; and even there, everything else in the painting including its frame or border constitute the house as what it is. Even if the "painting" consists of an entirely white piece of cloth in a frame, it still exists within the frame, and it would so even if there was no frame at all. In this way, John Cage's composition *4'33"*, the performance of which consists of a pianist sitting for 4 minutes and 33 seconds at the piano, hands on the keyboard without playing, performs "silence" against a ground without which the silence does not function as silence. I always encounter things in context, that is, against a ground whatever these might be. *This ground, the "other" part of the figure|ground dialectic, serves as the source* and *context for all figure that I may be conscious off.* It is only within a particular frame that a house makes sense *as* a house, a representation of some house, a notation for a house, and so forth. I experience the ground as much as the thing perceived, and it is only in the dialectical relation of figure against ground that a figure comes to make sense. The ground is constitutive of sense; it is not the figure that *has* meaning, but the sense of anything is the relation between it, as figure, and the ground, which constitutes a network of relevance relations. Because the experience of the ground is mediated by my past experiences, it constitutes what I experience as meaning or as source of meaning. *It is not that the* figure *is meaningful in itself but that the figure accrues to already existing,* familiar *ground, which I experience as meaningful* because *it is familiar.*

> As I am riding along, I primarily see the world not in a thematic way, not in terms of a collection of things, but I am aware of it in and as a unified whole. Some places, some things draw my attention, draw my regard to

rest for a while and inspect it as I am passing by. What I regard, observe, look at, I also guard, keep at bay, watch carefully.

Structure in a new environment emerges when I notice something as already experienced, something *as* something. And it emerges when the something is related to my ongoing activity. I may look somewhere without seeing what there is to see, as I may look at a wristwatch and not notice the time it displays because I have looked at the wristwatch for different reasons. What I perceive is related to *why* I am looking. The world constitutes ground for my actions; it exhibits normally only those structures that are related to the demands of my ongoing practical activity, as the following episode exemplifies. Thus, when I look into a particular direction, there are many different things to be seen—but not so simultaneously. Even if I only consider one plane of depth in my perceptual field, different figure|ground configurations may be apparent and other possible figures remain hidden.

> While riding my bicycle on a trainer—i.e., in the stationary mode—I sometimes measure my pulse rate or determine the cadence. To do so, I count the number of beats or revolution per thirty seconds using my wristwatch (Figure 3.3). So not to forget when I start counting, I always begin at the full minute, fifteen, thirty, or forty-five second mark. I am catching myself determining heart rate, only to return my gaze a few seconds later to find out what time it is or how long I have already exercised.

The episode clearly exemplifies how I have been looking at the watch without seeing the time it displays. Given that the watch is about 1 meter away from me, it completely falls into my angle of vision. Yet when checking the time to determine pulse rate or pedaling cadence, I only become aware of the second display. The current time of day entirely remains outside my consciousness. In these situations, the status of the second indicator is salient to me. I intend to determine the thirty-second period that ends my counting the heart rate or pedal strokes. Simultaneously, the chronological time, though it is a category that I am very familiar with, is not salient to me; had the time been salient I would not have needed to take another look for finding out the time given that I already have looked at the watch for a thirty-second period. That is, at the time I am counting heartbeats or pedal strokes, I am intentionally oriented toward determining the thirty-second period.

Figure 3.3. Although the entire watch was in my visual field, only the numbers indicating seconds tend to be salient when I set out to measure heart rate or cadence.

The current figure|ground relation makes salient the length of this period; but it does not simultaneously make salient the chronological time. To perceive the time of day I have to shift my intention, choose to look at the wristwatch within a particular context. The shift in intentionality mediates a very different figure|ground configuration. A similar shift in intentionality allows me to feel the thing I touch with my finger or the sensation the thing leaves in my finger but not both.

From a materialist perspective, I know that the image of the digital watch and numbers are on my retina. Other researchers can agree that there is a face of the wristwatch, structured in a particular way that people familiar with the culture can all recognize *as* something, numbers, names of days, and so on. They can provide time and spatial coordinates to locate particular features. Yet this physical perspective of the wristwatch is inappropriate for understanding my perceptual experience, or rather, it is only partially appropriate. Relevant to understanding knowing and learning are not the descriptions of entities and states that researchers agree upon but the ways in which things and events appear to me in my consciousness while pursuing particular objects of intention (i.e., motives). To understand that I do not know the time the firs time around, researchers also have to account for the motives and goals that orient what I do. Specific entities and phenomena emerge as figures against the material ground, mediated by my past experiences and by my present intentions.

It is also evident that I am not in control of those things that are emerging for me for the first time, though what emerges is constrained by my intentions. I am not even in control of my intentions, which I receive in my consciousness as the hospitable host receives his foreign guests. I cannot know in advance at what point a place becomes sufficiently familiar that I recognize it even when I come from an unfamiliar direction. Generally, I am simply taking much of the world for granted and without need to be made thematic. Those things that lie outside my awareness remain indeterminate ground, unattended to, though upon reflection they may be essential to the constitution of the situation as a whole.

> I notice that yesterday, my keys and my clothing have been transparent to me; I have not been aware of what I have been wearing and that I have had the keys with me on the bicycle trip. Though I have been thinking hard about the kinds of things that are more or less conscious to my activity of riding the bike and thinking about cognition, I have not thought of listing my clothing or the key chain, which, as I have noticed at other times, makes a bell-like sound that notifies other cyclist of my coming as I approach them from behind.

As this episode shows, many aspects of our lives are not thematic in everyday activity, though this does not mean that a setting cannot be structured such that these aspects come to constitute a figure|ground configuration. The bell-like sound of my keys alerts other cyclists and pedestrians, and without my clothing, I would be inappropriately "dressed" for most social situations (except perhaps nude beaches and European saunas). And yet, although I am not making my clothing thematic, it is essential to the societal situation in which I find myself. I do not go into most public spaces without clothing or dressed in a way that is inappropriate to the situation. Though my clothing contributes to defining and redefining these situations, and how they are and possibly can be constructed in new and different ways, I may be largely oblivious to them most of the day. Others, too, may or may not notice my clothing. A suit worn at a black-tie event hardly gets noticed. When I show up with a bicycle and in bicycle attire at a gathering during which the university president honors a grant recipient, my clothing comes to be noticed. In fact, it redefines the situation from the traditional black-tie event it was designed to be to something else, a new kind of gathering and event; or others present may redefine me as a rude or eccentric person. My clothing becomes and will be thematic, though normally it only "figures" in the ground, for example, at the weekly gathering of the local cycling club. *The indeterminate ground, therefore, is both the condition for perceptual experience* and *the indeterminate ground* against *which this experience takes place.*

The strange, contradictory expression "figuring in the ground" points to the possibility of something that currently is unnoticed to come to the fore, to become salient figure. Importantly, both figure and ground present intentions, and the spatial position of my body mediates (dispositions) the figure|ground structure of my perception: The figure corresponds to the focus of my gaze and the ground to what I compare it to as my eye saccades between figure and ground in imperceptible ways (Roth, 2005a). Furthermore, the perceptual surroundings can be differentiated into the immediate spatial context of the figure, on the one hand, and the indeterminate ground of the periphery, on the other, with the indeterminate ground including the marginal presence of one's own body (Pessoa, Thompson, & Noë, 1998). To see an object, therefore, is either to have it at the fringe of the visual field and to have the possibility of fixing it, or to effectively respond to the solicitation to do so. When I do fix it, I become anchored in it, *pre-positioning* me and thereby giving me an orientation. But this anchorage or stoppage is but one modality of its movement: I continue the exploration at the interior of the object. An exploration that earlier passed over all of them, in one movement, I close the landscape constituted by the face of the wristwatch as a whole and open the object, the numbers displaying the seconds. Even if I knew nothing of perception, the cones and rods in the eyes that make it possible, I would have to conceive of the necessity to disattend to the surroundings, which becomes indeterminate ground, to better see the object, which becomes figure; and I would have to give up to the ground what I gain in the figure. This is so because to study an object means to plunge into it, allow it to become my counterpart in the subject|object dialectic. *Objects thereby come to form a system where I cannot reveal one without also concealing others: In taking position, I pre-position, dis-position, and pre-sup-position myself.* All perception inherently involves a figure|ground dialectic. More precisely, the inner horizon of an object cannot become focal object without the surrounding objects become horizon—I perceive the seconds without perceiving the time.

SENSIBILILTY

My body constitutes me as being singular plural, which means, as body among bodies, as person among persons. I am always already in the world, I am continuously exposed to and participate in interactions with the world. I cannot imagine myself without the world, without which there is no air that can pervade me and provide me with oxygen, and into which I return the carbon dioxide that results from the burning of oxygen. However, my immersion is polythetic (plural) in the sense that I do not attend to most of these interactions in a conscious manner; I do not attend all other possible singular plural beings although the light rays coming off them strike my retina. Phenomenological thought has it that these influences constitute a layer of lateral experiences, pre-conscious and non-conscious that nevertheless contribute to constituting all experiences I can have. It is only in the conscious perceptive act that a particular impression is isolated and brought to the foreground and thereby becomes salient to my consciousness. That which is unattended in my experience and that forms the lateral correspondences is not available to conscious reflection and therefore to explication and explanation, but is a constitutive aspect of our perceptions nevertheless.

In the totality of my experience, from the ground, emerge some "aspects" that become salient. Some of these I attend to and some of these I later remember. There are many other singular plural beings also present, which I only notice at some later point (mileage signs along the highway); they nevertheless may be present to others in the world. They are not present in my lifeworld, from my position and disposition, the world I am oriented to—for once I begin noticing the white sign posts along the road, for example, I follow them, count down the distance, think about and with them: They contribute to that which I am conscious of and oriented to, which I check to see the next one, and so on.

My perception requires my actions, moving about and manipulating the world. But actions do not have a consequence if not something else is equally present, even presupposing action itself: *sensibility* (Levinas, 1978a/1998). In acting, I open myself to the world; but because I am sensible, open to being impressed and acted upon from the outside, my actions can have relevance to my way of perceiving the world. But sensibility does not mean that I perceive a world as it really is. What I come to perceive arises from this dialectic of agency and sensibility, the correlation of what I do and what I sense. Perception is the result of these interactions but not their precondition. The concept of agency insufficiently attends to the question of how structure—often theorized in terms of (a) material and social resources, on the one hand, and (b) individual, cultural-historically specific schema, on the other hand—arises in the first place. However, both agency and sensibility are possibilities that come with my body. My body therefore is not merely another or any material object, but it is the very condition for all other material objects, the foundation of all objectivity, that is, the primary object as such. My body is condition, as the sensible content of experience is inseparable from incarnation, of which it is the reflection or counterpart (Bourdieu, 1997/2000). My body therefore is both invested with consciousness, the seat and origin of consciousness, and a material object in its own right. The splitting of consciousness and body leads to the possibility of any other material object to exist. This same splitting underlies the splitting of sense from sound, and the privileged treatment of language as if it were all about sense (and meaning) completely divorced from its material embodiment in sounds, graphisms, letters, and so on.

Sensibility by itself is not a useful concept. To be useful, sensibility has to be constrained, for otherwise I would drown in a sea of stimuli that arrive at my sensory periphery. In this situation, then, my existing understanding of the world, my experiences that have left traces in the body and therefore are embodied in it as structured structuring dispositions, and my intentions constitute mediating filters. That is, language, culture, and sociability mediate the noticing of difference; but in turn, they themselves are made possible by my immersion (with my sensorial body) in the world. The noticing of difference depends on the situation (as remembering on my bicycle trips), for it is the entirety of the sensorial stimulus that allows particular knowledgeability to emerge.

Sensibility is intimately tied to my having a body, or more accurately, to the fact that I exist only in and through my body. Without my body, I would not be able to be affected by the feel of the things I touch, the smell of foods, the sense of heat and cold, or by the brightness of light. The nature of things depends on my own nature, the nature of the subject of experience, my body, and my normal sensibility to the world external to me. The body is first and foremost the means of all perception, it is *the* central organ (Gr. *organon*, tool) of perception; it necessarily accompanies all perception (Husserl, 1952). It is my body that allows a coordination and correlation in and through my senses between (a) an intentional orientation to the other (person, object) and (b) the orientation to a passive acceptance of that which is not me. The shift between the two orientations is fast and subtle so that I do not normally note it. But the difference can be experienced in my hands (double-) touching each other, and in this, each touching itself—with the touching hand, I can both feel the other hand I touch or I can intend it to feel being touched.

It might appear as if such an approach leads to solipsism, where my world and my knowledge about it are grounded just in me, that is, in my actions and sensations. But this is far from the case, as it can be shown that intersubjectivity is continually presupposed in the constitution of my body, which constitutes me, as body. Intersubjectivity is presupposed because being in the world is being singular plural, body among bodies, person among persons; whatever I do and think is thoroughly shared even before the first time that I am conscious of myself as Self. I make a distinction between other bodies and my own only when I discover that their bodies are similar to my own; it is in and through the bodies of others that I recognize my own (Franck, 2001). It is only because I discover in touching the touching of another that I can become a body and person in my own right. The bodily relation to the social and material world therefore is prior to the constitution of the material body as an experiential body; and the bodily relation to the other is prior to intersubjectivity, because it is based in the possibility to sense, through the corporality of my flesh, other bodies as flesh representing other egos (singular plurals).

Ecological approaches to perception specifically and to cognition frequently emphasize that my everyday perception involves no conceptual or theoretical intermediaries and are, in this sense, direct. Perception relates to the boundaries and qualitative gradients in those sides or portions of the world toward which my perceptual organs are directed at some stage and to which, speaking in evolutionary terms, they are tuned. It is a matter of picking out certain discriminated entities, setting them into relief against a more indeterminate and indiscriminate ground. This leads to an awareness of entities as units of existence, objects with identities, and grounds for perceiving change these entities undergo when transformed: in themselves or because I move. Situational differences subject perceptions to differences of granularity accompanied by different levels of organization.

The same part of the material world can be articulated in a variety of ways—where articulation means both the joints in and between the things I encounter in my perception and action *and* the way I describe and explain this world. What is relevant, salient structure depends on my present intentions, which predisposition me to the present project, and on my past experiences: I cannot presuppose learners to access a structured world, from which they are to extract specific observations, if they do not have prior experiences and are unfamiliar with the activity-centered intentions.

Ordinarily, perception is considered to provide the fundamental layer in our experience of objects; a phenomenology of perception is therefore basic to all further reflection on the relation between a conscious observer and his world. The value of reflection does not lie in some capacity to overcome perception but rather in its capacity to remain faithful to the senses from which perception sprang. I orient to and do and think what I do and think *precisely* because what I perceive is real to me. A phenomenology of perception must arise from an inner clarification of the given, not a criticism from an outside frame of reference. Through perception, the world is more immediately accessible than through re-presentation. I do not represent much of the world but rather am directly aware of relevant segments.

To sum up, then, consciousness arises where bodily movement becomes structured in a way that it allows for guided orientation of motions in relation to other objects in the world. Knowledgeability is not super-added to perceiving and perceived things, but is a relational structure that is relevant where human beings with their animate bodies come into contact with each other in specific sorts of ways and with other things. The sensual world, in which I live, upon which I act, and to which I react, is subject to constant evolution. The richness of my world is not the starting point from which I-learner derive abstractions but it is the end point, the product of a great range of abstractions that emerge from the transactions of I-learner-in-setting. This world, my lifeworld, emerges not as a consequence of a causal relationship with experience: I lay it down like a garden path that is laid in walking. My lifeworld is essentially contingent. In this sense, the qualities that I attribute to objects are not properties of the object, but sets of relation between the world I inhabit and myself. These are, in the final account, simultaneously the same and not the same: knowing me means knowing my lifeworld and knowing my lifeworld means knowing me. My lifeworld and I are two sides of one coin.

CHAPTER 4

EMERGENCE OF STRUCTURE

In chapter 3, I show that objects and situations are not given to me in the instant I lay my eyes on them; they are not given in propositional form, as observation sentences, and are given even less in the form of observation categoricals (generalizations). Perception turns out to be intimately tied to exploration. These statements characterize the possibilities to learn from perceptual experiences, not only my own but also those of other people, given that the reasons for these experiences lie in the way perception operates generally. To perceive something means to *allow* a figure to become salient against an indeterminate ground; it means to be *receptive*. This does not prevent me from looking, which may provoke perception. The same ground, however, lends itself to be organized in more than one way even when I am concerned with only a small fraction of the visual field—as seen in the example of perceiving the seconds indicated on a wristwatch but failing to perceive the time of day as a whole. *Being* always means *being singular plural*. This structure of the perceptual experience mediates what and how I can learn from observation and manipulation; it also mediates how my lifeworld unfolds rather than being given to me the moment I lay my eyes on it. Relative to teaching science this means that I can never be certain that a student has had *a* particular perceptual experience, *the one I-teacher expect,* so that my (teacher's) explanations may not be appropriate for theorizing what a student has *actually* perceived. The aporia lies in the fact that students presuppose that the teacher is attempting to provide concepts and theories for what they have seen; and teachers presuppose students to have seen what is explained by the concepts and theories articulated in teaching (lecturing). In chapter 1, I articulate this aporia, whereby students are asked to perceive something that they only really know as figure|ground configuration (Lat. *con-*, together, with & to figure) once they the discourse supported by the figure.

In this chapter, I show how even a simple thing such as a neon glow lamp (Figure 4.1) acquires its distinguishing features *in and through a historical process,* in

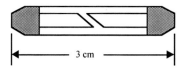

Figure 4.1. A representation of the neon glow lamp used by the students. This representation does not correspond to the students' actual perceptual experience, which did not (a) distinguish (in action or by description) between glass and metal ends, (b) note the gap in the filament, or (c) remark that the light appears left or right depending on the context.

the process of students using it extensively as part of their investigations. Thus, the structure of the filament, the composition of the housing (glass, metal ends), and the context-sensitive locations where it has to be touched to make it glow are not perceptual aspects apparent as soon as students "lay their eyes on" and "look (glance) at" a glow lamp. All these features emerge in the process of the investigation and within the context of many other figure|ground relations. I can observe such emergent features time and again on the tenth-grade physics tapes, including how structures and configurations emerge when students use metal-coated elderberry mark spheres, metal-coated table tennis balls, electroscopes (cf. chapter 11), and metal-coated roller blinds. For some of these devices, I have additional videotapes from an eleventh-grade course, which exhibit perceptual phenomena of the same nature, confirming my observation categoricals from the tenth-grade data.

From the perspective of the already knowledgeable physicist, the neon glow lamp works like this: Unlike a normal incandescent lamp, the neon glow lamp does not have a continuous filament; rather, there are two electrodes that reach into the neon-filled body of the lamp. When there is sufficiently high potential difference ("voltage"), electrons leave the negative electrode ("cathode"). As they are accelerated by the potential difference ("voltage"), most of which occurs in the vicinity of the negative electrode ("cathode"), the electrons become so fast that they energize and even ionize neon atoms. The energized neon atoms return to their normal state and release the difference in energy in the form of light. The lamp therefore always glows near the electrode with the electron surplus.

The episodes in this and subsequent chapters derive from a qualitative physics course on static electricity taught by a colleague—here referred to as *Tara*—in a tenth-grade class in a German grammar school ("Gymnasium"); a second colleague—referred to as *Tom*—interacts with students while they engage in small-group work conducting investigations in self-selected groups including transparency films, metal plates, pieces of wool and cotton cloth, small neon glow lamps, electroscopes, plates and tiny spheres made of Styrofoam, and (plastic, metal, PVC) rods. For each task, students are invited to plan and execute investigations of their own interest, but instructions for ready-made investigations are also available to those students who feel more at ease with specific instructions. The lead teacher, Tara, often demonstrates some effect, such as how rubbing objects against other objects creates certain effects in objects that make a neon lamp glow or attract elderberry mark spheres or table tennis balls. She then invites students to conduct open investigations of different materials and asks them to find out (record) as much as they can. The episodes in this chapter are taken from the videotapes featuring a group of four, approximately sixteen-year-old women (Brita, Clare, Iris, and Jenny).

EMERGENT FEATURES OF A NEON GLOW LAMP

In chapter 3, I provide a description of how different parts of my lifeworld change as I engage the world, repeatedly take the same ride, become familiar with different routes to the university, and come to discover a broken spoke. That is, although

I know that the light from the things I become aware off—the giant twin towers, second path, hotel, and broken spoke—must have hit my retina and therefore could be perceived before, I become aware of these things and their inner structure only in the course and as the result of my inquiries. Science educators may ask, "But how does this translate into classroom episodes?" In this section I provide an extended case study of how one group of students comes to discover the structure of a neon glow lamp. (Chapter 11 features another group of [male] students in the longish process of coming to perceive the electroscope as a structured assembly of distinguishable parts.) Initially, the glow lamp is but one of the pieces of equipment that the students have available. As other pieces of equipment, the lamp is not given to students at once; rather, it comes to have structure (whole|parts relations) in the (lengthy) course of a series of investigations. In and through students' investigations, structure emerges; that is, by opening themselves to be affected (touched) by what they touch and orient to (e.g., light), students evolve newly structured lifeworlds. Things such as the glow lamp or the electroscope (see also chapters 10 and 11) do not present themselves as structured things with features and properties, at once and for all; rather, they come to be things with properties and features *in and through their use as students engage the world*. The following three episodes occurred over a period of five weeks in the course of ten lessons during which students used the glow lamp. Initially, the lamp is but a tool that in glowing indicates the presence of static electricity. In my use, it does not have an internal structure, much like any other tool I use, and the very usefulness of which lies in its equipmental nature, that is, in its capacity to withhold from attention everything but the specific function it has been designed for. Just as my wristwatch becomes a stopwatch and reveals only the number of seconds that have passed when I measure my heart rate or pedaling cadence, the glow lamp reveals itself as a structured thing successively in its connection to all other things in their way of being singular plural.

Episode 1: Emergence of Filament Gap

In the course of the first forty-five-minute lesson, the four students bring into contact (rub, pull past each other, or re-used previously rubbed materials) two materials and subsequently tested them for charges 162 times (see excerpt in Table 4.1, where trial code A_n pertains to the n-th attempt in investigation A.). In some situations, students comment in some way on the outcome ("it worked," "it didn't work"), thereby providing an indication that allows me to understand what they see or have seen; but in other situations, they do not articulate what they see. The excerpt from the investigation in Table 4.1 shows that after bringing two materials into close contact sometimes brings about an effect (from the observer perspective) and sometimes it does not. Of particular interest here are those configurations that involve the glow lamp (italicized in the table). The students repeatedly attempt to re-do an experiment presented earlier by the teacher, who has provided proof for the presence of charges when the lamp glows. However, whatever they do and whichever materials they use, the lamp initially does not glow other than in trial

Table 4.1. Excerpt from the investigation of static electricity in one student group

Person	Trial	Material 1	Material 2	Action	Test Object	Observation
Iris	A20	Transparency	Ruler	Rub hard	Styrofoam	-
Clare	*A21*	*Transparency*	*Pants*	*Pull*	*Lamp*	*Light*
Iris	A22	Transparency	Rag	Rub	Styrofoam	+
Iris	A23	Transparency	Rag	Rub	Styrofoam	+
Iris	A24	Transparency	Rag	Rub	Styrofoam	-
Iris	A25	Transparency	Rag	Rub	Styrofoam	-
Iris	A26	Transparency	Rag	Rub	Styrofoam	+
Jenny	A27	Transparency	Ruler	Rub	TT ball	+
Jenny	A28	Transparency	Ruler	Rub	TT ball	+
Jenny	A29	Transparency	Ruler	Rub	TT ball	+
Jenny	A30	Transparency	Ruler	Rub	TT ball	-
Jenny	*A31*	*Transparency*	*Ruler*	*Rub*	*Lamp*	*No light*
Jenny	*A32*	*Transparency*	*Pants*	*Pull*	*Lamp*	*No light*
Jenny	*A33*	*Transparency*	*Pants*	*Pull*	*Lamp*	*No light*
Jenny	A34	Transparency	Ruler	Rub	Styrofoam	-
Brita	*A35*	*Transparency*	*Rag*	*Rub*	*Lamp*	*No light*
Clare	A36	Transparency	Ruler	Rub	TT ball	-
Jenny	A37	Metal	Ruler	Rub	TT ball	-
Brita	*A38*	*Transparency*	*Rag*	*Rub*	*Lamp*	*No light*
Tara		*Transparency*	*Pants*	*Rub*	*Lamp*	*Light*

Note: Those trials that involve the glow lamp appear in italic. The plus sign indicates an effect, the minus sign no effect.

A_{21}. When Tara passes their laboratory table after trial A_{38}, the students indicate that the neon lamp is not working.

Excerpt 4.1

01	Brita:	With this one, it doesn't work.
02	Tara:	What's wrong? It doesn't work? What could be wrong so that it doesn't work?
03	Jenny:	The lamp is broken! It is broken.
04	Tara:	What is broken? The transparency?
05	Jenny:	Yea. Perhaps it's the pants.
06	Tara:	((Pulls transparency through clasped knees, tests transparency with glow lamp: it glows.)) Did you see it?
07	Iris:	Yea, you could see it.
08	Brita:	What brand of pants do you wear?

From their experiments with the glow lamp, the students conclude at this point that it is the lamp that does not work, that is, they note the absence of light as a breakdown. Tara then provides a demonstration involving the same transparency students have used, which she pulls through her clasped jeans-glad knees, and the same glow lamp. She holds the lamp to the transparency, which makes it glow.

Jenny tries to copy the teacher but in her trial (A_{39}), the lamp does not glow. Iris repeats the procedure, which makes the lamp glow (trial A_{40}, A_{44}); Jenny and Clare try again (trials A_{41}–A_{43}) but fail to make the lamp glow. The students continue to fail to make the lamp glow and attribute the failure (breakdown) to the materials they use, the manufacturer of their pants, transparency sheets that are "worn out," and other possible causes. A new series of attempts (trials A_{53}–A_{56}) does not work for Iris despite having had a successful attempt earlier on. Here then a new question imposes itself, which from her position is something like: "Why have I been successful initially and why do I later experience failure?"

By now, the students have enacted a number of trials. They assume that the lamp should have been glowing but does not. In their search for the reason of the breakdown, they articulate the lamp as a broken piece of equipment. That is, the lamp no longer has its equipmental function. A broken state is ruled out, however, when the teacher uses the lamp to show that it cannot be broken because it does in fact glow. Being intentionally oriented to the glow lamp as object, its lighting is *objectively* given to all those present; it is a fact that it glows and therefore that it is not broken. The students now articulate a new object from the equipmental whole, including tool (glow lamp) and other equipment, and differentiate it in terms of characteristics. One difference between the equipment used by the teacher and students lies in the pants. Thus, the students hypothesize that the lamp works in the teacher's case because her pants charge the transparency film but their own pants do not. The difference between the different sets of pants is not so obvious, however, for everybody wears jeans. The only aspect that lends itself to be articulated as difference is that there are different brands; and with it, there are different types of material that go into the production of the pants. Someone comments that it must be the more expensive brand of jeans that charges the transparency and therefore makes the lamp glow. Here the background understanding of differences—predispositions and presuppositions—between cheap and expensive jeans comes in and is articulated as one possibility for the differences in the experimental outcomes; these are hypothesized as being caused by differences between the jeans.

The students' articulation of possible reasons for the non-working of the experiment may appear outlandish. But is it really outlandish? Let me think about this for a moment. If I do not know a domain, what can I do but use my existing understanding about how the world works and then come up with some tentative hypothesis? In the present instance, the most salient difference between what the teacher is doing and what I-student am doing is the equipment, not the transparency sheet or the glow lamp, but the pants that are used to charge the transparency. From my-learner perspective, right now any hypothesis is as good as any other—as long as it is consistent with the resources I have at hand. Given that two of the three materials involved in the teacher's demonstration and my own attempts are the same, and I-learner charge the transparency in the same way that the teacher does, so that the jeans are the only thing that is different, why not assume that this difference causes the differences in the outcome? The pants are the immediately salient structure for thinking about the non-working of the lamp, for everything else apparently is the same.

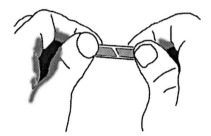

Figure 4.2. Brita intently looks at the glow lamp in her two hands. It is at that instant that the gap between the two filaments becomes salient to her.

After this interaction, Tara claims to know what students are doing that leads to the non-working of the lamp. In this comment, therefore, the teacher indicates to me-student that whatever it is that does not allow me to make the investigation work is such that it can be seen. That is, Tara is doing exactly what Toby Mory has been doing in Episode 2.2, flagging that there is something that can be noted but that is still hiding from me-learner. This in itself is startling because I think I am doing the same that I have seen her do. So, to break the equipmental whole, I may assume that the resistance comes from the materials or from my actions. But articulating the action, making it present again, thereby objectifying and representing it so that it can be analyzed, I have to articulate the equipmental whole in which my action is involved. Where the whole process has to be structured is not self-evident; it is not something my prior experience has provided me the resources with (predisposed me) to find out. There are no markings that have preceded the present session so that I could re-mark it as something that does not work.

To find the breakdown in the way I-student hold the lamp, the holding and the lamp in its detail need to be at-hand, present, and therefore become re-presentable. Only something that has been present once can be re-presented, can be made present again, can be re-cognized because it has been cognized (Lat. *cognoscere*, learn) at least once before. That is, I have to bring to the fore, make salient, the lamp as being composed of different materials. I have to notice that these materials have different properties and that the properties are relevant to my present concern; and the first and second instances have to be copresent to me presently. This is not self-evident. For, as with the laboratory table that is used to place equipment on, who is to know that it is or is-not interfering with the ongoing experiment?

Brita is the first to make a breakthrough, to make a significant discovery about the glow lamp. She repeats the teacher's demonstration (trials A_{116}–A_{117}). As the group has just written down the conclusion that the experiments do not work with old (i.e., used) transparency sheets, Brita suggests doing the investigation again using a new transparency. As she gets the lamp, she fixates it (Figure 4.2). She gazes intently at the lamp (1.8 seconds), then puts it back on the table and gets another lamp. She then pulls the transparency through her clasped knees, takes the second lamp, intently looking at it again (1.3 seconds), and then tests the transparency. The lamp does not glow. Brita looks again intently at the lamp (1.0 second), and then asks the teacher, "Is it not broken? Because this is not connected on the inside?"

In this episode, Brita articulates for the first time the internal structure of the neon glow lamp. The surprise noticeable in the way she communicates is an indication that she has seen the gap between the filaments for the first time, closely associated with articulating it verbally. This articulation is associated with two experiments that have not worked (breakdown) and the close inspection of two lamps; this process has brought the gap between the two filaments into conscious awareness. For the first time, therefore, one of the students perceives the lamp as broken. Rather than treating it as before in its equipmental whole, as something that glows, Brita links the possibility of it being broken with some feature on the inside of the lamp. Here broken-ness and the gap between the two pieces of wire on the inside (i.e., electrodes) go together. At this moment, the gap explains the fact that I-student do not observe what I thought I should observe.

Does Brita expect the wire to be continuous, such as in regular incandescent lights? She notices the gap, the particular feature of this lamp, perhaps in its difference to other lamps that she is familiar with. The lamp is no longer merely equipment, but once brought to the fore, in a new figure|ground configuration, the inside comes to be made thematic in terms of a lack of continuity. The gap between the two electrodes protrudes into conscious awareness and thereby raises the possibility that this is a piece of broken equipment. Here, the non-working of the lamp and the gap between the two electrodes come together and lead to becoming figure in perception and thematic to consciousness. If the lamp had glowed in the way it should have, it is not certain that the students would have structured it as such. Although Brita comes to notice the gap, she does not raise the possibility of the lamp to be broken until after the next investigation, which turns out in the same way many of their experiments have turned out before. It is in this nexus of the negative experimental outcome that the gap becomes a salient feature of the lamp.

Episode 2: Emergence of Glass and Metal Parts

In the third lesson on static electricity during the following week, Jenny makes a second significant, *noted because notable* observation. It begins with a sequence of tests (Table 4.2), in which she comments on the outcome of a test (no light) by saying, "I am sorry, but there is nothing I can do." In trial C_7, Jenny holds the glow lamp indistinctly, possibly partially on the glass. In the next trial, she ties a string around the body of the lamp and then, holding the string, brings the lamp to the charged object—no effect (Figure 4.3). During trials C_{12}, C_{13}, and C_{15}, the videotape shows Jenny holding the lamp on its metal end. She notes hearing a bristling sound; but the lamp does not glow. In the demonstration to Brita, Jenny says that she has seen the lamp glow, but Brita remains unconvinced.

Iris then gets another lamp from the supply area and conducted several tests, each time claiming to have heard a crackling noise from the lamp. Jenny also enacts another attempt (Table 4.2, C_{18}) and then announces that she has made it work ("Hey, it worked! Yeah, it worked!"). However, she is unsuccessful on subsequent

Table 4.2. Excerpt from the investigation of static electricity in one student group

Person	Trial	Material 1	Material 2	Action	Test Object	Observation
Iris	C6	Transparency	Pants	Pull	Lamp	-
Jenny	C7	Transparency	Rag	Rub	Lamp	-
Jenny	C8	Transparency	Rag	Rub	Lamp on string	-
Jenny	C10	Transparency	Rag	Rub	Lamp	-
Jenny	C11	Transparency	Rag	Rub	Lamp	-
Jenny	C12	Transparency	Rag	Rub (VERY long)	Lamp (tests all over)	-
Jenny	C13	Transparency	Rag	Rub (VERY long)	Lamp (tests all over)	-
Jenny	C15	Transparency	Leather	Rub (VERY long)	Lamp (tests all over)	+ {?}
Jenny	C18	Transparency	Leather	Rub (VERY long)	Lamp (tests all over)	+ {?} Brita not convinced
Jenny	C21	Transparency	Leather	Rub (transp. on table)	Lamp	-

trials (e.g., C_{21} [Table 4.2]). Several minutes later, Jenny excitedly calls the teacher, "It works, it just worked, Mrs. Tara!" As the teacher approaches, the following conversation ensues.

Excerpt 4.2

01 Tara: Did you establish what was going on with the glow lamp, the fact that it didn't work?
02 Jenny: Of course! ((She takes a glow lamp.)) You must not hold it like this. ((Holds the glow lamp as in Figure 4.4a.)) But you have to hold it like this. ((Holds the glow lamp as in Figure 4.4b.))
03 Tara: Exactly! ((Leaves table.))
04 Jenny: ((Places glow lamp on table.))
05 Iris: How do you have to hold it? ((She picks up the glow lamp, holding

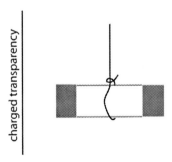

Figure 4.3. Jenny tries a new way of bringing the glow lamp to a charged transparency to see whether it lights.

it between thumb and index finger.))

06 Clare: How do you have to hold it? On the metal thing, ha? Or?
07 Jenny: ((Takes the glow lamp from Iris, brings it right in front of Clare's face.)) Like this, you have to hold it like this ((holds glow lamp at metal end as in Figure 4.4b)) and not like this ((holds glow lamp as in Figure 4.4a)). (Returns glow lamp to table.)
08 Clare: ((Picks up the glow lamp and holds it between thumb and index finger on one metal end.)) Like this, yes?

Here, Jenny articulates for the first time what needs to happen for the lamp to glow, "You must not hold it *this* way, but you have to hold it *this* way." The difference is expressed in the contrast of "Not . . . this way ((holding the lamp as in Figure 4.4a)), but . . . this way ((holding the lamp as in Figure 4.4b))" and the associated change in the position of her fingers on the glow lamp. From the utterance and the corresponding gesture, Clare is to perceive the core difference that Jenny wants her to notice in its noticeability, that is, something that can be noticed. (This is where constructivists get things wrong: I point out because there is something to be pointed out and because there is another who takes my pointing out *as* a pointing out.) Clare tests whether she has actually perceived and therefore understood what is the important difference. For all she knows, the difference may have also been in other noticeable noticed differences that are *not* relevant in *this* situation and therefore constitute ground, such as the shape of her grip. That is, Clare tests whether the difference perceived is making *the* difference. Here, perception is closely related to behavioral relevance: the co-emergence of the observation of the metal end and the action of holding the glow lamp at its end.

To render the events intelligible, it is important to structure the transcript so that it depicts the situation as it presents itself to the students. Otherwise, the reader is not confronted with the situation in the way students were. As soon as I-author write something like, "Jenny holds the glow lamp in the center, on the glass," a reader may assume that this is what Jenny *intentionally* and *consciously* has done: holding the lamp at the glass part. The point here is that for most part of the lessons up to that point, the glass and metal nature of the glow lamp is not salient in stu-

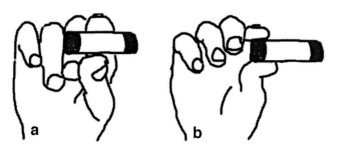

Figure 4.4. In Excerpt 4.2, Jenny holds the glow lamp in two distinct ways. It is at this very moment that the structure of the lamp—its metal and glass parts—becomes relevant in the actions of a student. The structure has a behavioral consequence.

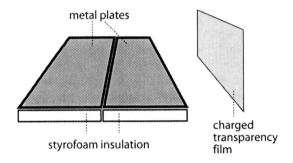

metal plates

styrofoam insulation

charged
transparency
film

Figure 4.5. In the featured episodes, the students are asked (a) to bring a charged transparency film to two insulated, touching metal plates, which are then separated, (b) to test the static electricity on the two plates, and (c) to explain the observations they make.

dents' actions and talk in the same way that the tear in my tire has not been salient to me prior to the second blow out. Thus, the students have held the lamp; they have not held the lamp *at* glass or *at* the metal ends. The possibilities for the existence of differences for the holding process have arisen *exactly* in this episode when Jenny articulates it for the first time and as a finding sufficiently important to announce it to her teacher.

Episode 3: Emergence of Asymmetry of Filaments

A third important feature of the glow lamp emerges ten lessons later, while the students are working on a task that asks them to test a pair of metal plates that have been charged by induction while in contact and then have been separated (Figure 4.5). The standard explanation goes like this: induction separates the charges so that one plate becomes positively charged while the other becomes negatively charged at its end. Separating the two plates at this stage leaves them (oppositely) charged. In their investigations, students initially simply note that the lamp glows when held to each of the two plates. Upon the insistent questioning of the teacher, students eventually come to notice that the lamp sometimes glows at the filament close to their hands, sometimes at the opposite filament. The first realization of the differences in the location where the lamp glows occurs precisely during a moment when they move from testing one plate to testing the other plate. That is, although the side of the lamp where the glow is observed has changed during their investigations before, this difference becomes salient for the first time after thirteen lessons of creating and testing charged bodies.

What We Learn from the Three Episodes

In the course of the three episodes, the glow lamp emerges as a lamp characterized by specific, articulated properties. That is, the whole|parts relations that constitute the glow lamp are an emergent outcome of extended investigations and repeated experiences of insight. It now has a filament consisting of two short pieces protruding from either end toward the center, has to be held at the metal ends to "work," and the glowing occur at the electrode close to the hand or at the other one away from the hand. It is true that students may have been vaguely aware of the glass body and metal ends much in the same way that I have noticed vaguely the tear in the tire. Asking students to draw the lamp even may have led to a diagram such as Figure 4.1 (seeking relevance in the question, students may have articulated certain aspects). It is a fact, however, that if they have been perceptually attuned to and visually tracked the lamp in the three episodes prior to the moments of discovery, these features have not made a behavioral difference in the same way that the tear in my tire has not changed what I was about to do; the tear, though after the fact I know that I have been vaguely aware of, has not changed my decision-making initially. In the present situation, even if one of the students is vaguely attuned to the structure of the glow lamp, she does not integrate this with thought and action-guidance. Such integration is a prerequisite for the relevant perception. This episode, therefore, is evidence for the agency|structure dialectic, where new structure—of the material glow lamp, my ability to perceive it—emerges in the process of active engagement with some part of the world. Part of the existing structure is further structured into new whole|parts configurations, whereby each part becomes new figure that stands out against a more diffuse and indeterminate ground.

When students begin using the glow lamp, they treat it holistically as something that glows or does not glow. The glow lamp has tool function, is an indicator of the presence of static electricity. There is no evidence that the students actually perceive the properties or aspects $x_1, x_2, \ldots x_n$ of the lamp just by looking at it and (initially) using it. Rather, the structured features of the glow lamp arise in the course of their investigations much in the same way that the twin towers or tear in the tire become part of my lifeworld in the course of extended experience. The relation between the lamp as a whole and its parts emerges while students *explore* the fact that "it didn't work" (breakdown); and in exploring, they *dis*cover. Students' articulation of glow lamp features is occasioned by moments in which resistance makes itself felt, much as the second tire blowout occasions my own articulation of the tear *as* tear (the singular as an instance of a plurality). The students actively discard other covariations that appear to exist (type of jeans, materials, worn-out transparencies) when tests with elderberry mark spheres show that their manipulations of charging the transparency indeed has the intended effect.

When I show videotapes containing episodes like the ones featured here, there are people who make negative comments about the students. Accordingly, there is something wrong with students who apparently repeat "the same things an over again" without being able to get the investigation to work or find out why the investigation does not work. Such individuals blame students for not "looking carefully" at the glow lamp and for not noticing its self-evidently noticeable aspects (whole|parts relation, metal ends, filament, relation between material and side that glows). If it happens that these students also do not have high marks, "low ability" becomes an explanatory resource. I suggest that such attributions are made because perceptual experience is not thought about from a first-time-through and first person perspective. If I were to make such an attribution, I would have forgotten what it means to learn something I do not know; and as soon as I-learner know what I have to learn, I forget that there has been a time when I have not perceived what I now take as a stable feature of the world. If teachers forget what it means not to know, then they have few resources for understanding why I-learner do what I do, which is always mediated by my positioned positioning disposition.

The analysis of my experience shows that the giant twin towers, for example, become perceptually salient at the moment I pass them for the seventh time. Then, the immanent nature of the towers turns into a transcendental fact; it is only when they exist in my consciousness that they also (and simultaneously) begin to exist for me as something in my world: as that which is uncovered in discovery. It is only at this point that I ask, "How could I not have seen these towers during my previous trips?" If I forget that the towers change from being immanent to being transcendental in nature, I may react in the way some people do while observing physics students "who do not see the obvious." That is, there is an *amnesis*, a loss of the story of the origins of perception and the world.

Even if students perceptually track the electrodes, metal ends, or location of the glowing, it is not experienced as figure. Just as in the example of the tear in my tire, it has been (if in fact students had the impression) a difference that does not make a difference. The glow lamp comes to be articulated—in perceptually and verbally articulated form—as students go about finding out why it does not work. That is, in breakdown, students are startled; and being startled positions them with an attentional disposition prerequisite for the articulation of the perceptual field, that is, for the emergence of figure|ground distinctions that may have salience to the problem.

Breakdown, which occurs *in action*, dispositions me to seek and notice things that right now are not apparent. The fact that something does not work (cannot be used) is discovered "not by looking and ascertaining properties, but rather by paying attention to the associations in which we use it" (Heidegger, 1977/1996, p. 73 [68]). When a student such as Brita "discovers" a particular property of the lamp, it is because of a need that arises from her inquiry—much in the same way I want to find out why the tire has exploded for a second time. Brita does not get her experiment to work. She has used different materials for rubbing but has not been able to get the lamp to glow. At one point she glances at the lamp intently. It is *precisely* at this moment that the gap between the two electrodes emerges, comes to be noted as a noticeable fact, as an articulation that can be verbally articulated. She consciously sees the gap for a first time, although she has been looking at the lamp repeatedly before. The lamp has been there, present to hand as something that glows or does not glow, but the internal structure that she discovers previously has not been available to her. With the gap, an association emerges between the lack of success in getting the experiment to work and a noticeable part of the lamp.

From these episodes, I learn that perception does not instantly provide a pre-given, structured world but that perception and world arise historically and biographically, in the course of extended engagement with a particular segment of the material world. Coming to see structure is a way of learning based on one's immediate apprehension of features of how the world in fact is. This process, which begins at birth, is indefinite and open-ended, making "vision . . . a continuous birth" (Merleau-Ponty, 1964, p. 32, my translation). The historical nature of perceptual processes in the school science laboratory is further highlighted in my own changes of perception over the course of doing this research. The perceptual processes that allow distinctions to emerge from the indeterminate ground themselves are emergent features. Through exploration of how something looks like, my perceptual field comes to be structured into recurrent figure|ground distinctions. Although some feature (figure) may be said to have existed all along, it is only when it becomes explicit part of my lifeworld that it can have behavioral significance.

A PHYSICIST (RE-) DISCOVERS THE GLOW LAMP

In the course of my career as teacher and researcher, I have been in many situations where someone explained the fact that students do not even see what they are supposed to see by saying that they are not really motivated or, worse, because they are "not the smartest kids in my class." The descriptions of my experiments with perception in the previous chapter already should have alerted readers that the structured world is not given to me (e.g., at birth), because I do not have those structured structuring dispositions that allow me to see the material world in a particular way. That is, prior to engaging with the world, I do not have the structured structuring dispositions that allow me to perceive structures. The structured world of my experience emerges in the course of my agency in an already structured material world—the only world to which I ever have access—that comes to be structured further or differently as a result. *It, my* world, is what is given to me in *my* perception; and because it is given to me in my perception, it is objectively present for me in what I orient to and what I do. It is what I perceive and use as resource in any decision-making. That is, I have never direct access to some material world existing independent of my being, but have access only through the way in which I experience it. And this experience I take as object-oriented, that is, as objective, even in those cases where I know that what I experience is the result of an optical illusion. Thus, even though I know I am deceived—such as in the Müller-Lyer illusion, where lines are of the same length (Figure 4.6)—my perception is objectively given. I know the two lines to be of equal length because I have measured them and yet they appear to me to be of different length.

When I do not know, anything salient may be used to explain what I see. This is not immediately clear to science educators, and it has not been clear to me. When I first observed the events surrounding excerpt 4.1, I smiled because the proposition that the brand of the pants might be at the origin of making the lamp glow or not appeared outlandish. Several days later, reproducing some of the students' experiments using the same materials, I all of a sudden find myself stating some of the same hypotheses students have stated. For example, after several failed attempts to charge a transparency, I switch to another one: it works. I realize that I am treating the old transparency as one that "has worn out" and I find confirmation of this in subsequent trials with a new and unused transparency.

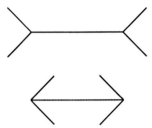

Figure 4.6. Even if I know that the two Müller-Lyer arrows are of equal length, they still appear to me as being of different length. When I do not know that something is an illusion, I take the way something appears to me as the way it actually is.

With respect to the glow lamp, I-author have undergone development, too. At the time when my research began, I have not taken note of the shape of the lamp interior. At the time, I do not note that a gap separates the two electrodes or pay attention to the particular shape of the glow lamp. I do not note that the glow is not distributed evenly but that the lamp glows either on one or on the other side. Indeed, this previous sentence I can only write today because *now* I know that the lamp glows on one or the other side. When I initially conduct the investigations with the same material that the students have had, the lamp simply glows for me, too. I treat it as a tool, as some indicator of the presence or absence of charges. I do not differentiate the glow because I have not yet perceived it as happening on one or the other end of the lamp. Therefore the only fact available to me at the time is "a glow" rather than "a glow at the near end the hand" or "a glow at the far end from the hand." I do not see the gap because I do not have the structured structuring disposition that *now* allows me to perceive the gap *as* gap and then to account for the gap in my actions. After the fact, I forget about my previous world, or rather, I provide all sorts of reason why I have not seen the light with all the features that are apparent to me toward the end of the initial period of investigation. Thus, at the time of the investigations I write in my research notebook:

> When I rub the transparency sheet and hold the lamp to it, I do not see at first that it is lighting up (possibly too bright in the room), but this is essential, for the preparation has to be right to see what I am supposed to see. Given that the room is bright, and given that I do not close the curtains, I cannot see what Tara wants me to see. Furthermore, I do not notice that the lamp is glowing on one particular side. I simply have focused on it being lit. When Tara talks about it glowing on the other side, I actually turn the lamp around.

In this research note, it is apparent that after the fact I come up with a number of reasons for why I could not have seen what I was supposed to see. But this statement also hides that as a learner, I could not even know that what I was seeing is not what I was supposed to see for drawing the kinds of conclusions that Tara wanted the students to draw.

The point is that science does not describe the world as it is; rather, science creates particular worlds and the descriptions and explanations that go with them. Science therefore works like this: *If* you set up an experiment using *these* materials in *this* way, and *if* you control the conditions in *this* manner, *then* you may observe something of interest to physicists, chemists, and so on. This something can be described in the language scientists create. That is, to know science means to create a particular world and take up a position in it, to control the particulars of the context in specific ways, and to use a highly discipline-specific, contextual language to describe the specially prepared events and contexts. Perception therefore is intimately tied to what I am doing and why I am doing it: I perceive (am sensible to be touched, impressed, affected) because I act and I act because I perceive. Agency and sensibility come as a pair, a unit, and they evolve as a unit as my agency exposes me to be affected by the unknown.

This, then, exhibits the aporia of learning. I cannot know what the something is that I will note some time down the road and yet, being in school, forces me to open myself to the new. The new, however, cannot be known in advance, and I-learner cannot even know whether what I perceive is that which I am supposed to perceive. This might make me want to hold back in situations where what I do is subject to assessment. Because I cannot control what new figures I will perceive and because what I will perceive mediates how I learn to explicate, I am exposing myself in and to a situation over which I do not have control. I therefore find myself in a precarious situation where I am assessed negatively because I have not seen what the teacher has wanted me to see. (And there begins the cycle of negative definitions: *lack* of ability, motivation, etc.)

Now in my case, it is difficult to attribute the failure—seeing the neon glow lamp in the way required and noticing the asymmetrical glow—to a lack of motivation or absence of cognitive ability. My position predispositions and dispositions me in particular ways: As a researcher interested in understanding knowing and learning, I am interested in understanding the events themselves; as a trained physicist I have had the required subject matter background, and as a learning scientist, I have had the required interests in understanding the structure of experience, the students' and my own. Science educators therefore need to take serious the fact that I-physicist, too, have not seen what Tara has wanted her students to see and to reproduce what she has wanted the students to reproduce.

STRUCTURING: AGENCY AND SENSIBILITY

In the episodes of this chapter, new structure emerges from the engagement of the student in the material world. This structure is dialectical in the sense that I have developed structuring structures—i.e., schemas—that allow me to see something in the world that other people also see; and, simultaneously, there is structure in the world that lends itself to be seen especially where there are boundaries (joints), which are different in kind and not fancy. These structures are resources for action and, therefore, are identical to what vision ecologists refer to as *affordance*. The resources (material, social structures) and my schema (structuring structures) are dialectically related in the sense that each presupposes the other. To see, I require appropriate schemas; but I have schemas, because I see resources. And whether anything can be a resource is itself a function of the material structure of my body.

To structure therefore means to identify joints in the world and things I experience where there currently is no structure. How can this be if I do not have the schemas to perceive this new structure? How can I get out of this chicken-and-egg situation where I need to be able to see the structures that structure my perception? Mere looking or staring at something does not reveal structure—the theoretical attitude alone does not give me a world in which I can act and live. Only praxis can give me a world; and it envelops all efforts to evolve a discourse that explains why I see what I see. In praxis, I manipulate and sense the world, and the two come to be correlated because manipulations, which I sense, lead to changes that I can sense and that I can attribute to the manipulations. It is *precisely* here that scientific method, if there is any, has its origin: a cause and effect relationship linking what I do with what I sense, noting in particular of any noticeable and notable, invariant figure against a changing ground or changing figure against an invariant ground.

Such structuring separates figure from ground, or rather, it leads to the emergence of new figure|ground configurations. Thus, for example, during many activities, the laboratory table is and can be taken as unstructured ground against which everything else happening on it can be taken as figure. Articulating the laboratory table as an object that has to be separated is unnecessary. In chapters 3 and 4, the main story is how we (students, I) come to structure something in the world. Structuring and therefore a conscious attention to the entity, for example, when I have the hunch that placing a transparency on the tabletop will mediate the process of charging it—the transparency may be charged or discharged by placing it directly on the laboratory tabletop.

The materials on a laboratory table—transparency, rulers, rag, pants—are salient, but other things are in the ground and do not enter the consciousness of the learner as things that might have to do with the outcome of their experiments. As art of the indeterminate ground, these other things do not exist as things; at best, there are possibilities for things to emerge. For example, in repeated trials, the students leave the transparency on the table (sheet of paper, styrofoam) while rubbing as if there is no interaction possible; or a student is rubbing the transparency while holding it on the backside with her hands. In these cases, the backing material is *transparent* to their activities, they do not attend to their hands as possible ways in which the transparency becomes discharged, and these entities and processes therefore do not yet have structure. These things and relations do not exist as things and relations in the activity and consciousness of the students. They do not stand out *as* something of relevance, that is, as part of the current relevance structure. They are part of the indeterminate matter (ground) that does not matter to the action; I-learner do not notice or include them in my active consideration of what to do next.

Differentiation emerges with noticing, itself happening when I find myself startled. Initially, the pants are just ground. However, when the students attempt to do the investigation in which a transparency is charged by pulling it through the clamped jeans-clad knees, they find that it does not work. The students articulate the possibility that it is the lamp that does not work. However, when Tara passes by, she demonstrates the investigation: the lamp glows. Iris uses the same transparency and lamp: it glows; but for Jenny and Clare, the lamp does not glow. In the discussion that follows it is the different type of material of the pants that becomes salient. Among the first features students notice are the differences between the pants—they use the same transparency sheet and lamp as the teacher. They only (material) thing that appears to differ is the material of the cloth which then becomes a central topic of their discussion. The pants, which are initially merely worn, pieces of equipment that nobody takes note of, now are made part of the investigation. Everyday equipment thereby becomes part of relevant experiences.

It is in response to the difference in the outcomes of their actions that students come to differentiate their field of experience, which comes to be structured (resource) as students evolve the associated structuring structures (schemas). It is in the relation of what they come to understand as having done and what they perceive to be the outcome of their actions that differences emerge. But for difference to be noted as different—recall the Australian students, who do not note motion *as* motion—students need to experience more than a noticing. Relevant difference emerges from a dialectic: the dispositioning nature of being positioned. That is, in one instant I see the world structured one way, in the next I see it structured differently; associated with these different structures are my own structured structuring dispositions that have changed my seeing. But how can this be? The answer is that the different way of seeing afterward already is contained as a possibility in my initially way of seeing. The impulse for doubting what I see emerges precisely during breakdown, when what I *do* is dissociated from what I *perceive*.

Already the philosopher Georg W.F. Hegel (1977) noticed that I cannot know my actions until after they are complete. I may formulate and know my goals, but because actions consist of chains of non-conscious operations, which are conditioned by the current context—including state of action, my body, position, material and social setting—my actions themselves have an emergent character. It is not surprising then that students understand what they have done only after their actions are complete. For example, following the differences in the cloth of the pants, another early differentiation becomes available in and through Iris' instruction to rub harder, followed by another instruction that the rubbing must not be too hard. Thus, Iris differentiates actions according to the vigor involved and how hard one had to push against the two materials involved. She also suggests that the Styrofoam balls—used as test elements—needed to be smaller. At this point, however, it is not clear whether and what students would retain as structure from the moments of success. For example, would the variations in the rubbing, which do not seem to make a noticed noticeable difference, be salient enough to be taken away as a result from their attempts? Would the fact that changing the size of the Styrofoam pieces does not make a difference be sufficiently marked to become re-markable (salient) at a later point? When I re-mark particular places, signs, aspects of my trip, I begin to notice recurrences over time. What aspects of the world (objects, actions, events) are salient so that they are re-marked at another point in time, at some later point? The events described in chapter 3 suggest that this seems to be connected to specific experiences, which I associate with different preceding experiences: events that I already have marked at an earlier time. How do structured features emerge into my world of experience? How do I come to notice patterns?

Here, from the complexity of the material world—complex because it affords so many, potentially infinite figure|ground configurations—students are to articulate a particular structure. Where to carve the world, where to articulate it, is not clear; it is not clear even in a limited domain such as the glow lamp and its relevance relation to other things on the table. The materials appear to afford only a limited number of variations. The students take for granted a number of things that, from a scientific perspective, are important in the preparation of the phenomenon. But in their lifeworlds, these structures currently are not articulated. How they hold the lamp is not salient. That is, in their lifeworlds, the lamp is to be held between the fingers and to the material. One of the options eventually raised is whether the lamp actually has to touch the transparency. That is, at this point then, the students begin to articulate a change in the way they conduct their test much in the way I might find a scientist evidently facing a problem say to himself, "I have to look at this a different way." For the young women, as for others in their class, the fact that the glow lamp has to touch for a current to flow is an emergent structure that results from their engagement. In the different operations of holding, no difference is made that would suggest a non-conscious taking-into-account of the structure of the lamp. The lamp glows. For us (students, me), the lamp initially glows and therefore works, or it does not glow and therefore does not work or the object is not charged. The way in which students hold the lamp shows that their holding does not articulate (distinguish) the glass and the metal end pieces, for they hold it sometimes at the former, sometimes at the latter. This holding does not differentiate the metal and glass parts. Thus, where they hold is not salient at this point: holding is holding the lamp. In the same way, the table simply is table, in the ground, a place to rest other equipment on. It is neither something that I need to spend energy focusing on nor something that might interfere with my experiment.

AGENCY: SOURCE OF VARIATION

Initially the lamp has a holistic structure because it is equipment; as equipment, the lamp is to glow. The teacher has shown a particular condition that makes the lamp glow. However, as equipment, the lamp has no characteristics other than exhibiting the presence of charges; its working and the presence of charges both are signaled by a glow. The nature of the lamp *as* lamp, with characteristic features, initially is not articulated into various constituting parts: the lamp is an equipmental hole. That is, the lamp is held in a particular way without that this way is salient to the agent; it is ready-to-hand until some point at which I am focusing on it, making it an object of my attention and intention, thereby making it present-at-hand.

To start with, students already have seen the teacher holding a glow lamp to the rubbed objects. The lamp glows. The teacher explains that the glowing is evidence for the presence of static electricity. Although they try hard, the four women do not get the lamp to glow consistently and when they anticipate it to glow. Furthermore, the teacher tells them at one point that she knows why the lamp does not glow and that they need find out. The students are then facing the task of finding out why the lamp does not glow although it should.

At this point then the students know that the lamp does not work and that they have to figure out how their preparation differs from that of the teacher. But they have to ask themselves, "How do I get the lamp to glow consistently?" "How do I carve the world to know?" To achieve this, I-learner have to muster my agency, because only in acting—even if this acting is reduced to the saccades and movements of my eyes—do I have any hope for articulating something new; but acting requires opening myself to being changed, sensing something that I am not yet familiar with. Acting for finding out, I allow myself to be vulnerable. But where do I begin when I know something does not work, and yet there seem to be no indication as to where to begin? I know my world is to-hand, and it appears to be unimaginable where to articulate it any further. Where should I carve? Where can I trench to add a new part to my world? Where do I place the cut that will detach equipment from its connections, which releases it from ground to become figure? And where do I articulate the practice of using equipment to reveal the damage?

New features of my lifeworld emerge, but emergence requires my agency. As differences in action are associated with differences in outcome, new features of the setting also come to the fore. This requires experiencing equipment no longer in its holistic nature, integrally woven into the ground, but as a separable entity. For new structures to emerge, actions have to be correlated consistently with perception. From the perspective of the person who does not know, any form of agency here is as good as any other. The more actions, the more likely new correlations and with it new structures may arise as noticed noticeable and notable features. That is, to evolve new structure, I *need* to act because acting, which always is a singular event, brings about variation—in action and perception—especially because it is repetition, which inherently embodies difference. These variations constitute the very possibility for new figure (structure) to emerge from the undifferentiated material ground and structure my structuring dispositions. Thus, changing a piece in the equipmental hole and making a different observation is at the origin of new structure. For example, after a number of negative events with a particular transparency sheet, Jenny gets a new one. She does with the new sheet what she has done with the old; and low and behold, she succeeds in producing a positive effect twice in a row. Here then, she links what is currently salient, the exchange (a form of agency) of the two sheets, the replacement, to the differences in perceived outcomes. That there are other changes associated with the exchange of the sheet is not salient, and therefore is not an available resource in her considerations. That these other things exist in the world of the observer is quite irrelevant to understanding what Jenny does and why she says what she says.

One of the aporias of learning school science from experience lies in finding the joints that are relevant to the physics that I am to learn and to articulate. It is evident that my teacher already knows what I am supposed to know. The question now is to find the way that the teacher knows—without my knowledge of how to get there because I do not know the learning object. What I am supposed to learn lies beyond my horizon, in the dark, waiting for me to be discovered and seen. To articulate something in a new way, I have to disrupt (a form of agency) my familiar way of seeing equipment, even when there do not seem to be salient ways of doing so. I need to *play* with the equipment to see whether it reveals joints, articulations, whether it reveals a place where it can be cut, and where it can be re-conceptualized. Because of the continuity of actions, it is equally and perhaps even more difficult to articulate them into component movements (operations).

Prior to knowing something theoretically, it is not clear what I am required to know. In the glow lamp example, not knowing why it does not glow leads students to enact variations. *Playing* is a form of acting without particular intent and direction, a way of exploring possibilities that the system (everything at hand that appear to belong together) exhibits when I begin to touch it in various ways. It is as if I am finding myself in a dark and unfamiliar room, and the only way to get to know my environs is by moving about, touching, and therefore producing structure. Thus, when I-author have a new computer program, I "play around," touching here, pulling a window there, pushing buttons in a third place, and so on. Over time, I learn how the program responds and what it allows me to do. By varying what I do, even though I cannot know what the variation does prior to enacting it, I increase my action possibilities. With time, I even may become an expert in the use of the program. In the same way, when I do not know why the glow lamp does not work, I have to "play around" with the hope that I notice something to understand the working of the device and its breakdown. Thus, in one situation, students begin holding the lamp in different ways toward the previously charged transparency sheet. Ever so slightly, sometimes consciously sometimes non-consciously (e.g., what looks like aimless playing around), they vary their interactions with the materials. In one of these attempts, Jenny suspends the glow lamp from a string wrapped around the center (Figure 4.3). When she then conducts the test, the lamp does not glow. This outcome then is a resource for concluding that the lamp does not glow if hung on a string wrapped around the center. It is in her next action, taking the lamp from the string, that the new structured action, "holding-the-lamp-at-the-metal-end" emerges and with it a structured aspect of the lamp—made available for all others to perceive in her demonstrative gesture (Figure 4.4).

UNSTRUCTURED GROUND AS SOURCE OF STRUCTURE

What I notice always occurs against an indeterminate ground that I do not clearly notice. When I notice something as something, I lift it from the ground to make it figure. Although the ground is indeterminate, it nevertheless is there and presupposed. The ground therefore is a possible resource for constituting structured figure, although it does not have structure when it serves as ground to any existing figurations. That is, structure is to emerge from something unstructured that already contains the possibility to become structured: it is structured and unstructured simultaneously. This happens only when the ground unfolds: a new figure emerges exactly at the fold, leading to the enfolding in the ground of a previous fold. Thus, when I conduct an experiment, I normally take the tabletop for granted;

I use it in a central way, while placing equipment, books, and materials. Yet at the same time, the tabletop *figures* as ground, I do not take it into account when doing the experiment—not unless there is reason to do so. Unbeknownst to me-learner, there may yet be, from a scientist's perspective, something of the ground that can be made relevant in making the phenomenon; yet this is irrelevant unless I can make the ground figure. But a reminder to look differently may jog my gaze. The process of looking at something before me differently is not unlike using a different lens, a different map in a geographic information system (GIS) for studying the same terrain—I explore this metaphor for learning in chapter 5.

Novices take as indeterminate ground what others may treat as salient. Jenny leaves the transparency on the Styrofoam plate, which she uses to rub the former against. She tests the transparency for any charges present. Here, the table and Styrofoam piece are mere equipment supporting the experiment. They are treated as transparent equipment that is part of the ground, where it does what a thing in this position would normally be doing. As learner, I do not have to think (and even less think twice) about wanting to rest something on a tabletop; it is part of my familiar surrounding that affords things being placed on. I normally pile stuff on top of the table, like a book, and without asking myself about Netwon's laws that make it possible for the books or stuff to rest in the pile without moving or falling vertically downward. As the materials are placed on the table without reflecting that these might fall to the floor, that is, the table a transparent background holding things at a comfortable height above the floor, so the table is also a place where to rest the transparency sheets when they are rubbed. The ground is not articulated, not seen as a separate thing in itself that might interact with the materials at-hand. In this sense, the table is ready-to-hand, not salient to the activity of making the lamp experiment work. And yet, the possibility of structure has to be there so that new structure may emerge in and through my agency.

From a physicist's perspective, having the materials on the table means that Jenny does not detach them as things from other things and the environment more generally. These things are connected and therefore interact with the environment. But detaching things from their surrounding is exactly what I have to do to make objects noticeable as scientific objects. To be a scientific object, a thing needs to be released from the indeterminate ground and made an object of intention; it must be separated from the natural environment and must be produced in the decontextualized setting of the laboratory. Thus, when Jenny places the transparency on the tabletop or on the Styrofoam plate resting on the latter, charges might be building up or might be conducted away. In Jenny's world, the world she inhabits an in which she acts, this possibility of charges being conducted away prior to her testing is not apparent. She uses the table as an equipment that transparently sits in the ground and allows her to rub in the way she does. The table therefore is part of the relevance relations that make the ground, unavailable for scientific reflection in its current state. Unbeknownst to her, therefore, the charges might already be gone before she ever conducts a test. In another situation, Iris rubs a plastic rod with a piece of cloth; she then takes a test object (a coated table tennis ball) to check the presence of charges; she notices no effect. To the physicist watching her, the case is clear: Iris has rubbed the center part of the rod, thereby charged it, but tested at the end of the non-conducting rod where there are no charges. It is evident that there should be no charges. The negative outcome is what she should have perceived under the condition. But Iris does not perceive the situation in the way the physicist does, who distinguishes center from end part of the non-conducting rod. For Iris, the rod constitutes an equipmental, undivided, and therefore unstructured whole. She rubs the rod and tests with the rod. There is no difference between where she rubs and where she tests. She simply handles "the rod."

But this problem is not just Jenny's and Iris': it is a condition whenever I am active in a domain unfamiliar to me. More so, this possibility of the setting to mediate what I do without my awareness always exceeds what I know, what I can know. *Because* the ground is indeterminate, without definitive structure, there always is an excess of structure and sense; and therefore, there is always an excess of possible effects of the setting on my actions that mediate (constrain, afford) my perception.

LAYERING AND THE DEVELOPMENT OF DISCIPLINARY LENSES

We must always tell what we see. Above all, and this
is more difficult, we must always see what we see.
Charles Péguy

Most of the time I navigate the everyday world without problems. For example, after deciding to shop some groceries, I make a list, take my bicycle, ride to the store, get the items, and return. When I have to attend some meeting, I simply leave home, ride to the university, attend the meeting, and return. This unproblematic nature of the everyday makes the real work necessary to act in a human environment invisible. This book is about this work, bringing to the fore what it takes to perceive, and showing how I use my body to produce a world, orient in it, and make myself at home with other bodies (people, objects). As part of my everyday material spiritual life, I not only do and produce things but also I emit sounds in the same way other people do when I interact with them. These sounds are part of the everyday world, and others hear them not just as sounds but also as words. But thinking about words and their "meaning" has mystified what humans really face when researchers study knowing in the everyday world in general and in science classrooms in particular. All of a sudden, psychologists depict human beings as intentional machines, who construct "meanings" and then attach them to words.

But theorizing my becoming a science teacher or a professor of applied cognitive science in terms of the construction of meaning entirely fails to describe my experience of becoming a core member in each of these professions—or of anything else that I have become competent in. I do not "construct" "meaning" in the way I construct a composting bin from familiar pieces of wood, nails and screws, and hinges; and it has not been like this historically. By and large I become familiar with a new world, and this includes becoming familiar with the sounds people produce; and this familiarity *emerges* from my engagement with the world. There is a level of passivity to this emergence that I cannot intent, and which the term "construct" does not capture. And if anything, it is not words that are meaningful but life, and words come to have a familiar, situated ring to them in particular situations. As I have become familiar with different (cultural, material, intellectual) parts of the world, I also have become able to anticipate the production and reception of particular sounds. Familiarity with the respective worlds, being able to navigate, also has come with knowing the sounds people use in a variety of settings associated with these worlds. Thinking in terms of sounds is more advantageous, as it also covers all the other things people produce with their vocal tracts that are not properly words, including "um," "ahm," "ooui," "whoosh," "cuckoo," or any other of the many onomatopoeias people generate as part of everyday life. Science educators have to begin to understand language through its cultural-historical historical origins, and understand that "meaning" is an add-on that figures on top of what sounds have accomplished originally and what they were for.

When I view a video of chimpanzees, I can notice that these animals produce a variety of gestures, body movements directed toward other animals, and sounds. These various productions serve as a means to do interaction work. The sounds do not have "meaning" in the human sense, that is, they are not used to refer to other things consistently and across multiple situations and settings. Rather, sounds are produced as part of being in the world and being with others. The animals use sounds to regulate aspects of their lives; for example, they emit sounds that are heard as warnings—approaching predators—or produce sounds to regulate their hunting. But they do not use these sounds to tell a story *about* predators or *about* hunting; they do not use these sounds to scare others to *believe* that a predator is coming. Rather, the sounds and the situation are connected in an irreducible way. In this situation, the material body of sound and the associated sense are one.

Some time in human evolution, in fact, just at the point of anthropogenesis, sounds came to be differentiated and used across situations to point to the same thing. Sounds came to be separated from and used independently of situations, and with it, a split was brought about between the material body of sound and the situation (sense). This parallels the way that a stick came to be taken from one location to another to be used as a tool, for example, to fish termites from their hills—up to that point, human beings, as chimpanzees today, left the stick only to break a new one when they needed it. That is, breaking a stick, fishing for termites, and eating all belong together. In the same way, sounds and hunting or sounds and danger belong together into an integral setting. But as soon as sticks and sounds came to refer to the same things *across* situations, they became tools and, with it, obtained semiotic (meaning-making) function. This new function can be understood as a new dimension of human life; in fact, it became a defining and constituent factor of human cultural life. Human life no longer unfolded in direct, unmediated relation with the environment. Rather, humans modified their environment, among others, by relating settings to other settings, which they achieved in part by carrying around tools that now were used across situations. Another dimension came to accompany the first, a dimension that could be used to refer to what was happening. It was a new dimension, because it involved a reflexive turn whereby early humans not only acted, but also had a way of presenting their actions again, in this situation or some time later. The sounds took on a new function: making another situation present again. Sounds had become a form of representation.

One can understand this second function as riding on top of the first communicative function that assists human beings, as animals, to point out things and get some other work done. This primary work, praxis, is associated with a primary perspective on the world, that is, the world as it is given to human beings in their perception. The other functions constitute perspectives that are associated with, describe, and explain the things and events that appear in praxis. Thus, scientists create theories and other forms of representations, and all of these can be understood as layers that are used to highlight entities in the world, something that is to be salient and of importance. Psychologists, for example, create language and representations *about* problem solving, designed to help understand the process of problem solving, but the language and representations are not *doing* "solving problems." The language and representations are material forms created to accompany the already existing material world. These different material forms are conceptual lenses that can be layered onto the primary perception of the world; these lenses constitute perspectives, which are the presupposed and presupposing counterpart to the material world. What is perceivable arises from the dialectical tension between the material world and what I see and articulate with a lens. The lenses therefore constitute ontologies and constitute particular sets of whole|parts relations.

Things, their environments, and their internal structure are a result of making and perceiving boundaries. These boundaries are joints in the world, its articulations, and constitute what I can articulate *as* something different from something else. I do not or seldom articulate a continuous surface: I perceive and denote a white unsullied piece of paper as *one*. Boundaries constitute a thing as something, as they separate the inner from the outer, the thing from the non-thing. Where the whiteness stops, I perceive the boundaries of the sheet of paper. Boundaries also constitute the internal structure of the things I encounter, the places where I can take them apart, perceptually or with my actions. Thus, there is an outside boundary that separates the neon lamp (Figure 4.1) from other things, the laboratory table, cloth, jeans, and transparencies. But boundaries are also possible on the inside of the object, which then define its parts. The lamp has metal ends, a glass body, and two electrodes. Each of these parts is associated with continuity, which defines its inside, and discontinuity, which defines the border with what it is not. The whole and its parts are mutually constitutive: (a) the whole presupposes its parts, for there is a glow lamp only when there are electrodes, metal end caps, a glass housing, and the neon gas on the inside; and (b) the parts presuppose a whole they constitute: the wires inside the glow lamp are *electrodes* because they are part of a glow lamp rather than of a coat hanger.

Boundaries have at least three characteristics (Smith, 2001). First, the material enclosed by the boundary to be determined is felt to have a coherent unity distinct from the material outside of the boundary. Second, the material provides a sense of connectedness, a connectivity within the boundary; this is contrasted by the opposing situations that give rise to a sense of discontinuity or disjuncture outside of the boundary. Third, the various portions of the material inside the boundary are co-relevant, relevant together and simultaneously, but the material outside the boundary is not. Whole|parts relations emerge along inhomogeneities in the material world that may serve to define boundaries, which shape actions in particular ways, or which are sensed differently. *And these homogeneities and inhomogeneities are not arbitrary, lending themselves to the constitution of structure, so that, unlike what (radical, social) constructivists sometimes claim, there are constraints on how the world can appear to me, or, in their discourse, how the world can be "constructed."* When I run my fingers across the keyboard, I can clearly sense differences, gaps, and particular movements and resistances. I cannot construct understandings that obliterate these sensible boundaries—although some radical constructivists once told me that my lived experiences were impossible because their constructivist-enactivist theory did not account for them. Between the keys, my touch does not easily depress the material, whereas what I name "key" easily yields to my touch. Structure therefore emerges along what I experience as boundaries where my agency and sensibility change in characteristic ways. I experience structure as allowing me to act in a particular way; this structure also has been termed *affordance* (Gibson, 1986).

From my interactions with the world, I come to be able to anticipate which structures support what I want to do and which structures constrain my actions. Affordances generally provide opportunities to act in particular, often-advantageous ways; however, affordances simultaneously hide other possible ways of acting, and therefore, actively suppress innovation. The more the holding capacity of needle nose pliers stands out, the more their capacity to be used to drive a nail into the wall recedes into the ground. Affordances generally are discipline specific: Physicists and engineers use a certain mathematical equation quite differently, which means, these constitute different types of resources in these disciplines. There are many studies that show how certain *boundary* objects are used differently in different disciplines, in each of which they exhibit a different structural properties. That is, depending on the activity I participate in, there are different, discipline-specific affordances that are more relevant than other structures. That is, sets of affordances constitute discipline-specific maps of the world. These maps define the relevant whole|parts relations for the discipline and constitute characteristic lenses that those in the discipline use to look at and find things in the world.

It is important to keep in mind that I always and foremost live in the everyday world and I do not make the maps I am using salient—I do not place feet but walk, I do not place my backside on some chair at some coordinates in three dimensional space, but I simply sit down, and I do not pronounce sounds whose meanings I look up in some databank but I speak. The world around me unfolds; and so does my life. Because everything is at its place, I do not have to monitor it, but simply abandon myself to whatever I currently do—right now, I do not worry about my desk and whether it holds my computer, keyboard, and monitor but I am focusing on writing and editing this text. That is, although I can think of my keyboard in terms of a map, it normally is transparent to me because I am focused on producing text on the screen rather than on searching specific keys. It is only when there is trouble that I begin to make a part of my lifeworld thematic, that is, I select a particular way of looking at and theorizing the situation as a whole and some of the things that are currently relevant within it. If a key of my keyboard begins to stick, I no longer write but think *about* the keyboard and possible reasons for *why* the key sticks and *how* I might fix it; and I search the map imprinted right on the keyboard itself to find the particular key that sticks. In so doing, I bring forth a theoretical attitude; and this attitude constitutes a lens, a map. I choose this map for looking; and this map constitutes what and how I perceive. Maps are lenses. In the context of science education, learning means, therefore, developing new sets of lenses that can be used as an alternative to the everyday way of looking at the world.

This chapter therefore is about the development of disciplinary lenses, which constitute maps that can be layered to perceive the material world much like the different maps of a geographical information system (GIS) are used for representing and understanding the same terrain in various ways. Many different maps are possible for looking at the same part of the world. But one perspective is privileged: The one that is associated with my perception of the world, that is, the world as it is given to me together with being in the world and being with others.

LAYERING ONTOLOGIES

Seeing the world through different lenses can be thought of in terms of the analogy of maps. There are different maps that portray the "same" geographical area, but they look rather different depending on the nature of what is being portrayed—here "the same" refers to some aspect of the material world and not how it is reflected in my consciousness. The map constitutes what I can perceive. Thus, an aerial photograph of my neighborhood differs from a map that features the roads, which differs from a map that shows the geology of the area, which differs again from a map showing the distribution of economic aspects, which will differ from population density maps of people of different cultural heritage, and so on. Maps do not just stand on their own. By establishing relationships between the different kinds of maps I can generate new forms of knowledge. For example, a map of the rainfall in my area at the moment I am writing these words (Figure 5.1a) looks very different from a map of the same area representing landmasses and water bodies (Figure 5.1b). If the two maps are correlated, for example, by overlaying them, I can see where it rained in my area and how hard (Figure 5.1c). Here, each form of root knowledge (map) actually corresponds to a different discourse or discourse community. Each map constitutes a different lens that provides a different perspective, a different reflection of the material word in human consciousness. Learning occurs when I move from one form of map to another, when I correlate them. Thus, for example, everyday talk about the sun constitutes one way of presenting our experience, which we express in observations such as "What a nice sunset!," "Look at the beautiful sunrise!," or "The sun disappears behind the clouds." Astronomers have another map according to which the earth rotates, allowing the sun to appear in the different regions of the sky according to the earth's orientation. That is, unlike the claims conceptual change researchers make, children draw on their primary map, which have a long cultural historical origin, rather than having or being besieged by *misconceptions*.

Each map actually does more than simply represent an area in a different way. It provides a different *ontology*, that is, an account of what is really there. The maps define inner and outer boundaries and therefore the inner and outer structure of things that are relevant to a particular form of activity. And each ontology comes with its own whole|parts relations, that is, cuts the world in different way. The map featuring rainfall looks quite different from the map featuring land and water. To show that two maps are actually related, the map creators normally place the geographical outlines of the land, which do not normally figure in the chosen represen-

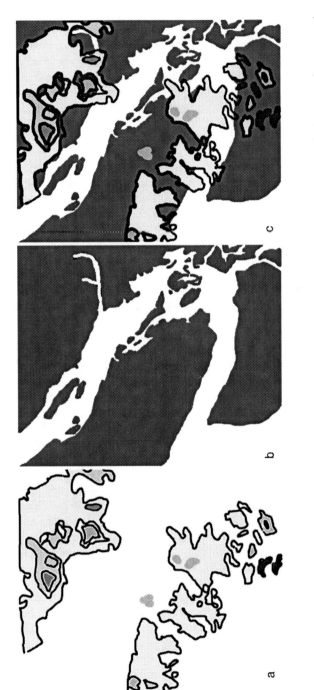

Figure 5.1. Example of two different maps of my area. a. A rainfall map based on the radar image provided by the local weather station. b. Geographical map contrasting landmasses and water bodies. c. Combined map allows me to understand where in my area it rained at the moment I created these maps.

tation. By understanding the similarities and differences between the ontologies of people—i.e., how wholes and parts of interest to them merge and split, how people and resources are mobilized to encroach on any one tiling—helps me understand regions of conflict and relative quiet. In a similar way, I show here that understanding the ontologies different participants bring to a situation helps locate difficulties in teacher–student transactions, the world as a whole and in its parts as salient to the individual students and therefore the environment towards which their (material and discursive) actions are directed, and so on. Trouble in student understanding becomes apparent, as do things that do not make sense to them, or things that they cannot embed in the networks of significance already established by them.

Experiential maps can be cut up in different ways: Each student looks at the world through his or her lens or set of lenses and teachers through theirs. These primary lenses of perception have nothing arbitrary about themselves, as the spatio-temporal thinginess of the world I experience constitutes the fundamental layer of all mundane experience. These personal experiences constitute concrete realizations of constituting the world such that the world springs forth everywhere and in each instant simultaneously (Nancy, 2000). The plurality of singular maps may go unnoticed because of the singularity of the (plural) world. When the maps students bring to class do not coincide with that of the teacher, trouble is in store, especially when the differences between these maps go unnoticed. Thus, in chapter 1, the physics teacher Tory is unaware of the fact that the majority of students see movement where he and a minority of students see none. The trouble emerges right here, because the teacher, in teaching a theory, articulates another map, another lens or set of lenses. This new lens interacts differently with the two given primary lenses (movement, no movement), and gives different images when they are correlated. For the teacher and those students who perceive no motion, the explanatory map interacts in a different way with their perceptual map, gives a different correlative map than it does when it is overlaid with the perceptual map that contained motion. Additional levels of contradictions may occur when interaction participants—students talking to students or students talking to the teacher—switch between layers without being aware that the switch is happening.

The analogy provides me with a new way of thinking about how maps serve as lenses for perceiving boundaries. That is, maps shape where I look to see the inner and outer boundaries in the area of interest because of some, often iconic, similarity. Thus, when a student holds his pencil parallel to one arrow depicted on a computer monitor while talking about "the arrow," the pencil-including gesture constitutes a map for finding on the monitor what the speaker is talking about (Figure 5.2); the student clearly is not talking about the other arrow that points to the upper right. To return to a GIS example, the map of northern Canada looks very different to a geologist interested in oil or gold than it does to a farmer interested in maximizing yields by associating soil types and crops to be planted. That is, each map constitutes and depicts different figure|ground relations in and of the same territory, that is, part of the material world.

In the following I show how talk and gestures embody and constitute conceptual maps that are layered on top of a world perceptually available to all those present

Figure 5.2. The gesture constitutes a map that allows other participants to find on the computer monitor what the speaker is talking about.

in the situation. I represent the episodes in such a way that they keep track of those things not evoked in the utterances, but that are perceptually present to the participants and required as part of the explanation. Furthermore, in the episodes, gestures enact movements that occur as part of earlier investigations and thereby represent themselves. These gestures emerged prior to articulated knowledge, from an indeterminate ground of work-related movements to which they maintain topological similarity.

LAYERING DIFFERENT MAPS

In this chapter I draw on a particular set of student investigation tasks. In these tasks, students are asked to bring a charged object, such as a transparency film, close to two, touching metal plates that are insulated from the table top by means of Styrofoam blocks. As the charged object—here a transparency sheet—has been held close to the plates (without touching), these are separated and tested for static electricity (Figure 5.3). This process is referred to as charging objects by influence and separation. When everything works as intended, a glow lamp lights up when the plates are tested individually; it glows twice as bright when bridging the two separated plates (Figure 5.3b3). One of the associated questions students are asked to answer is why touching the two plates leads to twice the brightness.

Phil and Matt attempt to show that there are equal charges on the two metal plates, which previously have been charged by induction and separation. The students repeatedly bring to the plates a transparency that has been pulled between their knees, then separate the plates, and subsequently remove the film. They bring the ends of a wire to the plate of an electroscope and then touch first one then the other metal plate with the other end of the wire. There is no deflection. After nine failed attempts to observe the anticipated deflection, they decide to test the plates using the neon lamp. They bring the transparency again to the plates, after having pulled it through the knees and separated the plates. Matt touches the metal plate with the lamp and comments, "very weak." They then repeat the sequence—they presume it to be the same and therefore a repetition—but use the electroscope with the wire as a test instrument. There is no deflection. One of the two teachers in the classroom suggests bringing the plates directly in contact with the electroscope, perhaps implying not to use the wire. The students repeat the experiment: again

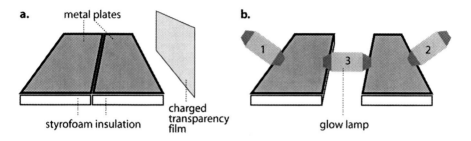

Figure 5.3. In the featured episodes, the students are asked: (a) to bring a charged trans-parency film to two insulated, touching metal plates, which are then separated; (b1, b2) to test the charges on the two plates individually and (b3) with respect to each other. They are then to provide an explanation for what they observe.

there is no deflection when they bring each plate into contact with the electroscope. Matt then touches each plate with the lamp but it does not glow. Philip also suggests that—perhaps—the teachers simply want to kid them. Phil inspects the wire. At its end there are plastic banana plugs. He asks Matt, "Could it be that you are touching the screw [on the plug]?" Matt: "I don't think so. Most often, I am holding here." Philip suggests that the same experiment "worked for the girls."

For students, the first difficulty is that they do not see what the teacher implies in his talk. Here, not observing what they are supposed or expect to observe involves the fundamental aporia already described in chapter 2: They not only have to produce some phenomenon but also they have to perceive the material world in a specifically scientific way. In both parts required for making the observation there is an aporia; or both parts are aspects of the same aporia—to perceive, I have to know that my actions produce what I am supposed to produce, but to know whether I am producing it, I already need to know that what I perceive is what I am supposed to perceive. *They must see that they see!* In such a situation, the two teachers in the class have an important mediating role. One of the observations they have to assist the students in this group to see is that the two discharges (the one with individual plates [Figures 5.3b1 and 5.3b2] and the one between the two plates [Figure 5.3b3]) are of different brightness and that touching each plate causes the lamp to glow on different ends. (In chapter 4, I describe the discovery of this phenomenon by the four female students.) Thus, although Philip and Matt do the experiment, they do not perceive what the teacher does. Consequently, they do not produce the observation sentences and even less the observation categoricals that physicists produce—who, in any case, observe something different. Once students get to the point of perceiving what they are to perceive, they still have to find an explanation for the fact that the two individual plates make the lamp glow less bright and at different ends than when the lamp bridges the plates.

Underlying the phenomenon are two systems, a mechanical and an electrical, each of which constitutes a map, a particular way of perceiving and depicting what is there. Electrically, the plates are neutral (before and after) overall. However, because of the electrical induction brought about by the charged transparency, an

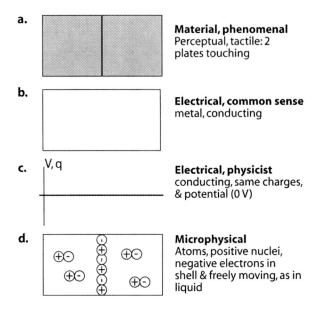

a.

Material, phenomenal
Perceptual, tactile: 2
plates touching

b.

Electrical, common sense
metal, conducting

c. V, q

Electrical, physicist
conducting, same charges,
& potential (0 V)

d.

Microphysical
Atoms, positive nuclei,
negative electrons in
shell & freely moving, as in
liquid

Figure 5.4. We can conceive of four layers that are co-present in the conversations about charging a plate by induction and grounding.

electrical gradient has been formed so that, after mechanical separation of the system into two parts, each half is associated with a different charge (q+, q-) though the total charge remains zero (q+ + q- = 0). When an individual plate is evaluated against the surrounding, a current flows either from the plate to ground or from ground to the plate. The total charge that has moved in each case is the same, that is, the value of the positive or negative charge: |q+| = |q-| (i.e., the vertical bar stand for "amount" such that this equation means: amount of positive charges is equal to the amount of negative charges). When the lamp connects the two plates, there are two currents. One flowing from the right to the left, the other one flowing from left to right. The total current therefore is given by the difference between the two charges, |q+ - q-| = |q+| + |q-| = 2 |q+| = 2 |q-|. To understand the phenomena in the intended way, students have to perceive the lamp glowing with different intensity and they have to perceive the lamp glow at different ends in the former situations. They then have to develop another disciplinary lens, which constitutes the explanation that fits on top of and is consistent with the perceptual lens.

In the case of charging metal plates by means of influence and grounding, there then are at least *four* layers, lenses, or ways of perceiving in operation here. Students usually find themselves looking at the plates through the first and second lens. Through the first lens, I see two material plates; they constitute a mechanical system (Figure 5.4a). I can touch the plates, move them, push them together, and pull them apart. Through the second lens, I see two conducting materials, which, when pushed together, form one continuous electrical system (Figure 5.4b). Through the experiences that follow in the curriculum taught by the two teachers, students are to develop two new lenses, the perspectives of which are to be layered on top of the first. The correct explanation within the discipline of physics requires a coordination of these different layers. If I look at the two touching plates through the third lens, I take an electrical view of the system that a physicist might take; I see one connected, electrically conducting, uncharged medium with an electrical potential of 0 Volts. If I touch the plate with the lamp, it does not glow because there is no current, which requires a potential difference ("voltage"). This potential difference does not exist because both the plates and ground, my body, have the same electrical potential.

The fourth lens is a microphysical one (Figure 5.4d). If I view the system through this lens, I see positive charges in the nuclei of the metal atoms that make the two plates, surrounded by electrons. Some of these electrons are not stationary but are free to move about in the material. On average, however, they are distributed throughout the material in such a way that there is no charge build-up in the system and all parts are electrically the same.

As an outcome of the lessons, students are expected to talk about the phenomena they observe (described in the previous section) in terms of these two new layers all the while considering the material constitution, that is, seeing the system in terms of a layering of the first, third, and fourth lens (Figures 5.4a, 5.4c, and 5.4d). The two plates do not interpenetrate and are likely separated by a few layers of various types of molecules (air, particles). Thus, at the material level there are two distinct objects that touch but—as shown by the mechanical properties—are distinct and can easily be pulled apart. At the electrical level, the touching is sufficient to make for one conducting medium. Currents may be passed through the boundary from one side to the other, though upon careful testing, some resistance higher than in the material might be detected due to the junction.

In discussing the phenomena students investigate, physicists normally do not talk about the interface between the two plates but treat it as one continuous surface, that is, they take the third and fourth lenses (Figures 5.4c and 5.4d) and in the process obscure (obliterating) the existence of the layers of different atoms and molecules on the interface. The metal plates are insulated from the table by means of Styrofoam pieces (Figure 5.3) or by supporting the metal plates on their insulated handles (not shown). Not thematized so far in my account are the surroundings. This is important, however, for understanding the tests, which are conducted in different ways (Figures 5.3b1, 5.3b2, and 5.3b3). Only in the third case (Figure 5.3b3) do charges move between the two plates.

In the investigation, students are asked to charge a transparency or other object and to bring it near the two touching plates. Depending on the lens I take, I see the system in a different way, well knowing that there is something material that I can see, touch, feel the temperature of, and so forth (Figure 5.5). On the material level, the two distinguishable plates still touch each other approached by a third material, a transparency sheet that has been rubbed in some way and (presumably) has been charged (Figure 5.5a). In the commonsense electrical view—taken by students, as the lesson transcripts show—charges flow somehow across to the metal that is electrically connected and therefore forms one whole (Figure 5.5b). For the electri-

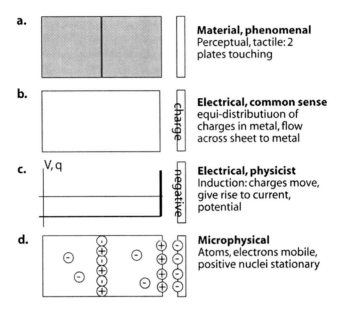

Figure 5.5. When a charged body is brought close to the touching double-plates, the four levels exhibit different properties and relationships.

cally more advanced person, the (positively or negatively) charged transparency is brought near the metal plates, where charge separation through induction occurs (Figure 5.5c). The opposite charges (equal amount) sit on the edge directly facing the film. Thus, the electrical potential is negative throughout the metal, but positive at the end facing the charged material. The microphysical view shows a separation of the movable electrons in the metal (Figure 5.5d).

In the investigation, I then mechanically separate the two plates in the presence of the charged transparency and then remove the latter. Through a mechanical lens, I see two material plates separated (Figure 5.6a). Through the everyday common-sense lens, the charges on the plates disappear when the charged transparency disappears (Figure 5.6b) or, if some of the charges are thought to have migrated (through the air) from the transparency to the plates, these charges still ought to be on the plates. From the sophisticated electrical point of view, a charge separation has occurred leaving one plate charged negatively (here left), the other plate positively with the same amount (Figure 5.6c). The electrical potential of the two plates (with respect to neutral ground) therefore is equal in magnitude ($|V^+| = |V^-|$) but has different sign (+, -). Through the microphysical lens, there is an excess of electrons on the left plate but an excess of positive charges on the right plate (Figure 5.6d).

When the students begin their investigation, they do not know about the different perspectives on the plates; most students come with everyday, commonsense views of electricity and electrical charges. Their task is to *infer* the new maps based on the events observed in their tests using the neon lamp as an indicator. If they use another indicator, such as the electroscope, they do not make a prerequi-

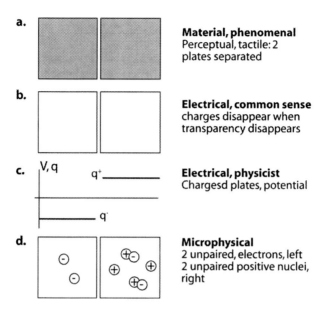

Figure 5.6. When the metal plates are separated while the charged body still is close, the separation of charges remains permanent in the metal plates.

site observation. However, given the aporias of perception described earlier, to make the desired inferences—itself a process that could occur in unexpected and undesired way—students have to perceive the events in the way physicists do rather than in the way they perceive it while untutored (Figure 5.7). But to perceive what scientists see, they have to enact the procedures, for which they need to know (as I show in chapter 2) that what they see is what they are supposed to see. To see what the scientists see, it is important that students enact the proper temporal sequence of first separating before removing the transparency. That is, time and the temporal evolution of the events is an important lens that provides me with yet another perspective, a different map for navigating the world.

Unbeknownst to Phil and Matt, they do not observe the sequence required for charge separation to occur in the way described (Figure 5.6). This, of course, mediates what they can perceive and therefore the models for the investigations that they create. Let me assume for the moment that students have enacted the proper sequence of events. The question now is how their observations compare to those of the teachers in the class—both of whom are trained scientists—who expect students to see what they themselves see. But the observations I describe in chapter 1 and 4 already should alert readers that this may in fact not be the case. (How I fared in my explorations of related phenomena is the topic of chapter 10.)

From the teachers' scientific perspective, that is, through the lens of the one who already knows, the issue is clear. When held to the two uncharged plates, the lamp does not glow (Figure 5.7a). There are no unbalanced charges and the plates are at the same electrical potential as the surrounding, which constitutes electrical

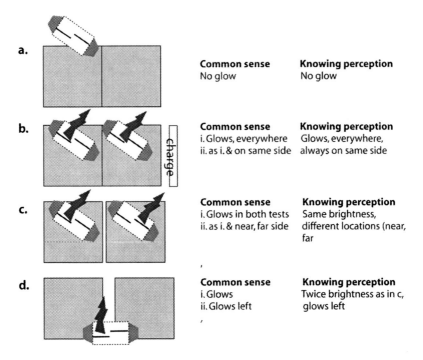

Figure 5.7. Testing the two plates with a glow lamp before and after charging by induction and separation is perceived differently by informed (knowing) and uninformed (common-sense) perception.

ground. If the plates are tested while the charged transparency is still near the two touching plates, the neon lamp glows in the same way wherever the test is conducted on the two plates (Figure 5.7b). Furthermore, the knowing person will be attuned to the fact that the lamp glows on one side, which, depending on the charged object, is either away from or near the fingers holding the lamp (see chapter 4). Once the plates have been separated and the charged body removed, three tests can be conducted. The first two tests concern the charges on the plates. In one instance, the lamp glows away from the hand, in the other near the hand (Figure 5.7c). The knowing person also perceives the same intensity in both instances. In the third case, the lamp is made to bridge the two plates. In this situation, the lamp also glows but the knowing individual perceives the intensity to be twice as bright as in the two previous cases (Figure 5.7d). Whereas it might be counterintuitive why this is so, the map depicted in Figure 5.6c clearly allows me to see and understand why the observation is as it is: The potential difference (voltage) between the two plates is twice that of each plate taken with respect to ground (zero line), and there are twice as many charges—i.e., twice the current—that move.

To provoke students into developing an understanding, teachers ask students to develop the advanced electrical and microphysical maps and coordinate those with the material and appropriately in the temporal dimension, the unfolding process of holding the charged transparent film, and the separation. I return to such temporal coordination of different layers in chapters 6 and 9. That is, if two layers (maps) are not aligned, then explanations that require appropriate coordination of two or more layers do no longer make sense, or produce a sense that is different from that of science. Such misalignment sometimes is flagged by the fact that evident boundaries on two maps do not fall together. Such would be the case when a human population map overlaps significant densities with water bodies. Readers may find it helpful to think in terms of the GIS maps of some geographical area (e.g., Figure 5.1). If the population density of my community were to be shifted by one kilometer westward, then people would actually come to live in the ocean inlet. Though such a feature is possible—there are people in my area living on boats and houseboats—it would be quite unusual here in Canada to have a town of 10,000 people living in this way—though this might not be so unusual in some other parts of the world, including in the vicinity of Hong Kong.

The videotapes from the tenth-grade physics classroom show that students do not automatically perceive the events as scientists do; this confirms the teacher–student differences described in chapter 1. From a commonsense perspective, the first case considered is unproblematic: like scientist, the commonsense perception does not involve the lamp to glow (Figure 5.7a). The scientific and commonsense perceptions may differ in the second case, where the latter is articulated by the statement "the lamp glows, wherever it is held on the connected plates" (Figure 5.7b). Through this lens, the location where the lamp glows may not be differentiated, as exemplified in the case of the four female students (chapter 4).

In the third instance, the commonsense and physics lenses yield different perceptions (Figure 5.7c). Students in this class perceive the lamp glow when testing each plate and some perceive the lamp glow on opposite sides, respectively. The students do not initially differentiate or make statements about how the intensities compare. Finally, the students in this class observe the lamp to glow or to glow on one side (Figure 5.7d); they do not make statements about the intensity of the glow, especially about how the intensity compares to that in the previous two tests.

This analysis of the investigation shows that it is much more complex than one might initially think. The separation of the four maps and what informed and uninformed spectators perceive using them shows how complex the underlying explanation is: it requires a coordination of the ways in which four different lenses cut up the material world. In the following, I analyze classroom events against this first analysis, which serves as a backdrop. I show how students articulate the world and how these articulations change as they interact with the teachers, who mediate their access to the world. Coming to know these phenomena in static electricity in the standard ways of physics means learning to coordinate the different perspectives, all of which are layered on the material world students manipulate.

CREATING AND COORDINATING LAYERS

Learning science does not simply mean to appropriate a discourse. Rather, it means using sounds, gestures, and body positions in a coordinated way while talking over and about phenomena and materials in the environment. That is, whatever is expressed using sounds, gestures, and other bodily expressions constitutes a layer that is aligned with the material world of which the learner also is a part. This is a world I-learner inhabit, and which responds to my actions, and which I sense as a consequence. The particular situation may be represented in the arrangement of materials that normally are part of the phenomenon created, and which students are supposed to learn to describe and explicate. Any changes in the configuration (events) need to be accompanied by an associated shift in the other layers, which serve as lenses to make certain whole|parts configurations stand out. Language then has the function to make salient particular dimensions and properties that are already shared and accessible to all participants.

Given the complexity of scientific phenomena generally and the electrostatic phenomena described here in particular, it is not reasonable to expect students to reconstruct science on their own. Interacting with other cultural resources, including teachers and textbooks, constitutes an important aspect of developing and aligning a variety of lenses for looking at the world. How the students in this classroom appropriate different lenses as exhibited on the videotapes is the topic of this and the following section. The frustrations one of the two teachers (Tom) exhibits are perhaps indicative of the difficulties to mediate students explorations and perceptions in such a way that they develop the new lenses required for looking at the material world and seeing it in very particular, legitimated and legitimate ways.

In this part of the videotape, there are four individuals sitting and standing around the two metal plates, Clare, Brita, Tom (teacher), and Iris (from left to right in Figure 5.8) Tom asks the three students to describe what is happening and then to explain. Clare begins.

Excerpt 5.1

01	Clare	If you hold it like this to it– ((Holds up the lamp.)) That is neutral. And when you go to the negative ((Holds lamp to the first metal plate as in Figure 5.8)), you get neutral negative and then ((Moves lamp to the second plate)) neutral positive.
02	Tom:	Um.
03	Clare:	And when you old it to it like this ((Attempts to bridge the two plates with the glow lamp)).
04	Tom:	Um. ((Nods.))
05	Clare:	Then it uses up more energy, because the negative goes through to the positive.
06	Tom:	Okay, so you say, used up, okay, so . . .

In this first excerpt, Clare begins her explication. She distinguishes the charges of the lamp from those of the first plate in terms of charges: neutral for the lamp, negative for the plate, yielding some situation that she denotes by "neutral negative." In her demonstration, Clare then moves the hand with the lamp to the second plate, denoting it by "neutral positive." Tom responds with a tentative "um" (turn 02), which allows Clare to continue. She takes the opportunity of having another

Figure 5.8. Clare (left) explains the phenomenon of charging by induction of two plates, in the presence of materials, gesturing where the tests with the glow lamp have to be conducted and what the observations are. Brita, Tom, and Iris (left to right) complete the scene.

turn to describe what happens when the lamp is held in such a way that it bridges the two plates and describes the situation as one in which more energy is used up because "the negative goes through to the positive" (lines 03, 05).

Tom struggles with finding a response or a way of continuing the conversation (line 06). Clearly, Clare has said something that he does not expect. Perhaps he is waiting for her to say something about the brightness; perhaps he wants them to compare the different intensities. I do not know; nor do the three young women. If he wants them to understand what he is expecting, he needs to articulate *for them,* and in this way, articulate it for me-analyst. From Excerpt 5.1 alone, I do not know just what Clare explains, that is, which of the various observations her explanation accounts for. To get the conversation back on track, Tom frames the situation he wants the women to consider. He begins by describing again the two tests they have conducted using a glow lamp as part of articulating the actions involved.

Excerpt 5.2

07	Tom:	So we said, if you discharge it this way ((Picks up the glow lamp)), one times in this way ((Holds glow lamp to the first metal plate [Figure 5.9a])).
08	Clare:	And then, and then . . .
09	Tom:	((Touches the second plate with the glow lamp [Figure 5.9b])) and then in this way, and then it is unambiguous, it lights up once at one side ((Points to one side of the glow lamp)) and on the other side.
10	Brita:	Because it is positively charged. ((Tom holds glow lamp near the two plates, as if bridging the gap between them.))
11	Tom:	Um.

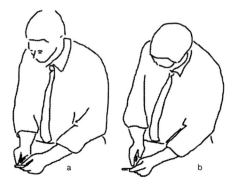

Figure 5.9. Tom articulates, oriented in particular towards Brita, the differences in the observations they should have made. The differences also are articulated in the body position, which shifts considerably with the shift in the referent of the pointing gesture.

12	Clare:	Then it just goes from the negative ((Points to the first plate, Figure 5.10a)) to the positive side ((Moves hand to point to the second plate)) across ((Figure 5.10b)).
13	Tom:	Yea, and then, yea, and what would you then– what *would* you then have to see? Does it light up on both sides or [only] on one side?]
14	Clare:	[NO!] [only on the one. This goes then–
15	Tom:	Should be seen only on one side! Or? ((Turns to Brita.))
16		(3.0)
17	Brita:	No, shouldn't it, oh I don't know.

Tom's articulation of the events is not neutral. Figure 5.9 shows that his right index finger points to the right-hand side of the neon lamp as he holds it in his left hand and to the two plates. He then moves the lamp to the second plate, accompanied by the movement of the index finger of the right hand to the left part of the lamp. Simultaneously, his whole upper body shifts from his right to left. That is, Tom not only articulates a description of the test in his words, but produces at least two indices for finding where the lamp is to glow: on the right in the first case, on

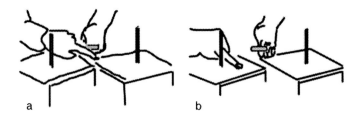

Figure 5.10. The movement of the index finger from one plate to the other presents the current flowing through the glow lamp, which the teacher holds right next to the two plates.

138

the left side and close to his left hand in the second case. He concludes by saying that the lamp "lights up once at one side and on the other side" (turn 09).

Brita talks first, followed by Clare. But they do not continue the preceding utterances. Rather, both articulate the charges and the movement of charges between the positive and negative poles. Tom struggles again, attempting to orient to the issue at hand and finding a way to respond. It is evident that he has not found an orientation toward the statements; his stumbling utterances buy him time until his next question comes forth: He asks the students about their perception generally then more specifically about the side on which the lamp glows (turn 13).

Here, then, he provides an articulation of just what he is expecting. The two women have talked about charges—which are names for things on a different map. After struggling for a few instances, Tom asks them about their observations, that is, descriptions of things from their primary map. That is, in this question he clarifies what he really wants to hear about rather than the charges that Brita and Clare highlight in their talk. Now the latter provides the sought-after answer, as is evident in the fact that Tom repeats the content of what Clare has expressed (turn 15). But he seeks to ascertain that Brita, too, is "on the same page," that is, is talking about the same observation rather than another one. But Brita articulates an opposition ("No, shouldn't it . . ."), thereby constituting the teacher question as a possible way of discrediting Clare's earlier response. Brita then expresses confusion ("oh, I don't know"): Tom effectively has questioned what has been certain until now.

Up to this point, Tom still seeks to clarify what has been observed and what is being talked about. Although he does not explain it in this way when I debrief him about it, in this situation he seeks to ascertain that the perception to be explained is the one he expects rather than possible other perceptions students may have in the situation. He appears to be aware of the fact that students sometimes see the lamp glowing but do not differentiate the position of the glow. Clare picks up from Brita.

Excerpt 5.3

18	Clare:	They are only on the negative side.
19		(3.0)
20		((Turns to Brita)) this is what I think.
21	Tom:	How is this?
22	Brita:	The positive ones. Because here, this is where we had the electrons ((Points to and touches first plate)) and they are, they are attracted into it, because ((Points to second plate)), no, there is electron lack, and there it is– ((Appears to be frustrated, abandons explication)).
23	Tom:	Isn't it that the electrons are only on one side, on the other side there are not enough of them. So all of them have to move into one direction ((Gesture of movement from one direction to the other, using his whole body to enact a presentation of flow, Figure 5.11)).
24	Brita:	Yea.
25	Tom:	And when you now discharge them individually (2.0) ((Manipulates the plates, prepares to set up the procedure)) when you dis-

Figure 5.11. Tom explains how the electrons move from one plate to the other. The lamp glows because electrons move through it.

		charge them individually, then there are here, for example ((Points to plate 1)) too many electrons, and they have to go out ((Gestures from plate toward the ground [Figure 5.12a-b])).
26	Brita:	Yea.
27	Tom:	And how is it here ((Points to plate 2))?
28		(2.0)
29	Clare:	Yea, then they come up.
30	Tom:	Then they have to go there like this. ((Gestures from floor upward and toward plate [Figure 5.12b-c].))
31	Brita:	Yea.
32	Tom:	Like this away ((Gestures from plate 1 toward the floor [Figure 5.12a-b])) and then like this to it ((Gestures from floor toward plate 2 [Figure 5.12b-c])). And this is why the lamp glows on different sides. ((Looks at Brita.))
33		[(2.5)]
34	Brita:	[((Nods.))]
35	Tom:	Right?
36	Brita:	Yea.

After Clare states that the lamp glows on one side only and ascertains her conviction (turn 20), Tom asks for an elaboration. Now Brita takes a turn, talking about the charge distributions in the two plates, using the terms "positive" and "negative" (turn 22). But she stops her attempt at an explication, making public her frustration to others at the table.

Tom takes over the turn at talk (turn 23). He structures his sentence such that we can hear it as a way of addressing the frustration: "Isn't it that the electrons are only on one side, on the other there are not enough of them." Tom attempts to make the women see the events through the fourth lens, the microphysical view, according to which electrons are in abundance on one plate but lack on the other (therefore giving rise to positive charges). He uses his body and hands to enact a movement, which, from his perspective, denotes the movement of the electrons from the plate to his left to the other on the right. But he does not make the differences between the layers explicit, in fact, blending them into one composite map.

Figure 5.12. Tom explains how the electrons move from one plate to the ground and from the ground to the other plate. Brita (right) and Clare attentively listen and watch.

Tom, who has moved so he now stands closer to the two plates, begins another explication (turn 25), this time concerning the events when the two plates are charged individually. As he describes the phenomenon, he layers an explication on top by enacting what can be seen through the microphysical lens with his body and hand gestures. Thus, the two different observations can be explained in terms of electrons moving from the plate to the ground (Figure 5.12a-b). (I deal with the question whether this picture of the event is in fact appropriate in a subsequent section of this chapter.) Brita simply indicates agreement and Tom requests a description of the events seen through the microphysical lens (turn 27). Clare suggests that the electrons ("they") come up from the ground, and Tom affirms this by enacting the movement that Clare just has described (Figure 5.12b-c). As Brita does not respond and the pause lengthens, Tom takes another turn, re-articulating the relevant observation to be described and explained.

In this interaction, the material perspective appears to be unproblematic. Teacher and students agree that the plates are separated. They do, however, differ in what they see: Tom wants students to articulate observations and then explain them when the events are seen through the fourth (microphysical) lens. The students talk about charges, perhaps viewing events through the second lens, the one yielding a commonsense electrical perspective.

After the fact I can see that the conversation continually is in a precarious state, as it is not clear just which lens is enacted and articulated. From my perspective, the situation is particularly precarious because the participants do not know that they are talking about different things. For example, when Brita and Clare point to the two plates, they clearly manifest what they perceive through their primary lens. Simultaneously, they talk about charges, thereby enacting a second lens, the commonsense electrical one. Tom also points to the two plates (e.g., turns 25, 30). Whereas at one level, he points to the material entities, his gestures enact what happens when looking through the microphysical lens. The two perceptions are layered in his performance. Because both students and teacher point to the material objects, they may assume to be talking about the same thing, when in fact only the part pertaining to the material separation is the same whereas the other part, the one each layers on top of the first, is different. Thinking in terms of maps that are fused, separated, or different allows me to locate where interactional trouble occurs and where participants take aspects of the world as shared. As a result, the interaction participants may be oriented toward each other as if acting in the same world, when in fact they are acting in different worlds—each understood as the result of the different layering processes. The analogy of maps and lenses highlights precisely how two maps are in or out of alignment and how any misalignment leads to communicative difficulties.

LAYERING AND TEACHER EXPLANATIONS

In the previous section, Tom employs gestures as part of his communication. Tom, as teachers generally (Roth, 2002), uses gestures as part of his explanations and interactions with students. In part, these gestures are the same ones found again in the explanations of students. In the previous excerpts, Tom interacts with a group of women. He also interacts with other groups, including a group of male students. The present episode is part of an explanation in which Tom attempts to help a group of male students understand why the lamp glows on opposite sides (different charges) when they test differently charged metal plates. Prior to the episode, students bring a charged rod close to the edge of one metal plate that is touching another metal plate on the opposite edge (Figure 5.3). After separating the two plates, the students bring the lamp first to one then to the other metal plate and, after some prodding similar to that described in the previous section, observe that the lamp first glows on one, then on the other side.

Because the students appear to have trouble producing their explanation, Tom offers one:

> In this situation, there are too many electrons on one side, too few on the other. The electrons have to go in one direction onto the other side. And when you discharge them individually, when you discharge it individually, then there are here for example too many electrons that have to leave. And how is it here? So they have to go there this way. Here they have to leave this way. Here they have to get to thus.

His body movement and hand gestures while uttering the last three sentences are depicted in Figure 5.13. The figure shows that Tom bodily enacts microphysical and mechanical layers at the same time that he talks. Because the conversation is about two plates, subject to a charging process, both represent themselves qua charged objects: they constitute the mechanical layer that serves as ground against which Tom makes available other conversational resources. The charges— phenomenally available by means of a test (the lamp which glows at different ends when brought to each plate separately)—are explained by means of entities not phenomenally available: electrons. The hands, moving from the left plate toward the ground and from the ground toward the right plate, confer a material quality to

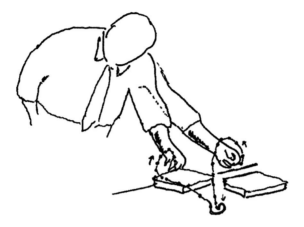

Figure 5.13. Tom explains to a group of boys how to understand that a neon lamp glows on different sides when held to two plates charged by induction and separation. Neither lamp nor action is thematized. The sketch traces the position of the hand during this excerpt, each dot representing the position of the hand on consecutive frames in the video.

these conceptual entities. In this, the gestures constitute a map that explains the different observations. The gestures have iconic quality in instantiating something like a trajectory (see the movement of the teacher's hand). This gesture represents the movement of electrons or electrical current, which are said to move to or from the plate and from and to the ground; in the process, they make the lamp glow. Confusion may arise because the same gesture has different qualities, iconic and metaphorical. On the one hand, the hand is part of the experienced world, and therefore part of the map in which the plates appear materially. On the other hand, the hand constitutes part of the microphysical map, which depicts electrons as particles that move from one place to another. The two maps interact, conferring the microphysical map a sense of materiality that a purely conceptual map does not have.

This depiction of the episode makes salient that there is much more communicated in the entire presentation than what is verbalized. There are several entities present (represent themselves) even when they are not referred to in talk or gesture. Those entities—evidently available to everyone in the situation—generally are not enunciated by means of words but pointed to or made salient through a gesture that enacts some conceptual content over and against it.

In this example, Tom in fact draws on *three* maps and therefore layers them to form *one* explanation. First, there are the metal plates as material objects, which are connected to the ground as intimated in the gesture. (Here, the plates are present, but the lamp is not used as a resource in the explanation.) The electrical ground, salient in the gesture that goes far beneath the table surface, is also perceptually available to students. Second, he talks about electrons that are moving from one plate toward the ground, or from the ground to the other plate. Finally, there is an electrical picture of "stuff" flowing from or to plates. The gestures suggest that the electrons, as material entities, actually move from the plate and into the ground, here represented by the table, which Tom touches midway on the trajectory from one plate to the other (Figure 5.13). In this explanation, each electron makes the entire journey, although in the accepted explanation, electrons are more like a fixed fluid, which as a whole moves a bit in the conductor until charge equilibrium is reached.

Electrons here are entities from a conceptual layer. Yet by pointing, using hands, moving hands along imaginary trajectories taken by these conceptual entities Tom attributes to these entities material quality. In this, these conceptual entities are attributed material qualities. These conceptual entities, when layered against the phenomenally available world, are said to explain what everyone can see, although they are never observable themselves. My way of representing the situation in multiple layers makes salient all those aspects of communicative acts that are not available when only words are transcribed. At the same time, my way of representing shows that knowledgeability displayed in communication is more complex than uttering and attending to words and propositional statements more generally.

THEORIZING IS ALIGNING LAYERS

In this chapter, I use an analogy involving maps, lenses, and layering to analyze the curriculum and classroom events in a classroom where students are asked to construct explanations of electrostatic phenomena. The analogy highlights the complexity of learning involved when complex theoretical frameworks are to be constructed on the basis of simple experiment, especially when the frameworks require different maps that have to be coordinated.

One can understand the entities present in the laboratory context as a stable but indeterminate ground that is not (does not have to be) represented in talk; it constitutes a primary layer. Deictic gestures and verbal deictic expressions can pick them out whenever necessary, such as when Tom stops with his hands on the table, which thereby is signified as electrical ground. Iconic gestures—or movements that are part of the action and deployed in the investigation—animate the situation but do not have to be represented in talk. Upon these perceptual elements as a stable ground, students graft other layers that together constitute the phenomena and explications the students learn and learn about. However, to make any sense, the conceptual layers have to be properly aligned with the phenomenal world given to them directly in their sensual experience: the required coordination work has to be learned and done. Gestures and deictic expression allow this coordination across multiple levels, as shown in chapters 6 and 7.

Laboratory investigations employed in science education therefore can be understood in this way: The experiential, sensual ground provides a base layer onto which further layers can be grafted that do not come from the experiential but from the discursive and other representational domains. Such grafting can be seen throughout the episodes, enacted by students and teacher. Thus, Tom explains the different (intensity, side) ways a neon lamp glows when held to a pair of aluminum plates electrically charged by means of induction and separation. In this situation, those aspects of the phenomenal world necessary in the experiment are present. His articulation—mostly gestures and deictic words—layer a microscopic explanation on top of the event already available perceptually to the students.

When different layers are involved, they may have to be made salient so that the different discourses and their connections can be made salient, too. Without the explicit articulation of these different layers, interaction participants such as Tom, Carla, and Brita may not be aware of the fact that they are talking about different things (entities, terms), or rather, that they are making salient different perceptions brought about by the different lenses that they are using and layering on top of the experiential one that they all take for granted and shared. It is the presupposed common nature of the base layer that allows the confusion to remain hidden, as it is the perceptually available one, whereas the others are conceptual (ideal). Gestures, which may be both part of the material world and signs that denote conceptual entities, allow the slippage between different maps and lenses. That is, gestures construe linkages between layers and partially fuse them, especially when conceptual entities, such as electrons and atoms, are reified as material entities that exist at the same level as the material stuff of which the worldly objects in the shared setting are made of, including the bodies of the participants. The coordination of and movement between different layers constitute changes in communicative forms that underlie the learning episodes described in the next two chapters. Words, too, allow such slippage to occur, when they are used to predicate material entities to stand for things other than themselves ("This [pen] *is the atomic shell*")—I return to this issue in chapter 6.

Gestures that embody conceptual entities—because of their inherently phenomenal, iconic, and metaphoric qualities—may lead to inferences and images that are not scientific at all. Scientists who already know adapt their presentations (utterances and gestures) to the requirements of the conversation so that the "essential" aspects are represented "correctly." Physicists and astronomers know when "to switch code" from everyday talk, "the sun rises," to Newtonian talk, "the Earth rotates"; they know when to don particular lenses. Thus, when Tom explains the discharging of the two plates via the neon lamp, he uses a gesture in which the hand moves from the plate to the ground. Simultaneously, he talks about "them," presumably the electrons that become the explanation for the charged plate (at no time does he speak about the current). The gesture evidently indicates something that moves all the way from the plate to the ground. Yet, physicists do not model what makes this phenomenon in terms of electrons that move along the entire trajectory of his hand, that is, from metal plate to ground. Rather, while there is an electrical current from the plate to the ground, individual electrons only move a little way along the conducting path metaphorically enacted by the gesture. Physics educators often use the image of a train that moves from the beginning to the end of the platform although each wagon only moves a bit.

The danger Tom's explanation embodies then is that learners may take his gesture as indicating individual electrons to move all the way from the plate to the ground (or vice versa). That is, Tom depicts a map (model) that is in conflict with the one that is to be developed only a few weeks later when the curriculum is concerned with electrical currents. The particle model as enacted here, where the electrons move along a conducting path from some source to some sink of electrons, is incompatible with the model of current electricity to be taught only a few weeks later. It in fact embodies a way of articulating events that conceptual change researchers have come to denote by the term "misconception." That is, although Tom is not likely to "have misconceptions" about electricity, his embodied communication articulates the phenomena in a non-standard way. As his communicative forms are all that he makes available to students, he is in fact teaching a "misconception."

In contrast to the learners, a person familiar with the field might read the gesture endpoints as deictic instantiations of *electrical source* and *electrical sink*, and the intermediate part as an instantiation of the topology of the conductor. A physicist may see in Tom's gestures a reference to a very different map, much in the same way that the science educator in chapter 1 meant the thumbs-up gesture to refer to the right-hand rule rather than to stand for itself to be taken literally. When asked about the actual movement of the electron, the physicist then draws on the standard model similar to the water pipe. Here, each particle does not have to move along the entire connection; rather, the liquid moves as a liquid column. That is, gestures obtain additional interpretive flexibility; when interpreted in words (translated into another signifying medium), there is a greater flexibility then when the sense-making process remains in the same medium (word to word) of the same culture.

The analogy of the maps allows understanding the difference between *sense* and *meaning*. Connecting different maps means connecting different ways of expressing one and the same thing. Here, the things to be expressed are phenomena. The new expressions derive from ways of communicating typical of the scientific community. Making sense, therefore, means coordinating layers, which constitute different ways of expressing "the same thing." Sense, if there is any, therefore is what students make. Students do not make meaning, as it is the condition of their being in the world. Meaning is constituted by the connectedness of a familiar world always already known through practical experience, in praxis.

PART III

WORLD AND LANGUAGE

Language often is treated as something special; and it is done so in an inappropriate way. Language is not *just* something special because it allows humans to do things that animals or plants do not do: talk about events that have taken place and about things that have been used elsewhere. I fully agree that language is something special in this sense. But language receives a special status, as if it were something special *ontologically*, as a being. Thus, gestures only sometimes are taken into account without given equal special status; but most researchers completely leave out from interaction analysis body orientations, as if these had nothing to do with the way humans orient in the world, to one another, and as if these had nothing to do with making interactions work. Similarly, the setting itself is part of what is being communicated without having to be articulated, *exactly* because it is perceptually available and therefore goes without saying (Roth & Pozzer, 2006). Thus, from a videotaped interaction, researchers may provide a transcript, as in the following excerpt spoken while the participants are oriented together with others toward an electroscope on the laboratory table (Figure III.1).

Excerpt III.1

01 Brita: Yea, the pointer always repels itself.
02 Tara: Yea, why?
03 Brita: Yea, because there ((Points to the electroscope [Figure III.1])) are
            also electrons.

Figure III.1. Tara, front, interrogates Clare, Jenny, Iris, and Brita (left to right) about the electroscope. Brita (far right) articulates their findings while pointing to the instrument.

To produce Excerpt III.1, I first have to parse a continuous sound stream coming from the tape recording and speakers; I am predisposed to hear the sound stream as words, just as I am *predisposed* to hear other sound streams as coming from birds outside my office window, the wind in nearby trees, my neighbor's dog barking, or my chicken's cooing. Thus, in a first, automatic translation, I am converting sounds into words. When I put these words on the page, it is generally assumed that this is what interaction participants really have said. Researchers then wonder about the "meaning" individual words have or the "meaning" that the participants "make" or "construct." In this situation, therefore, words have been abstracted from their material body in a first step, and then, in a second step, have given a particular quality. The material body, sound, and its signification have been split; and signification has been attributed a special quality. However, words do not have meaning; even when there are no words, human beings experience situations as meaningful. At best, words accrue to meaning, that is, are useful to articulate and be articulated in particular settings.

Let me therefore return to the videotapes. They provide sounds. To properly understand and theorize such situations, I have to begin with sound rather than with "words," lest I attribute special ontological status to the former (Mikhailov, 1980). That the words are but sounds is no clearer than in situations where I have difficulties hearing what is said. I can hear that somebody utters something, but all I hear is indeterminate sound. I cannot hear a word; the sound is not paired with sense. It is as if there is a hole in the flow of words that I can otherwise make out. (Question marks are often used in transcripts when words are inaudible, approximately one for each word unheard.) Under special circumstances, however, I may hear (much) later, what has been said. As soon as someone else provides a possible hearing, or when, after repeated hearing, I have a hypothesis about what it might be that someone says.

In this situation, therefore, I am confronted with the real entity that the video-tape provides: sounds—in addition, of course, I am confronted with images. But here, too, what it is an individual does is a matter of interpretation. Thus, I may wonder whether in Episode III.1 (Figure III.1) Brita is really pointing toward the electroscope or merely holding her hand in a particular way? Should I not provide an image of the situation in the way it is available to the interaction participants? For the participants, already the way in which they orient themselves in and to the situation provides a sense of what is going on. The configuration of the situation, who asks questions, who answers, how each is oriented, and so on all is central to practical understanding in situation. The danger in transcriptions such as that featured in Excerpt III.1 lies in the fact that everyday interactions are reduced to the discursive domain. "Everything is discourse," is the rallying cry of many self-described postmodernist researchers. Even when some researchers do not subscribe to modernism, they treat language in a special way, taking as an unproblematic tool that human beings use to make their provide thoughts and conceptual frameworks public.

In this third part of the book, I articulate a different way of thinking about language. Historically, language has emerged during and is co-constitutive with anthropogenesis. Initially, sounds accompanied much of what pre-humans did. They were fused with their situations such that sensible sounds and their situated sense were one. All I have to do is observe primates and I am provided with evidence that they too, produce sounds. Sometimes a sharp "cry" is followed by the dispersal of a group, and, when I am lucky, the video shows a predator prowling nearby. The dangerous situation and the sound are irreducible. The predator, sound, and dispersal all are part of what I denote by "dangerous situation." At other times, a large male animal stands erect, produce growling sounds with its vocal cords, and perhaps pound its chest like a drum. Another, close-by male distances itself. I may denote this by the term "exhibiting dominance." This shows that sounds already prior to anthropogenesis had the function to reveal an aspect of being. Sound production therefore is not reducible to the inner psychic working of thought.

The embodied nature of human beings, however, has allowed a split to occur at the moment of anthropogenesis, according to which sound and situation (sense) separated, so that the former could be used to refer to other situations (sense). Thus, the sharp cry has come to have the sense of "dangerous situation" independent of the dangerous situation itself. The sound of the cry refers me to something different, ephemeral, immaterial, and therefore ideal: sense. Similarly Human beings may be led to tell a story about dominance and communicating superior status, producing growling sounds without actually attempting to intimidate others present. But for the animals, the situation and sound are one: Male animals do not sit together in a group to tell stories about how they chased another animal away, reproducing the sounds but standing for another situation. When a big male growls, others distance themselves; when there is a sharp cry, others dissipate.

What these examples show is that already primates take up a position in their lifeworlds and use sounds. Taking position and producing sounds, moving about, making gestures, and orienting all are part of the way individual beings interact with other beings. Thus, while producing the sounds that I transcribed in Excerpt III.1, the teacher Tara and the students Carla, Jenny, Iris, and Brita are positioned around a laboratory table *oriented* toward the electroscope (Figure III.1). Brita stretches out her arm and index finger and brings them close to the instrument while talking. She is not just talking. Brita is taking up a position with respect to what all take to be the topic of talk: she orients her body, raises her arm and brings the hand forward and into a pointer configuration, and begins to speak. Others see in this an intentional act, and without much interpretation, know what is possibly intended. The others, too, are oriented toward the thing "being pointed to" and have taken up a position, here as attentive audience. Being in science class with the teacher and being oriented to a particular scene already constitutes a lens for understanding the ongoing event.

For human beings, sounds also have a second and even a third type of function: sounds are secondary and tertiary artifacts (Wartofsky, 1979) when they are used reflexively to denote the same sounds used in different situations. That is, sounds (words) initially produced as part of an *in-order-to* orientation can also be used in other situations (e.g., interview, moment of reflection, story) to refer to the original situation, that is, to talk *about* what happened then and there. When I talk about what I am currently doing, writing this book, I am *providing an account of* what I am doing. The relation of language with respect to the original situation is different in the two cases. A third situation can be thought of: one in which language not only is *about* the primary situation but also to explain the content of the account. In this case, language is used to theorize rather than merely to describe. It has become a tertiary artifact. The two ways of talking are not the same, though related; the difference is best understood in terms of *observation sentences* and *observation categoricals* (Quine, 1995), only the latter of which explain, whereas the former describe. These two different functions of language, too, can be understood as the results of looking at the world through different lenses and of providing different maps for understanding it.

In its function as secondary and tertiary artifact, language is derivative (Heidegger, 1977/1996). In its primary function, as discourse, it is *"existentially equiprimordial with attunement and understanding. Discourse is articulation of intelligibility"* (p. 161 [150], original emphasis). Here, I understand "attunement" as integral and constitutive part of the situation and "understanding" as *practical understanding* distinct from *theoretical understanding*. Practical understanding precedes all explication of itself and of the situation; it is the condition for theoretical knowledge, which cannot but explicate what is already understood. I exhibit my attunement to the situation, for example, through my physical orientation, making it available to others, who also make their attunement available to me. Heidegger is justified to say that discourse is articulation of intelligibility, *because* the situation as a whole is meaningful rather than because words "have" meaning.

In this part III of the book, I begin with the first function of language, its use *in order to* get something done. It is part of taking up and communicating a position and articulating intelligibility. More so, speaking does not require prior thoughts: speaking *is* thinking. When I speak in everyday situations I do not think of grammar, think of a topic, search for words, and then render what I have come up with by producing sounds. This is how computer scientists design computers. Everything a computer says is pre-figured in advance, has been assembled, and when ready, is pushed through the voice synthesizer. Human beings are not robots or artificial intelligence software. I speak in real time. When I begin a sentence, I do not know what the sentence will be that I will have produced in ending. I do not select words in my long-term memory but the words come to me as I speak. And when I have the sense that what I have said is complete, grammatically and topically, I may abandon my turn at talk. And yet, the sounds (words) I produce are not random even if they are not selected beforehand. Rather, when I begin to speak, I take up orientation and position towards the situation as I practically understand it, and in producing sounds for talking about something I also produce the situation as and for what it is. This is the topic of the first of the three chapters that follow. I am also concerned in this chapter 6 with how learners distance themselves from the situation constitutive of their experience and then talk about it, such as when students initially attempt to observe and create description and then stand back to produce a language for explaining what they have observed and subsequently articulate this for someone else.

The fact that I do not privilege language beforehand but regard it as something at the same level as other productions—orientation, pointing, iconic gestures, and perceptual configurations in the world—comes with theoretical advantages. Thus, I can ask myself how a scientific language emerges from situations in which students manipulate artifacts without talking at the same time. This attunes me to the forms of communication that precede *language about* something, including pointing gestures, things in the world, iconic gestures, and even manipulations—all of which are precursors of observational and explanatory written language. Thus, when students are asked to explain what they have found out very early in their explorations and investigations, they often say, "Look!," and then repeat producing the phenomenon. They do not talk about what they have done but rather ask the teacher to look. Such changes from initial manipulations to discourse about investigations and to written language are the topic of chapter 7.

In chapter 8, I take a look at the reverse trajectory from language to the world in the attempt to answer these questions: "How do I get from patterned ink traces on a page (i.e., text, words, letters), for example, instructions for preparing a particular meal, to something in the world, for example, a completed dish that my guests enjoy?" "How are words on a page or uttered by an instructor related to the things that someone does so that the latter (instructions) can be said to be the implementation of the former?" and "How do I follow instructions and under what conditions can I be said to have followed them?" I liken instructions to roadmaps because both provide me with resources for getting around the world. Both also require familiarity with the territory they describe—which contrasts the presupposition that we can learn *about* experiential things without experience of them. As I am writing these lines, I am thinking of the analysis of Brazilian high school science textbooks (conducted together with my graduate student Lilian Pozzer), which also contain texts about snow and particular ecozones where snow is frequent. I also know about the incredulous and exhilarating experiences all my Brazilian graduate students go through when they experience snow for the first time. All of their readings of snow have not prepared them—or their understanding—for this experience. That is, no instruction can prepare me for what I am coming to face when I actually (attempt to) do what it asks me to.

TAKING UP AND COMMUNICATING A POSITION

In the three chapters of part II, I describe how lifeworlds are disclosed in and to perception as human beings move about in them; or rather, I describe how the lifeworlds of learners expand, include aspects and phenomena heretofore not present; or rather again, I describe how individuals move about in their lifeworlds and in the process articulate them in different figure|ground configurations captured in and denoted by different maps. Although body and hand movements and manipulations are described, I have not placed them at the center of my descriptions. In this and the following two chapters, I am centrally concerned with how people take up a position in the world they know so well and, through their bodily movements and manipulations, bring to light new features of the setting, thereby enlarging or further articulating and refining their lifeworlds—what is apparent to them in their consciousness and actions. The position I take in the world is coextensive with my disposition, both a different position and a different frame of mind; position frames the way in which different communicative modes, each of which can be understood in terms of the layering of maps and lenses, come to be aligned and change.

In much of the literature on science and science education, the knowing person is described in information processing and machine terms: As in commonsense, the human body is described as a machine, and thinking in terms of the search, processing, and storage of bits of information not unlike the way in which computers and robots are constructed. There are mental models ascribed to me, and operations that are required to get from knowing A to knowing B, the difference of which is articulated in terms of the notion *learning*. The points A and B are characterized by different structures of mind, and the change therefore is thought of as cognitive or conceptual change. In such descriptions, knowing and learning are lifeless; they do not really pertain to me, a living human being. These lifeless forms of learning can be implemented in machines and artificial intelligence programs. Although science educators do not experience themselves as implementing a program for walking but walk, some do subscribe to ideas about knowing in terms of conceptions and conceptual frameworks. But do I behave and reason like computers, continuously weighing options, reasoning in the way I do when I defend and critique some argument? I know that I do not think and behave in this way. Rather as I orient in and to a situation, I am simultaneously given a world. This world, intelligible to me, I articulate in all its intelligibility to others by using discourse, itself always and already imbued with intelligibility.

For a long time, I-author neither thought about knowing in this way, nor understood that an overall orientation *in and to the situation* is so central to what human beings do. That is, until I have had experiences of the following nature, which I recorded during an ongoing battle with chronic fatigue syndrome and fibromyalgia, an experience associated with focus and concentration.

> I am frequently finding myself in the kitchen while preparing some dinner, needing a particular item for continuing in the recipe for the day. I turn about walk toward the wall, open a cupboard, only to find that it does not contain what I need. Rather, what I need is in a drawer below. That is, in all these cases, I have been turning into the right direction and oriented appropriately to that part of the kitchen. But I open the incorrect door or drawer. Sometimes I do not know what it is that I need, and yet find myself in some position. It is only upon reflecting that realize where I am in the preparation of the dinner and that the thing I need is in the particular part of the kitchen that I am currently oriented to.

I take this situation in a way that Harold Garfinkel (1967) made thematic with his breaching experiments, which take participants into situations where their normal ways of doing things no longer work so that they begin to exhibit precisely those competencies that underlie normal everyday behavior to deal with the situation of breakdown. In my situation, mediated by the illness, the nested nature of my navigation of everyday situation has become apparent. By turning around and walking into the particular direction until I am in front of the cupboards, I am taking up position, orienting toward a particular part of my kitchen and the things and needs associated with them, and only then focus on opening a particular door or drawer and subsequently begin to look for a particular tool. The orientation suitably limits (frames) the action possibilities and therefore the amount of considering I need to do for coping in and with the situation.

The point here is that normally there is no disjuncture between orienting and opening some drawer or cabinet door, just as there is no disjuncture between orienting and talking. In talking, I orient and communicate orientation; and my orientation communicates as much as my talking. This experience of the disjuncture tells me that orienting constitutes a larger frame within which particular goal-directed actions and conditioned operations are made available and constrained. The disjunctures have never occurred somewhere along all possible paths between my standing in front of the preparation and the position in front of the required item. Every time I have had such an experience, the disjuncture has occurred between the general position and opening the particular cupboard or drawer. Therefore, the things in my kitchen are not randomly distributed in space and my actions are not generated according to a master plan. I evidently do not know about the things by knowing their absolute coordinates, in the way a computer might store and remember where things are in my kitchen, that is, their spatial coordinates. Rather, the fact that I find myself in a particular position shows that things are associated with orientations; and my actions are associated with my orientations and the position the things are in. I do not have to plan opening the drawer, as getting to the kitchen knife implies opening and closing a drawer when I find it closed but does not imply opening when I find it open.

Coming to know therefore also means finding orientations, which constitute the frames within which particular actions (material, communicative) make sense. These orientations constitute frames for what I do and are both material and social in nature. What I say and how I say it depends on whom I am talking to and what the nature of the societal activity is I currently participate in; and I do talk without reflecting, like a computer that would search for "scripts." The situations are given to me, as and with my lifeworld, and with them, my orientations. These orientations, the societal activities, and my lifeworld are irreducible units. Therefore, the orientations, which frame the way I open myself to the world, constitute the very frames *to which* actions and words *accrue* as meaningful ways of behaving. In other words, it is not the material and communicative actions themselves that are meaningful but rather there are frames and orientations in and toward the lifeworld in relation to which material and communicative actions make sense. Meaning, therefore, is not something that gets attached to words and things. Rather, if there is any meaning, then it is in the densely connected frames and orientations, and actions and words come to be part of these existing meaning wholes.

When I— e.g., as a student—find myself in new situations, such as when I am asked to engage in some science laboratory task, I have to bring forth a world. Toward this world, I establish an orientation before I can develop a set of material and verbal actions that have any notable coherence. Jenny, Clare, and all the other students in this book orient themselves in this way; they have to find an orientation so that their actions and words can make any sense at all. They do so through their living bodies and lived experience, as human beings, not as thinking machines and computers that are made of "wet ware" rather than "hardware."

This chapter is centrally concerned with orienting and finding a stance, and therefore setting oneself up for acting, both manipulating the world and talking to others. Although I am describing students, and therefore write in the third person, Jenny (as her peers) always acts as from her first-person perspective, within her familiar lifeworld. Readers have to understand the following account as one through her eyes: I am looking outwards facing others and the material world, I am orienting and finding a position, I am articulating an idea, which comes together as I am talking about it. I do not completely know it in advance, but what is described comes to be articulated, takes on a figure|ground configuration.

ORIENTING, FINDING A STANCE

Communicating, above all, means to find an orientation that frames what I utter and do; this orientation, as I show in chapter 4, frames the way in which I take care in and of the situation. This is so because to the unity of the discourse corresponds a unity of perspective; and to the forms and articulations of the discourse correspond the forms and articulations of the perspective. Finding an orientation therefore frames both perspective and constitutes the condition for the unity of the discourse. The orientation—and the perspective that derives from it—does not stand beside the words, that is, in an external manner. Rather, in discoursing, I continually accomplish a perspective that fuses with the words and animates them from the inside (Husserl, 1929/1969). As a result of this animation, words, and discourse as a whole, embody the orientation and perspective and carry it within them in the form of sense. This can be seen clearly in the following episode, which derives from the first lesson on static electricity. The tenth-grade students have been invited to explore electrostatic phenomena after Tara (the teacher) has shown how the rubbing of two materials generates static electricity. Tara has told them that they may either design their own investigations or use prepared instructions. The students have available a variety of materials, including cloth from different materials (wool, cotton), rods (PVC, steel, plastic), spheres (with and without metal coats), and plastic transparency sheets. In the episode, Jenny gets ready and then articulates an idea for an investigation. She says:

> You can also do it like this. We have done it before. Then you hold it under the water tap. Then you hold it to the water tap. And then you can pull it away with it. And the water goes. And when the water goes thus, then the water goes this way.

Taken by itself, the text Jenny produces in this episode cannot be understood. This text is a typical instance of spoken language (discourse), which is always situated in the setting, as speakers do not have to articulate verbally all those things that go without saying, literally. Readers may be able to infer that Jenny talks about water and that it can be pulled in some way; there is also something about holding an entity to the water tap. Watching the videotape and hearing Jenny talk and knowing that the context of her talk is a class on static electricity, and perhaps knowing the phenomenon itself, allows me to articulate the central idea of her presentations in this way: I-Jenny can deflect a water current that runs from a tap by approaching an electrically charged transparency film sideways to it. But the text produced does not make this investigation or demonstration apparent. Jenny does not articulate verbally what a reader needs to understand what she says. Thus, whereas my re-statement of the idea may sound trivial, Jenny in fact makes a dense statement including physical phenomena (objects, events) that are produced by means of human actions, and explanations. The following more elaborate presentation of the event as seen on the videotape depicts how Jenny gestures three times the relative movements of water current and transparency film associated with different verbal descriptions of what should be salient at that moment.

Jenny begins by rubbing and thereby charging a transparency sheet. By means of gestures that make use of the materials at hand, and before the ground of other unused materials, Jenny orients toward the world and drawing on the resources at hand, develops new descriptions and explanations that have not existed before in this classroom. She is totally involved, bodily orienting toward and expressing a world that becomes present to her peers. She brings the investigation to life, enacts a description of it before and in the face of her group mates. This investigation is expressed in and through her body and cannot be understood as some conception as if Jenny was a computer with a program and memory where what she is going to say is already prefigured. Jenny is talking, communicating in and through her whole body, and as such, she is finding and defining a world, which she continu-

01   And then you can pull away with it

Figure 6.1. Jenny articulates, in gesture, body orientation, position, and talk how to conduct the demonstration.

ally develops. At each point, what she has already said and gestured becomes resource for what she is saying and gesturing in the flow of now. A story unfolds, in words and material and bodily configuration: She is the center of this story, which she unfolds around her and which thereby becomes available to anyone prepared to listen and watch. Here I take it that ideas and their productions cannot be separated from their public descriptions. It is in her embodied telling that Jenny brings the particular investigation into being, in and as temporalized and temporalizing narrative, not only enacted in talk and gesture, but also framing and framed by the current activity and its setting. (I return to this episode and its temporal aspects of knowing and learning in chapter 9.)

Jenny begins articulating an idea by rubbing and charging the transparency sheet. When she subsequently retells the idea, she omits this step; at this point it is understood that the transparency already is charged whenever students use a transparency as part of their explications. That is, although Jenny does not verbally refer to it as a charged transparency throughout her presentation, she unmistakably (to all participants in the situation) uses it as a charged film in her gestures while enacting the demonstration. Jenny then suggests bringing the prepared transparency sheet next to the water current. While uttering this statement, she still is rubbing the transparency—which lies on the tabletop—with a piece of cloth. However, she repeats the statement, accompanied by the gesture of holding the transparency in the air with her left hand, the right hand appearing next to it as she utters "water tap." Once she establishes her orientation, Jenny, in, as, and through her body, becomes an expression of the situation (Figure 6.1). (Running their eyes back and forth over the images, readers can animate the situation depicted.)

Jenny suggests that the water current can be pulled with the (charged) transparency. Her left hand moves the sheet away from the right hand, which thereby comes to stand for the water flowing from the tap. But as my drawing shows, her right hand stays in place across the three frames (Figure 6.1). That is, whereas her left hand, which holds the transparency sheet, moves back and forth, her right hand does not move. In her talk, she articulates something that is pulled. That is, Jenny is setting up a situation to which she orients and now she is in the process of articulating events as they unfold. However, just as I have been finding myself in front

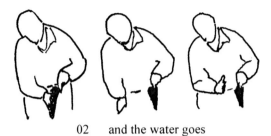

02   and the water goes

Figure 6.2. Jenny articulates again an action and the corresponding observation.

of a cupboard without knowing what I am looking for, Jenny finds herself articulating a story that contains a contradiction. On the one hand, she verbally articulates for her peers a water stream that is pulled. On the other hand, however, she
her gesture articulates a stationary water current. But in and with her body, she
does articulate an orientation, to the water tap and current, and the way in which
the charged transparency film has to be held.

At this point, it may still be unclear what exactly happens to the water. As can
be seen in line 02 (Figure 6.2), Jenny moves the right hand away from the film and
upward into a vertical position as if indicating the (inverse) water flow. Here, I am
not claiming that she deliberately makes this movement, as if she had calculated it
beforehand. Rather, the vertical movement of the hand, which comes to stand for
the water, is produced as part of the orientation; it is an integral and constitutive
part of it. It is the next thing to do, even without reflecting about it. Thus, the right
hand makes thematic not only the water but also its flow, thereby increasing the
number of resources available to others for making sense of her presentation. Here,
the right hand makes the flow thematic, and, because it is an integral and constitutive part of the person, it is Jenny, the person, who articulates these aspects. She
produces the articulation even if there were no conscious deliberations that preceded the hand movements. It is always in and through my body that I-speaker
express myself as much as I-speaker emerge from these expressions as an individual human being who articulates something for other human beings.

In the final stage, then, Jenny begins her description again by thematizing water,
its downward flow, the movement of the charged film, and the action of pulling
(Figure 6.3). In this latest attempt, Jenny does not have to re-thematize the charging process for this is already implied in the transparency stands for itself. It is recognizably available as a charged entity for any body else present in the situation.
Verbally articulating the charging again might have been taken as strange or exces-
sive. That is, although the representation merely shows the transparency, it has in
fact already been prepared and therefore represents (as a sense-making resource) a
more complex situation than the transparency by itself—that is, without context.

There are four parts to the entire episode, the first referring to the preparation of
a charged transparency (not represented here) and three parts in which the experiment is constructed. In the second part, the left hand enacts the movement of the

03   and when the water goes thus, then the water goes this way

Figure 6.3. Jenny achieves a coherent articulation during this third attempt.

transparency sheet whereas the hand representing the water stays still (line 01 [Figure 6.1]). In the third part, the right hand gestures the lateral and vertical directions in which the water moves (line 02 [Figure 6.2]), although in the reverse way in both instances. It is then in the fourth and final part that Jenny in, through, and as of her boy coordinates the two movements, assembling the results of her earlier actions. The water current moves vertically down and is deflected sideward in response to the movement of the charged transparency (line 03 [Figure 6.3]).

An inspection of the three lines of transcript provides evidence for the increasing complexity of the situation presented. The public description, having occurred for a first time, has been produced in real time taking about nineteen seconds. Jenny subsequently provides another description of this proposal after a group mate absent during the first presentation returns to the table. In this new presentation one can observe (a) a dramatic decrease in the number of gestures, (b) an increase in discursively represented entities, and (c) a decrease in the total time of the explanation to about eleven seconds. For example, she only gestures the movement of the transparency and subsequently indicates briefly the vertical downward motion of the water current in the second account. That is, more of the description of what she articulates as plan for a group investigation is expressed verbally. This then makes the gestures coincide when they appear, presenting redundant information, perhaps making the gestures ultimately unnecessary. In sum, therefore, after she has assembled the description into a coherent whole and while drawing on materials and gestures, these resources played a lesser role in subsequent presentations when the idea was presented to a greater extent in verbal form.

When watching the young women during this explanation of an experiment, it is clear that Jenny is organizing a world in which she orients toward the material objects and the unfolding narrative in which they figure. The two others present during the first articulation of the idea watch and attend to what she has to say (Figure 6.4). They, too, are oriented to the materials, watching Jenny first rub the transparency sheet, then following her gestural enactment of what the experiment is to show. Together, the three constitute the topic common to all, in their attention to one and the same articulation. Clare and Brita, therefore, are integral to the articulation of the event, not just Jenny as this might appear from my first account. They

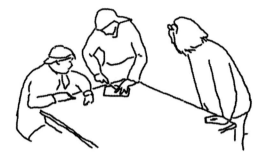

Figure 6.4. Jenny (center) is oriented toward the material objects and the description of the experiment she proposes. Clare (left) and Brita (right) attend to her demonstration.

are integral part of the constitution of the idea because it is for them and in a way that they find intelligible that the account takes shape.

More so, the situation as a whole has its place and is constitutive of a science lesson in a German grammar school at this point in time. What they do together, the investigation, they collaboratively articulate: Jenny through her presentation and Brita and Clare through their attendant orientation. They reproduce a classroom event recognizable as a hands-on, student-centered curriculum. This, too, is the frame that is both a resource for Jenny and her peers for orienting to the topic, and which they reproduce in and through their actions right then and there. The articulation clearly is a social as much as it is an individual one. Jenny, in fact, is not merely orienting to the materials and narrative. She says what she says for the others, proposing an experiment that they can do together. She uses words that already make sense to others, are intelligible. Jenny therefore returns these words to the other. Her orientation, which appears to be solely to the narrative and materials, is in fact embedded in another orientation—the orientation to others.

The social nature of the articulation goes even deeper. Jenny uses words, words others already are familiar with. She says, "you can do it like this," while rubbing the transparency film with a plastic ruler, which, as their previous actions have shown, produces static electricity. That is, when she says "you can do it like this," she presupposes and can do so legitimately, that she does nothing else but articulate something that others can already find intelligible. She articulates an idea that does not yet exist but that is already prefigured as possibility in the understanding of others, and Jenny simply highlights that they already share this understanding as a possible one. This understanding is shared because Jenny is not a monad, an independent singularity, but in being is being singular plural. What she says and does is a possibility not only for her but also for all the others in her group and in the course. This orientation toward the other, and others' orientation to her, can be seen clearly in one part of the presentation (Figure 6.5). These words are not only familiar to the others but also appropriate for the situation. These words constitute the situation as much as the situation constitutes the frame that mediates the sense attributed to words. Without this frame, without this orientation, it would be diffi-

Figure 6.5. Jenny reorients by looking at Clare to her right; both Brita and Inga have lifted their gaze to look at Jenny's face, ready to acknowledge her regard.

cult if not impossible for anyone to understand what Jenny has said. She therefore not only orients herself *in* and *to* the situation, but the situation in its entirety constitutes her orientation and communication. Others are oriented equally (Figures 6.4 and 6.5). Therefore, the structure of the situation and its unfolding in time constitute the narrative and the idea rather than the words alone.

Jenny's orientation toward the object and narrative therefore is nested within the lifeworld that the three young women take as shared, the physics classroom, within which their task is to construct experiments and explanations. They can legitimately take the situation as shared, because they are not independent singularities but singularities expressing plurality itself. Jenny expresses the plurality, shared understanding, with and through her being, only part of which is consciously available to her at any one moment in time. When her hands gesture, she does not control them consciously. There is no little person whispering into her ear to move her hands in this or that way. Rather, the hand movements constitute Jenny's idea as much as Jenny is the source of the hand movements. This is, to me, the sense of the notion of embodied cognition: I am who I am in and through my body, not merely a rational computer placed in a body that it animates. My gestures specifically and my body more generally animate me as much as my conscious thought animates my bodily self. I, my body, and my mind not only are indistinguishable but also irreducible; and I am an irreducible part of the situation so that who I am and what I do is as much an outcome of the situation as a whole as it is the result of my (intentional) agency.

Some readers may reject as self-evident the idea that the unit me-body-mind is irreducible. But if this is the case, then the self-evident frequently is not addressed in science education. Actions and discourse are treated as if these were expressions of intents already fixed in mind and oriented toward some object. Students are said to make sense of the experiment, or more frequently, that they make meaning of words, events, and the natural world. In such articulations, there is little to find about the orientation that students articulate not only to words, events, and the natural world but also to other participants that contribute to constituting the event;

and there is little about the mutually constitutive nature of individual and collective. Cultural-historical activity theorists on the other hand point out that one needs to analyze events in terms of three different levels, activity, action, and operation. Orientation toward the action, intending to describe an experiment always occurs within a larger frame. And only because understanding already exists in this larger frame do communicative acts in the form Jenny produces them here make sense.

DISTANCING

Talking, as writing, always occurs in some setting, always has a context. At one level, therefore, I bring forth words, as other forms of action, *in order to* do something. But sometimes, I talk about other situations that are distant in time and space. At these times, I am removed and, from the remove, talk about what is, is happening, was, or has happened at a different time or in a different place. My words and gestures, though they are about and pertain to these other places and these other times, are no longer uttered then and there. I use them here and now even though their original setting and context is not present. The words and gestures no longer have the same context and in this sense, they are decontextualized. They have been abstracted, taken away from the original situation and are used again in a new context and for new purposes. They are no longer in order to do the same something as before, but for a different purpose, to achieve a different activity. There is a distancing involved.

In the previous section, there already is some distancing between Jenny and the situation she describes. When Jenny explains the investigation her group should conduct, she, too, talks about a water tap, which is not present while she is speaking. On the other hand, the transparency sheet she would be using in the investigation actually is there. In her first articulation of what they ought to do, Jenny even rubs the transparency sheet extensively, thereby charging it, and then uses it as part of the description. Subsequently, when she articulates the description again, she does not repeat the charging process. Whether or not it is actually charged, the transparency now *stands for* a charged transparency. In the first situation, therefore, rubbing and charging the transparency is identical with articulating the rubbing and charging of a transparency. *The material form of the expression and its sense are one.* The second situation is different. Now, the transparency sheet stands for a *charged* transparency sheet. *The material form of the expression differs from the situation expressed; the material expression and sense have split.*

Standing-for something else is a crucial aspect of words and gestures that allows them to be used in some other situation where the original events are recreated, articulated, and talked about. In this, human beings differ from other animals: humans produce sounds and gestures as part of communications in a reflexive way; expression and thing expressed can have different material bodies and form. But to be able to do so, a distance is required from the normal absorption in the lifeworld so that the latter can be made an object of talk and inquiry. A split has to occur between expression and thing expressed. This requires the lifeworld, which heretofore was indeterminate ground (context) for my action, to become thematic figure.

Such distancing, partially observable in the previous episode, is even more salient in the ones that follow.

When the actual materials with which they conduct their investigations are still present on the laboratory table, students often pick up these materials and use them as part of their explanations. For example, to explain what happens when a charged transparency film is tested for static electricity, students actually pick up a film, rub it, and hold it up—as Jenny has done in producing the plan for an investigation. But there are moments on the videotapes of this classroom when students are asked to provide explanations of phenomena when these materials are no longer available. At this point, students frequently use other material objects to stand in for the original material. In this way, they take up position but this position is no longer in the world originally present. Rather, they take up position in a world populated with entities such as electrons, protons, atomic nuclei, and atomic shells; and these are denoted by a variety of materials taking the place of the inaccessible entities. These are not abstract entities, pure ideas; rather, these entities are treated as if they are material entities, extensions of the lived-in world. In the previous episode, Jenny holds the transparency without rubbing it, but everyone present knows that it *stands for* a charged transparency. The distancing is slight, but the split between expression and sense already has occurred. The distancing is more notable when Matt uses a plastic rod to stand in for and take the place of a metal rod. Here, the material no longer is the same and no longer has the same property, though there is a likeness of shape between the original rod and the one used to stand in for. The representational nature is iconic when Tara, the teacher, holds her right-hand palm above the electroscope to denote a situation where a charged transparency is held over the instrument. Here the shape of the palm suggests a transparency sheet. That is, she is making the distant situation present again by drawing on the perceptual similarity between the palm of her hand and a flat transparency sheet.

Distancing can—and has to, for communication to become scientific—lead to an arbitrary relationship between the material shape of the signifier and the thing signified. It is only when the two have become independent that the material world (praxis) can be modeled independently (theory), allowing different models to be compared and tested. This level of distancing has been achieved in the present episode. Jenny is asked to explain the relationship between the text that they just have read in her group and the investigations that they have completed over the course of the past two lessons. That is, Jenny is to explain why rubbing two objects against each other creates a phenomenon denoted by the term *static electricity*, and why the two objects appear to be charged oppositely, and therefore attract one another. Jenny begins by raising her left hand in which she holds a pen indicating that it stands for the transparency sheet (Figure 6.6). This is a direct link to the investigations during which she has extensively rubbed transparency sheets.

Jenny then uses a beat gesture—a quick up-and-down movement of the hand—to coordinate a specific hand and the things verbally articulated and denoted in the talk. That is, to attune her audience to what "this here" denotes, she produces a small but noticeable movement of one hand. In this way, the entity close to her and in her hand ("this here," "the pen"), which is the subject of the utterance, is predi-

01 This here is, the pen is the atomic nucleus, and this here is the atomic shell

Figure 6.6. Jenny articulates an explanation for the fact that rubbing two materials produces static electricity.

cated as the atomic nucleus ("is the atomic nucleus"). Jenny then raises the second hand in which she holds a second pen. She brings this second pen into play, that is, as resource into the discourse, by means of a verbal index, "this here." She predicates this pen (rather than the "this here"): "is the atomic shell." In this way, she configures the setting to include an atomic nucleus and an atomic shell. These entities now are physically present in and through the entities that denote them. Of course, anyone can see that neither pen *is* an atomic nucleus or *is* an atomic shell. Rather, through the predication ("is atomic nucleus," "is electronic shell"), these pens become signs that stand for what is articulated in the predicate. The "is" does not signify an identity but is the starting point of a predication.

At this point it appears as if the pens simply are non-verbal signifiers accompanying the words "atomic nucleus" and "atomic shell." As the following images on the videotape show, however, the pens stand for nuclei and shells *in the materials rubbed*. That is, there is a sliding transition between the materials used (i.e., the first of the lenses I describe in chapter 5), such as a transparency sheet and a plastic rod, and the microphysical processes said to occur therein (i.e., the fourth of the lenses I describe in chapter 5). There is therefore a gap, which appears when Jenny co-presents objects from two perspectives, one epistemic, as seen through the microphysical lens, and a phenomenal, available through the commonsense material lens. The atoms, their shells, electrons, and positive and negative charges are not what she has experienced during the investigations. Rather, her experience involved materials. It is therefore not surprising to see a second gesture in which she picks up a pen that—though this is not made explicit—stands for the plastic rods that she (as her group mates) has used extensively. As if she had jumped ahead of herself in the first utterance, Jenny backtracks and shows what is happening before unpaired atomic nuclei and atomic shell parts would be observed. Thus, in her next step, she articulates the process of rubbing (Figure 6.7).

Here, then, the elements from two maps are enacted simultaneously and therefore come to be layered: through the phenomenal lens, I can see the gestures iconically denoting the movements that previously have produced the static electricity. That is, Jenny moves her hands and arms in the *same* way that she has moved them when she was actually charging two materials by rubbing them. Simultaneously, she talks; and in this talk, she begins to articulate something else, something that is

02   Yea? Yea? And when one rubs them with this one here

Figure 6.7. Jenny articulates the process of rubbing, which produces the charge separation indicated in the first part of the episode.

to serve as an explication. This something else, the explication, constitutes a different lens, one through which the world is seen as constituted of microscopic entities. The two levels taken together constitute the phenomenon and its explanation.

From an experiential perspective, the gestures have a direct relation to the earlier investigations. Additional objects (e.g., pens) are used to bring in further distinctions and re-presentations). The rubbing is re-enacted and therefore links the discourse related to the perception of the world through the microphysical lens to the sensorimotor experience. In this way, words, orientations, body movements, manipulations and their recreation, and iconic gestures, all aided by beat and pointing gestures, come to be coordinated. Knowing lies in and arises from such coordination and coordination efforts. Together with the social and material setting, they constitute the situation in which particular forms of talk make sense and other forms of talk do not. That is, I do not require the notion of meaning as an attribute that words achieve or as an attribute that students attach to words. Rather, individual words and the utterances in their entirety constitute and find a place in the situation, which in part solicits and mediates the emergence of that very talk.

Importantly, Jenny is distancing herself from the original situation. She talks *about* it. Reproducing the actual movements that she earlier has enacted to produce the static electricity now are used to denote that earlier situation. This reuse constitutes a sort of bridge between "doing charging" and "talking *about* doing charging." Jenny has distanced herself, is in a new position, and yet talks about the earlier situation as if it occurred here and now. But this new and different (i.e., dis-) position also reflects a new disposition, where the articulation and its sense have split thereby rendering what is being articulated more theoretical. More so, she reproduces some of the talk that she has earlier used. She uses the same words, such as "rub," in situations that I denote by "talking *in order to* doing charging" and "talking *about* doing charging." Repeating the actual material, some of the discourse, and some of the hand movements, Jenny makes the original situation present again—she re-presents it—and layers upon this representation the discourse associated with a different lens.

At this point, Jenny has rubbed the two materials. In the course of the next two video frames (Figure 6.8), she then talks about the consequences of this rubbing. Here she shifts into the explanatory mode, that is, provides a description through

03   It creates here a lot of negative charge and

Figure 6.8. Jenny talks about the consequences of rubbing, the creation of negative charges.

the microphysical lens, imposing the map so created over the events she just has reproduced in and through her bodily orientation, stance, and gestures. That is, she has moved from the phenomenal to the discursive domain. In this discursive domain, there are electrical charges, negative and positive ones (Figure 6.9). At the same time, Jenny explains that these are separated in and after the rubbing. She therefore, in the following frames, separates the effect both discursively—negative and positive charges—and gesturally by locating one set of charges (negative) in front of her on the table, the other one at a substantial distance (see left-hand motion in Figure 6.9). In both cases, additional emphases produce pointers that coordinate the discourse and gesture. This emphasizes the distinction and difference between the two types of charges. The separation of charges, which is such a crucial aspect of the phenomenon, is a very clear result of this explanatory demonstration. The separation is more than merely talked into being. Jenny makes the separation present again by enacting a separation: She moves her right hand far away from the other; and she enacts the attraction by bringing together the two hands right in front of the middle part of her body.

Jenny gestures how the two have to be rubbed against each other (line 3 [Figure 6.8]) to produce negative (line 03 [Figure 6.8]) and positive charges (line 04 [Figure 6.9]). These charges, so she explains, produce the attraction between the two rubbed materials (line 04). As part of this explanation, she picks up a third, fountain pen (line 02). As she utters the proposition about the negative charges (line 03), she pulls the cap, places the body of the fountain pen with the "atomic shell"

04   here is positive charge. And therefore they attract each other.

Figure 6.9. Jenny completes describing the consequences of rubbing, the creation of positive charges. The two types of charges then attract each other.

pen to her right, and then holds up the fountain pen cap with the other pen, describing it as being positively charged (line 04). Her final comment relates the microscopic explanation to the macroscopic observation of attraction between the two materials, which she illustrates in her gesture that brings the two separated hands (holding the pens for the charged bodies) back together.

In this situation, the pens stand for various conceptual and material entities. In the process of constructing an explanation and as she represents the various entities, Jenny's explanation changes to become more scientifically correct. That is, Jenny does not just explain, using speech to make available some hidden thoughts, conceptual frameworks, and ideas. Rather, she *performs* the representation of the phenomena; the performance bears resemblance with the performance of the original investigation. The repetition involves slippage between repeating the investigation and talking about it. It thereby bridges the gap that has opened up between the two situations as she makes the original situation present again in a very concrete way. She performs the explanation, that is, she performs what can be seen through another lens, a different kind of map that bears constitutive relation with the other aspect of her performance. Initially, she performs the atomic nuclei with the pen in the left hand, the atomic shell in the left. However, a change over occurs in line 02, where she picks up yet another pen that stands in for one of the two rubbed materials. Then, at the moment she pulls the pen cap and separates it from the body, the two first pens stand in for the two macroscopic materials, whereas the fountain pen body and cap stand in for the conceptual entities: electrons and positive nuclei. This becomes even clearer when, in the final part of her performance, the two materials with the charges, visibly represented as properties, attract each other.

Here, as soon as Jenny identifies the pens as signifiers for the two materials to be rubbed, she does not need to verbally articulate them; holding up the pens and verbal deixis ("hier" [here] and "die" [they], line 04) is sufficient to make present again the materials. With the rubbing gesture, she makes present again (i.e., re-presents, represents) what previously have been manipulative and epistemic (resistance) movements, but which is a symbolic movement in the present case (line 02). Her final gesture, which enacts the attraction iconically, *stands for* the phenomenon that she had earlier observed between two charged materials (e.g., between two films or between rod and Styrofoam ball). Here, the verbs "rubbing" and "attracting" and the corresponding gestures coincide so that there is a certain redundancy in the information communicated (representations made available to the listeners); but this "redundancy" is nothing other than the conflation of material expression and sense. That is, in Jenny's performance, there is both a distancing moment and a moment of rapprochement. Her performance both stands for something else and repeats this something else concretely in the present situation.

In this, Jenny establishes a link between the discursive domain and the experiential domain. The experience of rubbing is re-enacted here. But it is not entirely clear how and why the transition should occur from the rubbing to the charge separation and from there to the hypothesized underlying structure linking positive and negative charges via the atomic model. *Embodiment* may be thought to exist in the phenomenal re-enactment, the rubbing; and even when she only uses words, the possibility of these actions and re-enactments "ring" in her body. Jenny has a personal phenomenal experience, which she re-describes in and by means of discourse. What is in the body therefore is the integration between the phenomenal and discursive experience. The separations that she enacts are metaphorical distances. As such, the origins of the relations that make these significant are to be sought in the historical development Jenny has undergone.

LIVED-IN ABSTRACT WORLDS

In the literature, it is easy to find statements about abstraction and decontextualization that are said to make it difficult for students to learn. In some situations, authors juxtapose the terms "real world," which is to be found outside schools, and "school." Are schools not real worlds for students? Do students not find themselves for large parts of their everyday lives in schools? Such descriptions run counter to a conceptualization that I always inhabit my lifeworld, including those aspects concerned with school and schooling. I am always in my dwelling, always at home with myself. How then can I understand the kind of environment that others denote by the aforementioned terms?

In the introduction to this book, I suggest that my lifeworld is my dwelling. It is what I see and it contains the resources for my actions. These resources (structures), though based on the same material worlds, are not the same for all people, differently positioned and dispositioned that they are and have to be: my kitchen provides different possibilities for acting to visitors, my wife, and me. That is, my lifeworld is some sociomaterial world seen through my primary lens. Because I cannot see without lenses—even those who do not wear glasses see the world through a lens, the eyeball, and through sensors in the retina that are tuned by other parts of my body, most notably the brain—all perception is mediated by some lens. My lifeworld therefore constitutes a world seen through a primary set of lenses. This is true not only for students but also for any researcher in the social sciences as well. It therefore comes as no surprise that Pierre Bourdieu (1992) warns sociologists that all they do is reify their everyday, commonsense perspectives unless they break with their original perception. The intent to rupture with the everyday commonsense ways of looking at perception and learning in science lies at the origin of this book.

Thinking about schools as institutions that inculcate new lenses then allows me to understand the notions of abstraction, decontextualization, and the distinction between school and "real world" in a new way. The intention of school science—besides reproducing inequalities necessary to provide differential access to scarce resources, such as spaces in colleges, workplace openings, and so on—is to allow students to develop new, disciplinary-specific lenses. With these new lenses, ideally, I come to see a world not accessible to me before. I expand my lifeworld and therefore see an aspect of my lifeworld in new ways or expand my lifeworld to cover new domains heretofore not present. In my own life, going to the university to study physics and subsequently teaching physics and researching students learn physics has led me to develop a new lifeworld, one in which Newton's third law, quantum mechanical entities, static electricity, charges, and electrical potential are constitutive structures. It is a habitable place to me, a familiar dwelling, where I move about in the same unproblematic ways as I move about in other parts of my lifeworld, including my kitchen and my garden. Yet when I invite others into this physics-related part of my lifeworld, they find it abstract, distant, different, an inhabitable world even in situations where I do not talk about vectors and tensors, about the differences in aging twins undergo when they travel at different rates.

Learning physics means, among others, looking at the world through new lenses, which are both my own, for I have to produce (repeat) them, and not my own, for there are already cultural-historical resources for making them (my repetitions are repetitions of something else). Both the materials for the lenses and the perspective through these lenses are different, strange. They come from and provide access to different worlds, inhabitable and inhospitable at first. The question now is: How do I-learner come to appropriate these resources and build and inhabit this new lifeworld? It is a new world, initially dark, so that I have to build it bottom up by shedding light on it. I have to make a clearing but also bring the clearing to light so that I can make it a part of my inhabitable and inhabited lifeworld.

Readers may already anticipate that the metaphor of layering provides me with the necessary anchoring point that allows the transitioning into a new lifeworld, that is, allows the emergence of new lenses and resources that eventually constitute a new aspect of my familiar world. For students, their everyday perceptions constitute the anchoring points upon which they are asked to graft another perspective, the world seen in a different way, but a world that may become hospitable.

In the videotapes featuring the tenth-grade students, the development of new lenses can be observed as students increasingly distance themselves from the original materials they have manipulated, the initial ways of talking about them, and the events they have created in the beginning. Initially, as described in the previous section, they still use some of the original materials from the investigations. These materials anchor the transition into the new world. Then students let go and replace some of the materials by other concrete things that take the place of, stand for, make present again, and therefore re-presence and represent the original materials and phenomena. Eventually even these materials disappear and students use but their bodies to enact accounts of and explain the events.

Even with the materials and instruments still present, and without using additional materials to stand in for the original equipment—as in the previous case study—students begin to present their descriptions and explanations. For example, after having worked for five lessons with the electroscope, Iris is so familiar with the instrument and her investigations that she produces an explanation of the electroscope without drawing on the device as a resource in her communication. With only the movement of the charges in the pointer suspension remaining in her gesture, she says, "by means of the transparency film, the electrons are attracted to the plate at the top of the electroscope." All relevant concepts and materials are made salient in the verbal mode so that no other expressive means are necessary. In the following episode, Jenny provides an atomic-level description to explain how two materials come to attract each other.

01 Jenny: The, the atoms, first, um, they repel something [there. The
02 Clare: [Electrons

Figure 6.10. Jenny begins to perform an explanation that no longer involves materials.

As a whole, Jenny explains that electrons are separated from atoms such that the resulting charge separation leads to an attraction. The episode shows Jenny as she begins her atomic-level explanation without making thematic the situation in which the electrons are removed; but she begins by sliding her hands against each other as if she was rubbing two materials in the way she has done earlier during the investigation (line 01 [Figure 6.10]). Jenny reproduces the hand movement, but whereas it originally charged two transparencies as she rubbed them against each other, she now *denotes* this process. Her hands are stretched out in the same way as when she had been holding the two sheets but now she denotes that process. It is as if I am talking *about* how to stir the ingredients while making a white sauce to a colleague at the university. In this situation, I do not have access to my whisk and pots and pans, so I may use gestures to perform a demonstration that denotes that other event in my kitchen. My movements are the same and in this way denote the original situation not only on their surface or arbitrarily—signs and signifiers denote other things in this way. Rather, my whole body denotes a situation by enacting part of the situation. My performance therefore denotes the making of a white sauce in a *metonymic* way, which means, my muscular actions, which are the same across the two situations, stand for the entire process of making white sauce. My body is the bridge between the kitchen, where I normally make the sauce, and the university, where I talk about making the sauce. In the same way, Jenny opens the door to a new way of seeing the world by acting in the same way that she does in her normal lifeworld, where and when she is exploring the materials and creating phenomena. These familiar movements provide her with the resources to create a new habitable place, even though it is going to be populated with (discursive) resources that initially are unfamiliar, strange, and therefore "out of this [her] world."

Here, Jenny's gesture represents the phenomenal level of what she has done. The process of rubbing the two hands against each other is an iconic and metonymic form of the rubbing of two transparency sheets, each hand representing one of these and the way they are held. As she begins to talk about the atoms, her left arm and hand move out in a "giving-away" gesture (line 01) as an instantiation of the near–far schema. Simultaneously, Clare interjects the word "electrons," which in fact supplies the referent of Jenny's "something" that is being repelled (line 02 [Figure 6.10]). Jenny continues by replacing her "something" that is re-

03 electrons are given away and afterward complement each other again.

Figure 6.11. Jenny performs the motion of electrons that would be seen through a micro-physical lens.

pelled with the conceptual entity "electrons," which are given off just as her left hand finishes the outward movement (line 03 [Figure 6.11]). Her giving-away or repelling gesture is completed some 800 milliseconds before the second verb comes forth, but coincides with the stressed syllable "o:::" in the word "electrons." In the final part of this episode, Jenny brings the hands together again just as she begins to explain that the charges "complement" each other again (line 03 [Figure 6.11]).

In contrast to the previous episode where Jenny uses pens to stand for conceptual (electrons, nuclei) and phenomenal entities (transparencies), there no longer are material objects standing in for the equipment that she previously has used in her investigation. Initially, Jenny has been taking these materials from one situation to another, she has been abstracting—from Latin *abs-*, away, and *trahere*, to draw—them from one situation and into another. In addition, she, too, has drawn herself away from the materials; she has been abstracting herself from the original situation and now begins to inhabit a new place, one that previously may have appeared "abstract," but which now is becoming increasingly inhabitable and hospitable place. The action that leads to the charge separation is embodied in the gesture. That is, the manipulation of the materials—an event that I denote by *ergotic* movement in chapter 7—and the causally related epistemic actions (attraction between materials felt, static electricity bristling against skin and hand) are now their symbolic equivalents. Beside this phenomenal experience and description, readers may note the newly acquired, conceptual component. This component is expressed in terms of the word "atom" and the late forthcoming word "electrons," which another student supplies all the while Jenny is still working on her utterance.

In this and the previous section, Jenny can be seen to evolve and inhabit an increasingly abstracted and abstract world as she learns to talk about what she has done independent of the situation in which she has done it. Initially she brings materials from that other, phenomenal world into the new situation. These materials provide her with a point of anchorage, as she begins to build a new space to be inhabited by and hospitable for herself. But the configuration of these resources in her lifeworld is both her own and not her own: these resources are of her making and yet, in her repetition, both originate in and return to the other. Jenny utters "electrons are given away and afterward complement each other again." This utterance is therefore hers: the words are from her *for* the other. But the utterance also is not hers, as all the words have come to her from other persons: they already have been in the world. And through her utterances, the words that have come from the other return to others, who already understand what she is saying *because* the words are also theirs. In this sense, not only Jenny but also her peers come to inhabit a world that they might have predicated previously as "abstract."

Some of the words that come to me from others may be unfamiliar and familiar words come in unfamiliar configurations. Each time this happens, the world evoked appears abstract, removed from my own lifeworld. They belong to ways of seeing worlds, to habitations that do not seem to be hospitable; they do not promise me to feel at home and become a host, to new ideas, to new ways of seeing, and to be host to even newer ideas, new configurations of my lifeworld. The contradiction in all of this is that I do not have any place to start with building a new lifeworld space other than everything else that I am already familiar with, my normal everyday lenses that both give me a world and give me access to it. New words only make sense—and therefore are said to be meaningful—if they somehow find a place in my existing lifeworld, including at the growth point where my lifeworld is currently in the process of expanding. In each case, new words presuppose an existing lifeworld, which constitutes a network of relevance that suspends to new words, to make sense.

DIS-POSITIONS ARE POINTS OF VIEW

Taking up position comes with a point of view on the world generally and with the manipulated objects in particular; position inherently implies disposition (frame of mind, mood, capacity [to view]), which derives from disposition ("dis-" denotes difference, separateness, singularity, privacy). Because I have a body, which is as material as the things I manipulate, the material objects become the point of anchorage. It is through these material objects that I come to perceive the world. Thus, when students use gesture to show what supposed microscopic entities and other invisible entities (electrostatic forces, currents, positive and negative charges) do, they position themselves in such a way that the perspective articulated is that of the object. In this way, their words describe a perspective on a world, which is also that of the object. Thus, it is not surprising to hear students say the electrons "want" to go up while the hand is moving up along the pointer suspension thereby indicating the movement of current in an iconic way, but also deictically making salient the purported trajectory. Or, in their accounts students become a part of the equipment—bodies among bodies, all *being singular plural*—that allows some current to flow between the device and ground leading to the observed phenomena of discharging through the neon lamp, the discharging of an electroscope, and, less visible but powerful as explanation, charging in process referred to in this course as "charging by means of influence and grounding."

In other situations, students' narratives emerge in and from the perspective of the investigator in the process of conducting the experiment, which is made salient, particularly with the materials and equipment still around. In this case, students enact the same movements that in an earlier situation have been used to charge or discharge and object, but now these movements constitute gestures that symbolize, signify, and denote something else. Already in the episodes presented here, there is a different origin of perspective (dis-position) for students' representation the phenomena in gesture, speech, and drawings. First, students always present actions from the position of the agent, that is, normally their own perspective and point of view. Students always gesture actions from their own perspective, in the way they have conducted the investigation and enacted the movements. There is a difference, however, for natural phenomena and the conceptual entities. Here, some students use object-centered perspectives where their gestures are from the position of the entity talked about. That is, Jenny presents the release of electrons, from a viewpoint of the atoms. The other perspective is that of the detached observer. Although there are some hints to gender differences in the use of object-centered and detached observer-centered descriptions, my data are insufficient to make any firm claims about such differences.

Considering knowing and learning through a lifeworld perspective allows me to understand why it is sensible to view the world from the perspective of a knowing person and from the perspective of the things that surround him or her. This perspective is always the one that the individual or some generalized other can take, but rarely the perspective from nowhere, the god's eye perspective that characterizes written scientific communication. Knowing is something personal, it means navigating a familiar lifeworld, *being singular plural*; it involves the process of enacting what I know. The difficulty in learning science lies in the fact that looking at the world through a scientific lens, the lens that scientist have developed over generations, means taking a look from nowhere and from everywhere at the same time. It is a disembodied look that contrasts the way in which I know and experience the world.

If teaching and facilitating the appropriation of a scientific perspective is the goal of science education, then the contradiction involved is this: learners have to develop lenses and perspectives that are unlike anything they know. And they have to do so bottom up, completely anew. These new lenses and perspectives, this new world, may be anchored in, though being radically different from, the lifeworld each student knows so well and is so intimately familiar with. How can I ever develop a lens that gives me a perspective from nowhere if all I know is a positioned perspective? How can I develop a perspective that is not a perspective at all because it is a perspective from nowhere and from everywhere at once? This is one of the aporias of learning generally and that of learning science in particular.

POSITION, COGNITION, AND THE GROUNDING PROBLEM

In this chapter, I describe how taking up a position in the world—and in fact defining what the momentarily relevant world is—involves my body, my orientation, my gestures, and my speech. Here, my material body is not to be seen as an independent entity, separate from who and what I am. I am who and what I am in and through my body. Through my body I am anchored and grounded in my lifeworld;

it is my host that provides me (my subjectivity) with a dwelling, which precedes my being the host. Thus, there is a law that "would make of the inhabitant a guest received in his own home, that would make of the owner a tenant, of the welcoming host a welcomed guest" (Derrida, 1999, p. 42). In this move, therefore consciousness *is* hospitality and "the *cogito* is a hospitality offered or given, an infinite *welcome*" (p. 48). This perspective of knowing and learning through a lifeworld lens sheds new light on the aporia of learning.

Human evolution has had a long history preceding the appearance of language and the concomitant phenomenon of culture. Not surprisingly, there are theories in which cognition, the human body, and its sensorimotor achievements—which are the results of selection processes during the (successful) evolutionary trajectory— play a central part. Among the different ways in which the body may be involved in communicative acts, my work has focused on gestures. In the following, I briefly provide an overview of some of the more influential work on the gestural aspects of communication. This then sets the context for chapter 7, in which I show how hand and arm movements during investigations become symbolic, that is, forms of expression, and thereby provide the crucial bridge between manipulations and reflective deliberation.

Gestures and speech have evolved into and constitute highly integrated communicative systems not only among aborigines but also among members of industrial societies. Talk and gesture are almost always copresent aspects of communicative action across all cultures. Although talk and gesture are sometimes considered as separate components of communication, there is no reason why this ought to be so. In fact, language emerged when hand and vocal gestures already existed, as they still do among chimpanzees and other great apes. These gestures are part of the great apes' being in the world, and it is probable that they have been part of our own communicative repertoire. In this, the hand and vocal gestures have always been tied to situations, such as when an individual member of a group has produced sounds that all others recognize as an alarm that warns everybody else that a predator is nearing. Pre-human communication has been something like this, too, and it has preserved this aspect, though it falls on the conceptual blind spots of many scholars. Yet in everyday situation, a lot of things are said to move the current activity ahead rather than to represent something else. The words—sometimes merely onomatopoeic sounds—are integral and constitutive part of the situation I find myself in, which is already meaningful. The sense given in and with hand and vocal gestures is largely of continuous nature contrasting words that denote categories. Continuous processes more easily expressed in gestural than in verbal form, because the latter requires re-coding into categorical form.

There is ample cross-cultural evidence that words and gestures are deep, constitutive features of human cognition rather than tools consciousness uses to make itself available to other subjects. Linguistic anthropologists who work with people as widely distributed as the Hai‖om Bushpeople in Southwest Africa, Guugu Yimithirr speakers in Australia, and Mayan peasants report on the interdependence of verbal and gestural deixis, iconic gestures, and spatial orientation. Knowing, body orientations, gestures, speech, and vocal modulations all are integral and constitutive part of every situation. In their cultural evolution, these traditional peoples developed orientation skills in which gestures, speech, and other aspects of cognition are deeply integrated systems. For example, indexical reference plays an important role in accumulating spatial knowledge among the Hai‖om Bushpeople and is embodied in the form of topographical gossip involving directional terms (Widlok, 1997). This irreducible interdependence provides strong support for the claim that gestures and language are not simply aspects of linguistic systems but of a broader communicative one, which involve the individual speaker to take a position with respect to the situation as a whole, including its material and social dimensions. That is, these peoples have undergone cognitive and cultural evolution in response to the need to survive in the particular (harsh) conditions of their surroundings, which have become familiar and inhabitable places; they have become hospitable.

In Western (like) civilizations, schooling has supplanted traditional forms of learning. Schools can be considered to be places where students are asked to evolve new forms of discourse, to learn new linguistic systems, which constitute new lenses, new maps, with which to create and navigate a world. When students learn in science laboratories such as in the present book—where they are explicitly encouraged to develop observational and theoretical languages based on their experience—a context is set in which new forms of communication arise by means of evolutionary processes. These new forms of communication are part of the new lifeworlds that become inhabitable places for the learner; and these communicative forms are themselves products of these lifeworlds. The two, forms of communication and lifeworld are mutually constitutive parts of the same unit tying together being and world.

The evolution of discursive forms in science classrooms has almost exclusively focused on *student-centered* learning environments. The term "student-centered" generally means that students are supported in developing their own expressive means; these may arise from negotiations both at the small-group and whole-class levels. This allows multiple lifeworlds and multiple discourses to emerge. Students themselves learn to recognize that only some of the discourses are viable in the long term, which encourages them to abandon the less viable ones. Rarely ever, however, are all scientifically (and mathematically) incorrect discourses abandoned. In *Talking Science* (Roth, 2005d), which is concerned with language development in student-centered science classrooms, I provide two case studies that show that even for the same objects (e.g., an arrow representing the concept "velocity"), students use ten to twenty different words before they have come to settle on what appeared to be viable ones. In the process, the particulars of the setting, negotiations with peers, and interactions with teacher and textbook, constrain the proliferation of different discursive forms. First, to get on with their activities and because of the collective nature of the products, students are constrained to find the most viable language they can use *together*. Second, interacting with the teacher and textbooks provides another constraint that fosters the selection of one among various discursive forms available.

In *Talking Science*, I also articulate conversations as multimodal events in which gestures and the indexical ground against which they occur have communicative functions and constrain the evolution of viable linguistic forms in student-centered science classrooms. Through this work, I have come to see the emergence of communicative competence as something closely tied to the physical arrangement between the participants and relative to the artifacts over and about which the communication takes place. That is, when students engage in manipulating materials and employ gestures, they quickly develop a viable discourse that allows them to constitute and navigate a new lifeworld; their communicative competence remains underdeveloped when the learning environment does not afford the use of gestures in communicative acts. Especially in the kind of classrooms I researched, the emergence of new discursive forms is best described by means of evolutionary analogies, for there is first an enormous wealth of new and different language productions among which a more limited number of viable ones remain, constrained and selected through interactions with other students and teachers. I explore the evolution of forms of communication in chapter 7.

Descartes is often blamed for having separated conceptions of the relation between bodies and minds. This separation is so deeply embodied in Western culture that I use a pointing gesture to my temples or head to indicate "thinking." Similarly, when I talk about emotions and feelings, I may use an expression such as "thinking with one's heart" and accompany it by a gesture to the named organ. That is, I do not just conceptualize and describe the separation between thinking, emotions, and living in the world, but I express it by positioning my body in particular ways and thereby enact the very separation that my talk is about. This separation then leads me to the question about how anything I think comes to be connected to my life, emotions, feelings, and needs. Artificial intelligence researchers and cognitive scientists denote this as "the grounding problem."

When I initially read about situated cognition, I was asking myself in which way the word "situated" could be used. I was thinking about neurons as doing the thinking and it made very little sense to me to say that cognition is situated. What is the connection, I asked myself, between the neurons and the environment? By now it has become clear to me that the resources for deliberations and communication are found in the setting. Away from my computer, there are many features I cannot explain, yet I competently use them when a computer is present. Furthermore, my being is always in some setting, difficult to delimit. As much of the literature on the topic has shown, it is more productive to draw the boundaries of analysis around the person-acting-in-setting rather than around the skin over a person's skull. This person, alone, would not be able to have a world. But the person I am writing about here, me, always inhabits a lifeworld: I am both a product of and produce this lifeworld, which both predates and antedates me.

In this chapter, I present classroom situations that show in which way I can understand representations to be distributed across the setting in different ways. First, the students use different modalities to communicate, especially during the phase where their verbal expressions first emerged. During this phase, the gestures facilitate communication because they symbolize the same motions previously enacted but then were intended to get things done in the world. Gestures support the articulation of descriptions and explanations because they constitute part of the communication, which therefore achieves greater complexity than if the students were speaking only. Second, by drawing on materials later, sometimes replaced by other objects, part of the elements do not have to be represented in speech or gesture but, being available to all members in a conversation, stand for themselves. They thereby function like scribbles in a notepad where salient information is kept and drawn upon just in time and as needed. That is, using a transparency sheet or a rod makes it unnecessary to say the word "transparency sheet" or "rod," and sometimes makes it unnecessary to say that these entities are charged. The use of these materials implies the state of being charged. By tracking the setting I can find the significance I need, much I track my word processing program and find what I need without having to store it in my memory. Again, this amounts to a decrease of what has to be attended to in the production of communication. And these ways change as individuals develop, as their lifeworlds grow. Pointing gestures in particular provide opportunities for the integration of external and embodied forms of representation (gestural and verbal modalities). This leads to an increasing independence of speech from the local context, and therefore to an "abstraction" of discourse from the setting.

A second important point is the relationship of the different levels involved in the students' presentations: there are materials and equipment phenomenally available to all and gestures and speech, which describe the phenomena and use atomic-level concepts to explain them. Here, deictic and iconic gestures allow a layering and coordination of the different levels. The phenomena thereby are visible to all present and do not have to be coded by any discourse or other communicative means: they are visible and therefore go without saying. They constitute communicative resources in the setting, and it is only when the events contradict what is available in the setting that interaction participants feel the need to talk (Roth, 2004b). *This setting as a whole and my familiarity with it constitute meaning; and in this setting I am always positioned, dispositioned, predisposed, and presupposing.*

There are many situations in my database where students do not comment upon the outcome of an investigation—I have coded more than 100 instances in each (a) the first investigation concerned with charging materials and (b) the investigations with the electroscope. With materials, manipulative (ergotic) and sensing (epistemic) actions, and observations as given elements of the environment, students could layer new conceptual-level descriptions on top of what they perceptually have available. The teachers often provide the new words, but it is only through students' embodied access to the phenomena that the words find a place in world immediately accessible to the students. Thus, this accessible world, in the phenomena produced and seen by the students, provides a stable ground for situating new conceptual talk. *Words therefore find a position in a familiar, meaningful situation rather than* "having meaning" *or* "receiving meaning."

In addition, because gestures more so than names of categories unfold in time and space, they are subject to the same constraints as other worldly phenomena.

Thus, when students gesture the motion of some entity such as electrons, the trajectories are real in the sense that they place constraints on what the conceptual entities can do. Deploying gestures therefore predisposes particular temporalities within communicative action. Furthermore, gestures are less codified than speech; they do not have the same (socially mediated) sense and are therefore much more interpretively flexible than utterances. Gestures are therefore more strongly dependent on the setting that serves as a ground against which gestures are seen and read.

EMERGENCE AND EVOLUTION OF
COMMUNICATIVE FORMS

At the end of the previous chapter, I suggest that there is an evolutionary trend in the way in which communicative forms develop not only at the cultural-historical level but also at the ontogenetic—that is, individual—level and at the level of the communications in a classroom as a whole. In this chapter I show how more abstract forms of talk arise from earlier communicative forms, which themselves are founded upon gestures that have their origin in the manipulation of material things and equipment. To find out whether manipulations, gestures, and discourse are related, and therefore constitute an important aspect of embodied, situated, and distributed cognition, communication has to be studied in sufficiently complex environments. School science (and perhaps mathematics) classes where students engage in hands-on activities constitute an interesting, everyday setting where the evolving relationship between manipulation of objects, gestures, and language can be studied easily.

It is well accepted that children develop *sensorimotor* schema while acting in and handling objects of the world. However, I am not aware of similar research that shows how the learning of abstract-level concepts (which, according to Piaget, are "formal operational") is supported by such activities. Thus, "hands-on" activities are based on the premise that *abstract* and *symbolic* forms of representation (e.g., scientific discourse) is supported by manipulating and handling materials; however, an existence proof for the supportive function of concrete activity in the development of formal language has yet to be made. If thinking is truly abstract, then engagement with the material world cannot be but a stepping stone that can be kicked as soon as a person has achieved the formal (abstract) level of thought. This, however, is not the case, because, as I have seen in my ethnographic studies of scientists at work, when there is trouble, they fall back on thinking in concrete forms. The concrete operations therefore do not fall away but remain constitutive of any formal thinking, if there is any. In this chapter, I show how formal science discourse might arise from and while interacting with and manipulating the material world. That is, I show a possible developmental trajectory, beginning with primary manipulations (ergotic hand movements) and sensing of materials (epistemic hand movements). These movements evolve into iconic gestures (symbolic movements) and from there support the emergence of discourse that describes the primary activities and observations; on these primary levels are lodged and evolve forms of talk about abstract entities.

When students attend school, their interactions with the teacher and the curriculum materials constrain what and how they talk. The "hands-on" tasks therefore can be viewed both as providing opportunities and constraints for forms of language to emerge that serve students to point to, articulate aspects of, and explain the lifeworlds they create in the process. At a second level, teachers hold students accountable for what they do and say; and this accountability, which is aligned with the particular curricular intentions that the teacher represents, constitutes the specific constraints for the evolution of any classroom discourse. As students become familiar with some domain, their modes of communication move from primarily external, perceptual, and gestural modalities to primarily spoken and written forms of representation. My earlier studies communication in school science laboratories focused on motion and simple machines, which allow students to investigated devices where concepts are at the "basic level of categorizations" (Lakoff, 1987), that is, categorization of things and processes that I phenomenally experience with my senses, including force, velocity, or acceleration. Symbolic communication involving basic-level categories arises from communicative forms in which objects in the world and manipulations support the rise of (deictic and iconic) gestures, which themselves support the emergence of scientific language (Roth, 2000). In this sense, it is possible to speak of the embodied dimensions of scientific discourse. But do gestures have any function in the development of scientific discourse concerned with conceptual entities that are inaccessible at a basic level? This role of gesture in particular and the body more generally is unclear when the core issues are microscopic events, or better, when macroscopic phenomena are modeled by means of discourse about microscopic and atomic events inaccessible to human experience.

THE INVESTIGATION

In this chapter, I draw on the events that occurred during the eleventh and twelfth lesson in the tenth-grade physics course. The students in the class were given different sets of materials with which to create and conduct an experiment. The four male students in the group receive a Styrofoam cup, a plastic ruler, a piece of cloth, and a metal-coated elderberry mark sphere on a string (Figure 7.1). In the first configuration, the sphere is supposed to touch the rod. Students are asked to rub the ruler with the cloth and then to bring it close to the end of the metal rod opposite to the sphere. If the ruler is approached without touching the rod, the elderberry mark sphere will move away from the rod—because both are charged in the same way, negatively or positively—only to return to its original position as soon as the ruler is removed. A slightly different experiment consists in leaving some space between the rod and the sphere. When the charged ruler is brought close to the other end of the metal rod, the elderberry mark sphere will first move toward the rod, touch it, and then remain at a distance permanently or bounce about for a while touching the rod in the process.

Through a microphysical lens (see chapter 5), the events in the first instance are explained in the following way (Figure 7.2). When a positively charged plastic ruler is brought close to the metal rod, the electrons move close to this end because they are attracted. Because the metal-coated elderberry mark sphere touches the

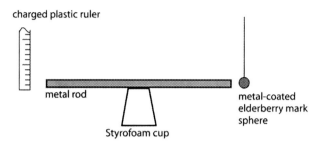

Figure 7.1. The students were asked to construct this set up, then to rub the plastic ruler with a piece of cloth and bring it close to the metal rod; they were to observe, then to describe and explain the events.

ruler, it either also gives off electrons. As a consequence, rod and sphere are charged positively. Because the sphere can move, it is repelled from the rod. The phenomenon therefore is exactly like the one observed on the electroscope—more closely described in chapters 10 and 11—where the pointer is repelled from the suspension on which there are the same charges.

In the second case, the charges at the end of the rod cause the charges on the sphere to be displaced, like charges will be more distant than unlike charges. As a result, the charges on the facing parts of rod and sphere are opposite, leading to an initial attraction. During contact, charges are transferred so that the sphere now is repelled from the rod. This leads to a bouncing movement from the beginning.

In addition to the tasks described, Phil also touches the rod with the ruler in the first configuration, which makes the sphere not only deflect but stay permanently in a deflected state. Phil also touches the rod repeatedly in the second configuration, which makes the sphere bounce around wildly, in large amplitudes, every now and then touching the rod, leading to further bouncing. The bouncing movement comes to an end only after some time.

In the following, I present excerpts from the conversations between two of the four students around a table of male students, Phil and Matt. The other two students (Chris, Marcel) are largely quiet, listening to what their peers have to say. Phil constructs an initial explanation as they watch the sphere bounce. Matt and Phil subsequently resort to gestures over the equipment but without actually charg-

Figure 7.2. This representation layers the microphysical lens onto the investigation in Figure 7.1, thereby explaining the phenomenon. Approaching the positively charged ruler makes electrons from rod and touching sphere to the left end. The sphere will be repelled, because it is positively charged like the rod.

ing the different bodies. In the course of repeated attempts in constructing an explanation, the students move through a trajectory of bodily expressions that increasingly emphasize verbal means independent of the equipment that figures in their early explications.

EVOLUTION OF HAND MOVEMENTS

In the following sections, I first show how students begin their first explanations by reenacting parts (or all) of an investigation; this re-enactment serves as the *indexical ground* of their utterances. By the term *indexical ground* I mean that students can point and otherwise refer to the setting and thereby bring it into the conversation as resource for making salient the issues at hand. Later, the materials and equipment still function as indexical ground but gestures begin to replace actual objects and events. Subsequently, students frequently employ a different object or gesture by itself to represent some relevant aspect of the event they talk about, and finally they represent all relevant aspects of objects and events in symbolic (abstract) form. I distinguish three types of functions of gestures in this development: In addition to the evident *symbolic* function that gestures have during speech acts, hand movements have *epistemic* and *ergotic* (Gr. *ergon,* work) functions.

Early in this development, therefore, we see in action a unity between the sign and the signified, the sensible and the non-sensible, and the bodily enacted and what it refers others to. That is, when students reenact an investigation and ask others (peers, students) to look, they make the event signify itself. This is the very condition under which pre-humans used sounds as part of their interactions and communal life. Only subsequently did they split "sense" and "meaning" from the production of sound and from the event. In the present chapter, a similar evolution is at work. As the communicative forms with respect to a particular topic evolve, students re-enact some of the same movements but now these movements stand for the movements in the event; the hand and arm movement signify another movement, one that had a different primary function: doing work. There is still some similarity in the two movements, which is the reason why the gestures are predicated by the term *iconic*. In the end, students describe and explicate the phenomena they observed in words, at which point language has been divorced completely from the situation: it literally is abstract. This split between the bodily faces (sensible) and spiritual faces (sense) of language in particular, far from being a negative aspect, is the very consequence of embodiment (Franck, 2001).

As to the *epistemic* function, the hands (as well as other body parts) permit a human agent to perceive qualitative aspects such as the temperature, form, texture, or movement of objects. That is, the hands in particular and the body more generally are endowed with sensibility, which opens us to the world. At the very moment that I intend to touch something, an intention that has been linked to agency, I also open up myself to being touched by what I am touching (Derrida, 2005). This aspect of being in the world, sensibility, is the forgotten sister of agency. It is forgotten but nevertheless constitutive of who I am and how I can learn anything from acting in the world. The *ergotic* nature of hand movement denotes the fact that humans change their environment, turn, displace, compress, or pull objects; in this way, I denote the transitive (intentional) aspect of agency. Epistemic and ergotic movements frequently go together taking on a symbolic function that increases human capacities for thinking by involving gesture and environment (Kirsh, 1995). Sensibility and agency, and therefore the epistemic and ergotic functions of hand (body) movements have to be thought together to eschew the reductionism implicit in the notion of agency.

The following episodes illustrate how, with familiarity, there are shifts along several dimensions. First, rather than explaining phenomena, students manipulate the original equipment. They subsequently use the equipment as indexical ground and simulated events by means of gestures. Gestures subsequently substitute for earlier presentations. Finally, students use verbal representations that subsequently show up in the form of written texts, which, as they develop, decreasingly are accompanied by iconic drawings. Second, associated with this shift there was a decrease in the total amount of gesturing over time. Gestures often precede speech production both when words are totally unavailable and when they are produced but follow the corresponding gesture with some delay. Indicative of development, however, any existing delays between gesture and speech decreases as part of the development and disappears when the two forms of representation overlap. Taken together, the two types of development can be understood as an evolution whereby a number of embodied representational modalities are coordinated and increasingly shifted into a verbal modality.

FROM ERGOTIC TO EPISTEMIC MOVEMENTS

When asked to provide explanations for phenomena at hand, students initially rely almost exclusively on redoing the investigations as part of their attempts to provide a description of the phenomenon and as a context for constructing atomic-level explanations. When the teacher asks them to explain what they have observed, they redo the investigation simply asking the teacher to "Look!" Upon a repeated request to describe, students again ask the teacher to "Look!" Perhaps because the associated events are too fast, students eventually simulate the events by moving the objects through the different stages of the phenomenon. This allows them to describe the observed objects and unfolding (simulated) events in real time allowing for a copresence of expressive means and aspects of the world.

Phil, Matt, and their two peers (who are silent during this episode) sit around their laboratory table where the steel rod is placed on a glass with one of its ends close to the metal-coated elderberry mark sphere hanging from a thin piece of thread on a laboratory stand (Figure 7.3). They repeatedly have done the investigation where they bring a charged object close to (or make touch) the end of a metal rod opposite to the covered sphere. As a result, the sphere bounces wildly. The students then attempt to construct a written report of what they have done and observed and to articulate an explanation. In this first of six recorded episodes, Phil and Matt collectively attempt a description and explanation of the phenomena.

Figure 7.3. Matt, Marcel, Phil, and Chris are in the process of articulating a description and explication of an investigation involving steel rod and elderberry mark sphere.

Rather than just talking about his previous investigation, Phil actually runs it again (line 1 [Episode 7.1]. He discharges the rod and brings the sphere to its resting position before charging a plastic ruler and bringing it to the steel rod.

Episode 7.1, line 1

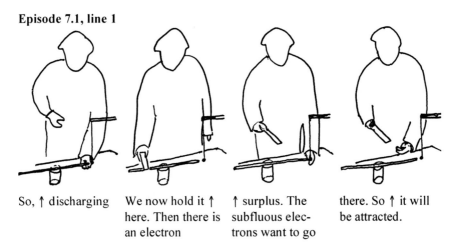

So, ↑ discharging   We now hold it ↑   ↑ surplus. The   there. So ↑ it will
                      here. Then there is   subfluous elec-   be attracted.
                      an electron   trons want to go

In his utterances (the arrows indicate the exact moment of the body configuration above the text), Phil attempts to construct a conceptual map that he can layer over his perceptual map. He uses his right hand to point (with the ruler) to the part of the steel rod where there should be, in his words, a surplus of electrons. His left hand first points to the end of the rod where "subfluous" electrons would move so that "it" (likely the metal-coated elderberry mark sphere) would be attracted. The language he uses serves the intentions embedded in the situation as a whole. It is a language that is inherently presupposed to be intelligible, and therefore is both his and not his language. This is so even in the case where he creates the word "subfluous" on the fly, without any apparent reflection, and without any one of his classmates objecting to this newly created word. Although this word has not existed in the German language, his peers nevertheless appear to understand, which indicates that this word is already a possibility shared in the group as a whole. In all its singularity, it also expresses plurality.

In the second part of this episode, Matt sitting on the far left from the observer and visibly being engaged in the task at hand (Figure 7.3) reiterates what might be happening at as viewed through a conceptual lens (line 2 [Episode 7.1]). His gestures stand for the movements of the electrons and that of the protons towards the sphere. His right hand demonstratively moves away from his body, iconically representing the way in which the elderberry mark sphere moves away from the sphere at the opposite end of the table from his perspective (Figure 7.3). In this hand movement, one can see how an embodied near–far schema, enacted by the hand, which is close and then far, comes to be applied to (layered over) the articulation of the perceptual near-far relations between the rod and the sphere. In his articulation, therefore, his entire body signifies the movement of the electrons from near to far and vice versa. This same metaphorical extension of the near-far schema is also evident in chapter 6, where I show how Jenny enacts repulsion using her two hands and thereby signifies by means of her body. The same type of repulsion is said to underlie the present phenomenon (conceptual map), and students use the same way of enacting the schema through their gesture. Here, the gesture bears visual, that is, iconic relation to the observation made previously.

Episode 7.1, Line 2

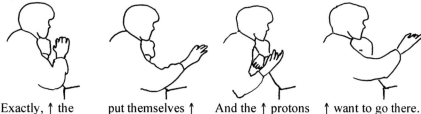

Exactly, ↑ the   put themselves ↑   And the ↑ protons   ↑ want to go there.
electrons   away

In this description, Matt describes the phenomenon from the perspective of the entities involved, as if he is telling the events from the perspective of the electrons, which "put themselves away" and the "protons [that] want to go there." Here the viewpoint of the microphysical particles makes absolute sense in that it parallels the performance of the near–far schema, where what is near is here, where I am, and far is there, away from me. In the final part, Phil takes the sphere in his left hand and, paralleling speech and gesture, moves it. Simultaneously, he describes observational and conceptual aspects of the event, that is, he provides a description that layers the perceptual and conceptual views (maps). Accordingly, the sphere approaches the rod, transfers "a part" then swings back, and returns to the steel rod (line 3 [Episode 7.1]).

Episode 7.1, Line 3

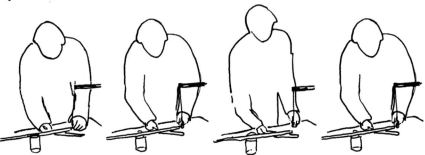

| Then this is ↑ coming there. | A ↑ part is transferred to here | then it swings ↑ back | And then gets ↑ to it here again. |

There are several dimensions in these three lines of communication that are typical for the early stages of communicative competence (complexity and temporal aspects are discussed in subsequent sections). First, students use equipment and materials, which they describe in observational terms. Second, their conceptual talk is often in a way that their teacher does not accept as scientifically inappropriate. Third, in the early stages, students often speak from the point of view of the inanimate entities involved and thereby portray these entities as animate. Fourth, their communication relies heavily on verbal and gestural deixis.

First, Phil reenacts the investigation while providing a phenomenal description of his actions and observations ("discharging," "hold it here," "it will be attracted"). As the event unfolds, he begins a first attempt to layer a theoretical description on top of what is unfolding before his peer's eyes. His movements are *ergotic,* because he is actually manipulating the materials, thereby causing changes in the world that are observable by others. However, these events are often too fast to be described simultaneously. Students begin to recreate the events, which allows them to coordinate speech with the perceived events. Here, Phil's gestures also are *epistemic* as he takes the elderberry mark sphere into his fingers and moves it through the trajectory thereby feeling the movement as he produces it in a form of cognition that is distributed across the setting. He moves an object but also feels the object, which is returning the pressure force that he applies to it—and, without doubt, leaving an impression, an experiential trace. While guiding the elderberry mark sphere through its trajectory, Phil is in the position to stop the motion at any point or move in slow motion so that his talk about coming, transferring, swinging back, and returning is in relative synchrony with the actual position of the elderberry mark sphere.

Second, given that students are to learn physics in this situation and that they have to begin with the language currently available to them, it is not surprising that they use words inappropriately and describe inappropriate physical events—as seen through the lenses used by the teachers in this classroom. In this case, Phil makes up a new word "subfluous." (In the original German transcript, Phil uses the word "unterschüssigen," which does not exist in this language. It is a neologism that builds on a contrast with "überschüssig," superfluous [adjective] in which the same verb root is paired with the contrasting preposition.) Matt describes protons as moving in the metal rod which, from the physicists' perspective is impossible for the nuclei, where the protons are located, are fixed in the lattice of a solid. Although these ways of speaking are not appropriate from the perspective of legitimate legitimating physics, they can be seen as initial attempts in creating a new discourse in a context where there are no constraints yet. Whether these new forms actually survive cannot be determined at that point in the events.

Third, in the early stages of learning about new phenomena and theoretical entities, students' speech and gestures frequently articulate an object point of view or portrays objects as animate. In this excerpt, Phil talks about electrons that "want to go" some place and Matt suggests that the electrons "put themselves away" and protons "want to go" some place. As I suggest above, this way of talking about the world may actually be much less demanding, because it articulates the world as it is available to you and me, rather than from a third person, god's eye perspective, which is the view from nowhere and everywhere simultaneously.

Fourth, in the early stages of students' examination of physical phenomena and their explanations, there was a high degree of verbal and gestural deixis. For example, Phil not only uses the deictic terms "here," "there," "this," and "it" but the referents of these terms shifts even in the brief episode displayed here. "It" refers to the ruler (Episode 7.1, line 1, frame 2), elderberry mark sphere (Episode 7.1, frame 4, Episode 7.1 line 3, frame 3), and steel rod (Episode 7.1, line 3, frame 4). From Phil's perspective, "there" both refers to the right end of the steel rod where there is an electron surplus, the left end where there was an electron deficit (Episode 7.1, line 1, frame 3), and the right extreme of the sphere's trajectory. The same referent also has been designated with different indexical terms: when the elderberry mark sphere approached the end of the steel rod it was both "here" (Episode 7.1, line 3, frame 4) and "there" (Episode 7.1, line 2, frame 4). Despite these variations and apparent inconsistencies at the verbal level, there is no problem apparent in the students' communication. With the materials and equipment actually before them, accessible to all students in the group, the respective listeners disambiguate the different indexical terms Phil uses. Furthermore—I return to this point below—the use of verbal and gestural deixis (pointing) provides students with resources make do with a minimal effort in the verbal mode, which at this point still requires extensive efforts to produce full descriptions and explanations that can stand independent of the context.

FROM EPISTEMIC TO SYMBOLIC MOVEMENTS

In a second stage, students use some of the materials from their investigations as perceptual ground over and against which they produce (i.e., layered) theoretical descriptions, which are descriptions of events through a different set of lenses as described in chapter 5. The deictic (pointing) and iconic gestures can be conceptualized either as distributing cognition around the setting or as bringing the setting into the conversation through its perceptual aspects (Roth, 2004b). Whereas students conduct the investigation or move parts of the equipment literally around as part of describing what happens and constructing a theoretical description in the previous event, students now simply produce and reproduce speech and gestures in one communicative act.

In this episode, Matt evolves another phenomenal and theoretical description of the metal-coated elderberry mark sphere and iron rod investigation. In the first line (Episode 7.2), he describes how holding the charged ruler to the end of the steel rod makes electrons move to the opposite end because of a repelling effect. His deictic gesture indicates the place in the rod where the electrons will go whereas his iconic gesture embodies the phenomenon and notion of "repelling," as his hand moves twice (he moves his hand) from near his body toward the end of the rod.

Episode 7.2, Line 1

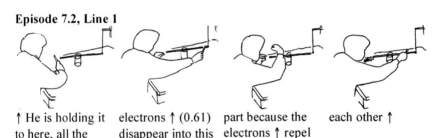

↑ He is holding it   electrons ↑ (0.61)   part because the   each other ↑
to here, all the   disappear into this   electrons ↑ repel

In line 2, Matt then describes and explains the effect of those electrons that are supposed to be at the opposite end of the rod (i.e., opposite from his position). He suggests that the elderberry mark sphere ("this uncharged body") makes an attempt to cancel the charge surplus and therefore pulled itself to the rod. His language is that of an involved observer, who sometimes takes his own perspective, sometimes that of the participant he interacts with.

Episode 7.2, Line 2

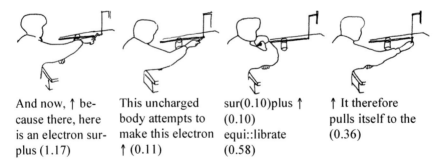

And now, ↑ be-   This uncharged   sur(0.10)plus ↑   ↑ It therefore
cause there, here   body attempts to   (0.10)   pulls itself to the
is an electron sur-   make this electron equi::librate   (0.36)
plus (1.17)   ↑ (0.11)   (0.58)

For example, Matt talks about an "uncharged body," which "attempts to make this electron surplus equilibrate" (Episode 7.2, line 2, frame 2). He thus describes the events as if he personally observes how someone before him engages in the effort of equilibrating an imbalance. He then produces an observational description according to which the elderberry mark sphere "pulls itself" toward the rod. In these descriptions, his concurrently produced deictic gestures accompanying the verbal deixis ("this," "it") make the elderberry mark sphere salient (Episode 7.2, line 2, frame 2, frame 4). His iconic gestures signify the notions of "equilibrate" and "pull to" as the hand moves from the stretched out position at the end of the rod all the way in front of him. This movement continues into the final phase of the episode, as Matt makes the iron rod thematic one more time.

Episode 7.2, Line 3

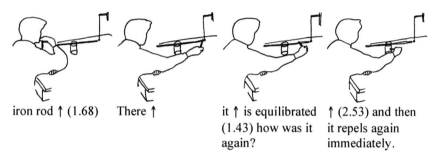

iron rod ↑ (1.68)   There ↑   it ↑ is equilibrated   ↑ (2.53) and then
                                    (1.43) how was it   it repels again
                                    again?   immediately.

Toward the end, Matt begins to hesitate about how to complete the description. There are frequent, lengthy pauses and he asks reflexively about how "it was?" This suggests that he is aware of the unfinished nature of his explanation and that his communicative act is still incomplete. It also supports what I argue for throughout this book: in most everyday situations a speaker does not prepare in advance what he or she says. My ideas come to be formed as I talk and gesture to articulate them not only for others but also for myself. The articulation and the idea it articulates are one. There is no fully fletched idea prior to speaking, but the idea is articulated and articulates itself in the unfolding communicative act. The idea comes into being as speakers signify through their bodies, making salient aspects of the material world. But speakers are part of the material world; listeners, too, are part of the material world, and so are the things and events signified. That is, in a very fundamental sense, *through speakers and audiences the world signifies itself to itself.*

Familiarity with the world provides the speaker with a framework for deciding when his (or her) act is complete or can be considered to be complete. Here, given that there are longish pauses, which the others do not use to take the turn at talk away from him, there is evidence that they, too, consider his idea as available in the articulation, is yet unfinished. At this point, Matt's theoretical ("equilibrates") and observational descriptions ("repels") stand in the air without relating to each other. He has not yet arrived (as it will happen later in the lesson) at a conceptually complete explanation for the process in which observation and theoretical discourses are coordinated.

In the evolution of students' language, this example is further along than the previous episode where students actually are observing the event or moving the objects around to be able to describe them and their relations to each other in the various configurations. Here, what is being done as part of the investigation and what can be observed is described and enacted and therefore made available to others in and through gestures. Over and against—i.e., as a new layer—the objects present and the description of actions and observations, Matt produces a description of the events *through* a theoretical lens. Materials and equipment, viewed through a phenomenal lens, serve as ground, as a first layer, and in some cases are replaced by arbitrary objects. Here, a pencil in the right hand (Episode 7.2, line 1, frame 1) replaces the original charged ruler, as Matt shows how the latter is brought to his end of the metal rod; he subsequently uses the pen as a pointer (remainder of Episode 7.2, line 1). These materials or their substitutes allow students to point to particular aspects without the need to name or describe them in words. Matt does not name the iron rod other than in line 3 (frame 1), although he repeatedly refers to or implies it gesturally. Thus, when his right hand moves back and forth along the rod, others see that he is moving along the rod rather than randomly in space; and similar to his peers, I-analyst can see his hand move back and forth along the rod, thereby implying its presence in the communicative act. Furthermore, he does not name the metal-coated elderberry mark sphere; he enters the object in to the communicative act by means of verbal ("this" [Figure 3.b.ii], "it" [Figures 3.b.iv, 3.c.iv]) and gestural deixis.

Here, it is evident that communication is a distributed phenomenon. It does not just start out in somebody's mind and then gets converted into words, which are transmitted to others. Rather, communication is a phenomenon that takes into account the situation as a whole; the variants and invariants in the situation as a whole, including sounds, body orientations, body positions, gestures, and talk together constitute what is being said. To know what is being communicated, I need to be attuned to the situation and I need to be aware of its variant and invariant properties. A gesture therefore is not a signifier in itself but becomes a signifier in its relation to the remainder of the setting. Because we are in the setting together, the others and I-speaker can take it as shared and therefore make reference to it indirectly and still know what it is that is to stand out. Thinking, too, does not occur in the head, but is distributed across the setting (Roth & Pozzer, 2006). Thus, when Matt's hand is located away from him at the far end of the iron rod, this constitutes a particular state in the emerging and unfolding idea. It is not yet complete, but the next phase in the description is relative to this state currently enacted in the situation: the charges being distributed in a particular way. Their redistribution has to be relative to its current state. But because this state is available in the configuration of the setting, it does not have to be reflected in its entirety in the mind; it merely has to be available perceptually to all those present.

As in the previous episode, the same indexical terms have different referents; because of the logic of the underlying event to be described and explained, these indexical terms are therefore disambiguated. Thus, "it" refers to the charged ruler (Episode 7.2, line 1, frame 1), elderberry mark sphere Episode 7.2, line 2, frame 4)

(Figure 3.b.iv, 3.c.iv), iron rod Episode 7.2, line 3, frame 3), and the explanation itself ("how was it again" [Episode 7.2, line 3, frame 3]). In the same way, both ends of the steel rod are designated by the deictic term "here" and the opposite end of the rod is also "there" Episode 7.2, line 2, frame 1; line 3, frame 2). At this stage, the visible objects and invisible entities are animate, and they engage in intentional action in the explanation. Thus, the elderberry mark sphere "attempts to make . . . equilibrate," "pulls itself" or "repels . . . immediately." Furthermore, the iron rod "equilibrates" and the electrons "repel each other."

Toward the end of this episode, Matt's description has become more independent of the indexical ground constituted by the material setting, though Matt still makes use of indexical words and gestures to designate the things at hand. He does not need to fully describe those things visible to all. They "go without saying" and it is sufficient for the situation at hand to designate the relevant objects, entities, and events by pointing to them or expressing them by means of iconic gestures. Over and against the material ground, perceptually available to all, the theoretical discourse, which constitutes a view through a different lens, takes its hold. The sounds produced find their place in the material situation as a whole, signifying as other material aspects, including things that can be seen and touched, gestures, and body orientations. In these first episodes, speakers take the point of view of the entities involved. They talk from a position of material participants among these other materials, from the perspective of someone sharing a world.

In the evolution of communicative forms, speaking from the perspective of a world shared with objects actually may be easier. I-speaker describe the world from my perspective and relative to the other, which may be a person or an object. My talk is not deficient—as captured in the negative connotations when educational researchers write about the anthropomorphic and anthropocentric language children use—but rather addresses the generalized other in the second person. This generalized other first and foremost is a different material body, being singular plural in a different position, which only subsequently is unfolded differentially into *merely* material body or another *human* body, endowed, as I am, with agency and sensibility. To talk about the objects and entities as if these are imbued with agency requires moving to a dispassionate and non-animate perspective from a third-person perspective, the one from nowhere and everywhere. This only happens once learners are very familiar with the events viewed through different lenses.

FROM SYMBOLIC MOVEMENTS TO SPEECH AND TEXT

When students become very familiar with the objects, equipment, and phenomena they produce with them, they no longer require the presence of the materials in their observational narratives or as ground over and against which they produce and layer theoretical descriptions. At this point, arbitrary objects often serve as signs to stand in for some object or entity. Thus, in chapter 6 Jenny uses pens to stand for *any* charged object. If these pens stand for other rod-shaped objects, like to plastic rods, the relationship between signifier (pen) and signified (rod) is iconic.

In earlier forms of communication, iconic relations predominate, that is, relations that build on the perceptual similarities between two situations. For example, when a plastic rod is used to signify a metal rod, the two shapes are related; similarly, if a pen or pencil is used to signify a metal rod used as part of the investigation, there is a perceptual similarity between the investigative materials and the thing used to signify them some time later during the conversation where an explanation is to be evolved. If these pens stand for cloth or transparency sheets, then the relationship between the shapes (and materials) does not bear perceptual similarity. In this case, the relationship between signifier (pen) and signified (cloth, transparency) is more arbitrary—though there still is a lasting entity rather than a more ephemeral sound standing for another thing. Jenny uses a third, fountain pen to stand for an atom that is separated into a positively charged nucleus and (negatively charged) electrons in the rubbing process. Her gesture is iconic in the sense that it bears a perceptual and therefore motivated relationship to the process of rubbing; but the entities used in the process, the pens, bear an arbitrary relation to the things that have been rubbed. As a result of the rubbing, the pulling apart of body and cap of the pen is a material instantiation of the idea of *separation*, the separation of positive and negative charges that are central to the perception of the events through the microphysical lens. In this, Jenny uses her entire body and some material elements from the setting to signify separation; but this signification only makes sense because it occurs against the ground, which is implicated in the communication and without which signification does not occur. In a similar way, toward the end of the second lesson on the steel rod–metal-coated elderberry mark sphere investigation, Phil produces the following explanation and uses a PVC rod, which has not figured as a material in their original investigation.

In this episode, Phil and his mates work on constructing an explanation for the phenomenon of induction on the metal rod and the elderberry mark sphere so that they can produce it as an entry in their laboratory notebook. Phil picks up some PVC rod on his laboratory table and then produces an explanation, in gesture and speech, over and against the rod. This PVC rod symbolizes the metal rod and, with it, the experiment as a whole. Here, the material (PVC) is no longer the same as during the investigation; in fact, if the investigation is conducted with the PVC rod, it does not work because PVC does not conduct and therefore does not allow the presupposed electrons to move freely back and forth. The relationship between the PVC rod and the metal rod therefore is arbitrary; but it is also motivated, because both entities share perceptual properties: they are both long thin rods. The second type of relationship is metonymical, whereby something, which is a part of a larger entity, comes to stand for the entity in its entirety (Lakoff, 1987). A typical, everyday example of a metonymic relationship is between a ham sandwich and the person eating a ham sandwich: two servers may therefore talk about "the ham sandwich" when they talk about the person eating it. In the present situation, the rod stands for the entire investigation in which a rod has been used. The part is a placeholder for the situation as a whole. As Episode 7.3 shows, Phil's gestures and speech articulate two layers: the phenomenal, perceptually available events and the presumed entities and their relations that explain the phenomena; and these two layers exist over and against the perceptually available materials on the laboratory table. That I can observe the two layers to exist does not mean, however, that they are salient to Phil while he is speaking.

Episode 7.3, Line 1

↑ You hold the   ↑ everything is   Now comes the   Comes here ↑
rod here therefore   going here let's   little animal ↑   Goes
                     say, repels

Phil shows with his right hand where the (charged) ruler has been held relative to the rod and, with his left hand, how "everything" has been repelled inside the rod toward the other end. As a consequence, the elderberry mark sphere moves toward and then away from the end of the rod. At the same time, there are events that his gestures re-enact over the rod and that therefore are attributed to the steel rod in the original investigation. His right hand enacts movements of "everything" (or "they") in the rod moving to his left (Episode 7.3, line 1, frame 1, 2). He then uses his right hand to show how the "little animal" "comes here," as it moves from the position just off the far end of the rod toward the rod (Episode 7.3, line 1, frame 1, 2). If I just consider what he utters ("Now comes the little animal, comes here, goes"), it is impossible to understand *what* he says, that is, what his narrative is about. But his words describe an image that can be thought as iconically related to the things at hand: the elderberry mark sphere is very small, about 1 centimeter in diameter. "The little animal," therefore, is an imaginative figure for the sphere. Furthermore, relatively to the rod, it figures exactly in the place where the sphere previously has been located with respect to the iron rod.

The term "relative" here shows the mutually constitutive nature of the rod, gesture, and speech in creating a visual but ephemeral image that symbolizes what has happened before. Some of the relations between the situation as made presented again here and the original situation are arbitrary, others are based on perceptual and therefore motivated iconic relations that better articulate the existence of a relationship than does an arbitrary one.

As the episode continues, the right hand then changes its signified as it becomes associated with talk about some entities (they") that distribute "themselves again." The utterance "distribute" is produced simultaneously with the movement of the right hand over and against the rod, from its left to right end from Phil's perspective (Episode 7.3, line 2).

Episode 7.3, Line 2

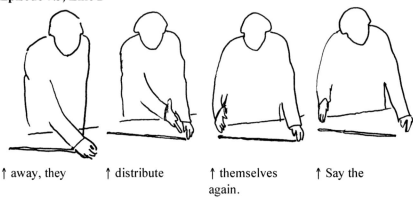

↑ away, they   ↑ distribute   ↑ themselves   ↑ Say the
                                     again.

Here again, what Phil is really communicating can be understood only considering the setting as a whole, including words, gestures, and material configuration. By itself, the utterance "they distribute themselves again" tells us very little. But coinciding with the gesture over and against the rod, I come to understand how the charges ("they") distribute themselves in horizontal direction and along the rod.

Phil then articulates a "piece" that has been charged by the experimenter ("you"), which "pulls itself." Whereto it pulls itself is left open as Phil stops talking all the while continuing to gesture (Episode 7.3, line 3, frame 3). For a stretch, then, the communication consists of gestures only (Episode 7.3, line 3, frame 4–line 4, frame 3), the significance of which is obtained from their relation to the rod, which itself stands for the rod observed earlier during the experiment that now is to be explained.

Episode 7.3, Line 3

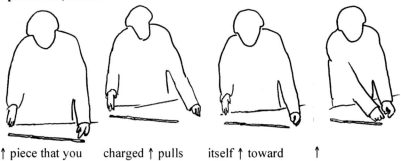

↑ piece that you   charged ↑ pulls   itself ↑ toward   ↑

While Phil talks about "the piece" that "pulls itself," his left hand moves toward and away from the rod in the same relative position that the original metal rod and elderberry mark sphere previously have had (Episode 7.3, line 3, frame 1–3). Here, the former "little element" has transformed itself into "the piece that you charged." This transformation, though not indicated otherwise, is consistent with the fact that the hand movement is identical across the two moments and with the fact that the designated entity is the agent that approaches the rod, at first "going" then "pulling itself." Here, then, although the signifier has changed from "little animal" to "the piece you have charged," I can understand both as signifiers referring to the same entity (signified), because of all other sense-making resources in the setting that have stayed the same. That is, communication involves tracking the variant and invariant aspects of the setting as a whole, not just the words or word–gesture combinations.

Episode 7.3, Line 3

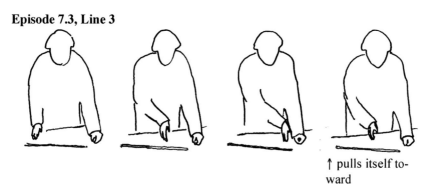

↑ pulls itself to-
ward

In this episode, the PVC rod stands for the steel rod that has been part of the original investigation and, metonymically for the experimental configuration as a whole. The PVC rod functions as (material) signifier for some other object. Resembling the steel rod in shape and size, it has an iconic relation to the object it signifies. In this, the right end from Phil's perspective corresponds to that end where the ruler was approached, the left end to that where the elderberry mark sphere was found earlier. He is positioned with respect to the rod in the same way that he has been during the original investigation. That is, he recreates a constellation and configuration that is very similar to what his group has experienced before. Placing himself in this position iconically but metonymically creates the conditions for an orientation in which is grounded any subsequent theoretical and by the teacher acceptable, scientific explanation.

The perceptually recreated and intimated events constitute a first layer against which the explanatory layer, the perspective through a different lens, is constructed. In this latter perspective, there are atomic level events, which Phil creates and intimates by means of gestures. Because the gestures occur over and against the rod, the processes are intimated to occur inside the rod by means of the perceptual similarity. A crucial and also the most difficult part of the explanation is the articulation of what happens at the atomic level after the elderberry mark sphere initially is attracted and repelled. Phil does not yet have a verbal explanation, but his gestures enact a process according to which there is a cyclic process of movements (perhaps equilibration) across the rod (Episode 7.3, line 3, frame 4 to line 4, frame 3). The finding that Phil enacts a process gesturally prior to producing a verbal account does not surprise me, given that I have observed similar cases in very different domains—students conducting computer-based simulations or designing architectural structures (e.g., Roth, 2002). Changing to representing the elderberry mark sphere with the left hand while depicting the atomic level movements with the right hand also clarifies the referents. As in the previous episodes, Phil imbues the objects and entities with agency in the same way that humans are imbued with agency. This attribution takes us to the fundamental situation where the material body shares the world with all other material bodies, human and non-human alike—being is being singular plural. Phil therefore articulates the material entities from the perspective of his own material involvement in the world, which he constitutes and shares with other material bodies. This puts him into (and reflects) a position of a being talking about other beings and interacting with beings no different than himself. Material bodies have a position; and this position, as evident throughout this book, comes with a disposition. When I am among things, it is easier to talk about what I do and what others do in relational terms, as dispositions, and in terms of what we do together. Another step is required to remove situated and situating human agents, you and I, from the descriptions, which then represent everybody's and nobody's perspective simultaneously, taking a viewpoint from everywhere and nowhere simultaneously.

The entities used as part of the gestures make the event to be explained present again in metonymic form: they take the role of additional representations, additional layers and perspectives. They track objects and entities that constitute a ground, which does not need to be represented in mind. They are perceptually available to all participants in the conversation and therefore "go without a saying," which names or describes them. These objects exist as signified available for future reference and as long as they are needed. They serve as indexical ground over and against which students gesture without the need of a description. In this way, communication is spread across the setting, reducing the need for mental representation and cogitation. Each time students change the representational form— i.e., the lenses they use for looking at the events—the production of an explanation becomes more difficult again. Students have to replace previously existing physical representations by discursive or gestural representations.

INCREASING VERBAL ARTICULATION OF EXPERIENCE

The sequence of episodes, which follows the explanations of one group over time, illustrates how students became increasingly independent of the actual objects and equipment in the production of their observational and theoretical descriptions. Initially, the students' accounts are partially articulated in modes other than the verbal one, including the original material objects, new and arbitrary material objects that bear metonymic and iconic relation to the original ones, and iconic and metaphoric gestures. This development therefore constitutes an *abstraction*, a pulling of sense-making resources away from the original situation; and it involves students who moving away from and talking about the situation.

When students no longer do the full demonstration but only some material objects or arbitrary objects, they can be thought of as enacting a simulation. For this

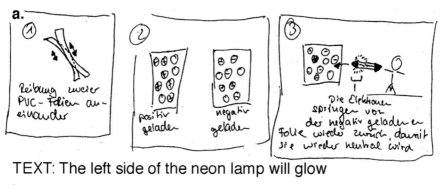

TEXT: The left side of the neon lamp will glow

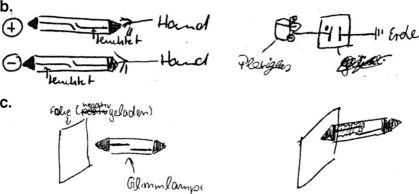

TEXT: Touching causes glow on the transparency side

Figure 7.4. a. Iconic representation of production of and test for charges. b. Various aspects of the iconic representation are now replaced by words or other symbols for charges. c. Even more of iconic representations are omitted and replaced by text (not shown).

investigation, all videotaped episodes exhibit students using some form of material object representing the original situation. I cannot state any hypothesis about how their communicative forms concerning this investigation has continued to evolve, especially when there no longer are materials to stand for, such as, for example, when students describe the investigation and the explanation of its phenomena. But there is evidence for such a development from the initial investigations students conducted with static electricity also described in chapter 4.

One of the question on the test asks students, "How can you test whether the charge on a rubbed transparency film is negative." The teacher has told students that they can make drawings if they want. Copies of some of the student responses are depicted in Figure 7.4. The results not only provide a cross section of responses in the class, but also show how students find themselves at various points in the trajectory of representational articulation. That is, as in the discourse situations earlier, the inscriptions (inscribed representations) change from *more iconic* (topological) to *more textual* (categorical) forms. In the top row, the student represents in iconic form the events of rubbing two films and how he tests for the charges, recording his observation as a glowing neon lamp (Figure 7.4a). Also represented is the conceptual level explanation: rubbing leads to charge separation, leaving one transparency positively charged, the other negatively. The student (Matt) has drawn a stick figure, which holds a glow lamp to one of the two transparency sheets. Matt suggests that electrons jump from the glow lamp to the transparency to make it neutral again. Although he does not articulate it in words, this jumping of electrons is associated with a glowing of the lamp.

In this situation, there is an entirely figurative articulation of the events that lead to the charging of two transparency sheets and the test that proves the presence of charges. The depictions constitute iconic re-presentations, and, in the leftmost image, the name "PVC film" has been inscribed on the image itself. It both names and denotes the nature of the drawn figure as representation of the material object that Matt has used. In the center drawing of Figure 7.4a, Matt depicts two transparency sheets, one with positive and the other with negative charges. This depiction is equivalent to but more iconic than the explanation Jenny gives in chapter 5, where I show how two pens come to stand for the two transparency sheets and the cap of a third pen for the positive and negative charges. Matt, on the other hand, represents the two transparencies iconically; and he provides metaphoric representation of the charges in the form of small round circles with a "+" or "-" sign inscribed on the inside. This constitutes a figurative representation of events as seen through the microphysical lens, which provides an explanation for the fact that charges are present. One notes that each of the first two representations represents a perspective through a different lens: through the phenomenal lens, I see the action of rubbing two sheets, none of which has microscopic particles inscribed; through the microphysical lens, I see small charged particles—as distinct to a charge that might be a macroscopic entity, distributed throughout. (I am thinking here of the differences between representing atoms as nuclei with small negative spheres revolving around them like planets around the sun versus representing the nuclei with negatively charged clouds surrounding them. Matt's representation clearly is a view through the microphysical rather than, for example, a quantum mechanical lens.)

In the third image, Matt returns to the phenomenal level as he describes what happens when a glow lamp is brought close to one of the transparency sheets. Notable is his depiction of the inside of the lamp, which iconically represents the lamp, and the glow, which clearly is associated with one side rather than the lamp as a whole. But a second type of representation can also be noted: the transparency sheet includes small circles inscribed with "-" signs. This image therefore can be understood as presenting two perspectives on top of one another, achieving a layering that is not unlike my weather map (Figure 5.1c) that results from the superposition of a rain map (Figure 5.1a) and a geographical map (Figure 5.1b).

The renderings of the process of testing an object for charges are less figurative in the center row (Figure 7.4b). In the left of the two images, Winona has produced a layered representation that includes elements taken from each of two different perspectives. On the left side, there no longer are figurative representations of the objects involved in the rubbing. These objects are denoted by a circle inscribed with a "+" or "-," respectively. The neon glow lamp is depicted iconically, including its inside and the characteristic shape of the two electrodes. On the right-hand side, stick hands and the German noun word for "hand" indicate that during a test for the presence of charges, the investigator holds the lamp on this side. The glow, however, in contrast to the way Matt depicts it, is denoted by the verb "lights" ("leuchtet"), with an arrow pointing to the near and far side of the lamp with respect to the hand.

Vanessa, who denotes the charged object by means of a square and the word "Plexiglas," has produced the second example at this level (Figure 7.4b, right). She renders the glow lamp less figuratively, that is, more abstractly than either Matt or Winona: it is a square with electrodes that have little perceptual likeness to the ones in the lamp and as depicted in the previous example. The depiction bears likeness with the drawings of electrical elements in certain professions. On the right-hand side of the drawing, the grounding process is no longer depicted as occurring through the human body but in terms of an icon that can be found on circuit diagrams and the word "ground" ("Erde"). Whereas Matt depicts the events figuratively by means of some of the salient aspects that can be observed and literal representations of the microphysical perspective, Winona and Vanessa describe and explain the events less figuratively in a form of development that also characterizes the talk in the laboratory. Vanessa's rendering shares similarity with Jenny's explanation during the lesson, where she used the three pens to depict how transparency sheets are charged by means of rubbing: the non-verbal elements in the communicative act no longer are related iconically to the original materials. In Winona's rendering, a mix of iconic and non-iconic representations can be observed. In both cases, the inscriptions are layered as they include both phenomenal and microphysical elements.

Resembling the decreasing reliance on non-verbal elements in the discourse situations, the iconic renderings disappear in the written test. This can also be observed in the test papers, which, as said, represent a cross section of students at different stages of the representational trajectory. That is, the drawings become increasingly abstract, decreasingly bearing perceptual similarity, and finally omitting most of the detail. Thus, although Phil has drawn the transparency sheet and glow lamp figuratively, he no longer represents the charges figuratively or the events during the unit test. The hands have disappeared as has the fact that the charged object is grounded—either through the stick figure, hand, or abstract electronic element. Instead, just above the drawing of the transparency sheet, he writes "sheet (negatively charged")" and in the main text, he notes "touching causes glow on the transparency side" (Figure 7.4c). In this instance, therefore, important elements of the observation and explanation have been rendered in verbal form, which no longer bears iconic relations to that which it describes. The drawings disappear altogether leaving all explanations to the text. Thus, on the test some students do not even use drawings at all but render descriptions and explications in the verbal mode only.

These examples show that when students inscribe observations and explications, they make use of depictions that also show a range of perceptual similarity (iconic relation) with the phenomena initially but become less figurative and, for some students, eventually completely verbal. This development mirrors the one in discourse situations described previously, where hand gestures, body movements, body orientations, and positions (configurations) play an important role in the transition from accounting for observations in the situation where they occur versus accounting for them some time later and without any of the original material objects present.

Much like the figurative drawings, gestures therefore play an important role in locating objects and entities by means of deixis, and animating the movements of these objects and entities by means of iconic gestures. However, the iconic gestures also have deictic function. When a student moves his hand from left to right across a rod while talking about the movements of electrons, he does not just gesture motion (as this might happen in those communicative contexts where the topical situation is not at hand). Rather, he also represents motion in a particular direction and along specific trajectories. Gestures are over and about the material objects that are their topic. Gestures thereby encode information not necessarily available in contexts where these objects (or their representations) are absent.

Taken together, material objects, gestures, speech, drawings, and written text constitute different modalities for situationally making ideas present in and during communication. All of these entities, including verbal language, constitute the exposition of the world of bodies as such: it is in and through these forms that the world takes form. These communicative forms are used to exhibit and expose the different ways in which the plural singularity of the world. They exhibit the entirety of being "as its meaning, which is to say, the originary sharing according to which a being relates to a being, the circulation of a meaning of the world that has no beginning or end" (Nancy, 2000, p. 84). In these days, schooling is such that it favors verbal (written) representation. This feature of schools therefore constitutes an environmental pressure that mediates shifts in students' representations from situated (material, gesture) into situation-independent (symbolic, abstract) modalities. This has implications for how teachers teach the explanations and theories of events that require quite different lenses, with objects and events that bear little likeness to anything in the phenomenal world.

The trajectory from more to less figurative representation described here also is a trajectory of layered representations that initially include more figurative elements to less figurative elements, that is, including more elements as seen through the phenomenal lens to more elements through the lens or lenses used in standard physics. In the videotapes of this tenth-grade class, the teachers permit students to use all representational modalities they have at hand. This possibly mediates their development in the sense that it decreases the mental effort and increases the rate in which they can make the transition between the different representational levels, especially, the transition to forms of representation that have little to no iconic relation to the events described.

EVOLUTIONARY TRENDS

There are important evolutionary (temporal) dimensions in the relation of setting, gestures, and speech as representational modalities in students' communication. Although I return to time and temporality in chapter 9, a first look at the temporal dimensions involved in evolving communicative forms is appropriate here. In this and the previous chapter, I show how students initially gesture phenomena that they do not yet express at all in the verbal modality. Students then express phenomena verbally, but the verbal mode lags behind the gestures. As students become familiar with the phenomena on the one hand, and the production of descriptions on the other, the lag all but disappears so that gestures and speech are perfectly coordinated. Finally, the overall time for producing observational and theoretical descriptions decreases significantly, which therefore parallels the previous form of development.

In evolutionary terms, the individual-level changes normally associated with the notion of "development" reproduce gesture-speech relations that are thought to characterize human (cultural) "evolution." Whether or not one agrees with the "ontogeny repeats phylogeny" assumption, the data from this and other studies support the notion of language development as an evolutionary process (at least in the type of settings researched). In the shifting levels of representation from things and movements in the world, that is, ergotic and epistemic movements to symbolic gestures to spoken and written text, student communication undergoes evolutionary trends. From a first-person perspective, I-learner experience such trends as increasing familiarity with things, events, and relevant communicative forms. Although I may not think of development, I experience myself as having an increasing number of action possibilities, including ways of talking *in order to* do what has to be done and of talking *about* the things I am doing. How is such a development or evolution best to be described?

Some cognitive theories regard environment and individual as a unit, which integrates the two into an irreducible, dynamically and structurally coupled whole. The episodes—presented in this and the previous chapter—illustrate events whose emphasis shifts from environment to increasing symbolic representation within the individual student. Initially, communication relies on the ergotic and epistemic function of hand movements accompanied by little speech; the teachers frequently consider this early speech inappropriate as learning outcome. Those aspects that constitute representations in the setting increasingly shift to internal representations, spoken and written text and drawn images, that signify things that are of a different logical type, a different conceptual layer, than the gestures and things in the world. That is, although signification is achieved in material form, that which is signified has split: signification and sense no longer are the same. More advanced forms of knowing are made possible to the students by communicating in contexts that afford other modalities than speech alone. Thus, because material objects and instruments are present and visually available to all participants, they "go without saying" and therefore do not need to be talked about (unless one or more participant notes the presence of conversational trouble). At the same time, the material setting puts constraints on how gestures can be understood, because in communication, gestures, and the aspects of the ground made salient have to coincide to yield intelligible communication, to make the situation as a whole signify in a non-contradictory way. These aspects therefore are simultaneously resources for making sense of the gestures and constraints on possible senses the gestures may have.

The episodes underscore how students produce many different descriptions and how only some survive. Other descriptions disappear altogether, such as the notion of protons that move throughout the material initially proposed by someone. This talk is consistent with thinking of positive and negative charges globally but inconsistent with the perspective through the microphysical lens, according to which positive charges are found in the nuclei of atoms, which are stationary in solids, and electrons, some of which can easily be removed or are entirely mobile (e.g., in metals). Still other forms of expressions, such as the "subfluous electrons" subsequently change, here, for example, into "electron holes." These results are consistent with my observations generally that focus on the emergence, stabilization, and extinction of discourse in science classrooms. Whether a particular description survives depends on the number and quality of other descriptions of the same phenomenon, the degree to which it is taken up by others, and the level of support it receives from teachers. That is, there are identifiable situational factors that allow, at a minimum, a descriptive model of the linguistic changes in a physics classroom.

For the described form of evolution to occur, "pressures" or "constraints" are required. In the present context, the most obvious pressure is associated with students' (meta-) knowledge about the activity of schooling, which mediates what and how they learn: at some later point, they have to produce written or verbal explanations. This ulterior goal mediates what students do and the representational trajectories they obliquely aim for and undergo. For example, laboratory notes and written tests require context- and gesture-independent descriptions and explanations of phenomena. This constrains students, who react by evolving verbal forms of communication. There is therefore a pressure towards a specific communicative form built into the curriculum that provides students initially with great freedom to evolve communicative forms, but ultimately constrains them to allow only one (or a small number of variations of verbal forms). The ultimate goal that teachers aim at is the written production of science rather than the modes of communication observable in any laboratory, which, as shown, include numerous indexical references to the setting.

Materials and gestures as representational forms allow students to think publicly; this thinking is articulated in and through the materials, gestures, body positions, and talk. The thinking is expressed in the setting, through and through in material form—sounds, arm and body movements, and material things perceptually available to others in the setting. That is, these different resources are situated and distributed across people and setting. Using the world as its own representation and later to gesture over, about, and against the objects visibly available to the conversational participants reduces the effort that is required to produce stand-alone verbal descriptions. There are many sayings around the world about the fact that someone's lack of access to gestures interferes with his or her communication;

and there are theories about the function of gestures in speech production that would predict difficulties in communication, especially in and about unfamiliar topics (e.g., Butterworth & Hadar, 1989). Whereas I do not subscribe to these theories, the fact is that parallel resources including natural language, gestures, visual representations, and natural objects allow different types of communication integrating the categorical (designating) and topological (dynamic) aspects of phenomena and the theoretical discourse laid over them. The multimodal communication is thereby made available for inspection in its dynamic parts in a much better way than if the participants are exposed to the symbolic, verbal end state only. Finally, there are constraints on the objects and events when they are enacted through ergotic and epistemic movements, or when they appear as symbolic gestures above the materials than by manipulating mental images. Because it takes time to produce gestures, to move material things (e.g., pens, rods) about, signifying with and through the body as a whole produces a different temporality than if speakers only produced sounds. This temporality needs to be accounted for in the analyses, because it makes discourse differ from written texts—which have no temporal beginning or end but are given in their entirety at once, allowing the analyst to treat any part of the text as if it was produced simultaneously with any other part of the text. In chapter 9, I deal with some of the aspects arising from the temporal nature of being, discourse, and learning.

An important issue for educators and educational researchers is the representational point of view. In their (verbal and gestural) communication, students often take the perspective of the objects, which are imbued with agency. Sometimes researchers treat such talk as primitive and animist. But such a characterization misses the point because these forms of talk decrease communicative effort particularly in novel and unfamiliar situations. Thus, even physicists—said to be the most abstract-thinking scientists—are known to use object-centered talk and the researchers become part of the world of entities that their work is about. The lore has it, for example, that Albert Einstein imagined traveling with objects at the speed of light while articulating special relativity theory. Furthermore, the Nobel Prize winning Barbara McClintock used alternative, animate language invites the perception of nature as an active partner in a more reciprocal relation to an observer, equally active, but neither omniscient nor omnipotent. This active partnership is explicitly theorized when being (verb) is understood as being singular plural. The subject-centered perspective appears to provide advantages over abstract perspective because it decreases the effort necessary for producing a non-indexical representation. I-centered perspectives and indexical representation characterize everyday cognition—perhaps *because* they require less cognitive effort.

FOLLOWING INSTRUCTIONS

In vivo the manual offers a reader anything but just what is needed.
(Garfinkel, 2002, p. 205)

In the two previous chapters, I show how students evolve communication generally and language particularly over and about investigations into phenomena that they either designed themselves or conducted following teacher instructions. The two chapters show (a) how students initially manipulate original materials as part of their accounts of what they have seen and (b) how they theorize these phenomena. These theories are perspectives on the event that can be likened to sets of lenses that provide different maps for the experiential reality. This perceptual reality, as I show in chapters 3 through 5, is itself not given at the moment I lay my eyes on them, but emerges in the form of new figure|ground configurations that add to, subdivide in whole|parts configurations, or sublate previous figure|ground configuration in the same domain. The overall development is one from agency in the world to verbal language, which serves *in order to* get the investigations done and which is *about* the investigation and explains what can be seen. In this chapter, I take the reverse trajectory: How do I-learner get from an instruction, articulated orally or in written form, to actions and products in the world?

In science education, instructions for doing a laboratory investigation or, for my present purposes, any instruction that a teacher gives to students, are treated as unproblematic. When students do not do what a teacher intends them to do, the latter frequently blames the former und uses low motivation, disinterest, and other negative terms to explain. Students, on the other hand, frequently complain that the instructions are not sufficiently well constructed, and therefore, "not meaningful"; they often blame the teacher for not being clear. (Many evaluation schemes university students use to assess their professors and instructors include an item intended for rating the quality and clarity of instructions.) My descriptions in chapter 2 already show some of the problematic issues that exist for students as they attempt to do what the teacher wants them to do. Even exemplifying what to do does not guarantee that students do what they are supposed to do, as exhibited in chapter 4 where students struggle to get the neon lamp to glow. In part, knowing what I do means knowing that what I see is exactly that which I am supposed to see; but seeing something specific is the intent underlying the task. I therefore find myself in a double bind that to follow an instruction, I already have to be able to do what it says; but I follow instructions exactly because I need them as resource to act when I do not yet know what has to be done next. In this chapter, I go beyond this everyday practice of blaming instructions or instruction followers when things go wrong, that is, when intended outcomes differ from actual outcomes.

PERVASIVENESS OF THE PHENOMENON

Instructions and instruction following are pervasive features of everyday life. When I buy a new watch, computer, VCR, or camera, I generally use or refer to a set of instructions that come with a device to make it work. I find a new recipe in the daily newspaper or weekly magazine I subscribe to, and, finding it interesting for one reason or another, I use the instructions in the attempt to (re-) produce the dish that looks so appealing in the photograph provided with the recipe. I know that it is not easy and sometimes impossible to understand instructions. Elsewhere I describe a situation where it has been impossible for me initially to (learn to) prune fruit trees and bushes, although I have had the finest book available to me, as I have attested repeatedly since I know better how to prune and what pruning is about (Roth, 2005d). The difficulties a set of new instructions poses to my understanding are especially enormous when I read them without also engaging in the attempt to do what the instructions ask me to. Thus, when computers first became widely available, I attempted to read the manuals prior to using the software, with the result that after the first few pages, a sense of not having a clue was arising within and overcoming me. Some (perhaps many?) individuals react to such frustrations by blaming themselves, and I have heard frequently comments such as, "Oh, I am just so stupid when it comes to computers?" or "I just don't like cooking too much." Such statements are consistent with the way some science educators have been talking about scientific literacy. Only a little over a decade ago, advocates of "Science for All" deplored the general illiteracy, using the general commonly experienced difficulties to program a VCR to exemplify illiteracy. But there is more to following instructions, as I know from my own experience, and it is difficult for anybody to attempt explaining my failure in terms of illiteracy, scientific or otherwise. In this chapter, I track these problems, which I formulate as an aporia in chapter 2: How do I know that I have followed the instructions, especially when I do not know beforehand, what the result of my actions are to look like? What does it take to follow instructions?

In school science, too, there are many situations where students are faced with instructions that they are expected to turn into a series of actions—e.g., an investigation, a laboratory task—the result of which are the teacher-intended lesson or learning outcomes. In any such situations, common lore views the discovery of the relation between the projected outcome and a corresponding course of action on the basis of given instructions as a *consequence* of someone having followed instructions rather than as a *condition* for doing so (Amerine & Bilmes, 1990). Following instructions therefore is like traveling with a map (chapter 5). The view I take here is this: Successfully following instructions means constructing a course of actions such that, having done this course of action, the instructions will (a) serve as a descriptive account of what has been done and (b) provide a basis for describing the consequences of such action. However, like instructions, this description leaves undefined the practical skill, the embedded activities, and the background knowledge, in other words, the competence by means of which constructing courses of action in accordance with sets of instructions is accomplished.

Following instructions should be of particular interest to science educators, who frequently use laboratory investigations as part of their curricula. Yet how people "follow instructions" and especially how people successfully do so is an underresearched and undertheorized phenomenon. Doing investigations by repeating the methodology someone else has described is an important aspect of the sciences, which. Though said to be about the world, investigations really are about designed and constructed worlds, that is, the world as it exhibits itself under special conditions. The methods sections of research articles are designed such that others can take them and repeat the experiment. The laboratory is the place where scientists create the world apart from the world. This world apart from the world is so crucial that only a laboratory allows a researcher to "raise the world" (Latour, 1983). Knowing that it is not easy to follow instructions while knowing that only instruction following creates the phenomena that physics describes, Michael Faraday built equipment for his peers, which he sent together with instructions. In this way, he felt more certain that they would see what he has been able to see, and therefore, that they accept his way of theorizing electromagnetic phenomena.

APORIA OF INSTRUCTION FOLLOWING

Following instructions, as phenomenon, has been of interest to ethnomethodological research for quite some time, especially because following instructions appears so innocuous; and yet the phenomenon involves some fundamental aporia to the person who is following instructions. How do people follow instructions in everyday situations and what embodied skills do they bring to the task that make the work involved disappear when instructions are experienced as unproblematic? Ethnomethodological studies of *instruction following* highlight the indexicality, incompleteness, and ambiguity of rules and instructions and considers these properties as necessary and essential rather than as incidental and remediable (Suchman, 1987). Indexicality, incompleteness and ambiguity between an instruction such as "Do X" and an action to which an observer ascribes the observation "She has done X" constitute a gap that no improvement or changes in the instruction can remedy. This gap between the statement "Do X" and the execution "Doing X" is an ontological one: the instruction and the action are of a different logical type. In everyday practice, I usually do not notice this gap. Yet beginning teachers, first-time cooks, first-time assemblers of furniture, and so forth experience it almost as a matter of course. Ethnomethodologists use terms such as "unremark-able" and "unnotice-able" to make salient—i.e., figure against ground—the efficacy and mundaneity of our everyday competence in dealing with this gap.

Instructions such as "Do X" not only indicate to me that I am to engage in some action X, but also serve as *prospective* accounts. That is, if the action is successful then the instruction serves as an account of "what has been done." When things "go wrong," on the other hand, an assessment highlights that the instruction has not been followed. Often, such as when following the instruction to do a science experiment or in following a recipe in the kitchen, it is not clear after completing an action or even a series of actions whether or not the instructions have been followed. In chapter 2, I show how twelfth-graders struggle—without knowing it so—acting in such a way that they can be said to have followed instructions. This is, because the checkpoints that may serve as controls often integrate over series of actions: Only some time down the road can I assess that the experiment does not give the expected results or that the dish does not look like the photo in the cookbook. As I show in chapters 2 and 5, in such cases the actors find themselves in a double bind that I have framed for following instructions. I state the aporia of following instructions in two, incompossible but mutually presupposing statements:

1. to find out whether I have done what I was supposed to do, I need to know that what I observe is what I was supposed to observe; and
2. to know that I have observed what I was supposed to observe, I need to know that what I have done was what I was supposed to do.

The perceived problem between instructions and situated action can be turned around. Rather than build a theory of action based on a theory of plans (instructions), the aim is to investigate how people produce and find evidence for plans in the course of situated action. Studying instruction following as a phenomenon is made more difficult in situations where there is a culture of blaming others for the gaps between actual and intended outcomes. It is too easy to fault high school students for not following instructions. I therefore use my own experience of following instructions as source for a first-person study of the phenomenon.

ON MAKING CHOUX PASTRY GOUGÈRE

Being an avid hobby cook, I spend a lot of time in the kitchen, among others, trying out new dishes when I see an interesting recipe. Each time I make a new dish following some recipe, I face the same gap that exists between the recipe and the completed dish, between the instructions (descriptions of preparation) and my actions that realize the dish. This gap is sublated in my praxis of cooking. Although I have a lot of experience cooking, and although there are times when I say to myself, "there is something wrong with the recipe," the fundamental gap does not go away. The account was written only hours after cooking a dish by following a new and unfamiliar recipe.

A First-Person Account

> I have decided to make a gougère. It is a dish that, as its name suggests, has French origins. It involves two major components. There is a ring of choux (or puff) pastry surrounding a filling made from smoked haddock or tuna in a white sauce that also includes onions and mushrooms and is topped with grated firm cheese.
>
> The ingredients for the choux pastry, calculated for a meal for four persons, include: 1 cup of bread flour; ¼ teaspoon salt; 6 tablespoons cold, diced butter; scant 1 cup water; 3 eggs beaten; and 5 ounces of grated Emmental, aged Cheddar, or Gruyère.

My wife and I normally have an appetizer with dinner, and because we are only two, the recipe needs to be adapted. I am thinking about making one-third, which, in my experience, would be a sufficient quantity, but then I decide to make one-half, given that I have more fish than the recipe calls for and given that my wife can take the remaining as lunch to work. The instructions read:

1 Lightly grease a shallow ovenproof dish. Sift the bread flour and salt onto a sheet of waxed paper. Place the butter and water in a medium saucepan and heat gently. As soon as the butter has melted, bring the water to a boil. Immediately pour in all the seasoned flour.
2 Beat the mixture hard until it comes away from the sides of the pan. (It will look alarmingly lumpy at first.) Remove the pan from the heat and cool for 5 minutes—this is important.
3 Gradually beat the beaten eggs into the dough until the mixture has a good dropping consistency and holds its shape. You may not need all the egg. Stir in two-thirds of the grated cheese.

I put half a cup of water on the burner, set to about 6 on the dial, take out half a cup of flour onto a waxed sheet, and then turn to cut the three tablespoons of butter, which, because of experience, I can estimate and cut pretty accurately without additional help. I wonder why the sheet needs to be waxed; for a moment think that I could have the flour in a bowl, too. All of a sudden I realize that the water is boiling, I add the butter, only to note upon returning to the cookbook that the recipe reads to add the butter right away and to heat rapidly only after it has melted. I ask myself, "What is the relevance of heating strongly only after the butter has melted?"

But there is no time: the butter is melting and I need to add the flour quickly. I vaguely remember having heard before that it needs to be added all at once. I wonder about the instruction "beat the mixture hard." What am I to beat it with? An eggbeater? A whisk? There are no instructions, but two of the photographs on the page show a person handling a pan contents with a wooden spoon. So I grab a wooden spoon, asking my wife, "Which one am I supposed to take?" and "What do they mean by 'beating hard'?" There is no time to deliberate. I am beating the mixture with the wooden spoon, turning it, then hitting sideways again. Within seconds, the dough forms a ball. What does it read? "Beat . . . until it comes away from the sides . . . " Does what I am looking at constitute "coming away from the sides"? I continue beating the dough sideways and in a circle. "Is this what 'coming off the sides' looks like?" The pan and dough don't answer. I place the pot on the stovetop, setting the timer for five minutes.

I return to the cookbook, reading the instruction about the beaten eggs. I have prepared two, because the instructions say I might not need all of it. But then, I know that because I use whole grain spelt flour instead to the normal bread (fine wheat) flour called for in most recipes, everything changes anyway. But what does "dropping consistency" mean? What am I to see? And how is the dough to look like? Is it to drop from the spoon? But it is quite firm now.

After the five minutes are over, I begin to add the beaten eggs. I beat the beaten eggs into the mixture. I add, wondering how the dough will change to take on "dropping consistency." I go back to the cookbook thinking it might be saying "drooping" rather than "dropping"; but no, I got it right. I continue, wondering whether my beating actions correspond to the beating required making the choux dough. I know that some actions are such that little variation will lead to failure. Choux pastry puffs up, and not doing it correctly may lead to a dough that does not puff and remains a big blob while baking it.

I continue beating in the beaten egg. The recipe says I may not need all, and because I am making one-half, I should anyways need only one and one half eggs. I look out for changes in the consistency, asking myself, "is this what 'dropping consistency' looks like?" But there hasn't been much of a change. So I add more, beating the mixture. It holds its shape, but I perceive nothing that could be described as "dropping"? I add more and realize that I have added all of the two beaten eggs. I beat more. When I lift the spoon, the dough does move downward, it is not just a hard ball.

I turn to prepare the filling. I butter a shallow ovenproof dish and add some of the dough. I am about one quarter around the dish when I realize, "Oh no, I forgot the cheese." It is sitting on the cutting board, already divided into two piles. I return the dough from the dish to the pan and then add the cheese. Do I need to heat? Had I put the cheese into the dough mixture right away, it would have been at a higher temperature, and the cheese might have melted. I do mix then place the pan on the stove plate at low heat. I use the spoon and turn the dough, which mixes the cheese into it. Am I to stop now? Should I wait until the cheese melts? As I turn, the cheese seems to disappear. Is it melted or just covered with dough? I stop although I think that a lot of the cheese has not yet melted.

It turns out to be a wonderful gougère. My wife and I decide to have another one quite soon. But the question lingers, "Have I made a gougère that tastes like the one that the cookbook instructions intend me to make?"

Aporias

My account, written soon after I have prepared the gougère, highlights my experiences of making the dish. This account is as different from the actual making as the instructions that preceded the process of cooking. Now, several weeks later, I have acquired some distance from the original event and I can ask myself questions about the account, where it hides some of the work involved, where it highlights some of the potential trouble, and where it provides insights to the fundamental aporia of turning instructions into situated courses of actions. The difficulties emerge even prior to doing anything, being related to the indeterminacy of any manual (e.g., about quantity) with respect to its referent.

At a surface level, the account points out some of the contingencies that require the adaptation of the descriptions for the situation at hand. Thus, the recipe states the ingredients for four persons, but at the time, I am cooking for two; more so, because I make an appetizer, too, I can do with even less for the main course. I do not (have to) know how much of the normal recipe I need exactly and then calculate the equivalent amounts of each item. Doing so is a typical schoolbook text problem, which in this way never poses itself in the everyday world of a cook. Rather, there are constraints within the recipe that mediate how much I am going to make. For example, the recipe calls for eggs, which my chicken lay in wholes and keeping part of an egg does not improve its value. So I usually make dishes that use one, two, or three eggs, that is, an integer rather than a fractional amount.

Other constraints, too, are external. I do not use wheat flour in my cooking, substituting spelt for it instead; I also do not use fine flour but only flour made from the whole grain. Similarly, I use grey sea salt, which is a bit wet, rather than the salt that comes in large quantities and is completely dry and "free flowing." In these instances, just what does it mean to take 1 cup or ¼ teaspoon? How does my 1-cup spelt flour and my ¼-teaspoon salt compare to how much the cookbook author uses which she describes as 1 cup of flour and ¼ teaspoon of salt? A reader may be tempted to say that the problem lies in my using different ingredients than the ones called for in the recipe. But this objection only skirts the real issue: whatever I use as flour or salt, it never is the same as the one that the cookbook author had used and is using. A repeat performance *never* is identical to the original; repetition inherently constitutes difference (Deleuze, 1968/1994). The question whether a performance constitutes a repeat performance therefore has to remain inherently open. More so, there is openness with respect to the measures and ingredients themselves. Because the ingredients have traveled, they have also settled, and they may have settled differently from other ingredients depending on their origin, composition, and previous processing. The point is that not only the instructions to be followed but also the list of ingredients pose tremendous challenges. They embody instructions and work that are hidden: the text "1 cup bread flour" or "¼ teaspoon salt" does not just denote an entity, a certain amount of substance but rather the end result of a course of actions, *measuring out* a certain amount of a specific ingredient. The result of the action of measuring 1 cup bread flour or ¼ teaspoon salt is therefore as contingent as the action of measuring itself.

The account of the experience of making gougère also allows me to understand why it is nearly impossible to make sense of instructions before actually making the dish. Thus, the instruction "beat the mixture hard until it comes away from the sides of the pan" presupposes my perception of the mixture at all times during the process. What I observe prior to the moment marked by "until" is not stated explicitly in the recipe. The recipe does state the possibility that I observe something that "is lumpy." But this, too, is not a shortcoming, because even if it is described, there are other aspects that are not. This is just what a set of breaching experiments exhibited (Garfinkel, 1967). The instructions ask students to write down any brief conversation they overhear in their daily life; they are then to explicate "what really has been said." In successive attempts, students build up extensive explications only to find that however detailed they provide an account, a fundamental gap remains between the utterances and what really has been said or meant. The same can be said of instructions. However detailed they are, the gap between the text and my embodied actions remains. This gap is an irremediable feature of the instruction–situated action relation.

After I pour all the flour into the boiling butter-water ensemble, I am to "beat the mixture hard until it comes away from the sides of the pan." As an indicator, I am provided with the description of what the mixture might initially look like, "alarmingly lumpy." If I ask myself prior to beginning the process of cooking, "What does lumpy mean?," I may struggle. I know many situations in which my use of "lumpy" will be appropriate. I have mixed concrete and grout while laying ceramic tiles and seen situations that are "lumpy." Porridge may have lumps in it, when the texture is not smooth; so does polenta. But what will "lumpy" look like in the present context? My description of the events after the fact does not refer to a state of lumpiness. Perhaps I have not observed this state? That is, whether "lumpy" is a useful term for describing what I see can be done only when I actually look at the materials *at the moment, then and there,* when I am in the state corresponding to the actions described. Whether what I see is a lumpy mixture or whether the use of "lumpy" is inappropriate in the present situation is something I can establish and know only after fact. Even the description of what I might see does not overcome the essential problem of matching an observation and a description, especially when this description has been articulated in language form, which inherently has no (iconic) likeness with the thing it describes. That is, I have to find in my actual observations, then and there, the relevance of the observational description "lumpy." The instruction warns me that I *may* observe something lumpy, but the assessment whether what I am looking at *is* lumpy is a situated accomplishment the results of which are known only subsequently.

"Until it comes away from the sides," too, is an observation sentence. It sounds innocuous enough, and I might envision the mixture to come off the sides in the way plastic wrap comes off a box. But dough is not plastic wrap, which becomes clear as soon as I look into the pan. When I stir, there is always some coming off the sides. Just what is the sense of "coming away from the sides"? At what point is what I am seeing an instance of "coming away from the sides"? All I can do is "beat hard" and look, well knowing that I may miss the point at which the cookbook author might have stopped the process of beating. I do not know beforehand what "coming away from" looks like, I can only find it in what I perceive. Without observing instances of stopping too early and too late, I do not really know what the exact point looks like when the mixture comes of easy. That is, I really have to make this kind of dough repeatedly before I can know what "coming away from the sides" means, for it simultaneously requires me to understand what the state just prior to and after "coming away from the sides" looks like.

Throughout making the gougère, as it is whenever I follow a recipe, I am engaged in the work of matching perceptions and text, attempting to find whether what I see is "coming away from the side," "drooping," or "lumpy," whether I am not there yet, or perhaps whether I am already too far. The observational descriptions set me up for observing something, thereby mediating my perceptual work, without ever being able to tune me *exactly* to the relation between the entity I see and the description. The description in itself is insufficient to allow an assessment with certainty that I recognize in my perception the thing being described. This uncertainty remains even if there are iconic descriptions available, for example, in the form of photographs, as these only represent *other* repetitions rather than the one I am in the process of realizing. In fact, studies of the classification of birds show that field guides with drawings and diagrams appear to make the job easier than photographs (Law & Lynch, 1990). That is, observational descriptions inherently are insufficient to guarantee that I perceive what is being described even if an experienced person might recognize a match. That is, I can make such assessment only with and through my embodied experience of repeating the instructions a number of times.

Ultimately, then, the sense of instructions and associated perceptions (observations) can be made only after the fact. I can know the sense of an instruction only after already being familiar with the situation that it brings about and describes— for example, after successfully having made gougère. Only after knowing that I have seen some phenomenon can I know that what I have perceived *is* the phenomenon; that is, only when I know that what I perceive is what I am supposed to perceive do I know that the phenomenon described actually looks like. Or rather, only when I know that what I perceive what the phenomenon looks like can I make a match between a verbal description and the experience it is said to describe.

My account also highlights an issue that I discuss more closely in chapter 9: cooking is an activity, which is realized by series of actions, themselves realized by sequences of operations. At all levels, activities are characterized by time and temporality, and achieving the intended results (those described in the cookbook) means acting appropriately in time. Thus, the recipe requires me to enact certain instructions at particular points in the evolving dish so that I find myself under pressure to act without having much time to reflect. Through my agency, the different materials are brought into relation, but because of their materiality, they are associated with particular constraints that I, too, am subject and subjected to. The appropriate coordination of my movements in time and space is itself an achievement that I acquire over time—in the same way that the coordination of gestures, speech, and body position have been achievements that Jenny made in the course of repeated articulations of the proposal for an investigation.

APORIA OF TRAVELING WITH MAPS

In the previous section, I show how instructions not only mediate action but also perception; they tell the reader of instructions what to look for as necessary condition for engaging in action ("beat the mixture hard until it comes off the sides of the pan") and what to ignore. Thus, following instructions is a lot like traveling with a map. A map not only tells me how far I have to go, when to turn left and right, but also what I can expect to see—a park, a monument, a train station. This analogy between following instructions and using a map allows me to make a link

Figure 8.1. My neighborhood viewed through two different lenses. a. A roadmap denotes what I can find, usually in terms of streets, roads, and lanes that a car can take. b. Through the lens of my camera, I see and experience the neighborhood in a very different way.

between the phenomenon of *perceiving something as*, taking particular lenses to look at the experiential world, in fact, layering the two (chapter 5), and the phenomenon of following an instruction. In this way, then, my work of following instructions becomes that involved in getting somewhere using a map. The problem is the reverse of that faced by students in chapters 6 and 7, who go from the territory (their experience in and of creating investigations and phenomena) to creating maps, whereas in the following of instruction, I move from a map to the territory it is said to describe. This process of getting to an unfamiliar place using a map, too, is fraught with aporias that are of the same order as that of following instructions. What I am essentially asked to do is moving about the world in such a way that the trip planned on the map will have been a good description for what I have done with my body on the terrain. But what does it mean to travel with a map, or to be good at reading maps?

To get a first grip on the problem, consider two different ways of looking at my neighborhood (Figure 8.1). Through the lens of the street mapmaker, I see an arrangement of locations (Figure 8.1a). I know that the footpath that allows me to get from the cul-de-sac directly to the street south of it is not available. Checking the map, I note that none of the footpaths in my neighborhood has an equivalent on the map, though I also note that wherever I can go by car finds its representation on the map. A roadmap gives me a particular perspective: it is one useful for drivers (and cyclists) allowing them to anticipate where they can go, how they have to go, when they have to turn, and when a cul-de-sac requires them to turn around. It is not a good representation of my neighborhood from the perspective of someone talking a walk, for none of the walkways and trails has been included.

A very different perspective on part of my neighborhood can be found in the second plate, a view through the (literal) lens of my camera (Figure 8.1b). It shows houses, trees, and in the distance ocean water, islands, and even a volcano. The photograph, too, is merely a map rather than the real thing, a particular perspective that is mediated by the lens through which it has been achieved and by its unstated point of origin (position). It too serves well some but not other purposes. But it is much closer to what can be experienced when I am actually in the place from where the photograph was taken. I shall treat the photograph *as if* it is what I experience, an iconic re-presentation of how the world is given to me when I am actually there.

It is evident that the two lenses allow me to see very different things, make figure very different entities and relations, while leaving other things in the ground. When I travel with a roadmap to get somewhere, I am therefore using one map (Figure 8.1a) to find my way about the world (Figure 8.1b). Successfully using a roadmap means to bring the two maps to overlap to such an extent that the correspondences between the two *can be established* at every moment. Many readers will have had the experience that they do not see what they anticipated to see, do not get to a turn-off that they anticipated to reach, do overshoot a turn-off but know so only long after the fact, and perhaps even do get lost as a consequence of the inherently ambiguous relation between two maps.

The map stands for something else, some territory. But what is it that it stands for? and What is the relation in which it is standing to what it is standing for? The map is *not* the territory—and therefore must not be confused with it (Bateson, 1980). In chapter 3, I write about the bicycle trips I have taken while staying at the *Hanse Institute for Advanced Studies*. As always in an unfamiliar environment, I have used a roadmap to get around, especially initially. When I want to get from where I am to some other place, I am setting a goal. The map is a resource for me to get from here to there in the same way as the recipe instructions constitute a map of getting from the ingredients to the finished dish. Whether and how I achieve this cannot be determined from the fact that I have a map. (By implication and perhaps even more so, giving students instructions cannot ever guarantee that they get to where teachers want them to get—though "learning objectives" do pretend so— and even less how they get to wherever they eventually arrive.) What I-learner do when traveling with a map, how I do it, and what the relationship between the outcomes of my actions and the map I use are therefore is an empirical matter.

Navigating (with) a Roadmap

In my bicycle example, the map not only tells me how to go but also stands for my prospective experience in the world. It stands for the roads I am to take or which I have taken. The map is a recipe that I use to get where I want to get. In this sense, the map has a double function. It both stands for the particulars of my travel, tells me the check points, stands for the streets I am taking, the park I am seeing, the overpass, the round about, and so on. At the same time, it tells me what to do, how many left and right turns to take.

Initially, I have no idea what it might look like where I will be passing. What I see with my eyes, such as a turn-off or intersection, could be any intersection on the map. And the map does not prepare me for the kind of perceptual experience I will have other than in some abstract sense. Figure 8.1a does not prepare me for the particulars available in Figure 8.1b. That is, making a match between the map and the world I experience *always* is a contingent achievement. I do have prior experiences with maps, and therefore have developed some competence with roadmaps in general, in the same way that I have had prior experiences cooking when I set out to make the gougère, and therefore with cooking more generally. These experiences allow me to go back and forth between the roadmap and the world. Eventually, I do not even need the map to get and find my way around. But, when it comes to showing someone else on the map how to go from A to B, I can point to it, talk about my experience in terms of the map, and in terms of the revisited images of my actual experience. My relation to the map changes with my experience. The roadmap now relates to my personal experience of having been at the train station, at a particular round point, at a particular park.

> I meet a couple on the cycling trail north of Delmenhorst; they seem lost. They stop me to ask for the directions to "Altenesch." I pull my map and find "Altenesch." I am sure that I have been through the village some time ago and that I have now passed some intersection, which I show to the couple on the map. But as I look up, I see a road sign that points ahead of us, "Altenesch 2.5 km." Am I wrong, have I passed another village thinking that I have come through Altenesch? I am confused.
>
> In my own estimation I was certain to be somewhere specific, which I located on the map as being past a certain intersection. But the nearby signs indicated differently. What I pick from the environment, as information, is different from my own sense of where I am. In the end, I trust my intuition and assume that someone has turned the pole on which the road sign is mounted thereby pointing in the incorrect direction.

This account of my experience during one bicycle trip highlights some of the trouble users of maps experience. On the one hand, I have the sense in that situation that I have already passed a certain village ("Altenesch") and so that on the map the village has to be behind me. On the other hand, the road sign bearing the name "Altenesch" points ahead of me and in the direction the couple has come from. This experience therefore highlights something already stated in the previous section: If I do not know the recipe and what it intends me to perceive, I do not know whether I have reached a certain point ("until it comes off the sides"), have passed it, or have not yet gotten there. I cannot know where the contradiction arises, whether it is in the territory, on the map (instructions), or in what I have done. My disorientation is due to the fact that there is an incongruence between the different experiences, having passed a village and finding a pointer to the village, and finding the corresponding locations on a different map.

Navigating with a roadmap involves similar processes as using a cookbook to make a certain dish or as following the instructions to produce a phenomenon in the science laboratory. It may appear as if using a roadmap simply requires converting an instruction—this is what a roadmap really is, a set of instructions telling me to keep straight, turn left or right, and telling me what I can anticipate to see, for example, a two-lane highway rather than a simple road, a cul-de-sac rather than a thoroughfare, and so on—into a course of action. But the episode with the couple shows that there actually is a two-way relationship, where each of the two maps presupposes experience with the other: To know where I am requires me to bring to coherence my perceptual map and the roadmap. These difficulties of bringing the two maps into coherence lie partially in the fact that they represent different orders of things, and different aspects of possible experiences:

> There are many things I cannot know when I go to new places even with a map: I am leaving my place, estimating the distance from the map. To the university it is about twenty kilometers. I think that I should be able to do it in about forty minutes, give or take a few minutes because of traffic. However, what I cannot know beforehand is the condition of the road that it is at times in bad condition, has washboards, and therefore slows me down. The wind is terrible, blowing head on. I am slowed down by the traffic lights. Then I get out of my rhythm and it is harder to start again.
>
> When I take a roadmap that is at a large scale, new contingencies arise: I cannot know what the details of the roads will be, that it is muddy rather than the beaten agricultural roads. The map does not contain the muddy potholes filled with water from the last rain. Further, I find myself at intersections that are not indicated on the map. Thus, I have to continue without knowing whether I am continuing on the path that leads me out of the thickets. To get out of the situation I use my sense of direction, from the brightness of the sun through the clouds (or the position when it is actually visible, or can be estimated); that is, I use my practical understanding of the world to navigate in a new situation that I do not yet know.

Ultimately, therefore, navigating *with* roadmaps also involves navigating roadmaps themselves. That is, there are at least two types of efforts involved. On the one hand, a roadmap is a resource that I can use to get from A to B, from the *Hanse Institute* where I live to the university and back or on a circular ride from the *Institute* to the North Sea and back. There are experiences in the world; and the roadmap provides indications what I need to do when I come to a turnoff, intersection, etc. On the other hand, using a roadmap also requires navigating the roadmap itself, finding my way around the different signs and symbols, relating them to one another: It means navigating a different world, one seen in and through the roadmap lens. Ultimately, therefore, knowledgeably navigating the map becomes indistinguishable from knowledgeably navigating the world as I experience it.

Navigating (with) Science Textbooks

The experiences with roadmaps and perceptual maps described in the previous subsection make me think about students, who find themselves in situations when they follow laboratory instructions. They are not likely to know that they are disoriented; they are not likely to have a sense of where they are and where they are to go. Whereas I am going into the unknown, I also have a map. I am not traveling completely into the unknown, but have the map, and ultimately know that I can ask specific questions to get back to where I have come from. The students, however, do not know where they will arrive. The purpose of their journey is to understand something that they do not yet know: a blank on their (experiential) map. In the process they discover how a white spot on their current map should be structured and how this structure refers to the territory that they encounter. Also, whereas my map provides me with the possibility for anticipating how I get to where I want to get, the students have to take instructions one at a time, trusting that what they do is getting them closer to where they are supposed to go, without recourse to resources that allow them to assess whether they are "on the right track." It does not surprise therefore that so many students ask, "Am I right so far?"

Science textbooks are maps, systems of sign and sign relations; these maps relate practices and the equipment (material aspects) that go with them. Instructions for investigations that students find in their textbooks are much like the roadmaps I use for navigating the area around the *Institute*, and from the *Institute* to the university that I am associated with. These maps provide both a lay of the land, when they describe what should be seen—as in my kitchen example, the instruction "beat the mixture hard until it comes of the sides of the pan" involves an observation in addition to an instruction. As a whole, even where they are not about laboratory investigations, science textbooks constitute maps of the world, which provide particular perspectives, much like a roadmap provides only one of many different and potentially infinite number of maps of the same area (see chapter 5). This world that my science textbooks provide maps of frequently is not the world surrounding me in my everyday life, but is special world that exists only through my making in a special place, the laboratory. That is, like my roadmap of northern Germany, the science textbooks constitute roadmaps that allow me to navigate the terrain that I experience with my body, but which also requires a different kind of navigation, one involving equations, language, images, or diagrams that make a particular science book. When I learn a new subject (physics, chemistry, biology, earth science), I am involved in navigating both worlds, the one in the book, and the one in the world mapped by the book in a different way. Learning science involves, therefore, learning to navigate the characteristic texts of the discipline and creating and perceiving the world through perceptual lenses—see chapter 6.

What does it mean to be able to read a map other than a roadmap? To be good at reading maps, or using them to navigate the world that is given to me in my perception, I have to have a sense that my anticipations of what might come if I were to go into a certain direction are realized: I actually see things of the type and category as those that are indicated. It also requires me to have a sense of direction, plus a familiarity with translating from the sign world into the experiential world such that a particular angle means that I am navigating in a particular direction in my experiential world. Having navigated a lot is possibly similar to having navigated a lot of books or computer programs, which, after some time, seem to be alike in many ways. There is a common structure, a common sense of what it means to write and use a book or program such that the more books or computer programs I use the more easily I learn using new ones.

To be familiar with reading maps, I already need to be familiar with what such maps may mean in specific situations. I need to be familiar with maps so that I can anticipate a forest or park where the map exhibits a green splat. That is, I already have to be familiar with the kinds of things that such sign assemblies may mean in such circumstances, though the particulars are never specified and always underdetermined by the map. I am familiar with the kinds of things that *this* map and *such* maps mean in such situations as in which I found myself. This leads me right back to a fundamental aporia. How is learning possible if I need to learn both map and territory and if how I perceive the territory depends on the map I am using? Simply doing investigations therefore does *not* provide sufficient ground for learning science, the investigations I engage in to learn presuppose the very knowledge and perspectives—which issue from my positions and dispositions—that I am to learn.

Maps allow me to anticipate types of things, circumstances, and categories. But they do so only if I am already familiar with what these *types* of things—entities, circumstances, and categories—look like. That is, maps work for me as maps because I am familiar not with *a* map but with maps in general; and maps work for me because they refer not only to one thing, one intersection, one alley, or one four-lane highway, but because they refer to *types* of things, intersections, alleys, four-lane highways. Reading a roadmap with four-line highways while living in small rural villages, where toilets were outside the homes, without sewer systems, no tractors but oxen-drawn carts, the concept of a four-lane, paved or concrete highway ("Autobahn") was not only foreign but also difficult to imagine. How could I understand what might be meant by "four-lane highway"? What might be its sense? To what extent could I develop anything of an understanding of "four-lane highways" prior to having seen and experienced traveling on such a feature? To what extent can I say that students understand nuclear power when all they have available is a textbook, a map, without ever having had experiences that the textbook map describes? And even when I have had these prior experiences, I have to recognize *this* situation as one of a *type* of situation that would be denoted by the particular feature of the map.

It is only when I am familiar with all of these features that I can anticipate with any certainty what lies ahead of me. In the case of a roadmap, I can already classify it in a particular way, a forest edge, a river, a bridge, a park, and so on although I am not familiar with *this* forest edge, *this* river, *this* bridge, or *this* park. Reading a book-type map, I already anticipate the possible ways in which the argument develops and perhaps even the way in which *this* argument develops. I read the map under the auspices of my involvement in, and familiarity with, the circumstances under which such maps are created, and under those circumstances, by appeal to knowledge of how maps and the world they denote operate. I know about the gaps between particular map features and the specifics of places, of what kinds of things I can actually perceive rather than conceivably perceive, of what as a matter of fact I did perceive and do in connection with the map, and so forth.

Readers of maps arrive at definitive conclusions about what these say, and they do so despite the fact that the contents of any individual map may be only marginally adequate to what its readers regard as necessary for determining the meaning of a particular feature. Furthermore, there are no definitive and uniquely specifiable methods for reading maps. Their readers contrive ways for dealing with the inherent difficulties and do this because they draw on their understanding of what may happen in such places, possibly and actually. Everyday users who read some map may encounter the indeterminacy of its contents—much like I encounter the indeterminacy of a recipe instruction. But this indeterminacy is an *occasional* rather than a chronic problem. Normally, users of maps elaborate the indexicality, indeterminacy, and ambiguity through their actual course—the praxis—of reading.

Given these requirements, it is not surprising if many individuals do not read or do not read well a variety of maps, including those related to science. Learning to read a map involves effort, agency (my possibilities to affect the world), and the possibility not only to learn but also to fail (because of my sensibility, openness to the world). I have to have a sense of future payoff to engage in the effort and produce the required energy for learning to navigate not only my world in new ways but also the world described by the different maps, and to correlate the two in ways that I come out of the experience with new resources for acting (and experiencing). However, if I do engage in the effort and eventually become familiar with and competent in navigating with some map, the difference between map and the world disappears. The map becomes transparent such that looking at it, I see the world, and looking at the world, I know what a roadmap conceivably looks like. That is, becoming familiar with a map, learning to navigate the world with the map and navigating the world of the map makes the distinction between map and its territory disappear. This is also true when the map largely consists of language so that knowing a language is no longer distinguishable from knowing one's way around the world more generally (Davidson, 1986).

FOLLOWING INSTRUCTIONS: A THEORETICAL ACCOUNT

For the longest time, I-author thought that the problem between instructions and situated actions disappears when learners frame goals themselves so that they can do *exactly* what they plan to do. I was thinking that the problem was lying in the difference between a person's intentions, obliquely pointed to by means of the instructions, and his or her own. I realized only recently—while closely studying a set of tapes from the ethnography in a scientific laboratory—that goal setting does not remove the inherent gap between intended actions and the situated actions that they are (not) descriptions of. That is, there is a gap between my own intentions—formulated in my goals—and my situated actions, which I can fully know only *after* the action is complete. A tennis player may intend to play the ball into the right back corner, but knows what she has done only after the ball has been caught in the net. A golf player may intend to sink the ball and knows only after the ball has bypassed the hole that he should have done something differently (holding the putter, how hard to hit, etc.). In cultural-historical activity theory I have found a framework that allows me to understand *why* I cannot know what I am doing *until after* have done it.

From the perspective of a human agent—a perspective that is always singular plural—an action is intentional, directed toward some specific, conscious goal. When making a gougère, I decide to pour the flour into the boiling water-butter mixture, and then pick up the materials and pour. But my "pouring" involves many components, which I do not consciously plan—though at some stage I may. I bring my hand to the paper that holds the flour, I close my fingers, I lift the paper such that it forms a gutter-like entity, I shift my body so that my hands come over the pot, and then with a little jerk, I dump the flour at once. But although I articulate these components of my action here, when I do "immediately pour in all the sea-soned flour," I am not actually conscious of my arm and hand that do the picking up, the fingers that hold fast and shape the paper, and I do not have to think "dump it" to actually bring about dumping. I am not aware of these *operations* in the same way that I am unaware of my fingers while typing these lines, where my intentions are directed toward producing a text; nor am I aware of my hands that bring the fingers close to the relevant keys. All of these components of an intended action— at present, writing this sentence—are non-conscious and therefore different from the goal that I have consciously formed. This goal is conscious, but its realization is achieved through the enchainment of non-conscious movements. In cultural-historical activity theory, these movements are denoted by the term *operations*. That is, whereas I am conscious of the goal—pouring the flour, writing a sen-tence—the operations that concretely realize my action are not; the former serve as referents for the latter to come about. The operations therefore are not produced willy-nilly; the desired goal-directed action *constrains* but does not *determine* them. The setting (tools, materials, current state of the object) and the moment along the trajectory that realizes the action mediate these operations.

The relation between a goal-directed action and operation, therefore, is a dialec-tical one: they mutually presuppose and constitute each other. On the one hand, an action only exists in and through its realization by means of operations: an action presupposes the operations that realize it in a concrete way, as there are no actions without operations. On the other hand, operations presuppose an action and the goal it aims at achieving; it is only because of a goal-directed action to be realized that I produce the operations through embodied and bodily engagement. That is, in and through my bodily self, I bring forth operations *because* I have formed a goal that I want to achieve. The specific operations I enact presuppose that I have some goal. The goal-directed action therefore serves as a referent for the operations.

The relation between an action and the operations it realizes is dialectical. The goal therefore *mediates* the operations I bring forth but does not *determine* them. In other words, the operations arise in the dialectical relation of current state and in-tended outcome. This dialectical relation makes plans (goals) and situated actions both identical and non-identical simultaneously. It is the non-identical aspect that allows for new forms of actions to emerge; it introduces the possibility for (cul-tural) variation that deterministic, one-to-one relations do not allow. Because the operations occur at the non-conscious level, I cannot know what I have done until after I have done it and begin to reflect about what has happened. Thus, for exam-ple, the entire event of "immediately pouring in all the seasoned flour" lasts but a fraction of a second, too little time to build a mental model and decide whether what I am doing is what I intended to do. At best, that is, in a situation where I have formed a goal, I can assess whether I have done what I intended to do after having completed the series of operations that realized my action. I can then make it present again, re-present the events and material objects at hand; and I can make an assessment as to the extent to which they correspond what I wanted to have done at this stage.

With instructions from the cookbook, however, there is an additional problem. The description of actions and observations are those that the cookbook author has used to describe what she has done and seen. But to what extent can I reproduce *her* actions and *her* observations given that I only have descriptions thereof? To what extent can what I do be counted as a repetition, which is both the same as the original and not the same? These original descriptions, at best, serve me as resources for action; whether or not my actions, which I cannot know in advance with certainty, actually can be described by the same sentence that I find in the cookbook is therefore an empirical matter. I have to engage in making the dish from the recipe; and I have to find in my actions the relevance of the descriptions of actions and perceptions that the cookbook author provides. It is only once I know that I have made the dish successfully that I can say that I have followed the recipe. Yet the sequences of actions and operations necessary to prepare the dish presuppose the recipe. The relationship between plans and situated actions, therefore, is the dialectical situation articulated above.

This really is a good analogy for how our actions always are both cultural and individual. Human beings learn what an instruction or observation statement means by finding themselves in situations that allow them to discover the possible relevance of an utterance, bodily action, gesture, photograph, diagram, or other signifier—all of which are cultural and available to all others—in their own embodied, singular experience of the world. It is in this sense that I am a singular plural, doing, understanding, perceiving in and through my body but also in terms of descriptions that are not my own. As there is no guarantee that the relevance I discover in my actions and perceptions is the same of another person, interpretive flexibility of cultural objects exists as soon as there are humans and, with them, the dialectic of language.

The example of making a gougère shows that the nature of what I have done also is a function of perceiving the outcome of an action. Thus, I know that I have sufficiently beaten the mixture *when it comes off the sides* of the pan, and I know that I have sufficiently beaten when the mixture is no longer lumpy—should I have perceived it as such. Thus, my perception of the material state mediates my understanding about just what I have done. My action denoted by "beating hard until the mixture comes away from the side" and my observation denoted by "the mixture comes away from the side" presuppose each another. There is no coming off the sides without beating, and there is no end to beating without coming off the sides. What it is to do "beating the mixture hard" cannot be known prior to perceiving the mixture come off, but what it means for the "mixture to come off the sides" can only be known by sufficiently "beating hard" for a sufficient amount of time. What this time is and what the results look like presuppose each other and, in the absence of prior experience, have to be determined together in the practical realization of both.

Following instructions, particularly following a set of instructions for the first time—whether these are the instructions in a cookbook, roadmap, or science textbook—requires me to make leaps of faith, that is, to launch myself into actions and to open myself to receiving the response from the environment. It is a form of ad-hoc action, where I find out after the fact whether I have done what I intended (was supposed) to do. Similarly, I have to find out what something looks like to assess the extent to which an observational description is useful for describing what I perceive. It may appear as if these ad hoc features are a nuisance that better instructions can take care of, that is, as if anybody was justified complaining about the incompleteness of *these* instructions or instructions in general. However, complaining about the incompleteness of instructions "is very much like complaining that if the walls of a building were gotten out of the way, one could see better hat was keeping the roof up" (Garfinkel, 1967, p. 22).

WORLD AND LANGUAGE

In the first two chapters of this part III, I describe how students learn to navigate the world and in the process evolve forms of communication that are useful for describing and explaining their experiences, perceptions, and actions. I show how language is only a (temporary) endpoint of a trajectory through multiple and inter-acting communicative forms, which also draw on the things in the world, pointing and iconic gestures, and arbitrary objects before discourse (and later written language) emerges that can stand on its on. I liken (science) language to a map, which, for it to work, is coordinated with the experiential map of the user.

In chapter 8, I articulate the inverse trajectory, along which I (singular plural) have to move to go from some state with stuff to a finished meal by following instructions, formulated in and through language, to experiences in the world. Here, too, language is a map that bears a relation to the experiential world as other maps. To be useful, language has to be coordinated with the world it describes and in which I use some aspect of it. This, as I show, requires me to learn how to navigate the map (language) itself as much as it requires me to learn to navigate my experiential world *with* the map. The two are related. The map is a resource that allows me to anticipate where I am going and what I see and, in this, mediates what I open myself up to, experientially and perceptually. Thus, the map shapes my anticipation and therefore tunes me to see and act in some ways rather than in others. In the limit, therefore, knowing the map (language) and knowing my way around the world generally becomes indistinguishable; there is therefore no need to make language something special. It is but another feature that allows me to cope with the world. When it has become indistinguishable from finding my way around the world, language, as map, and the territory it describes, have become so close that it is easy to confuse them. When I do confuse them, I am no longer able to recognize that I am wearing a set of lenses—I am like the proverbial fish that does not recognize the water in which it swims and which affords swimming in the first place. I am trapped in an ideology when I do not recognize the water, that is, when I do not recognize that what I am seeing is a result of the particular kinds of lenses I have donned.

Confusing the two, language and the territory comes with great dangers, especially in education and other social sciences. When names and the everyday life experiences they are used to denote are not held separate, then educational research becomes a tool in and for the reproduction of ideology (Smith, 1987). Terms such as "single parent family," "Standard North American Family," "Poverty," "learning disability," "scientific illiteracy," and "misconception" come to stand for and designate realities despite the fact that they are the lasting and reified outcomes of social relations. This book therefore is not only about high school students learning science but also about the learning of social scientists and educational practitioners, who can benefit from understanding the nature and role of perception in human experience.

Democratic and enlightened citizens ought to be able to engage with others who perceive and act in the world very differently; and they ought to recognize that their own ways are shaped by the lenses that normally are transparent just as my glasses are transparent so that I do not notice wearing them most of the time. Learning science therefore should involve learning to follow instructions or to parrot some words and sentences from a science textbook. Science should allow students to look critically at the particular lenses that the subject constitutes and learning to evaluate the advantages as well as the disadvantages. To do so, they need to be able to distinguish between their primary map, the world as given to them in their experience, and their secondary maps, the different languages and representational forms that are used to describe and explain experiential phenomena. More so, science education ought to allow students to realize that even primary experience constitutes a map, the shape of which presupposes other maps. In a sense, therefore, science education ought to be integrated in a larger endeavor of making students epistemologically literate; this form of literacy then allows them to be democratic and enlightened. But the consequences of these ideas would lead me beyond the purposes of this book. Interested readers might want to refer to some other work (e.g., Désautels & Roth, 1999) where I have articulated ideas about addressing the blind spots that inherently come with any kind of lens (map) I chose or did not choose to done.

PART IV

KNOWING AND LEARNING AS EVENTS

Time, temporality, and the flux of experience have been major topics of philosophy because they are central to understanding human nature and consciousness. *Being and Time* (Heidegger, 1977/1996), *Creative Evolution* (Bergson, 1969), and the trilogy *Time and Narrative* (Ricœur, 1984, 1985, 1988), and *Time and the Other* (Levinas, 1987) are but some examples of studies that show how my very being, the possibility of experiencing myself, others, and the world in the way humans enact it collectively, is tied up with time. It is not that I am simply exposed to time as something external to me—such as physicists or experimental psychologists might think of this dimension of being. This form of thinking was proposed by Immanuel Kant, who thought that time was a precondition of experience, from which a rational mind could then learn and construct knowledge. This, however, as shown in more recent philosophical work, is not the case. The experience of time is itself a particular form of experience rather than its precondition. As a result, time now is understood to be the result of human praxis; the scientific mode of time, as indicated on chronometers, is but a mode of a more general category of time, which arises from human experience in the world. Thus, the experienced time unfolding for Sean, Jon, and Rhonda in chapter 2 cannot be measured suitably with a wristwatch; their search for patterns in the movement of the rolling and sliding entities is better characterized by pulsations and pauses, moments of absorptions, and moments of waiting. Only when the teacher calls students to order and gives them one or two more minutes of chronological time do the three students hurriedly come to an end with their investigations.

Clock time, or chronological time as I refer to it here, serves to coordinate and construe an external measure to what human beings do. Thus, the teacher Toby Mory has fixed a certain amount of chronological time for the inquiry independent of the fact how long it would take students to come up with patterns, independent of their absorption while doing a focused inquiry, and independent of the fact that no new patterns were arising after the initial observation. But then, given only a couple of minutes to end their search, Sean, Jon, and Rhonda engage in more frantic investigations, being absorbed again as they abandon themselves to the object of the task. Thus. I produce time, temporality, and flow to the same extent that I am subject to them. And, as Emmanuel Levinas points out, difference itself is tied to time. I cannot experience difference itself but only difference as it arises from time, and producing time is producing difference—between the other (person, material object) and me.

Educators think of time mostly in terms of curriculum planning; thinking about the role of time in knowing and learning does not or only seldom figure in published research accounts. Yet the production and reproduction of time is pervasive in everyday life. The two dimensions of time—being subject to time and producing it—are evident from the following excerpt from an interview about graphs and graphing. Annemarie asks Daniel to give her a hint, but Daniel apparently does not want to respond. By uttering "um" repeatedly, he stretches and buys himself time, on the one hand, time that he is subject to; the longer he waits and does not answer, the longer he breaches the in social interaction inherent convention that questions are followed by answers.

Episode IV.1
01 A: okay ask me a question then . . . where is your hi[nts?
02 D: [um, u::m:,
         [um ((clears throat))
03 A: [it seems to me [you're in very good shape up to he[re
04 D: [em   [okay.
05 A: but as soon as it begins to turn and come down you need to look at the situation as far as conservation goes because if that goes on for long=

Annemarie continues to talk, venturing a hypothesis about what the sense of the graph at a particular location is (turn 03), but Daniel only produces sounds, which acknowledge that he is listening but that do not add to the topic at hand. Simultaneously, he makes (produces) time as his hesitation modulates the temporality of the unfolding interview/think aloud session. By not answering, or rather, by producing the utterances by means of which he takes a turn without responding to the query, he slows down the unfolding of the event. He makes or stretches time for orienting and finding a position—see chapters 5 and 6—which frames his subsequent production of a turn. How much and how long he can avoid responding to the query is not something determined by chronological time but rather is a function of human praxis and therefore itself a situated accomplishment. To successfully participate in conversations such as Episode IV.1, I have to have a sense of the game, feel what is right, know when I have waited too long, and have a sense for how much I can avoid answering without making the situation an affront. That is, the speed of the unfolding event changes and therefore also how long it will last depends on the accumulation of such temporal and temporalizing events; it is characteristic of the events and the participants' situated understanding and use of uncertainty to make the situation signify itself as something particular—e.g., into an interview or a tutoring session. Whether and when the event can be ended then is itself an accomplishment in and of producing time (Roth, 2005a).

Most research on knowing and learning in science does not take into account time and temporality, to the point of taking the language of the written text as the paradigm for analyzing language in use—i.e., discourse—despite its apparent temporality and emergent quality. Taking text as the paradigm erases all time, all temporal modes of producing discourse, whereby even the speaker does not know what he or she will be saying next and what they will have uttered when the turn of talk goes to someone else. Taking the written text as a paradigm for the analysis of discourse makes all parts of a conversation the same, although this is not what has happened. That is, the relationship between what has been available at any one point in time is inverted, as the analyst presupposes that what is being said at the end has the same status as what has been said in the beginning or middle of an utterance or conversation. In such an approach, however, the text of a conversation is treated not only as the transcription of the stuff people are said to have in their heads but also as if this stuff in the head existed there unchanged from the beginning to the end of the utterance or, worse, from the beginning to the end of the conversation.

On both cultural-historical and ontogenetic levels, discourse precedes written language. Discourse therefore is primary. If anything, discourse should receive special status and written language ought to be treated as a derivative, a special mode of discourse. The special features and powers of written texts to culture can then shown to be the constitutive results of cultural-historical processes that turn inherently dynamic processes of talking and understanding into timeless written statements. These powers are associated with shortcomings, which are not often discussed, but have been a philosophical topic from Plato to Derrida (1981). They are also notable in the problematic relation between timeless mathematical equations—which, in equations such as "$a = a$" presuppose the possibility of identity—or scientific equations—in which time is presupposed to be linear and bidirectional, such as in $x = v\ t$—and the inappropriateness of such foreshortened notions of time for describing human experience (Müller, 1972).

In this part IV, I present a variety of issues that are not static like written texts but that unfold in time, including lessons and the tasks someone is asked to do. Currently there is little discussion in the discipline of science education concerning the match between the time foreseen in curriculum planning—at the level of number of concepts per year, the amount of time individual students need to develop a familiarity and understanding with a concept, and the durations and flow that I-learner may experience when I am really involved with some task. Yet it is already apparent in Part II of this book, which deals with perception, that I do not know at what time something becomes apparent to me, stands out, and becomes figure above an indeterminate ground. This raises many questions including, "How can science educators at large plan lessons, that is, predetermine the rate at which students learn if so little is known about how learning unfolds in real time?" If a teacher observing me repeatedly taking the same route on my bicycle had asked me about the gigantic twin towers at the roadside, or posed a problem in which perception and knowledge about them was required, I might have failed utterly until the seventh trip (recall, I never recorded having seen them until this trip). Similarly with the other experiences described in chapter 3, and even with the neon glow lamp, for example, in chapter 4: I have begun to note the particulars of its structure only after my colleague Manuela Welzel has made reference to it. That is, prior to this moment I might have failed any exam questions pertaining to the internal structure of the glow lamp. How can one plan for such moments of insight, which are inherently spontaneous, sudden, emergent, cumulative, and therefore outside the maps that lesson plans constitute?

The upshot of these questions and aporias is that a closer look has to be taken at how activities generally and learning tasks more specifically unfold in time, how they produce time, their temporality, and the flow experienced by those fully involved in accomplishing it. In fact, flow is an experience few science classes can bring about among their students, though I repeatedly have been privy of student comments in my open inquiry courses that suggest their having had such an experiences. When a student says, "What, the lesson is already over, we have only begun!," he articulates that "time has gone by" without him noticing so. Thus, whereas classes of are experienced as interminably long, some experiences in some courses are such that students get so absorbed that the temporal mode of the experience changes significantly. There are presuppositions that students cannot engage in a lesson for more than an hour and that they need frequent change. But this contradicts everyday observations that the same students can practice for hours on end the same moves on their skateboards, play the same electronic game for an entire day without stopping, or watch television for an entire weekend. The presupposition that students cannot engage in an activity for a long time therefore is unfounded. At the moment, science educators do not have a discourse that would allow description and articulation of such learning experiences.

TIME AND TEMPORALITY

Everyday *praxis*, unlike the theories that are used to describe it, has a temporal character. It unfolds in time, is non-linear, and irreversible. Its temporal structure—rhythm, tempo, duration, metric, flow, movement, directionality—is not only constitutive of its meaning but also the central element that distinguishes praxis as a lived experience from praxis as it is reflected in theory (in terms of *practices*). Yet learning takes place at a level of temporal immediacy that does not allow stepping back and taking time out in order to reflect and therefore theoretically understand the situation to make a decision based on rational choice.

It was above all the philosopher Immanuel Kant (1968), who determined time as precondition of all sensation and experience: Only when time is given can there be simultaneity and succession; only under this condition can there be something at the same time or at different times and therefore possible to be experienced. Time, in this view, precedes the possibility to have any experiences at all. Phenomenological philosophers and philosophers of difference show, however, that the opposite is the case. Time arises in and with sensibility and experience. The origin of phenomenological time, which is the ultimate form of all things experienced in general, presupposes the body and its capacity to sense (Franck, 2001). A phenomenology of learning through bodily experience therefore also requires me to investigate the role and experience of time, not just chronological time, but all the other modes that have gone lost in the reductive process.

APORIAS OF TIME IN SCIENCE LEARNING

Despite the considerable philosophical interest in time and temporality as constituent aspects of human experience, learning theories generally do not take them into account. It is as if time and the temporality of experience generally and the temporality of learning more specifically did not exist. If there are any considerations at all, chronological rather than experienced time is at issue. Thus, in science and science learning, time is measured along a linear scale of chronological time, and schools are operated and organized like factories. The cycles are lessons, which mostly last somewhere between forty-five and sixty minutes. Learning is to occur within these time frames rather than within a frame of the need of human beings as physical organisms that live and change in time. The factory model also underlies curriculum theory, according to which lesson plans can be written with achievable and to be achieved objectives within the confines of the clock-determined lesson. For example, a lesson plan for third graders on motion, which has the purpose of teaching that speed can be derived by reading the slope of a {time, position} graph is slated to be accomplished in forty-five minutes. The instructions to the teachers read:

> First, mark equal positions on a hallway (use tiles or pace off the increments). Assign students to each mark and distribute stopwatches at each mark. Instruct the students to start their watches when the car starts, but not to stop their watches until it crosses their assigned mark. Repeat these steps with the car set at a faster setting. Return to the classroom and compile the data in a table. Then have the students work in pairs transferring the data from the table to a graph. The position (number of marks) should be plotted on the Y-axis, and the time in seconds should be recorded on the X-axis. The two speeds of the car should be plotted in different colors.
>
> The students should then draw two straight lines, each suited for the specific data speed. Begin with the slower line, and explain that we can now see how much the car travels in a specific amount of time. Ask them to count how many marks (change in position) the car went in a 10-second time period (10–20 sec). Now ask them to use that information to find how many marks the car went in 1 second. This is the speed at which the car is moving.

In this lesson plan, there is no reference to what students might be experiencing, and how their lived experiences unfold in time and thereby mediate what the teacher has intended for them to learn. There is no room for students who might become so engrossed with their investigations that these could go on for the entire day without their realization that hours are passing by. The difference between the chronological and experiential perspectives turns out to be exactly that between a planned lesson and an enacted lesson, between plans and situated actions. The lesson plan is without life, it does not address children's learning, which unfolds in real time activity, unfolding within the constraints provided by their prior experiences and the field. As any other form of text, it is itself outside of experiential time, analyzable for its internal consistency and coherence. Learning theorists take an equally atemporal perspective of learning, by mapping prior knowledge and subsequent knowledge in an atemporal space, much like mathematicians conduct mathematics in a space that has no time.

The psychologist who does not go back to the sources and takes temporalization as already completed will see consciousness in terms of a multiplicity of facts between which he or she attempts to establish a report of causality. And all these facts, though produced by the person in time, are laid out simultaneously as signifiers (representations) that the psychologist moves about and puts into relation irrespective of any temporal ordering in which these conceptions might unfold. Thus, conceptual change theories describe learning in terms of a change of structure without any temporal dimension at all (Figure 9.1). These structures are described outside of time and outside of the situations that might occasion them. This approach to knowing and learning, therefore, is atemporal. It does not even question what the role of time is in the construction of such a structure, what the differences in time experiences are between students, and what possible constraints exist that limit the structuring and restructuring of such frameworks. I have found no refer-

a.   **b.**

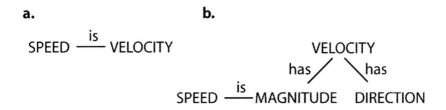

Figure 9.1. In a conceptual change perspective, there is no temporal dimension to learning; there is only a change in the relations between concepts, indistinguishable from semantic structures. With the suppression of time, knowing as lived phenomenon has been evacuated from the theory of knowing science.

ence to the time and temporality in the establishment of such conceptual frameworks from its constituent parts. When two such conceptions are involved, researchers sometimes speak of weak and strong restructuring that is required without actually articulating how an earlier structure comes to be undone, how the new structure forms, the time required for the construction of the new structure, and the temporal modes that students experience in the process. Any stonemason knows that you cannot just throw materials at a construction side to have a house. Building a house has its own temporality such that the pouring the basement walls and basement floors unfold in time, time is required for the concrete to be worked, and time is required for the concrete to settle and dry. Learning theorists discuss *construction* processes outside of any consideration of time. The models of conceptions and conceptual change, embodied here by the concept maps, are as atemporal as the mathematical models of nature, whereby one-to-one relations are established between the natural and mathematical world, which, as pointed out above, exists outside of time.

All consciousness manifests itself in action, experiences, and "psychological facts" in which it recognizes itself. How does a living person change from consistently saying "velocity is speed" to consistently saying "velocity has magnitude, equivalent to speed, and direction"? Let me think for the moment of knowing in terms of cognitive structure—rather than patterned actions or praxis. The students have connections that make them think of speed as velocity. If the model of conceptions and conceptual change is to have any purchasing power, I need a theory about the connections and how these connections and structures change as a function of students engagement with the world, and particularly, how such connections turn into different connections. That is, what I require to predict learning in the classroom is a theory that describes the breaking up of one set of connections and reassembly of a new set of connections, that is, from the structure represented in Figure 9.1a to another structure, for example, the one in Figure 9.1b. I also need a theory that describes what students will say at the different moments in time when they are in the deconstruction and reconstruction processes, and how the conceptual structures are related to the different forms of (first, second) language students are familiar or unfamiliar with.

Such theories that would articulate how conceptual change occurs in time, however, do not exist despite more than two decades of research on conceptions and conceptual change. My guess is that such a theory is not likely to be created any time soon. This is so because the conception and conceptual change model fails to capture the experience of knowing and learning in real time. It is erroneous to leave out time in knowing and learning, because even knowing can be assessed only in processes that also occur in time. I can only ever know about what someone knows through a *process* of assessment never through the taking of an instantaneous picture. What I know, I can only show through a knowledgeable act, which is in time and makes time, as seen from a subsequent episode in which I inquire into the electroscope.

In chapters 6 and 7, my descriptive accounts make apparent a number of temporal issues that are important in learning—there are important temporal dimensions in the relation of context, gestures, and speech as representational modalities in students' communication and there are evolutionary aspects that always occur in and through time. A phenomenological perspective differs radically from the other approaches discussed so far. Being cannot be thought independently of time. Being is time. In acting, I temporalize myself and thereby produce time at the very same instance that my action unfolds *in* time. It is in this that time operates, exposes being and thereby discloses itself in and as experience. Knowing is knowledgeably acting, and, because acting is a process, inherently subject to temporality and time as all processes are. Knowing therefore cannot be understood in terms of stuff in my head but, at best, as the temporalization of knowledgeable structure. I need to think about knowing and learning in dynamic ways, as being-in-the-world that continually unfolds in taking stance and changing with the requirements of the present. Time is the main point why classical models do not model well cognition in the everyday world:

> The heart of the problem is *time. Cognitive processes and their context unfold continuously and simultaneously in real time.* Computational models specify a discrete sequence of static internal states in arbitrary "step" time (t1, t2, etc.) Imposing the latter onto the former is like wearing shoes on your hands. You can do it, but gloves fit a whole lot better. (van Gelder & Port, 1995, p. 2)

To get by in life I need to be able to act adaptively, in real time, in a relatively unconstrained environment (compared to the world of a chess board). There is no time out; and every action produces time as much as it is subject to it. The temporal issues are quite apparent when it comes to music, where playing slower or faster makes a big difference, especially when participating in a jam session but also when participating in a conversation generally. Time makes a difference in sports, where being a little faster or a little slower make the difference between winning and loosing, catching a ball or missing it, achieving synchrony in a rowboat or being asynchronous and working against teammates. The notion of synchrony may be transferred into other domains, such as noting the achievement of mutual understanding and intersubjectivity by expressions such as "being in sync."

TEMPORALITY AND FLOW

In schools, teachers and especially students engage in tasks inherently knowing that there is a limit to the amount of chronological time available for what they are doing. This chronological time, though it constitutes a very reductionist view of time and temporality, becomes the meter and master for how I act in the world—although it is well known that students do not learn at the same rate, a school year exactly is about 200 school days long, no shorter and no longer. I have often said to colleagues that I could not engage in research and writing if I had to work under the same conditions that students are asked to learn under.

Real inquiry is subject to different rules, it has its own temporality, generally not subject to chronological time. And although the reports of heroic discoveries often exhibit how one group of researchers won the race against a competing group, the same reports make salient that discovery itself cannot be forced. Difficulties arise unforeseeably and insights come suddenly, both punctuating and drawing out time. Thus, as shown in many engineering studies, there are often problems that have not been considered and that emerge some time later when discovery and solution finding are subjected to chronological time (e.g., Bucciarelli, 1994). The emergence of ideas and invention operate differently, cannot be planned and mapped against a form of time that inappropriately theorizes the temporality of human experience and the temporality of praxis.

Teachers, on the other hand, frequently chastise students for not working quickly enough or for not trying sufficiently hard to get an inquiry done prior to the end of a lesson. The following episode from my notes describes an event where I engage in investigations of static electricity with the same materials that the students in the tenth-grade physics class use in the videotapes. Whereas they have exactly one lesson, I end up spending many hours working through it. What is happening to me there is better described in terms of absorption and flow. I am taken up so much by the (self-selected) task that there is a fusion of subject and object of inquiry, leading to the irrelevance of chronological time to my experience. It is only after the fact that I can map in some approximate way what has happened onto the chronological time displayed on my wristwatch. The episode shows me repeatedly enacting "the same" manipulations, vary consciously and non-consciously what I am doing, noticing only after the fact what I have done.

> I rub the PVC rod, get a deflection, but cannot rub off the charges onto the electroscope so that they stay. At least, there are not enough. I try again, and try again. Perhaps there is a cumulative effect? Nothing works. I change to the woolen cloth, change my approach to rubbing, a deflection of the pointer, but nothing stays.
>
> I rub the metal plate, taking it at the handle, on a plastic film. I rub long, long and hard. I put the plate to the electroscope and get a giant deflection. I rub it off and it stays.
>
> I change to the transparency. I rub it with the cloth: no effect. I rub it with the leather: no effect. I rub the film at the electroscope and, as I rub, observe no effect. I push down hard onto the transparency. Perhaps it's a

matter of getting a better contact with the other material. No change, no deflection. I continue rubbing, pressing harder. Nothing. What am I doing wrong? I pull the film, and wow, I get a giant deflection.

I attempt the finger thing. Bring my index fingertip close to the pointer of the electroscope (Figure 9.2): it moves. When I move my finger, the pointer follows. I go back and re-do it. The pointer follows my finger. Perhaps the water in my finger gets oriented so that it is polarized? This new issue draws me in; I leave my previous attempts by the wayside, pursuing this new type of event.

I rub the top plate of the electroscope with the transparency that I have used before. I take it off. Nothing. I repeat the process, taking the transparency off. Nothing. I do it again. Nothing. I change the transparency and wow, giant deflection. Perhaps there is something to the story of the used films that the tenth-graders have come up with in my videotapes?!

I reflect. I do not trust my own approach to doing this investigation. I begin to question my observation of the students: Is there anything negative in their repeated attempts of doing something without apparent change in what they do? Here I have been repeating the same action at least three times without apparent change in what I have been doing before I start changing, to vary something in my procedure. I am surprised about myself. Why do I repeat what I am doing although I do not observe any effect? Why do I do the same manipulation over and over again without varying what I do? But each time I repeat is also different. Perhaps I am attempting to check whether the null effect is something consistent? Is a matter of detecting variants and invariants?

I see the pointer still a bit deflected. How far can I pull it? I bring my finger close, it moves (Figure 9.2). I don't want to touch the pointer and yet make it move. I come close again, the pointer moves towards my finger, I pull away so that it can't come to close, but it falls back. I bring my finger close to the pointer and pull it again: I have it almost twice the angle, against gravity! The pointer follows quickly and I can't get my hand

Figure 9.2. I bring my finger close to the pointer of the electroscope: it deflects.

away fast enough. The pointer deflects three times its original position, touches, and goes back to zero.

I am surprised about my focus. I experience an original and originary surprise. It is a first-time experience. It is amazing how far the pointer deflects just with my finger coming close. I check whether the uncharged pointer does anything, though I know it won't or shouldn't. I am filled with a sense of discovery.

In stepping back to reflect what I have done during the episode, I notice that the described episode has lasted several hours. Yet it has seemed to me as if only minutes have passed since I first pulled the electroscope close to investigate some fuzzy idea that had thrust itself into my conscious awareness. In the episode, I conduct many manipulations repeatedly, abandon them, and return to doing same "same" things again. But the second time I do something, it is no longer the same, I am manipulating the equipment having done something like it before, whereas the first time I have not had prior experience. The second doing is a different doing, it is later than the first, but its outcome appears to be the same. That is, to note that something does not work or does not bring about an effect requires temporal difference as much as it takes a temporal difference to note a difference in the result. That is, difference and time are linked. There is no knowing and learning outside of time, the temporal mode that characterizes mathematics, where statements such as "a = a" can be made without somebody raising doubt—although even the establishment of this identity requires my eye to saccade first to establish each "a" as "a" with respect to ground and then to establish the identity of each with the other. In fact, the knowledge required to make a statement about identity is so advanced and requires considerable time to evolve that it cannot serve as the starting point for a reasonable epistemology.

My experience during such episodes is quite strange indeed. It involves the sense both of intense involvement and of "being lost in time" or "having been in a time warp," as the popular expressions go. I am in a different temporal mode, having abandoned myself to the rhythm of the inquiry: bringing the finger close to the pointer to make it deflect, "pulling" it so that it deflects more, and letting it go. Bringing the finger close, pulling the pointer to deflect more, and letting it go. In acting, I produce difference; difference is the requirement for time to be felt. But acting occurs only in time, acting and time are the same all the while being different. Acting, difference, and time are dialectically related, mutually presupposing each other. I cannot think of one without having to thematize the other. But this time is different from the one I observe while gazing at my wristwatch. In fact, gazing at my wristwatch—as I have experienced many times while attending high school—makes the day long, interminable. The more I gaze at the watch, the slower time appears to pass, or in other words, the less change there appears to be.

In the episode, however, time is difference, time is different but not in the same way as chronological time. I am caught up in a flow, which itself is the result of my actions. I am conscious of what I am doing, pursue lines of inquiry, yet I am not conscious of the chronological time indicated on my watch, though I use it at other moments to coordinate actions with others. At the end of the episode, I have the sense of having learned something, knowing more and knowing more about static electricity now than I did before. The activity is punctuated by its own demands, repetition, and difference, difference in repetition. There is no clock or timekeeper that attempts to synchronize me with an external, impassive world; time and temporality are subject to and arise from my actions. When I do research and write, I experience the same modes of time. And I cannot ever predict at what time I will have an insight, the sense that I have learned, the firm conviction that my consciousness has changed as much as my body.

In this episode, the flow of activity is all there is. Such situations are the result of the shift of intentionality from its normal orientation toward the object to the sensation itself (Levinas, 1978b). As a consequence, the existing separation between me, the participant, and the situation in which I participate disappears: one term in the subject–object distinction becomes the other. In such situations, the existent (i.e., entity) participates in existence, becomes verb and looses all its substantiality. In such *flow* experiences—for this is what they are—doing unfolds into doing, and the material world, including my own body, vanishes into the ground. As a consequence, the temporality is that of the experience itself rather than its abstraction, chronological time, which is only one of the modes of temporal experience. This experience, in which the subject–object distinction has been sublated, is the present here, that is, this here and this now: it is the hypostasis of being. But the now constitutes a stop; it interrupts the course of time to proceed from itself. The present mediates pure duration because the contact with the being that constitutes it does not take place in the passage from one moment to the next (Franck, 2001). The essence of the moment, therefore, is the stance, the orientation, which I introduce chapter 6 as the central aspect that frames communication.

In this episode, I experience outside of chronological time. Such absorption is the expression of temporality, which reveals itself as the meaning of authentic care (Heidegger, 1977/1996). In such moments of absorption, I really am outside of time, I am outside of myself, in and for myself. Thus, "*[t]emporality is the primordial 'outside-of-itself' in and for itself*" it is the "*ekstatikon par excellence*" (p. 329 [302], original emphasis). Past, present, and future therefore are the *ecstasies* of temporality, the ways in which time presents itself to a conscious being pondering temporality. This outside-of-itself constitutes primordial temporality and is the principle of all subsequent forms of exteriorization.

In praxis, where I actively deploy my body, I-learner temporalize myself. Many readers will have experienced lessons, in which time did not seem to progress, days seemingly unending in their slowness. They will also have experienced moments in which time appeared to race, where there is no time to reflect, and no opportunity for a time-out to choose among alternative actions. In such moments, there is no time for me to comprehend my situation in a removed way, to deliberate whether to do one thing or another. Even waiting and doing nothing or, as Sean, Jon, and Rhonda in chapter 2, repeating an observation over and over again, constitutes an action. Practical time "is made up of islands of incommensurable duration, each marked by its particular rhythm. It is a time that presses on or drags, depending on what one is doing, that is, on the functions assigned to it by the actions that are performed in it" (Bourdieu, 1980/1990, p. 141, my translation). In praxis, there is a practical investment that brooks no delay, because not acting is also a form of acting.

TIME IN AND TEMPORALITY OF LEARNING FROM EXPERIENCE

When I know where I go, for example, from home to my office at the university, I know approximately how long it will take me. I know the number of traffic lights on the way and how long I therefore have to wait. I also know that bad weather and taking the mountain bike will slow me down compared to the road bike. Because I have a clear intentional object, getting to my office, I have a good sense of the amount of chronological (clock) time the trip is going to take. My control of my actions in time is similar when I prepare a familiar dish for dinner. For example, to make pasta, I know that it will take about ten to twelve minutes to mix the flour, salt, eggs, and oil with a fork and then to knead the dough before putting it into the refrigerator to rest for at least half an hour. Even if I become absorbed in these events so that I do not notice the time as unfolding, I nevertheless operate in a particular framework of chronological time.

The amount of chronological time taken when I explore an unfamiliar territory or when I make a new dish from a recipe is not only longer than for an equivalent trip or dish, but also indeterminate. I cannot know what events and processes intervene, what I discover in the process of traveling or cooking, and how much time it takes me to coordinate my bodily engagement in the world and reading the map (roadmap, recipe). In both instances, however, I have a more or less clear idea about what I intend—traveling and exploring or preparing and serving a new dish. Science students, on the other hand, generally do not know that much. They come to lessons where they are asked to do things to arrive somewhere and generally do not have the faintest idea about where they are going or how to get there.

Traveling in unfamiliar territory does not allow me to predict with any certainty how long it will take me to get to some endpoint or where someone else wants me to arrive. I cannot know the amount of time it will take me, because I travel in *unfamiliar* and *uncharted* territory. Conversely, the teacher cannot know how long it will take *me*, as the point at which something becomes apparent to me is indeterminate—as apparent from chapters 3 and 4, which articulate perceptual experience in unfamiliar terrain. The intended object is out of my reach, inherently, because I do not have to learn something that I already know. If I do not know what it is that I will have learned some time down the road, I cannot have control over my actions in the same way as I do when I ride to the university or make a familiar dish. In previous chapters, I describe the realization of something new, a new perception, as an emergent phenomenon. But inherent in the notion of emergence is the idea of temporal indeterminacy: I cannot predict when something such as an insight will happen. Although I can wait for it to occur, and although I know that something will happen, I may not know when.

These considerations show that the model of learning as the outcome of an intention is flawed in a double sense. First, I cannot intend the real object of learning, because it lies beyond my present horizon, beyond my familiar and charted (mapped) territories. Second, I cannot intend learning, because perception and the world it provides me with are temporal processes; insights, too, lie outside the realm accessible to intention—intentionality and temporality come to run apart:

> Attempting to remember something does not always lead to the intended results. I may try to recall the name of a former classmate, but I may not get it. Now I have found a way of approaching recalling long forgotten facts (e.g., names, words) that in many instances eventually leads to success, though I cannot predict exactly when the intended fact will emerge into my consciousness, if I recall it at all. For example, I may think of moments that I have spent with the classmate some 40 years ago or go through the alphabet attempting to generate some of the first and last names of other peers that I have had at the time. I engage in what I think as "trying hard to remember." After about ten minutes of doing so, I deliberately attend to something else. I may read, continue with an ongoing activity, or focus on the conversation I am having with my wife. Then, all of a sudden, some time later the intended fact surges into my consciousness, and I call out, "I go it!" or simply state the name or word that I have been looking for. In terms of intentions and time, this type of event lies between the two previous ones, where I am either completely in control over the object of activity or not at all.

When students engage in laboratory investigations the outcome of which they do not yet know and as a result of which they will learn something that they currently do not yet know, they have no control over the instant that they come to perceive something novel, when they will have done what the teacher intends them to do, or when they have the insight that constitutes their learning. In a previous section, I describe my own involvement while investigating the electroscope and how I repeat certain manipulations over and over again. This takes time. But I do not know how often I have to repeat something until I know that I have controlled all possible aspects of an action that I can think of before moving on? How can I know whether this type of action will lead to my insight or whether I have to try something else?

Until I-analyst looked at the videotapes featuring the tenth-grade students exploring static electricity, I never thought about learning in time. I was puzzled seeing the students apparently doing the same actions repeatedly (e.g., chapter 4). But recognizing something as repetition means recognizing something in the experience as the same all the while experiencing it as something different. It is only *in and over time* that I distinguish some behavior as different and not repeated and other behavior repeated, that is, being the same despite apparent differences. This then allows me to understand what looks like repetition in what students do. For example, a tabulation of some of the events during the first two lessons shows which materials the four female students employ, how they test for the presence of static electricity, and what they state to be the results (Table 9.1). Iris rubs the transparency five times with a rag and then tests with a piece of Styrofoam (which

Table 9.1. Excerpt from the investigation of static electricity in one student group

Person	Trial	Material 1	Material 2	Action	Test Object	Observation
Iris	A20	Transparency	Ruler	Rub hard	Styrofoam	-
Caren	A21	Transparency	Pants	Pull	Lamp	Light
Iris	A22	Transparency	Rag	Rub	Styrofoam	+
Iris	A23	Transparency	Rag	Rub	Styrofoam	+
Iris	A24	Transparency	Rag	Rub	Styrofoam	-
Iris	A25	Transparency	Rag	Rub	Styrofoam	-
Iris	A26	Transparency	Rag	Rub	Styrofoam	+
Jenny	A27	Transparency	Ruler	Rub	TT ball	+
Jenny	A28	Transparency	Ruler	Rub	TT ball	+
Jenny	A29	Transparency	Ruler	Rub	TT ball	+
Jenny	A30	Transparency	Ruler	Rub	TT ball	-
Jenny	A31	Transparency	Ruler	Rub	Lamp	No light
Jenny	A32	Transparency	Pants	Pull	Lamp	No light
Jenny	A33	Transparency	Pants	Pull	Lamp	No light
Jenny	A34	Transparency	Ruler	Rub	Styrofoam	-
Brita	A35	Transparency	Rag	Rub	Lamp	No light
Clare	A36	Transparency	Ruler	Rub	TT ball	-
Jenny	A37	Metal	Ruler	Rub	TT ball	-
Brita	A38	Transparency	Rag	Rub	Lamp	No light
Tara		Transparency	Pants	Rub	Lamp	Light

Note: This table reproduces Table 4.1

is attracted to charges) whether there is static electricity (A_{22}–A_{26}). She does not articulate what she sees to share with others, but on the videotape *I* see that a little Styrofoam piece sticks three times to the transparency, twice it does not. The third positive trial follows on the heels of two negative trials. Similarly, Jenny conducts eight consecutive investigations (A_{27}–A_{34}). At first, she rubs the transparency with a plastic rule and uses a table tennis ball to test for the presence of charges. During the three first trials, the table tennis ball is attracted, providing evidence for the presence of charges. But then in her fourth trial, the ball is not attracted. Jenny then substitutes the lamp as test object for the table tennis ball after having rubbed the transparency sheet with the rule. As in the preceding trial with the table tennis ball, there is no sign for the presence of charges. Jenny then changes one of the materials: She places the transparency between her jeans-clad knees, pushes the knees against one another, and pulls the sheet. In both instances, the lamp does not glow.

In this situation, students are doing something but it is unclear whether what they do constitutes repeat instances. To know why they do what they do, however, we need to know whether *they* perceive what they do as repetition or as change. Learning occurs when students recognize regularities that correlate what they do with what they sense (see, feel, hear). In both of the present cases, chronological time goes by, as students *appear* to struggle making their investigation "to work." But then I put myself into their shoes, having a flashback to my own experience of investigating the materials. Thus, I can imagine Iris in her investigation experiencing the situation much as I have experienced my own:

> I am rubbing the transparency with the rag, test: the Styrofoam sticks. I am doing it again: the Styrofoam sticks. It seems to work. I am rubbing the transparency again: uh? The Styrofoam does not stick. What happened (with my theory)? I am doing it again: it doesn't stick! Does this mean it doesn't work? Rubbing the transparency with the rag doesn't produce static electricity? But why did it work the first time? Perhaps there is something wrong with the Styrofoam. I am going to try again. I rub the transparency with the rag: it sticks. It works when I use transparency and rag.

In this example—which needs to be read as an approximate account of what really is a fleeting sense—making something work for a first time does not mean it is a consistent phenomenon. Because the next time, whatever it is I want to achieve might not be the observed outcome. At what point can I stop knowing or at least be vaguely aware of the fact that it works all of the time—unless I am doing something wrong and know what it is that I have been doing wrong when it does not work? In a similar way, how is Jenny to know what is going on when after three positive trials (A_{27}–A_{29}), she does not repeat the observation (A_{30})? Is it her rubbing that differs from the previous instances? Is the absence of an effect due to the testing material? Has the transparency sheet changed? Has the ruler changed? To know the answers to these questions, Jenny has to continue investigating, by consciously varying known parameters or by *playing*, hoping to note something that clarifies how to produce a phenomenon consistently. To know that she has achieved to enact a repetition, she "must enact it, play it, and repeat it until the acute moment that Aristotle called 'recognition'. At this point, repetition and representation confront one another and merge, without, however, confusing their two levels, the one reflecting itself in and being sustained by the other" (Deleuze, 1968/1994, p. 15).

If I am really intent on finding out, if I allow myself to be absorbed, then a different modality of time reigns. Chronological time no longer pressures me. The quest for an answer is all that counts. My object of inquiry absorbs me. I no longer think of "me," no longer have an identity apart from the object, but fully engage in the flow of the activity, determined by the rate in which my actions unfold and enchain. How is anyone then to predict at what point in chronological time I can be certain that what I observe is what I am supposed to observe and at what time I will know that what I have done is what I am supposed to do? How is anyone to predict at what time I observe that the lamp glows differently under different conditions, sometimes close to, sometimes farther away from my hand?

EVOLUTION OF TEMPORAL DIMENSIONS OF GESTURE AND SPEECH

Communication through and through is a temporal phenomenon, and yet, educators do not explicitly account for this fact in their theories of engagement and learning in general and in student-centered tasks specifically. In the preceding chapters, I show how communication is dispersed over people and situation, and therefore involves the coordination of various forms of operations spread across bodies, gesture, speech, and setting. The coordination of processes always means coordination *of* something *in* time; it also means that it is something that has to be achieved. When there are many different signs and processes involved, coordination cannot be expected to occur the first time I attempt to communicate something but requires a process of learning during which I come to coordinate the different means of expression such that resulting expression is coherent across the various means. Thus, in chapters 6 and 7 I articulate several features of learning to talk about physical events that require coordination, which itself is the product of a process, and therefore occurs in and is the result of time.

Learning is an evolutionary process that has a variety of temporal characteristics, occurs in time, and produces time. In this section, I articulate three temporal dimensions of communication and learning observable in the set of videotapes from the tenth-grade physics course. First, students gesture phenomena that they do not express in the (school-, teacher-) desired verbal modality. Second, when students begin to express phenomena verbally, the verbal mode lags behind the corresponding gestures. As students become familiar with the phenomena on the one hand, and the production of descriptions on the other, the lag all but disappeared so that gestures and speech come to be perfectly coordinated. Third, the overall time for producing observational and theoretical descriptions decreases significantly; this evolution occurs in parallel to the previous processes.

General Description of Evolutionary Dimensions

Throughout the curricular unit, there are examples of situations in which students do not produce, or produce slowly, the teacher-desired (scientifically legitimized and legitimizing) verbal articulations. However, their gestures already forebode scientific articulation in that they embody the topological and indexical relations to the macroscopic objects. In one particular instance, Phil does not produce a verbal description, but his right hand moves across the PVC rod denoting the metal rod in the investigation, syncopating a temporal succession that parallels the periodic motion of the metal-coated elderberry mark sphere intimated by his previous gesture (Figure 7.3, line 3, frame 4 to line 4, frame 3). Here, the visually available periodic back and forth of the metal-coated elderberry mark sphere is represented in the syncopated back and forth movement over the PVC rod of the left, "electron" hand. This is an instance of situations in which learners gesturally articulate what they only subsequently express in another modality: discourse or text.

Students' increasing familiarity with the materials and phenomena is accompanied by a decreasing amount of time required for explanations to be constructed in real time. Over time and related to specific phenomena, there is a decreasing reliance on the materials at hand, the manipulation not only provides resources for communication but also imposes constraints. Frequently, only the central material or equipment remains part of students' descriptions and explanations. For example, several episodes feature Phil explaining how an electroscope is charged. Initially, the videotapes show Phil rubbing several transparencies and holding them above the electroscope. Subsequently, he merely uses a transparency sheet without rubbing it. Still later, he holds an arbitrary object above the electroscope (notebook, sheet of paper). Finally, he merely brings an open palm above the electroscope. The deployment of these resources occurs in time and space, and the spatial organization to be achieved occurs in time. It is therefore not surprising perhaps that the decreasing reliance on objects and events as resources in his explications is associated with a decrease in the amount of time it takes to articulate observations and explications pertaining to the phenomenon. However, as the descriptions in chapters 6 and 7 render evident, these materials provide resources for communicating at students are not yet ready to produce using words (language) alone.

In another instance of development, Matt explains the changing charge concentration on an electrical capacitor made from two metal plates. Initially, Matt repeats the entire experiment. Subsequently, he merely lifts one of the metal plates involved. Still later, he enacts a gesture against the two metal plates as an indexical ground without touching them. Finally, he provides an explanation in which the two metal plates and the distance between them are entirely expressed in words. Thus, when asked to explain why an electroscope attached to two charged metal plates increases its pointer deflection when the plates are pulled apart, Matt, without drawing on the two plates and electroscope within his reach suggests the following (gestural beats indicated where they occurred relative to the utterances):

> The upper one is like, in the normal situation, so ((beat)) when it is like this, the lower positive ((beat)) ones attract the upper negative ((beat)) ones or vice versa ((beat)). And when you take them apart ((beat)), can– ((beat)), they have to distribute in a better way, because there are so many electrons, it is difficult to explain ((beat)), so there are so many electrons and they repel ((beat)) each other, and that is why their density is larger and there is more voltage.

In this instance, an increasing abstraction from the situation can be observed, which ends with this presentation where beats are the only form of gesture deployed. Immediately thereafter, Matt uses diagram and text to write down his understanding of the phenomenon, which he subsequently reproduced during the exam with a corresponding item.

Paralleling the decreasing use of materials, there is an increase in more abstract representations (especially in the verbal modality) and a decrease in the amount of time that students take to explain something. For example, from his earliest attempts in explaining the phenomenon to the above presentation, Matt reduces the time required to produce the description from 48 to 30 seconds over the course of one lesson. In the same lesson, Phil initially takes 25 and finally 14 seconds to explain the same phenomenon; concurrently, he decreases his bodily involvement from showing the investigation while explaining it to using only one iconic gesture as part of the explanation. In a similar way, Jenny's first presentation of a proposal for an experiment lasts 18 seconds and involves several gestures including the expected outcomes of approaching a charged film to a current of water from the tap. In her second presentation of the same experiment to a student previously absent, she explains the investigation in 11 seconds and the gestures are reduced to the iconic representation of the movement that had to be conducted with the film, and the direction of the water current. Finally, Jenny's explanation of how objects come to be charged process (chapter 6) decreases in length from 20.75 to 6.97 seconds. This reduction in time is directly associated with a shift from gestural and manipulation-related communicative modes to communicative modes base on words and other signs bear an arbitrary relation to the things they denote.

Articulating an Idea in Real Time

Let me for a moment analyze in more detail the episode in which Jenny articulates an investigation with the charged transparency sheet held next to a fine stream of water running from a tap. Figure 9.3 depicts Jenny's body position in one-second intervals for the entire 20-second episode during which she articulates the proposal for the first time. In situations such as this, I-learner have a rough, vague, fuzzy, underdetermined, and indeterminate idea. Having an idea does not mean I have something like a photographic image that I then describe with words as I might describe by just naming the different parts and relations. Rather, it is more like perceiving a vague and blurry image of a dripping faucet and a transparency sheet held somehow next to it. I am in a situation much like when I ride my bicycle through an unfamiliar area for the first, second, third, and so on time (chapter 3). Much like the gigantic twin towers, which only appeared when I passed a particular stretch of the road for the sixth or seventh time, my idea comes to me as I articulate it, takes on firm features, in and through the process of articulating it to my peers. Its details are worked out as I am beginning and getting through my account, which articulates the idea that comes to life in and through the articulation. It is a continuous process of articulation of a figure|ground relation that has begun with a blurry image that is worked out in its detail in and through my account, much like a sculptures statue increasingly takes shape as she chips pieces of the initially indeterminate block. My account establishes the figure that makes the ultimate proposal; the proposal does not exist in a finished form in my mind only to be translated into speech. Here, I retell the event as if I had attempted to articulate the idea for the first time, gathering resources and me together into a coherent story.

> I am first orienting to my peers and the idea by announcing, "You know what one can also do?" (Figure 9.3, first two frames). In talking and addressing myself to the others, I announce that I am in the process of articulating something. My announcement orients the others to what I am doing, which includes a preparation of a ruler and an overhead transparency. In this preparation, I exhibit my orientation to the topic, the extent of which is only becoming clear, to others and myself, as I am going along.
>
> I now have readied myself to some extent, have oriented to articulating an idea, and have prepared my peers that something is forthcoming. Using

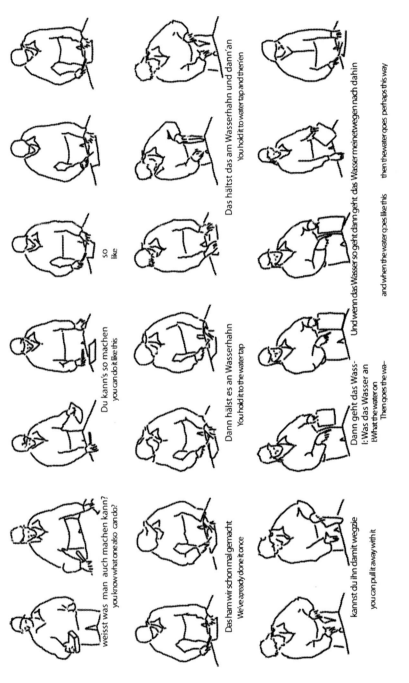

weisst was man auch machen kann?
you know what one also can do?

Das ham wir schon mal gemacht
We've already done it once

Dann geht das Wass-
i: Was das Wasser an
i:What the water on
Then goes the wa–

kannst du ihn damit wegzie
you can pull it away with it

Du kann's so machen
you can do it like this

Dann hälst es an Wasserhahn
You hold it to the water tap

Und wenn das Wasser so geht dann geht das Wasser meinetwegen nach dahin
and when the water goes like this   then the water goes perhaps this way

so
like

Das hälst das am Wasserhahn und dann'an
You hold it to water tap and then'en

Figure 9.3. Jenny produces time as much as being subject to it while articulating a proposal. (The last frame in one row is identical to the first image in the next row.)

an idea, and have prepared my peers that something is forthcoming. Using the materials, I begin to rub the transparency with the ruler and describe, "You can do it like this" (Figure 9.3, line 1, frames 3–5). I pause speaking but continue rubbing, just as I have always been rubbing when I want to get the transparency charged. I then announce that I have seen it done before ("We have done it once"), still rubbing, because I have to rub hard to make the transparency charged. I have rubbed for a while and now announce that one can hold the transparency to the tap, but I continue rubbing to move to the next part with my demonstration only subsequent to it.

In my rubbing, the idea of the investigation begins to take on specific form. *I am gathering, and I am gathering myself* together. I now move to the next step, holding the transparency to the tap. This step begins to become figure in the process of charging, which immediately precedes the step, and therefore readies me for what is to come.

Here, then, my bodily action of charging and my speech have run different courses. I am still showing how to charge the transparency but I am already articulating what is to be done with it once I have finished charging. So when I am done charging and begin a demonstration showing how to hold the charged transparency sheet with respect to the water that I denote with my other hand, I am articulating again in words what is going on. Here, my speech has waited for my bodily demonstration and repeats what it has articulated, therefore aligning my different modes of communication again. I then show how the stream of water can be pulled, but now the left and right hand operate independently at first, my left hand shows how I pull but my right hand does not yet follow. My articulation of what I anticipate to happen gives shape to my anticipation, such that I re-articulate when what I have communicated does not fit my own initially vague anticipations. I attempt again, and then again, finally coordinating the down and leftward movement of the stream with the sideways movement of the charged transparency.

This episode articulates the sense Jenny might have had during the event. In any case, it articulates some of the features that are vague and then salient as I-learner attempt to articulate an idea. I do not know in advance exactly what I will be saying, but know that what I have said was what I wanted to say when I am done speaking. When something I have said does not appear right, I begin again, or re-articulate an aspect of what will be the ultimate account. As I am producing my idea for a first time, I have to gather together and bring into alignment the different pieces of my story. Some of these pieces, my demonstrations, are enacted, and these have their own temporality and temporal constraints. I can rub only so fast, and to show that I have to rub hard, I either have to articulate it in speech or demonstrate it. In words, I may already have said what is necessary, so that my speech, if it is to be aligned with the other parts of my articulation, has to wait. When my manipulations and gestures are ready, I may repeat what I have already said once simply to produce a conjoint account in the different modalities at my disposition.

My articulation of the idea for an investigation therefore is an achievement in time. I produce the idea in and through the verbal articulation. I do so for a first time, as I have to gather together all the necessary pieces; and I have to gather together myself. When I do articulate the idea a second time, it is a repetition, sameness in difference. Now it has some likeness with how common sense (psychology) thinks about communication: a finished product is read out, made public, as I am speaking. But if it had been a finished idea prior to my first speaking, why would it take me less time when I articulate the idea again? As other research involving gestures suggests, there are no or little changes in rate or production of gesture after the first time an account has been produced. That is, the initial articulation *is* the first time the idea is articulated, it does not, in most cases, predate the first articulation as a mental model of the thing.

Speech–Gesture Coordination

In chapters 6 and 7, there are episodes that show how speech and corresponding gesture may be produced at different moments in time, and coordination occurs with familiarity. In fact, familiarity and perfect coordination are two different ways of explicating the same phenomenon: When I am familiar with the thing I communicate, my gestures and speech are coordinated; and conversely, my gestures and speech are coordinated when I talk about something familiar to me. When students produce descriptions while moving the objects around to produce a slow motion representation of the actual event, talk is normally coordinated with the movement. However, during their attempts in constructing observational and theoretical descriptions of the phenomena students produce in their investigations, there initially is a lag between the main, signifying part of the gesture (technically, the *stroke*) and the corresponding word. In this database this lag ranges from 400 milliseconds to 1.40 seconds. For example, Jenny's explication of the investigation involving water flowing from the tap and a charged transparency sheet (chapter 4) initially includes temporal shifts and conceptual incongruencies between the gestural and verbal mode.

Similarly, there are such shifts in the early explanations other students produce for these and other observed phenomena. As seen in the episode with Jenny, when new to a topic, my gestures and my speech are shifted with respect to each other—my gesture generally runs ahead of my speech, though in Jenny's case, she was talking about bringing the transparency to the water tap prior to actually showing it gesturally. In some instances, there are delays between gestures and corresponding words that range from 2.01 to 2.53 seconds. Thus, Matt's gesture representing the movement of electrons and his deictic gesture indicating their final location is completed 0.80 seconds before the stressed part—the marker used by linguists interested in the gesture–speech relationship—of its corresponding word "disappear" (Episode 7.2, line 1, frame 2). The endpoint corresponding to "this part" was reached 1.23 seconds before the associated utterance. Matt's gestures run ahead of his utterances, which appear to be "facilitated" or "jogged" by the gestures that precede them. In the entire database, there is only one student whose gestures are nearly always coordinated perfectly (within the 40 milliseconds accuracy of the video track) with speech, though there are often long pauses before the simultaneous production of both.

These differences in the temporality of gesture and speech indicate a dispersion of the communication over and across the body of the individual. The different ways of signifying, to make a communicative act coherent, have to be gathered together and coordinated. The coordination these different movements, as the case study featuring Jenny shows, is an achievement *in time*; once it has been achieved, repeating the communicative act takes much less time. Thus, when I communicate, it simultaneously is a single I and not a single I who speaks. It is not a single I in the sense that there is no one conception made public by some central processor. Why would there by temporal delays if there were a central processor, a core ego, that is in control of the communication? There therefore is not a single ego in the sense that this "I" is distributed over my body and consciousness; I therefore have the ability to speak differently at the same instance. I is a dispersed I, it is spectral, a one and a many simultaneously.

The episodes featured throughout this book show that at the early stages of producing an explanation, there often are considerable delays between the stroke of a gesture and the verbal equivalent (stressed part in novel contribution). This observation differs from other research, which reports that gestures coincide with their verbal equivalents (McNeill, 1992). I observed—across a number of studies conducted in very different data sets recorded in different countries, content areas, and type of activities—that delays are almost always present when students talk about unfamiliar phenomena; the delays decreased when students became more familiar with the words describing the phenomena.

TEMPORALITY IN AND OF INTERACTION

Interactions inherently occur *in time*; they also contain a substantial element of emergence, as I cannot know what the person opposite to me will say or respond to what I have said. I do not even know what I will have said and how long I will speak once I have taken a turn. I cannot therefore know what my next contribution will be once I have another turn at talk; and I do not know when this next turn will be, particularly if the interaction involves more than one person. Conversations therefore are emergent beasts not only with respect to their content but also with respect to the processes; conversations are of a different order as they are outside the control of any individual and therefore come with yet another aspect of temporality. Let me take a look at the second part of Jenny's proposal, beginning at the third to last frame in line 2 (Figure 9.3). I have transcribed this part including the pauses to the tenth of a second in Episode 9.1, which begins when Jenny says that "this" (transparency) is to be held to the water tap.

Episode 9.1
01   Jenny: Das hältst das am Wasserhahn (0.39) und dann'an (0.20)
                        ((This you hold to the water tap and then'en))

02		kannst du ihn damit wegziehn
		((can you pull it away with it))
03		(0.83)
04	Iris:	Was [das Was]ser an
		((What the water on))
05	Jenny:	[Dann geht das Wass–] Und wenn das Wasser so geht,
		((And goes the wat–)) ((And when the water goes like this,))
06		dann geht das Wasser meinetwegen nach dahin.
		((then goes the water perhaps this way.))

The transcript shows the pauses that separate the different speech elements. Jenny appears to come to an end point once she has articulated that "it" can be pulled away. She pauses. Pausing generally means that someone else may speak. Pausing means that I indicate readiness to give up my turn at talk, especially when the pause is lengthening. However, whether an instance without a word is a pause that I need to reorient to continue or whether the pause is to be a transition point is itself an achievement. Here, after more than 0.80 seconds, Iris begins to speak. She may seek clarification about the water, but Jenny begins to talk again. Apparently she is not yet done; but she also clarifies the issue with the water.

The transcript shows that Iris speaks more slowly than Jenny, two syllables (turn 04) overlapping with four (turn 05). The former exhibits no hurry, compared to Jenny, who, by speaking fast, indicates the wish to complete the turn she has had before someone else speaks. Jenny also indicates that she has not finished the idea, that something is lacking, something that she wants to complete before anyone else is to react to it. In this situation, Jenny not only speaks faster than Iris, but also faster than she normally does. Thus, Episode 9.1 and Figure 9.3 show that she articulates more syllables in a three-second period following Iris' intervention than during any other moment of her presentation. The rate with which Jenny speaks therefore is also mediated by contextual features, here her own leaving a pause and Iris' beginning a new turn. Jenny then accelerates, and therefore shortens the overall time that the utterance might have taken had Iris not started to speak. More so, Jenny might have let the pause get even longer followed at the preceding speech rate, thereby lengthening the total time the account. This shows that the measures I-author provide in previous sections for overall production time to produce a particular account only are approximate measures, for it is variable depending on numerous contextually emergent features that inherently cannot be predicted. Speaking rates, though they mediate how fast students speak never are taken into account when educators analyze learning that occurs in and through interactions. Students' utterances, which are given in their entirety in the transcription, are treated like text rather than as unfolding and temporalizing discourse. What students say is treated in an atemporal manner, consistent with the idea that their saying is an articulation of something already stable and fixed in their minds, such as an idea, conception, or conceptual framework.

A phenomenological perspective takes into account the temporal features of talk and the possible ways in which the results of situated talk are mediated by the con-

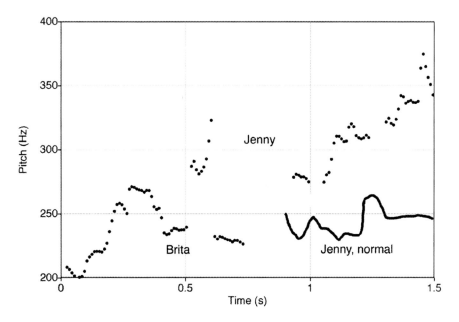

Figure 9.4. Pitch level changes occur when speakers compete for the speaking turn.

textual nature of the talk as process. What students say cannot be analyzed in the same way as written text: what they say unfolds in time and whatever they become aware of in the process of speaking mediates what they say, when they say it, and at what time they stop. Contextual features mediate the process of talk, and therefore also what and how students learn in a given period of chronological time.

There is a further temporal moment to which researchers have paid scant attention, but which is an important resource in and for social interaction. When I speak, there is a certain dominant frequency with which my vocal cords vibrate; these vibrations, a temporal phenomenon, determine the pitch of my speech. It turns out that pitch is an important feature of interactions. For example, when students disagree on a point or compete for a turn at talk, their pitch rates drastically change. In one instance, Brita is explaining some phenomenon but Jenny disagrees, vying for a turn at talk. Figure 9.4, which presents the pitch of the two students in this situation as well as Jenny's normal pitch range, shows how Jenny begins at a much higher pitch rate than Brita, a range that is much higher than her normal range. Whereas Brita continues speaking at her rate, with a dropping pitch as this is normally observed at the end of a speaking turn, Jenny continues to produce utterances at a pitch that is much higher than normal. I observe such features of talk across a considerable variety of situations, both in and out-of classrooms. Thus, teachers are particularly successful when their pitch levels blend with those of student utterances; observers in such classrooms talk about the considerable levels of synchrony that appears to exist without being able to put their fingers on why this is the case. On the other hand, conflict is generally associated with (sharply) rising

253

pitch levels, which, in really difficult moments, reaches shrill outbursts. It is also related to the acceleration of speech rates, and with an overall increase of the rate of temporal phenomena.

In the case of the rising pitch levels, the person as a whole seems to speed up, not only in the rate of speech, that is, the rate at which words are articulated, but also in the process of the articulation itself, the vibrations of the vocal cords, which are observable as a rising pitch. Everything appears to go faster, and, in a different context, I have seen that this increased rate also is visible in features such as students' rocking of their legs, pounding a pencil on the desk, and so on. As the conflict aggravates, even those not involved accelerate in their rhythms, only to slow down as the conflict subsides or is ended by the suspension of a student.

There are therefore many levels at which time and temporality mediate how and what students learn in any classroom. These temporal features are not inherently linked to chronological time, that is, the time that is outlined in the curriculum, which, as text, is itself a timeless feature. Learning is presupposed to occur as a result of what teachers plan, and therefore is articulated in a deterministic framework. Such a framework is inherently incompatible with an emergent approach. The temporal aspects can be identified at many levels, from the very microperspective of pitch to the level of interacting with others and speech production, to the production of an entire explication, to the realization of a variety of features of a glow lamp—which, as I show in chapter 5, is taking the four young women ten lessons to achieve.

UNDERSTANDING IS ALWAYS A PRESENT THAT HAS BEEN

Theoretical understanding implies a temporal order that is radically different from absorbed copying in the world exhibited by the participants in classroom events, students and teachers alike. This is so because theoretical understanding inherently *follows* practical understanding that always already exists and which, in fact, constitutes the very condition for theoretical understanding (Ricœur, 1991). Without practical understanding there cannot be theoretical understanding. Present understanding—the stuff I know that I know—is always in terms of historically and experientially constituted horizons, and therefore a practical understanding of the world that "has been." Because of the action|operation dialectic, I cannot "know" what I do until after I have done it, so that my actions already display knowledgeability before it can be known to me. Biographical experience always precedes and exceeds that which can be objectified, and objectification itself is a process in time. Learning, therefore, is a process in time, not only because I experience in time but also because my experiences alone do not provide me with all that is to knowledge. There is a process by means of which experiences are transformed to become knowledge that I can talk about and therefore make the theme of my talk. That is, learning means historicizing experience in and through the process of making it present again, re-presencing or re-presenting it, that is, representing it by means of signifiers that stand in for it. Learning occurs when, following Aristotle, I recognize something that I have already known, when I cognize again, re-cognize. Un-

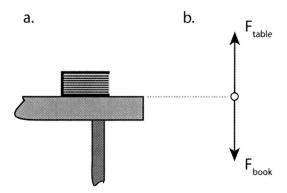

Figure 9.5. I experience books on tables in a phenomenal realm, describing it in everyday terms. Physics has a different way of describing and theorizing such experiences, thereby objectifying the things that normally surround me in absorbed coping.

derstanding, therefore, always is an understanding and presence that already have been. In chapter 3, I foreshadow this temporal mode of learning in my use of the prefix "re-" in the notions *re-cognition, re-presentation, re-member* or *re-gard*.

Thematic understanding therefore only deals with events that already "have been," which have passed. This involves a freeing of the things that surround me, things that are characterized by their availability, things that are at-hand, and making them subject to an objectifying gaze. That is, for useful things that I employ and deploy in knowledgeable practical action to become theoretical objects, I have to free them from their involvement with other things in time and articulate them in a space, where they become and are subject to manipulation and transformation as toys are in a child's hands. They do not themselves undergo transformations but are building blocks or elements.

There is a changeover in the way of relating to a situation when my circumspect taking care turns into objectification, deliberation, and ultimately theoretical description. I elucidate this statement in the following discussion of an example from teaching and learning of Newton's third law of motion. Physics and physical science teachers (as well as textbooks) often use a book on a table (Figure 9.5a) as an example that illustrates Newton's third law of motion, "Every action has an equal and opposite reaction" (Figure 9.5b).

In my circumspect use, books are used for reading and tables are to put books on and places I work at (or, at home, where I eat). In their daily use, books are not occurrent in and as objects that have mass, that are heavy or light. Students and teachers, in their daily use, might recognize and deal with the "the book that is heavy." But the statement can also mean that the being before me—e.g., the book with which I am familiar as physics book—has a weight or mass, and has the property of heaviness. As such, it exerts pressure on the table, itself an instance of beings that in their everyday use are not recognized as a "something that supports something else," but are circumspectively used. I experiment at a laboratory table without ever consciously thinking about the table as such. Similarly, I do not think about the dining room table during dinner, but simply rest my arms, place the spoon, knife, or wine glass. The table is there (materially) but also not there (in consciousness); it figures in the ground against which everything else that I use becomes figure. I do not thematize the table *as* table; rather, under normal circumstances it is transparent to me as I am using it. As such, if I jerk the table so that it is removed from under the book, I "know," even without thematizing it as such, that the book falls.

But there is a shift as soon as I begin to thematize the book as something that has a mass and therefore a weight (force) that exerts pressure on the table. In this move, I change over from the circumspective use of book (as something I read and draw information from) and table (which I use to put books, notebooks, pens on). What is now in my perceptual field are the book and the table, not as tools that I circumspectively use, but as thematized corporeal things with properties that are subject to the laws of physics, here gravity. In this case gravity is not available in some form other than a sign that is associated with my experience of things dropping, the book dropping from the table. My circumspect (transparent) use of the table to put my office stuff on has changed to talk about heaviness and gravity. Circumspect talk about a heavy book no longer has its original meaning because it is no longer in the mode of an *in-order-to* relation that I am enacting with the book when I find it "to be too heavy."

When I talk *about* the book and its heaviness, my relation to it has changed from how I normally use it. What I am talking *about*, the heavy book and the table that supports it, does not show itself differently because it is at a distance from absorbed use, but because I am *looking at* the thing at hand. By *looking at*, the book, as any other thing, is encountered in a different way, as a thing that is objectively present to me, my consciousness; it has become an object of my attention and intention. In this shift from transparent use of the things to *looking at* these things, and the corresponding shift from nonthetic to thetic presence constitutes a shift in the nature of the thing that is at the origin of the difference between praxis and theory. This shift is encountered in my everyday being in the world as a breakdown, and, at a greater remove from transparent coping, as theoretical understanding of practice and world. In a statement that attributes weight to a book, its ordinary character as a "thing-to-be-read" or "thing-to-find-word-problems-in" recedes into the ground; it no longer is ready-to-hand in ordinary activity of reading a textbook or doing a word problem.

In making the things surrounding me objects of my conscious thought, that is, in objectifying them, they loose their place in the experienced whole and become "released," that is, they are pulled (Lat. *trahere*) away (Lat. *abs*-), abstracted from the whole. But such abstraction is always a thematization in a particular way such that the totality of what is objectively present to me is thematic: re-presentation in its very nature constitutes a particular point of view. It is in this release, when the reduction that occurs as the nonthetic changes into the thetic, in the thematization that understanding of being is modified. Thematization is a projection that aims at freeing things encountered in the world and its temporality so that they can become objects; thematization objectifies and frees things. It frees the things in such a way

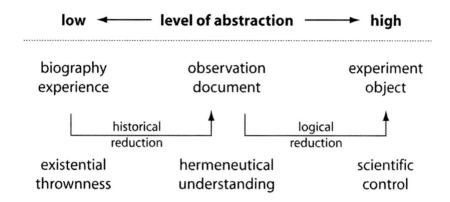

Figure 9.6. The turn the experience of phenomena into scientific knowledge requires radical transformations in our relationship to the world.

that they are *objectively* available and subject to questioning and definition. And it frees the things from the temporal order that they normally are implicated in, that implicates them, and that these things implicate in turn.

When a teacher stops what she is currently doing (e.g., enacting a whole-class interaction over and about Newton's third law) to think about how to deal with an inattentive or disruptive student, she objectifies her situation in terms of descriptions and thereby already makes a basic kind of theoretical grasping. For the students, of course, there is a problem in that they too have a relation to the book and table. Furthermore, the forces as shown (Figure 9.5) are not available to them: they are not and cannot be occurrent. Whereas it may be a minor step from drawing an arrow downward to designate gravity, it is not at all self evident to have another force pointing upwards. For the table, in everyday mundane perception, is not pushing: it is just holding.

Experiencing something and knowing *about* the same thing therefore constitute different forms of *relating-to*, and they involve different modes of time. When I use the curriculum materials from the lessons on electrostatics to create and explore phenomena, I encounter these as part of my existential throwness, as part of my biographical experience. Thus, for example, I use the neon lamp to check for the presence of static electricity. The thing exists as tool, has the character of *in-order-to,* existing in the present moment of the biographical experience of existential throwness (Figure 9.6). When for some reason I stop to think about the lamp *as* lamp, for example, because "it does not work," then my relationship to it has changed. It no longer has its usual *in-order-to* character but has become an object of my attention and intention. I now *look at* something that I have always already encountered in a different mode. That is, my observation of the lamp as something that has two electrodes or that is made from glass and metal end caps constitutes a historical reduction. The qualities and features of the thing emerge from a hermeneutical process that figures the world into things and their properties, which come to stand against everything else.

In a second, logical reduction, the properties of the things discovered and brought to light are now related as factors (Figure 9.6). This involves a second shift in the temporal mode from the ever changing, historical interpretation to the timeless correlation of properties, which are external to the things and therefore no longer implicated in the temporal order of the things. That is, to learn anything related to science about the book, for example, Newton's third law of motion, I first need to make table and book thematic *as* something that has *weight* and *mass*—see my discussion in the epilogue of how children come to properties in and through experience. Similarly, the table has to be made thematic as something that can push (rather than merely "hold up" something) prior to any science that can be learned. This second reduction, then, constitutes a logical reduction in which I come to relate to the world in yet another way. Whereas in the first reduction, I become aware of the things *as* things with their properties, the second reduction makes connections *between* properties rather than the things themselves, that is, the things I experience. The previous chapters also provide evidence that practical understanding precedes theoretical understanding. Brita, Clare, Iris, and Jenny use the neon glow lamp prior to their theoretical parsing of the device into something consisting of two electrodes, metal caps, and a glass body.

In the process of learning from experience, two major shifts in temporal modes occur. First, practical understanding precedes the articulation of things *as* things; it occurs in time. That is, prior to making some thing and any of its properties the object of thought and investigation, I have to have some experience with it. Without experience, there is nothing I can articulate—but it is true, without articulation, there is nothing I can experience. The point here is to go further than my current articulations, to learn, I already need to have some practical experience with the things I am asked to learn about. The experience then can be articulated in the form of observation statements, which constitute documents that inherently have historical dimensions in the way I understand them. Scientific understandings, however, is constituted by atemporal relations of properties, which makes the logical reduction both requisite and a process of change in the temporal mode. It does not surprise me therefore to see that students have had difficulties defining and controlling variables, which inherently involves change in the experienced temporal modes of being.

During the 1960s and 1970s, and even during the 1980s, science educators focused a lot on science process skills. Controlling variables emerged as one of the quintessential skills scientists were said to have. The pendulum constitutes the paradigmatic investigation during for students to learn and demonstrate the control of variables. Thus, students are expected to control variables prior to any extended exploration. But this expectation, I have been able to experience ample time as a teacher, is not justified. Most students coming to the pendulum for a first time do not control variables, do not even frame relevant variables. Rather, if they are to control the variables, they first need to engage with the equipment and material, then, in a moment of hermeneutic reduction, frame properties, before they can relate anything like two variables and control others. The framework I just outlined allows me to understand why this is so.

Before I can relate the two gigantic towers at the roadside into my (scientific) experimentations and investigations, I have to become conscious of them, encounter them as things, as outcomes of a historical reduction. *Before* I can use the white posts in figuring out my speed, relating distance and time given by my wristwatch, the posts have to be given to me *as* regularities, and the distance between them *as* regular distance. *Before* I can perceive the tear as something that allows the inner tube to protrude and explode, it has to be given to me in my perception, which itself requires my engagement with it, an engagement from which the tear *as* tear can emerge. This engagement precedes any historical reduction, because something becomes figure as the results of my eyes jumping back and forth between some point on the inside of what becomes figure to something on the outside, which will be the indeterminate ground against which the figure figures. If the image of some object continually falls on the same place on the retina, I am no longer able to see it, and "I," the subject, fuse with the object (Cole & Levitin, 2000).

These examples show that historical reduction always precedes the scientific approach involving the same material entities. This, as my ethnographic studies show, is also true for mature scientists when they work in unfamiliar terrain (e.g., Roth, 2004a). But the historical reduction itself is preceded by a practical encounter of the things in the world. In the same way that the properties of the neon lamp become occurrent to the four young women (chapter 4) or the different qualities of the rolling and sliding objects to Sean and his mates (chapter 2), the pendulum string, bob, suspension, etc. *become occurrent* to the student who is finding out about the thing. That is, these things are *not given immediately* but *reveal* their properties in a process of exploration, itself given and unfolding in time. At this point, then, students are in a position to make the first, historical reduction. In a second step, they can relate the different properties to one another, control them, generate hypotheses about relations, and then test them. This constitutes the second reduction, which, as should be evident, has both experience and first reduction as its prerequisites. Prior to the logical reduction from which science springs forth, experience and historical reduction unfold in time. Then, logical reduction unfolds in time making experience and the results of the historical reduction its topic, objectifies them. And in this way, I arrive at the initially mysterious claim: understanding always is (practical) understanding that already has been.

TOWARD A PHENOMENOLOGICAL UNDERSTANDING OF TIME AND TEMPORALITY IN SCIENCE LEARNING

Temporality is the central distinguishing feature between praxis and any subsequent theory intended to describe and explain this practice. Yet there is little research that has concerned itself with the temporal aspects of teaching. In this chapter, I am concerned with the phenomenological structure of time in the experience of learning. Students continuously act in time (even sitting in a chair and dreaming is an act), without having the luxury of *time-out* for deliberating every action and without any opportunity to turn the clock back (*irreversibility*). That is, learners continuously *commit* themselves to the implications of their acts to the recipients for which they bear full responsibility, for which they are *answerable*. Each act therefore has not only practical but also *moral* aspects. These moral aspects, which derive from considering the temporal modes of being, have not been addressed in science education. But these aspects deserve treatment in a discipline dedicated to the training of specialized personnel in the development of tools that mediate human access to the world. One difference between experienced and new science practitioners lies in the sense of the former for doing the right thing at the right time (moral aspect). Another difference lies in the experienced practitioner's ability to intuit the potential implications of his acts and therefore to avoid situations in which their room to maneuver is constraint. This aspect remains to be explored by science educators

This chapter shows how learning is an event (process) in time and how any learning outcomes are the results of historical processes at very different levels. Not only is learning a process in time, it requires time. When I am involved in some investigation, I am subject to a different mode of temporality than that given by chronological time, the time of a clock and the calendar, that is, the modes of time that characteristically figure in curricula and lesson plans. Time and temporality underlie learning to a tremendous extent, especially the unintentional aspects of learning that occur in moments of flow. Time and temporality mediate when and what I can learn, that is, when and what particular scientific knowledge emerges from my experiential thrownness, through which I encounter the world, and my historical reductions, that give me the basic level things that I can subsequently make the objects of my inquiry. In the two following chapters, I articulate learning as it occurs in time, following its own beat, while students (chapter 11) and I (chapter 10) are attempting to create and understand electrostatic phenomena. Before moving on, however, I articulate some key concepts arising from phenomenological considerations of time.

Three Modes of Time

There are two forms of experienced time that characterize human experience: phenomenological time and chronological time. Chronological time is associated with objective experience, arising with the human capacity of reflection, that is, with the reflection about the relation of past and future. Phenomenological time is related to the experience of the moment, which philosophers often refer to as the experience of being-affected. The former is accessible objectively, in reference to the passing of day and night, the regular advance of the hands or digits of a wristwatch. It is the time that I am feeling subjected to when I reflect on my being. The latter is related to the living presence. It includes the sense of "not-yet" related to the future and the "no-longer" of the past, both of which are opposed to the pure and simple is of the present. The no longer of the immediate past is necessary for being able to experience difference, because what is now can be experienced as different from the preceding moment only if this immediate past is still available in the present: Although the moment and its contents are past, they also have to be present or I would not be able to establish their difference. And I cannot have an intention unless there is some immanent future to which I am oriented and which I want to reach. In a positive way, these modes of time appears in language as the "will be present" of the future, the "was present" of the past, whereas the present is reflected in itself. This living present is therefore characterized by imminence. The two forms stand in a relation of complementarity so that they cannot be thought together.

Phenomenological time is characterized by a sense of duration, imminence, which includes a sense of immediate past and future in the present. The philosophers Edmund Husserl and Maurice Merleau-Ponty expressed these as aspects of time as *retention* and *protention*. These forms of time are referred to as the past and future of the present. Imminence, the recent, constitutes "intentional relations, internal to the present, not by any means transitive intentional relations, turned toward objects sighted outside, as it were, but longitudinal relations constituting time as a continuous flux" (Ricœur, 1991, p. 210). The notion of intention focuses attention on what I make happen rather than on what happens as event in objective time, which I experience because of my capacity to be sensible. This dimension of time arises from a phenomenology of perception, which links present and future in the duration of visual fixation of an object and links present and past in assuming the existence of an object prior to its appearance in consciousness. It is in this sense that I can speak of the human body as making and secreting time instead of being subjected to time.

Chronological time is the time of physics, a time that is represented as a point on a line. This time is external to me: it is the time that I experience passively, a time to which I am delivered and subjected to. Chronological time is thought from the present in such a way that it allows making logical connections between the past, present, and future. In this sense, theory fundamentally requires the simultaneous presence of objects and events that in practice never occur simultaneously. Logical connections, as in scientific theories, can only be made when "the present becomes threefold: the present of the future, present of the past, present of the present" (p. 210). Theory, is but one aspect of human experience—though the part that can easily be objectified—being-affectedness because it is inaccessible to reason and rationality lies outside formal inquiry.

The act is a moment of beginning: I make something happen that I do not entirely have control of. Taking initiative means to engage in action that marks the beginning. However, to speak of initiative is also to speak of responsibility. All speech acts commit their speaker through a tacit pledge of sincerity by reason that I actually mean what I say. But each act is tied into past and future; each act is only an aspect of a series of *inter*action. The two forms of experience are united in praxis, through the actions I take. The human body, seat of the "I can," my *agency,* here becomes the mediating element between the objective order of the world and the course of subjective personal experience. The connection between the living present and the anonymous instant is performed practically in the initiative that has its seat in my body. Praxis, therefore, is the location where the two moments of time are mediated and united.

CHAPTER 9

Experiencing Time

In *Being and Time*, Heidegger (1977/1996) articulates the relationship between time and myself, the experiencing subject: temporality and subjectivity are one. I have to understand time as the subject, and the subject as time. I do not think the passage of the present into another present that currently lies in the immanent future. I am not a spectator of this passage. Rather, I produce it, I am already in the present which will come in the same way as my gesture already contains its goal, I am myself time, a time that dwells rather than the time that flows or changes.

Far from being a condition *a priori* and transcendent to historicity, time is what practical activity produces in the very act whereby it produces itself. Because practice is the product of schema that are themselves the embodied products of the objectively experienced, immanent regularities and tendencies of the world, my schemas can anticipate these tendencies and regularities, that is, a nonthetic and non-thematic reference to an immanent future inscribed in the immediacy of the present. Time is engendered in the concrete realization of my intentions through actions, which is by definition a making present and letting become a matter of the past, that is, the "passing" of time according to common sense. Practical activity—in so far as it is felt and makes sense, that is, in so far as it is engendered by my schemas adjusted to the immanent tendencies of the objectively experienced world surrounding me—is an act of temporalization through which I transcend the immediate present as I mobilize the traces past experiences inscribed in me as resources and through which I practically anticipate the future inscribed in the present as objective possibility. Because praxis implies a practical reference to the future implied in the past of which it is the product, my schemas temporalize themselves in the very act through which they are realized.

Experience, acquired first hand or vicariously, always is a matter of overcoming something foreign, of something acquired becoming sedimented in my schema of perception and action. The notion of "space of experience" then brings to mind a layered structure, composed of clusters and stratifications, which allows the past, built up in this way, to escape simple chronology. Anticipation is possible when the future-become-present turns toward the not-yet. The notion of horizon evokes the power of unfolding as well as that of surpassing attached to the notion of expectation. Anticipation can never be derived from experience—the space of experience is never enough to *determine* the horizon of the anticipation. Action is therefore related to a third dimension of temporality, which has the persistence or accumulation of the past in the presence (experience) as one pole, and which has the open future (expectation), "the future-become-present turned toward the not-yet" (p. 218) as the other pole.

Activity in a world of realistic complexity is inherently a matter of *improvisation*. By "inherently" I mean that this is a necessary result, a property of the universe and not simply of a particular species of organism or a particular type of device. When I engage in something as the result of which my action possibilities increase—i.e., I am learning—I cannot know at what time and how quickly I become aware of what it is that I am to learn or what I learn despite of what a teacher intends. As I engage in some task, I find myself in a present, a now that continuously recedes into the past. "Now" is infinitesimally narrow, so that I capture events, or moments, only as something that has some extension. To be able to re-present it, it has to be something that can be grasped, the nature of an object; "objectification" means that another aspect from the dynamic continuum (e.g., material sign, object, mental image) can be used to re-present it. From this follows that the present does not exist as such, as an objectified entity, for it does not have an extension. It is always and already available to me as a limit to that which has occurred and that which will occur in a future tense. The now is also a horizon that limits what is available to me for objectification, as fact. It separates the not-yet-available from the already available and objectifiable. It is only at some future present that the now as event is objectively available to the reflections of the agent.

These temporal capacities of human beings are painfully absent from theories of knowing and learning in science, and they are equally absent from the repertoires of expert systems that are built according to the classical information processing paradigms. Processing explicit information is also the central underlying character of reflection. Hence, there is at least some plausibility to the suggestion that rather than looking for time-consuming general-purpose perception and planning explanations of human behavior, one might look for some mechanism underlying ongoing activity that is a somewhat rough-and-ready affair dedicated to the just-good-enough real-time completion of certain specific behaviors of high adaptive significance. The absence of my temporal capacities from theories of knowing and learning leads to the fact that the experience of learning—such as that occurring while I investigate the electroscope—is absent, too. I am in and through time, I am absorbed in the task and lost to phenomenological time: I experience flow. But I cannot know when I learn something that is yet beyond the horizon, temporally and conceptually. I cannot therefore intend to know the thing that is beyond my intention, because as object, I cannot yet grasp what it is that I will only grasp at some future time. Learning is an event and process, yet is depicted in terms of outcomes in curriculum documents and research articles. I urge science educators to attend to and theorize the processual nature of learning. Learning as event and process is at the heart of the following two chapters.

Chapter 10 is primarily concerned with understanding the phenomenon of flow. In the course of two nights, I have been engaged in pursuing a contradiction between my observations on the simple device, the electroscope, and my understanding of charge distributions. The fact that I spent two long nights, more than twenty hours "on the same problem" shows that *real* learning and understanding cannot be planned and cannot be made to fit into 60-minute slots that are allotted to science lessons. My experience is not singular, as I know the kids on my street do spend many hours practicing "the same moves" on their skateboard. The experience allows me to understand the anachronism of schooling, which tries to package and plan learning and, in this, achieves anything but learning.

Chapter 11, too, is concerned with the temporality of learning, but here in the constrained space of a 90-minute double lesson in a German physics class.

Changes in perception and knowledgeability unfold in time; they appear at unpredictable moments and sometimes out of what looks like mere play.

FLOW OR HOW A PHYSICIST DISCOVERS CHARGE DISTRIBUTIONS

In chapter 9, I articulate some of the temporal features of knowing and learning. I end with a conceptualization of learning that distinguishes between biographical experience, observation (achieved by means of historical reduction), and experimentation (requiring logical reduction). During biographical experience, I enact practical understanding of the world, using but not making thematic things that surround me and stand to the world in terms of *for-the-sake-of-which*, *in-order-to*, *what-for*, and *what-in* relations (Roth, 2005c). That is, the world is available to me but not in a thematic way: I relate to the world but do so not by making the relationship thematic. Thus, I may use a glow lamp like a tool and all I observe is whether or not it lights. When I am framing my basement as part of expanding my living space, I have to do a lot of hammering, but never do I think about the hammer as hammer. I am aware of hammering but not of the hammer or myself. All that is salient in the experience are the nail and getting it into the wood to fasten it to some other wood or concrete. Absorbed engagement, which some articulate by the term *coping* (Dreyfus, 1991), does not require a thematic world and therefore does not require information processing. But even if there is no conscious information process that I experience, my absorbed coping cannot be reduced to automaticity. When I hammer a nail *in order to* complete the doorframe, I am not an automat, but a living human being experiencing its thrownness in a nonthematic way. Nonthematic is not the same as automatic—or highly competent practitioners in both intellectual and sports domain would not be distinct from robots. The fact that such distinctions can be made clearly shows that the two are not the same.

Nonthematic involvement with the things at hand is equivalent to the disappearance of subject and object; all I experience is *process* without awareness that anything like a process is unfolding. I am aware without being aware of myself—especially as something different from anything else. In this condition, I do not exist outside time, exposed to it in its chronological dimension. With the loss of the subject as separate from the object also comes the loss of time as separate from being. There is no time that I can objectify ("Time is money!"), it is not something that I can or cannot have ("Got no time!"), and it is not something that impinges from the outside on and constraining my activity ("Time is running out"). Rather, being and time are inseparable. And with the disappearance with chronological time, the related differences in the world also disappear.

Nonthematic involvement does not mean that no concepts are available. In fact, scientists may be nonthematically involved in their everyday affair, for example, theorizing the results of their last experiment. But they do not make thematic their own involvement in the world, they do not question how they use the concepts they use. These issues become clearer in the present chapter, in which I analyze my own learning concerning the distribution of charges in objects that presumably are charged by induction. My initial object is the charge distribution, but the subject–object distinction fades away as I become engrossed in the search for an answer to the question about charges that ought to be there but that I cannot find when testing for them. How can one understand this kind of experience, which others sometimes denote by the term *flow*?

During the months that I initially investigated the videotapes featuring the German tenth-grade students explore static electricity, it dawned on me that all the models of learning science currently circulating in science education do not take into account the (singular plural) experience of learning. This learning is always mine for somebody, always a concrete particular experience thereby realizing the very possibility of such experience that exists not only for me but also for other persons denoting themselves by the pronouns "I" and "me." The existing theories of learning make thematic frameworks, structures, and processes that I do not experience; they do not describe *my* reasons for acting and therefore cannot explain why I learn what I learn by engaging in the way I do. These theories, for example, the one embodied in (radical, social) constructivism, therefore cannot be used to describe why I do what I do and therefore why I learn what I learn. These theories cannot be used to describe *learning* as a temporal phenomenon, though the very concept has to do with difference, difference between action at one point in time and another, more knowledgeable action at another point in chronological time.

I learn by engaging; in engagement I learn. But I learn because I open up to being affected—by something or somebody outside myself. My agency and my sensibility are but two faces of the same coin. Each moment of agency is a moment of sensibility (welcome): in touching something, I allow this something to touch, affect, and impress upon me because I welcome the object. In thinking about an object (agency), my thinking has welcomed the object. "Intentionality, consciousness of . . . is attention to speech or welcome of the face, hospitality and not thematization" (Levinas, 1969, p. 299). In other words, "Intentionality, attention to speech, welcome of the face [i.e., the other WMR], hospitality—all these are the same, but the same as the welcoming of the other, there where the other withdraws from the theme" (Derrida, 1999, p. 22–23). What then does it mean to learn (science)? And how does such learning unfold as I engage in some inquiry?

While I watch the German tenth-grade students "wrestle" with the electroscope, I see their repeated attempts in charging a particular combination of materials through rubbing. I decide to re-produce a particular event, for example, to test whether something students have done can or cannot be done. Immediately absorbed by the activity, I initially do not notice that I, too, "wrestle" with the same materials and with the same concepts. When I become aware of what I am doing, I already have completed five equally "futile" attempts in charging the electroscope with this same set of materials. In the process I discover that transparencies that have been used for some time do not seem to work anymore. Whereas I have been smiling with incredulity when I overheard students say that the transparency was "used up," I all of a sudden find myself with the same "phenomenon" that the students have encountered.

To develop a better understanding of how learning unfolds in such situations where the learner does not know, I sometimes videotape myself in novel activity. I also have kept detailed notes during the different stages of my inquiries, although I could not know whether what I am finding out is something that will hold up to the scrutiny of my colleagues in the physics department at the university. Yet this is exactly the kind of engagement and learning that I strive to understand, describe, and theorize. It is the kind of learning students do as they engage in their favorite activities—which often are not those that they are confronted with at school. In the following, I account for some of the discoveries I have made using the same materials as the students based on the detailed notes that I have recorded in the process. In part, my own experiences articulate how in the absence of knowing what is supposed to be the result, I have no resources for judging my "intermediate" results, and I have to continue knowing that anything I do and know may have to be abandoned should I find out something that undermines anything I have thought so far.

While engaging in a chosen task, I often get lost in it, loose track of chronological time—much like the kids on my street loose track of time when they practice the same moves on their skateboard for an entire afternoon. They spend the afternoon evidently without a notion of chronological time that others might hold them accountable to. In both instances, the learning subject becomes so engrossed with the object that the subject–object distinction disappears. Because the object is also the motive of activity, being engrossed in it means that I completely identify with it (motive). A psychologist might say that I am "motivated," though, as evident in my articulation of the phenomenon, there is no need for motivation as a psychological concept. Any time a subject takes up and therefore identifies with a motive of activity—in fact, is identical with the motive because of the subject|object dialectic—he or she is "motivated." Being absorbed catapults me out of chronological time, allowing me to pursue what I am doing according to the temporality of the activity itself. In this sense, in this loss of time, I gain the freedom to explore something in a way unfettered by the temporal constraints students are subjected to in schools. A sense of flow and duration is all that "I," which no longer is an "I" separate from its object, am vaguely aware of.

EXPLORING THE MICROPHYSICAL (PARTICLE) MODEL

Late one evening, a question emerges and grows within me, which I then attempt to answer over two sleepless nights, using the same equipment that the students have had available. While observing the students in the videotapes, I all of a sudden realize that nobody has checked whether the charge distribution—that is said to occur in a metal when a charged object is approached—actually is observable. Both teachers present in the class never bring up the issue with the whole class or in small-group investigations. The issue, nevertheless, is pervasive, as many investigations students conduct in the videotapes are based on charge separation, including the investigation with steel rod and metal-coated elderberry mark sphere (chap-

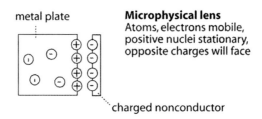

metal plate

Microphysical lens
Atoms, electrons mobile,
positive nuclei stationary,
opposite charges will face

charged nonconductor

Figure 10.1. When negatively charged nonconducting material is brought close to a conductor, the electrons in the latter are said to be repelled, leaving the positive nuclei at the edge facing the nonconducting material.

ter 6) or the investigation involving the two metal plates first charged and then separated (chapter 5). Figure 10.1 illustrates the problem, according to which the electrons in the metal plate are said to be repelled when a negatively charged nonconducting material is brought close to its edge, leaving the positive charges on the edge of the conductor. If this picture (i.e., theory) is appropriate, then it should be possible to prove the presence of negative charges in the body of the metal plate but the positive charges on its edge using the neon glow lamp. The lamp is a suitable tool, as it glows differently depending on the type of charges tested. (This is an after-the-fact articulation of the rather vague idea about the situation and its implication for testing the different charges involved.) I decide to pursue this question, keeping both written and diagrammatic records of what I am doing.

In the following notes, written in the course of and shortly after the investigation, I account for three experiments that I conduct using an electroscope, a metal plate, a transparency (not shown), and a neon glow lamp (Figure 10.2). All investigations involve the following elements: I rub a metal plate on a transparency and then make it either touch (Figure 10.2a) or bring it close to (Figure 10.2b1, c) the top plate of the electroscope (a process physicists know as charging by induction). In all cases, the charges are tested using a neon glow lamp. The experimental setups and outcomes in diagrams sometimes were recorded diagrammatically in the same way I had diagrammed student investigations. Where would the lamp to glow in the third instance? After observing the lamp glow in c.1, the plate is removed (c.2). The pointer deflects. I test it. Where will the neon lamp glow?

> I conduct a series of experiments involving the rubbing of a metal plate on an overhead transparency sheet and then charging the electroscope either directly or via induction. As I am working, I notice that the metal plate I am using is charged less and less. I also note that there is a build up of grey material on the transparency sheet. Further, I am checking repeatedly the electroscope suspension, rattling it mechanically because it might be sticking and therefore show fewer charges. The stickiness is salient now, and I blow at the pointer to loosen it. I rub many times. I am vaguely aware of the students I have seen on the tapes, repeating their attempts over and over again and then focus on the metal plate again. Several times I note that there is a spark, based on a bristling noise I can hear. I become

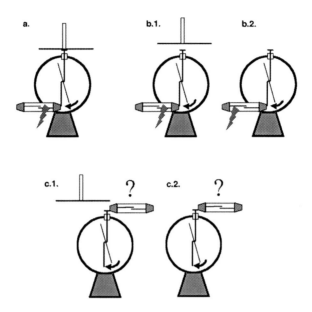

Figure 10.2. In such drawings, I articulate the different experimental procedures, observations, and questions for further experimentation.

conscious of the fact that I am too close with my arm to the setup and that there is a spark between the metal plate and the electroscope. Once I note that the spark actually goes to my arm as I approach the plate to the electroscope. I can feel it in the skin and hair. I become aware of having made an angle to the handle of the plate and thereby come too close.

I register something like frustration though at the moment I do not thematize it as such. I become more frantic, impatient with the little things that do not seem to work, and that I cannot handle all pieces of equipment at the same time. I have to bring the plate close without touching. I also have to rub, get the glow lamp, do everything quickly. I think that this is an investigation best done by at least two people.

I am flabbergasted by the results. Though trained as a physicist, I do not have an explanation. I use my everyday reasoning that I also have seen enacted in the classes of the videotapes that I have been studying for the past five weeks now. The lamp glows at the side where I do not expect it. I repeat the investigation, over and over again, testing every aspect (as in the sequence of the diagrams noting the experiments [Figure 10.2]). The most difficult one turns out to be experiment [Figure 10.2] c, for I have to leave enough space to get the lamp in without discharging the metal plate, and to get charging by induction. Common scientific lore wants a macroscopic separation of positive and negative charges (Figure 10.1). Here, the outcome indicates that even on the top plate I get negative charges from the electroscope—at least as a result of the way I conduct the experiment. That is, that there is no difference when compared to the situation in [Figure 10.2] b.

With my previous experiences, I theorize the problems as originating in the charging process. I note a correlation of amount of charges on the metal plate and the build up of grey stuff on the transparency: "Is the metal rubbing off?" I turn the transparency until it appears to have the same problem. I frantically search for the other transparency sheet I know to be around. I finally find it after continuing a little while with what I have at hand.

I am completely absorbed. I once emerge from the absorption and think that I should take notes of my experience, but let myself become absorbed again. Only at the end, "when I was done" do I thematize my job again and sit down to write about the experience and prepare the drawings.

In the beginning of this account, the reference to an almost frantic engagement with the materials can be noted; this engagement is associated with my subsequent frustration when things apparently do not go as anticipated. I have had in mind to conduct a simple test, but already the first step, charging the metal plate—subsequently to be brought to the top part of the electroscope—becomes problematic. Over time, the same amount of rubbing seems to yield fewer charges, while simultaneously there is a build up of a grey substance. But there is a moment of uncertainty: if the electroscope pointer jams, the diminishing charges may just be an illusion. Mechanically, the electroscope does not appear to work in the way it should. Of course, it is not evident at all whether there is in fact a problem and where any problem might lie. It is clear, however, that what is initially merely noticed faintly eventually becomes salient figure, because there is a sense of breakdown, a sense that things are not working the way they should.

In the first paragraph of these notes, I articulate phenomena that I have not been aware of before. There are bristling noises, which I attribute to sparks and discharges made possible because my arm is too close to the materials. The static electricity clearly can be sensed in the arm and the perking hair on my skin. In this instance, I become aware of a phenomenon that I have not intended. It emerges into my consciousness—made possible because of the sensibility that allows me to be affected while acting to find out about something I do not know. That is, one clearly sees here the link between agency, manipulating the materials and wanting to find out; it shows how agency sets me up to find out things that have not been intended and yet are central to the phenomena at hand.

I then state to be flabbergasted by the results, which have not been articulated in words but are available in the diagrams I produce. The results of the first investigation are taken to be unproblematic. If, for example, the charges on the plate are negative, touching the electroscope allows some of the electrons to move onto the instrument. The neon lamp should glow on the side of the electroscope, which is precisely what I observe together with a decrease in the pointer angle (Figure 10.2a). When the charged plate is brought near the electroscope without touching, the model (Figure 10.1) predicts the electrons in the electroscope to be repelled from the top part, so that testing should make the lamp glow on the electroscope side together with a decrease in the pointer angle (Figure 10.2b1). If first the glow lamp and then the plate are removed from the electroscope, the model predicts a lack of electrons (which have left the instrument through the glow lamp and my body), and the pointer should increase its angle. A renewed test should make the lamp glow on the side opposite to the instrument and decrease the pointer angle (Figure 10.2b2).

All of these investigations both confirm the anticipated results and are necessary to get a handle on the equipment. They confirm what I have been thinking and provide me with the certainty that I still understand what is going on. I am not completely in the dark. This state is the starting point for what turns out to be the more difficult part. My notes show that the third part of this series of investigations involves manipulations and preparations that are difficult. Figure 10.2c1 exhibits the source of the problem I experience: It resides in the fact that the charged plate is to be brought close to the top of the instrument without touching and yet leaving me sufficient space to bring the neon lamp to the top part of the instrument. As my notes show, the sequence of actions—manipulating the materials, charging the plate, then picking up the lamp, and bringing everything into the test situation—turns out to be challenging, especially because the distances involved are too close and discharges occur in my arms. Here, the material world constitutes a constraint, that is, resists to be brought into the anticipated configuration.

To my surprise, the third experiment (Figure 10.2c) turns out *exactly* like the second (Figure 10.2b), the lamp glows first at the electroscope end, then on the opposite end. I am puzzled, and write about "common lore," which is common lore among physicists. I note that the results are consistent with negative charges on the top plate, in contrast to the positive charges I have anticipated according to the microphysical model (Figure 10.1). This is puzzling me at the time; in fact, I describe the situation as being "flabbergasted." What might be the problem? In the first instance, I attribute it to my preparation. That is, rather than accepting the results of my investigation as true results, which contradict the anticipated results, I attribute my observations to some error in the preparation and configuration. I treat my results as artifacts rather than facts. The notes confirm that I make thematic the charging, which, as described earlier in the text, has led to a build up on the transparency sheet, the grey color being indicative of some metal residue.

The notes show that at one point, I am vaguely aware of the fact that my own process of inquiry, the repeated rubbing of the metal–transparency combination and the repeated configuring and testing, resembles what I have been observing in the videotapes. Just as the tenth-grade students, I am apparently repeating actions and tests that already have yielded results without recognizing the repetition *as* repetition, that is, as the same in its difference. It is as if I do not trust what I have done and redo it, attempting to constitute the results as facts and making sure that they are not artifacts. That is, I appear to be seeking a separation of variant and invariant aspects, ascertaining the stability of the phenomenon in the phase of the minor variations that I notice as occurring. This noticing of the similarity between the behavior of students and my own ultimately shows that there is an underlying, structural commonality that exceeds the differences between the much younger and much more inexperienced students and me. That is, whereas I am pursuing investigations that students have not done, which may be a function of my previous training, the *structure* of my investigation exhibits considerable similarity. My interest in what is at the heart of this phenomenon leads me to conduct the studies described in this book.

Near the end of the episode, I describe the frantic search for a new transparency sheet. The old one appears to give out. It is with this sense of giving out that the grey matter on the transparency sheet becomes particularly salient, much like the exploding inner tube has been a central element in the process that has allowed me to make the tear in the tire wall apparent. That is, the grey matter initially does not stand out or is thematized as such (i.e., grey matter). Rather, I have been vaguely aware of this matter in the same way that I am vaguely aware of the trees while driving down the highway. I am *vaguely* aware, because, when asked a question about the type of trees or any other aspect one might think of, I am not able to respond. But the problem with the diminishing return from my rubbing correlates with what I notice to happen on the transparency. My becoming aware of the correlation mediates the process of making the grey matter thematic.

This part of the episode is particularly interesting as it and the recognition of the similarity between my action and those of the students eventually leads me to a very different appreciation of what they are doing. Prior to that moment I have analyzed already the tape of the first two lessons—featuring the four women in the attempt to find out why their lamp does not glow in the way the teacher has shown (chapter 4). The students attribute their failure to make the lamp glow to the differences in the brand of jeans they wear and, in an instance not described in chapter 4, to the wearing out of the transparency sheet. I still remember that I was smiling when hearing the insinuation. (As an instance of the passivity of experience, the smiling overcame me rather than being intended.) Perhaps I have had a sense that the "wearing out" sounded silly, a commentary made because they have become frustrated with their failure. Now, during the night described in the notes, I am finding myself in the same situation: I catch myself thinking, "the transparency is wearing out." The transparency is giving out and I frantically search for the second sheet I know to be somewhere in my office. What is at the heart of this experience? Why do the students and I (during the night) consider something as a feasible cause of the problems we face, which, by others (including me at the moment watching students on videotape), is heard as an outlandish comment? To understand, a first-person perspective has to be taken.

In these situations, the students and I are facing trouble and apparently cannot find out why we do not get a phenomenon to work as anticipated or as shown by someone else. Not knowing the phenomena at hand, which become phenomena only in and through our (student, my) investigations, any aspect salient in our investigations is as good as any other. It is not surprising that I am finding myself in the situation that I have observed students to be in: attributing the problems to one of the material entities I have been manipulating. It is not farfetched to assume that the problems arise with the materials I manipulate or with the way I manipulate these. The contrary is the case. The fact that I attribute the problem to the transparency exhibits the intelligibility of this possibility, the very opposite of being a far-fetched one. That is, in this situation, the students and I experience the transparency as a potential source of the problems as an intelligible concretely available possibility; an understanding of learning, therefore, requires a consideration of the emergence of such possibilities in our consciousness, even though they might look outlandish from the outside, for example, from the perspective of the knowing teacher or researcher. The very fact that it is considered at all articulates wearing-out as a collective possibility that others may repeat.

The episode ends with me I leaving the curriculum materials and sitting down to write the notes reproduced in part here. At the end of these notes, I am writing about the absorption, the fact that I have not taken note of my environment, and especially have not taken note of chronological time. The final paragraph shows that I have had the sense that I was onto something in terms of understanding engagement and learning, and that I needed to sit down and write about it, which I have done just prior to writing the paragraphs that precede it. Such absorption sometimes can be observed in classrooms—usually under circumstances where students pursue objects of their own interests and when there are few external constraints (e.g., Roth, 1995)—but not so frequently in others, where the experience of being subject to an external clock mitigates against much, or any, true engagement. This type of absorbed engagement constitutes an investment that seeks a resolution in achieving intended outcomes, which requires students to formulate goals or identifying with the activity-defining motives. The process of resolution, however, cannot be anticipated, especially not the amount of chronological time it might require. The prospects of being jerked out from the middle of the investigation mitigate my engagement—I personally do not even begin to write unless I know I have a substantial amount of chronological time at my hand so that I can immerse myself in the object I want to write and write about.

Although the account given so far provides some interesting details about how the inquiry unfolded in time, the beginnings of the investigation are more or less in the dark—which may be a characteristic of all beginnings (Derrida, 2005). I do not know what it is that makes the particular problem of the charge distributions salient, but all of a sudden it appears. I have no control over its emergence; I can only receive it in a passive way. But certainly, intensively investigating the phenomena and attempting to understand what students do while investigating the same phenomena, what they know, and how their knowledgeability changes has prepared me for the image of the problem (Figure 10.1) to emerge and for concretizing it into a problem. The second point that lies outside of my control is the intention to investigate it, not just to note the issue nobody appears to be wondering about, but to actively pursue the question about the charges. I have not intended my intentions; these, too, I receive passively. Once the intention is present to what I do, it becomes the driver for what I do. More so, because the intention is tied to its object, here the problem framed, it is the motive of the engagement so that the question of motivation becomes irrelevant. The motive of the activity and the potential payoffs, emotional valence that comes from the resolution of the problematic issue, are all that is needed to understand why I am engaging in the are all that is needed to understand why I am engaging in the self-forgetting way apparent from the account. But how the motive becomes activity-driving motive, too, lies outside of consciousness. This, then, lies at the heart of the aporia: "Intentionality, consciousness of . . . is attention to speech or welcome of the face, hospitality and not thematization" (Levinas, 1969, p. 299). That is, *intentionality* and *consciousness of*, by their very nature, precede intentionality and consciousness of. I cannot but welcome them, as they precede and antedate all thematization.

MORE EXPLORATIONS CONCERNING THE MICROPHYSICAL MODEL

The previous episode ended with my sitting down to take notes of what has happened during the preceding hours. This movement toward the computer to take notes makes for a shift in activity. Before, I have been involved in finding out something about the electrostatics and electrostatic phenomena. Primarily I have not thought about engaging in a phenomenological inquiry of learning through my setting up the situation. Rather, I have wanted to find out the question about electrostatics, and so engaged in it, only becoming faintly aware of what is going on in the process of my working with the curriculum materials. This faint awareness included a sense that what is happening to me also is of interest from a learning point of view. "How do I learn?" "How do I experience the explorations?" "What is happening to me?" and "What is salient to me as I am going along?"

When I sat down to write, however, a different set of concerns mediated what I was doing. I produced a record of what just has happened to me, what I noted, and what I have been aware of, faintly, and what has become salient in my writing about it. This change in the object—i.e., motive of what I do—constitutes a clear shift in intentionality, away from the electrostatic phenomena. I know that such radical shifts away from on activity into another sets me up for the process of *letting go*, which is of central importance to phenomenological inquiry, especially to the process of becoming aware (Depraz, Varela, & Vermersch, 2002). I know that after such shifts, when I explicitly let go of one intention and pursue another, the solutions to problems I have worked on hard for some time all of a sudden emerge into my consciousness. Such shifts include those from academic work to a different kind of activity, sports, garden work, or cooking. All of a sudden, while equally immersed in the new activity, an idea pertaining to the problems in the previous activity thrusts itself into my consciousness, although and perhaps despite the fact that I have no awareness of having thought about it. My technique for remembering long forgotten facts, recounted in chapter 9, is an example of this process of the relationship between *letting go* and *becoming aware*, or, in passive voice, opening myself to be host to a new insight.

That night, the shift to writing constituted a significant shift away from the problem that I had framed concerning the distribution of charges. It may not come as a surprise that while writing about what was happening to me I was having insights about how to continue with the previously aborted investigation. My next note, recorded immediately after the episode, in fact, ending the investigative epi-

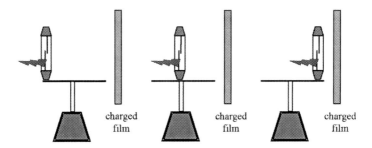

Figure 10.3. Wherever I test the plate, the lamp glows on the same side—the charges are the same in contradiction to the results anticipated according to the microphysical model.

sode, begins with an insight that leads me to shift from writing notes to continuing the investigations in electrostatics.

The idea is this: I simplify the tested object, here the metal plate with handle, to stabilize it and configure it so that I can diminish the sparks I observed before. But, as the account shows, the discharges continue to occur. Reimmersed in the investigation, the possibility to bring about variations emerges in my consciousness, and I enact these new possibilities, such as moving the configuration to the edge of my desk. But the changes do not improve the situation; I continue to observe discharges and other "weak effects." I need to get rid off these uncontrolled effects if I want to be able to make a point in the meeting I will have later in the day with a group of physicists at the university institute that I am affiliated with.

> As I am writing along, an image emerges of a simple plate that I can do an induction experiment with. At first, I leave the plate on the Styrofoam, on a table, and bring a transparency film close ((as in Figure 4.5)). But I get discharges. After a few trials, I move the Styrofoam over the edge of the table to bring about a separation. But again, in about five attempts I get many discharges and weak effects but nothing as strong as I would like. I then think of the base of the electroscope as something that I can use. I unscrew the ring and then place the handle of the metal plate into the base, screwing tight. I am faintly aware of the fact that I want to isolate this effect from all other influences. I want to talk about these things with the physicists I am going to meet later in the day, and therefore want to be sure so as not to make a fool myself. I want to have a clean fact rather than an artifact. I conduct the experiment again according to the sketch I have made (Figure 10.3).
>
> I get the discharge spark always on the same side of the lamp, no matter where I test the metal plate. In all cases, when I then remove the charged transparency and test the plate on its own, I get the spark on the other side as I would expect it from a plate that has been charged by induction and grounding (Figure 10.4).

Figure 10.4. When the charged transparency is removed, the lamp glows on the other side.

> These experiments confirm the earlier ones with the electroscope. This time, I have a sense that I have had a better control over the potential problems around the space between the two plates (electroscope, charged plate).

The notes document the emergence of a new idea: fixing the metal plate in the base of the electroscope allows me to isolate it from the environment much better than having it rest on the Styrofoam plate. Here, therefore, something that normally is only indeterminate perceptual ground—the Styrofoam, table, and closeness of the charged transparency to Styrofoam and table—has become salient figure. That is, the desk and the insulating material have been in the background, noticed and included in my action, without being thematic. They have allowed me to do what I did without drawing attention to themselves. I have related to these things as tools, which are useful and, as such, have withdrawn into the perceptual ground. The fact that I want to discuss my results with the physicists clearly is mediating the events in the way the future communications (articles) mediate the activities of any scientist. I do not want to make a fool of myself. The notes provide evidence that I want to show that the observations I have made in the previous episode on the electroscope are repeatable, identical in their difference (facts rather than artifacts); and I want to make sure that I have considered every conceivable mediating influence. But at the outset, I cannot know what these influences might be. To know, I may have to disclose what has withdrawn into the indeterminate ground. Simplifying the equipment and equipmental configuration and eliminating the discharges constitute aspects of a first step of making the phenomenon repeatable and independent of the particulars of the setting. I repeat the previous investigations but now with a new set up, in which the metal plate is surrounded only by air and all other material aspects of the setting are considerably removed (Figure 10.3).

Even without thinking about it, I have been acting scientifically in the sense that I have attempted to control the context of the investigation as a whole. It is not that I am more scientific than the student. Rather, I see in this form of acting a type of behavior inherently human, but which in the scientific community has become part of *the* position. Becoming a scientist means taking up position, inherently involving a particular form of disposition. This disposition is already there, available in all human beings, where it might constitute primarily ground, though during involved engagement it comes to the fore.

As in the previous investigation with the electroscope, I test the metal plate in many locations, including at the edge closest to the charged film. The test results, as with the electroscope, are the same. My diagrams show that the neon lamp glows on the side of the metal plate, which, according to the microphysical model, should be charged negatively. But the lamp glows in the same way when I am at the edge near the charged transparency contrary to the anticipated results. Why does my test not provide evidence of the positive charges opposite to the charged transparency? The final test I conduct follows the tests with the transparency close to the metal plate. Once it is removed and I test the plate, I detect the expected positive charges (Figure 10.4). The notes show that at this point I realize that I have confirmed my previous investigation with a different setup. I am more confident that I have been able to better control the problems with the discharges that previously occurred while I was investigating.

This episode shows how from a variety of ways to engage the material, certain configurations emerge into consciousness and then are tested. As the students in the videotapes, I attempt to understand why I do not observe the anticipated results. In chapter 4, the anticipated results included a neon lamp that glows, but which does not despite many attempts at holding it to materials that have been rubbed. Here, my investigations exhibit a concern with controlling the setting. But the concern itself and the source of the ideas that surge in my consciousness are not subject of my intention: I am a host to them and have to receive these ideas and intentions as they offer themselves to my consciousness. In fact, each time I write about something new the involuntary nature of the idea stands out. I have the idea of moving the metal plate on its Styrofoam bed to the edge of the table, which I do once the idea is conceived. But there is no indication that I intended this idea to emerge. In fact, I cannot, if Levinas (1978a/1998) is right, because having an intention is like hospitality: it precedes my intention. I can have an intention or have an idea *because* I am open to receive something as an object of intention, which at the moment is not yet mine and therefore foreign and strange. A fundamental attitude appears to be required before all requirements: willingness to confront the unknown and a high threshold to failure.

Any time I seek to understand something I do not know, I am confronted with the risk that I may not understand despite the investment made in and through engaging with the object. That is, willingness to learn is associated with the potential risk of not knowing, though the nature of future knowledgeability is uncertain and out of reach. Learning in the inquiry mode means willingness to confront the unknown, which implies that what I currently know may become obsolete. It means confronting the risk that despite all the investments I make, I may not come to know any better or more than I do before. And this risk exists even in the absence of grades, which mediate learning in school contexts generally leading to defensive learning (Holzkamp, 1993), learning just to avoid punishment (i.e., low grades).

Following this night of investigation, I meet with several physics professors and physicists. I talk about the phenomena I have been producing and the fact that it contradicts the explanations that they teach. I also indicate that I am more concerned with the way in which such findings mediate lessons if the students came up with them on their own. I tell them the story of Christina in the Australian classroom (chapter 2), who had evidence that disproved the teacher's theory as a result of her investigations nevertheless instigated and made possible by the teacher. My colleagues laugh at me, saying that what I had seen was impossible. When I insist, they suggest that I am not considering the whole system, that is, the fact that all the materials and configurations, including the table, the floor, and my body are part of the system mediating what I can see. But they do not provide me with a satisfying alternative, that is, an explanation including diagrams showing the charge distributions in terms of the microphysical model (Figure 10.1) superposed by a phenomenal representation of my experiment. If anything frustrates me at that moment, it is their lack of engagement with the issues that I truly find problematic and at the very heart of learning theory. At that moment I feel the need to know more about the phenomenon and my lack of understanding raises questions about the very fact that static electricity and its explanations are part of a tenth-grade curriculum. I know that I cannot expect students to come up with appropriate explanations if I, a trained physicist, cannot get a handle on explaining this phenomenon myself. More so, how can I expect them to come up with such an explanation on their own? I already spent an entire night exploring the phenomenon without being or coming any closer to an explanation. Not knowing *the* answer, I cannot know how close or how far I am from finding one at all. But I do know that what I am observing is not the result of a singular case but a consistent phenomenon in its own right.

PLAY, OR GETTING TO KNOW THE ELECTROSCOPE

Two nights later, I find myself again in the situation of conducting experiments involving the electroscope. The beginning of my first note of that night indicates that I continue to pursue the idea that the particle model of positive and negative charges (Figure 10.1) is inappropriate. I do not know where the intention to pursue the investigations is coming from, but I do find myself pursuing related questions: the intention has arisen from somewhere; now I simply act on it. I have noted that the electroscope pointer deflects when the charged transparency is brought to the side of the instrument (Figure 10.5a). While the particle model appears appropriate to explain the configuration that the teachers refer to and talk about in the class (Figure 10.2a, b), it is unclear to me why the instrument should indicate the presence of charges in this new configuration, which apparently puts into question the rationale for designing the geometry of the device. If I use the particle model, how do I need to diagram the positive and negative charges so that the resulting diagram *explains* the phenomenon? I venture the hypothesis that the charges have to be shifted sideways—if the particle model is to be any good at all. But even in this new configuration, I get exactly the same results: the lamp glows on the instrument side. I even push the transparency between the outer ring and the pointer (Figure 10.5b), and, as my notes show, still get the same effect: I cannot find the charges said to sit on the surface facing the charged transparency sheet.

It is another sleepless night. I am conducting electroscope experiments, pursuing the idea that the particle model might be inappropriate. The transparency is negatively charged, the lamp glows away from my hand. (a) The experiment also works when the transparency film is brought to the side of the electroscope (Figure 10.5a). At that place, the charges should be shifted sideward (if the particle model is any good). (b) I can discharge the electroscope on the side of the transparency and still get the negative discharge, wherever I do it on the electroscope, near the end to the film or far end. (c) I can go from side to pointer and from the narrow end and still get the effect (Figure 10.5b).

It thus appears that unless the posited positive charges exist outside of the material body itself, I cannot explain this observation. (a) If the charges were outside, then the electroscope is negative all over and I would have access only to the negative charges wherever I measure. (b) If the charges were not outside, the symmetry of the experiment would have positive charges on the pointer.

The effect even occurs when the charges are seemingly pulled into the pointer (Figure 10.5b). When, for example, the transparency is brought near the upper part of the pointer, but from the side so that one would expect the positive charges to be on the outside of this part of the pointer. If it is charged positively, the negative charges are equally distributed throughout the electroscope—they should be, as one can ground the system anywhere connected to the central suspension, and still get charging by means of induction.

Here, there should be positive charges on the upper left and bottom right of the pointer, negative on the remainder of the electroscope, and I should get an attraction. (Perhaps the attraction from the film is stronger than that between the pointer and the remainder of the scope, one could argue.) I can even ground between the pointer and the transparency to discharge, always get negative, and get the induction.

So until now I have tested: (a) Induction from top, discharging everywhere, even between film and plate (metal plate, film through pants [seems to give me more consistently charges than metal on film]). (b) In-

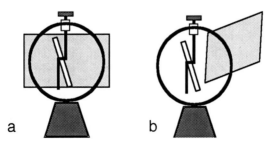

a   b

Figure 10.5. As part of my inquiries, which are not mediated by teacher instructions about what I can or cannot do, I explore different ways of making the pointer deflect.

> duction from side (plate to get symmetry, film) charging from bottom left, bottom pointer; top right, top left. There is a discharge between pointer and transparency. I make five to ten repetitions for each attempt. Making sure nothing has been touched, that the effect is repeatable. Testing charges on film, on scope.

These notes testify to the variations that I have been enacting in the process, without knowing what the variations will yield. I have not even (consciously) intended variations but they appear to have sprung forth from my engagement. If it were certain that some configuration only reproduces the previous results, then it would not be necessary to conduct the repetitions—which therefore are not repetitions in a strong sense. Given that I have been testing these configurations means that I have had the need to test them and that I could not have been certain of their outcomes. With variation comes certainty, because the phenomenon—same negative charges wherever on the inductively charged object and whatever the shape of the material—appears in a consistent way, is an invariant feature despite the variations in the material preparation.

By the second paragraph of these notes, it has become evident that the positive charges, so evidently facing the charged transparency in the model (Figure 10.1), are not "materializing" in my tests. I am considering an "outlandish" explication, here, that the positive charges somehow are "outside" the material. In this case, the results of tests would become intelligible: wherever I test, the lamp glows on the side of the metal and away from my hand, which means the former is negatively charged. I even have tested configurations where the positive charges would have to be on the pointer, and thereby change the arrangement. Thus, approaching the pointer from inside of the ring (Figure 10.5b) should lead to positive charges a change in the effect to be observed, but I am observing the same outcomes as before—negative charges. According to my thinking at the time, the positive charges on the pointer should lead to an attraction of the pointer to the suspension, but I am not observing this—though the possibility that the attraction between the negative charges on the transparency and the positive charges on the pointer being greater than the one between pointer and central suspension has been considered.

These notes therefore provide evidence for the underlying procedure: I produce many variations in the configuration. I evolve ways of configuring the transparency–pointer relation so that there should be changes in the observations pertaining to the deflection of pointer and test with the glow lamp. Like the students on the videotape, the variations include using and deploying the electroscope in ways that it was not built for, for example, bringing a charged object to the electroscope from the unshielded side or inserting the charged object between ring and pointer (Figure 10.5). In part, these variations create new configurations to be explained and in part different usage may create different observations. Prior to being deeply familiar with a system there is no way that I could predict what happens, because prediction implies that I have a causal model, that is, a type of knowledge that has preceded by biographical experience, hermeneutic reduction, and logical reduction. At that moment in my investigation, however, I am still attempting to produce order the field, that is, acting to see how the system under investigation behaves.

This way of proceeding has a lot in common with *play*. Here, I do not use play in the sense of play-acting, such as when children use a toy kitchen to play at cooking. The latter form of play is intentional, geared to reproduce existing forms of action for which the child is still too young. Nor do I mean to intimate the dimension of diversion that is often associated with the term play. Rather, *play* involves both intention and non-intention, it is *intentional|non-intentional* engagement. Thus, creating ever new configurations with the materials at hand, some of which are accidental, both has an object—that is, variation of action that is to be correlated to observations—and is non-intentional in the sense that the outcomes of the actions are not or cannot be anticipated given my knowledgeability at the moment. Observing students in the videotapes, someone may be tempted to describe the actions as *mere* play, for example, the seemingly non-intentional creation of ever-new variations of using the materials, when in fact the non-intentional aspect is a precondition for creating new figure|ground configuration that can be described (hermeneutical reduction) and then articulated in terms of features, which are then correlated with other features (logical reduction). But during my research career, I have found many instances—several shown in the next chapter—where students appear to merely play but make profound discoveries in the process.

Having kept notes of numerous instances where I become familiar with some domain that I do not know or know little about, I know that the term *playing* has a lot to offer as a positive descriptive term. Learning about some system that I know little about requires me to act without knowing or anticipating the outcomes of my action, which is a contradiction in the sense that actions normally are goal-directed. But not knowing the system at hand requires me to do something and to be open to perceiving what happens, that is, the reactions of the system. For example, I describe elsewhere how I use mathematical modeling software to find the solution of a word problem (Roth, 2005d). Not knowing the solution or even how to go about the solution, I *play* with formulas and numbers, while being open to perceiving results without knowing what I need to be open to.

In this form, play is not frivolous or mere play but very serious business. In fact, it appears to be a central aspect of science. When I find myself in a play mode or observe students in such situations, I generally think of James Watson and Francis Crick, who created cardboard models of the different chemical bases that they know can be isolated from DNA molecules. They laid their cardboard cutouts on a table and pushed them about, playfully bringing them together to see how they might combine. At one point, Watson realized that certain pairs of bases when held together to form a compound yielded the same geometric configuration. But he did not trust his cardboard cutouts. So he prepares cutouts from sheet metal, which does not easily deform. He then used these new cutouts to repeat what he has done before, and lo and behold, pairs of bases formed identical configurations. He concluded that these pairs are the rungs of a ladder-like structure. That is, at the heart of one of the most-hailed scientific discoveries of the twentieth century there has been play involving material shapes.

At one point during the night, I stop and reflect. I notice after the fact that I have been vaguely aware of the intention to have the experiments consistent so that I can show the results to the physicists and physics professors I am currently working with. Perhaps because they laughed at me on the previous day, I want to create the phenomenon *as* consistent phenomenon so that it holds up to their (potential) criticism.

> I also note upon reflection that it is good to have done the investigations at night. With the lights turned off, I can see the slightest light flickering in the lamp. Sometimes, even when the electroscope pointer does not show anything. I can see light glowing weakly. I can see sparks from my pants to the transparency or from the transparency to the pants when I pull the sheet between my knees. Chills run down my back. It is like real discovery work. I am faintly aware of self, there seems to be a dynamic that has nothing to do with person, it is all process. There is no "I" no person who proudly would tell an achievement, not author, not a subject that is separate from its object. There is just process of inquiry. I now know this to be the phenomenon that is commonly described as *flow* (e.g., Csikszentmihaly, 1997).

Flow denotes a state of being completely involved in an activity, where the ego falls away, where I am not aware of chronological time, where every action, movement, and thought inevitably follows from the previous one. This state is experienced when a person works at his or her limit of skills in a highly challenging environment. It is a state of ecstasy, which literally means standing outside oneself, that is, when I have stepped outside the subject–object opposition that characterizes reflection, thought, and deliberation. In phenomenological thought, flow is theorized in terms of ecstasy, which defines the *Moment*:

> We call the *present* that is held in authentic temporality, and is thus *authentic*, the *Moment*. This term must be understood in the active sense as an ecstasy. It means the resolute raptness of Dasein, which is yet *held* in resoluteness, in what is encountered as possibilities and circumstances to be taken care of in the situation. (Heidegger, 1977/1996, p. 338 [310])

In the *Moment*, I am therefore both resolute—which connotes thematic—and rapt—which connotes absorbed. That is, in this brief quote, temporality and knowledgeable, everyday non-thematizing coping are but two sides of the same coin. This mode frequently is found among athletes, children, artists, and Zen Buddhists. But, as apparent from Zen Buddhism, it is a mode of being that may characterize any everyday activity—where I experience it as timeless absorption in gardening, cooking, cycling, and writing. The absorption is timeless, because there only is here, now, and unfolding event. This mode of temporality and knowing contrasts *making present*, which always constitutes a making present *again*, or representing, and therefore constitutes a different modality of time. The shift between the two modalities characteristically is experienced at the limit of breakdown, for example, the not working of a tool. At this moment, the hammer, which previously has withdrawn into the hammering event, now becomes present as an object with properties, where the properties are the result of my having shifted the relation. Science becomes what it is exactly in this limit, where I make things thematic (inauthentic) in absorbed coping (authentic activity). That is, although science is concerned with rendering the world explicit and to represent it, which is not an originary moment of knowing, it does so in and through activity that frequently is thoroughly authentic—as seen in the description of my personal discovery work.

FIRST EXPLANATIONS

Up to this point in my inquiry, my actions are characterized more by the manipulation of materials than by the creation of a theoretical model that would explain my observations. The particle model has always been in the background of my attention, but I have not yet moved any further in creating a suitable alternative. My description thus far, however, makes evident why this state of exploration is necessary. It is necessary because the various investigations not only provide a better (practical) understanding of the system under investigation but also create constraints that limit what kind of model can be evolved, as any model will have to account for *all* the observations made. This active concern with the theory itself then defines something like a next stage.

On the one hand, with the investigations I have explored the limits of the particle model in the way I understand it. As much as I have tried, I have not been able to find the positive charges induced on the metallic objects (plates, electroscope). At the time, this therefore constitutes an endpoint of the inquiry. If I want to go any further, I have to seek new and different avenues toward different solutions. These new avenues arise from a conflux of my present concern for understanding the physics of charged objects and an interest in the things I encounter in the world and their inner nature—a topic that philosophers refer to as *ontology*.

At the time, I am interested in the notion of lifeworld and how in our everyday world we come to experience objects and how these objects come to obtain structure in terms of whole|parts relations—a domain some refer to as "naïve physics" (e.g., Smith & Casati, 1994). The philosophical domain concerned with the nature of things is *ontology*, and the philosophical domain concerned with whole|parts relations is *mereology*. At the time, I have come across some papers concerning the nature of boundaries, which define the limit of things and their parts. The problems raised in these disciplines are interesting, for they arise in the attempt to provide answers to questions such as "Who owns the boundary between two countries?" This interest, and based on the few articles I read on the topic, mediates how I am going about solving the puzzle concerning the particle model and the results of my observations. I do not know how the connection between the two has come about, but the very fact that the particle model predicts the positive charges to sit on the boundary certainly makes a possible link between my problem at hand and the topic of mereology probable.

A first rather radical step I take is the supposition that the charges are to be thought as sitting outside of the object itself or on the boundary, where they have to be considered to belong simultaneously to the inside and the outside, just as the border between two countries belongs to both countries. In taking a step, I change

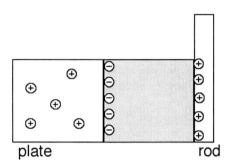

Figure 10.6. Based on my reading about boundaries, I hypothesize that the electrons have to be thought as part of the electrical field (grey) between plate and rod rather than as part of

position and disposition, which comes with a different supposition. The notes from this part of my inquiry that night read as follows:

> To me, it looks more and more as if the particle model (the part that makes the charges move around) actually does not explain the phenomenon. (a) One possibility is that the positive charges are thought to be somewhere outside of the electroscope, on the boundary, but no longer effecting the electroscope with its charges, so that the metal is negatively charged throughout.
>
> I am not sure such an explanation would fly. One would have to draw recourse to the science of parts and wholes (i.e., mereology) and explain how it comes that the positive charges move outside, become part of another whole, now inaccessible to being shown. I tried something else earlier in the night, with another area, the air column that could be identified in terms of one of the surfaces as in my diagrams of the charging by induction and separation drawn yesterday. ((See diagram [Figure 10.6].)) But the direction of the charges does not make sense.
>
> When I think about it now, why should the electron holes have a homogeneous but low density in the material, whereas there is such a high concentration of negative charges on the boundary? I guess one could say that in this way, the material is "shielded" from the field and there can be equidistribution of charges. There can be no field inside the material either. So, for the electrons to be shielding they would have to sit outside, really on a boundary inaccessible to the material on the inside. This would then explain the situation. But in a physical metaphor, it is difficult to accept that one could not get at the electrons on the surface. They would have to be above the surface. Thus, even if I wanted to do a test, the electrons would be said to float on the surface. Good. But the argument would not hold for the lack of electrons, the holes to be outside the material. Or are they on its surface?
>
> I remember something. There cannot be electrical fields inside a container surrounded by conducting material. Thus, on the surface I have to

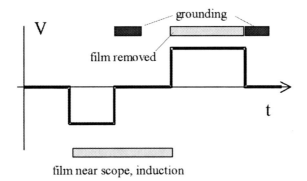

Figure 10.7. My experiences with different representations of potential energy allow me to think about the situation in terms of potential energy. Bars indicate duration of events.

have an arrangement such that the field inside can be zero. Mereologically, it is as if approaching the rod now brings in an area to be considered in the equation. We cannot say there is nothing, but there is a field and air column. The system now encompasses all three, the plate, the rod, and the field. Now, the charges on the surface become part of the middle part, the column though they are on the boundary. But as Smith (1997) writes, boundaries are funny beasts, there can be two shortest (coincident) lines between two points, they are at the boundary of categories. So now the electrons in my figure belong to the middle part, the field, as do the protons (electron holes) on the right. So this means, the electron holes ((i.e., positive charges)) have to be actually on the surface of the material and would rearrange if I brought a testing medium in between the film and the surface of the plate.

In effect, this then is consistent with the view that the potential has been moved up in the metal as described [earlier] below. The two models are consistent again.

Another alternative comes to my mind: a potential energy model. Charging the transparency changes the potential of the electroscope. In the present case, the potential goes down such that electrons are flowing off the electroscope when grounded. When the transparency is taken away, the potential moves back up and now will be above zero. In this case, I would observe "positive" charge on the scope after the transparency has been removed. The diagram ((i.e., Figure 10.7)) shows this. During the first grounding, the charges observed would be the same as on the film, negative (away from body), and the opposite during the second grounding.

The notes I kept that night show a diagram, in which the space between the charged rod and the metal—in which a charge separation is induced—is shaded grey (Figure 10.6). I have begun to think in terms of an electrical field, and this field is made thematic in my text. Thinking in terms of electrical fields rather than particles or thinking the two together constitutes a first step away from the particle model itself. In this diagram, the polarities are reversed with respect to the experiments I have conducted—the rod is charged negatively. But whereas it appears reasonable to assume negative charges on or outside the boundary, the reverse, a lack of electrons (the "holes"), or rather, positive nuclei outside of the material does not make sense—they do not move according to the model!

In this second paragraph from my notes recorded that night, therefore, a new aporia comes to be formulated. The provisional model may work for electrons but certainly not for positively charged nuclei, which do not move. The diagram leads me to further considerations. For example, I am writing about the "shielding" effect that I know to exist when a metal cage (Faraday cage) or wall (e.g., car) surrounds a space that remains unaffected even in the presence of very high discharges (e.g., lightening). This shielding effect keeps the electrical field from penetrating the metal, where the charges can be distributed equally and at low density. The outer ring of the electroscope is intended to shield the pointer, which moves in the same plane defined by the ring.

But I have doubts: the model does not work for the positive charges, as the microphysical model would forbid the nuclei to be outside of the material. Equivalently, if the electrons were to be *on* the boundary, testing with the lamp would allow them to flow and therefore make the latter glow. The issue with the positive charges may be resolved temporarily, as soon as I begin to think in terms of "electron holes," a standard way of talking about semiconductors that I am familiar with.

My thinking then pursues the issue of the fields, and to derive an explanation in terms of the absence of electrical fields within the metal. I do not know why and how the idea of the field has arisen; I have not been searching for it in my memory. But when it is there, I pursue it. I begin to redefine the parameters and extend the entities that appear to be involved, including the air column (space) between the metal plate and the rod. This then allows me to think in terms of the two boundaries, one between plate and column, the other between column and rod. With this middle part, the charges can be attributed to it, as in the case of each of the two boundaries; they belong to both phases involved.

Yet another possibility arises into my mind as if from nowhere; it is related to Figure 10.7. *Although I have not intended this possibility but passively received it, I begin to explore its implications.* I am thinking in terms of the electrical potential that exists between electroscope and electrical ground. Initially, the electrical potential is zero. When the charged object is brought close to it, its potential drops to some negative value (induction). When the electroscope is touched—e.g., with glow lamp—and thereby grounded, its potential returns to zero (same as ground). Then, when the transparency is removed, its electrical potential moves to the equal but opposite value as it has had before (Figure 10.7, white bar). Grounding then returns its value to zero (second black bar). Because of the difference in electrical potential, a current is flowing through the lamp, making it glow at opposite sides because of the opposite direction of the potential difference.

In this phase of my inquiries, new terrain is made possible by bringing together two very different disciplines. On the one hand, there are philosophical considerations concerning the nature of things and the whole|parts relations that define them. On the other hand, there are the physical investigations and their results that I have been taking care to note. Relating the two is highly speculative, it is a play in and with ideas, an apparent attempt to explicate a phenomenon that appears to escape the standard approach. It certainly is an attempt to deal with an aporia that any science (physics) teacher might face when a student begins to ask the kinds of questions I have been asking myself. (When I was a student, I did ask such questions despite the fact that I was far from having the best grades.) More so, for me there is the issue of teacher knowledge: how can I teach something that I do not thoroughly understand? A statement that the particle model breaks down in this instance does not suffice, as it does not yet explain why it breaks down.

The ideas *have come* to me; I *have not* intended them. Though when I became aware, I accepted them and pursued the implications with respect to my current understanding. This *having of ideas* is not well captured in the transitive verbs used in the reigning theories: to construct, to enact agency, to learn. There is a level of passivity to learning that future theories need to capture; it is a level of passivity that transcends all passivity. Yet despite passivity, my agency may prime and prepare me for having of ideas. More so, once I have welcomed a new idea, I engage with it like a host welcomes and engages an unfamiliar guest. Here, I evolve a new way of thinking about the situation constitutes yet another lens onto the phenomena, providing a descriptive model for the phenomenon at hand. The cognitive resources may come from the discipline of physics and the traces long-passed courses have left. They now resurface while I am struggling to constitute a frame that allows me to *explain* why the presupposed charges facing those in the nonconducting material cannot be detected.

At this point, then, the particular way of drawing the situation, the actual diagram (Figure 10.6), and the emerging understanding of the problematic issues concerning the nature of boundaries, have taken me into uncharted waters. Here, two of the conditions that *flow* researchers deem prerequisite clearly are present: the high level of challenge and the deployment of skills at their limit. Where skills are at their limit, skilled behavior actually turns into unskilled behavior. This precarious situation between skilled and unskilled behavior defines the possibility of success and failure. There therefore is also risk: possibly and perhaps likely failing to come up with satisfying answers, investing oneself (and time) without any prospect of success, unless the "rush" of the experience itself is considered enough reward.

A REFLEXIVE TURN

All of the actions described so far have occurred in a state of absorption, in a state of flow, focusing on the investigation the intent of which is to find out how to explain the outcomes of testing for charges and the suitability of the particle model. Some of the notes are part of this experience. When I then write down and think about what has happened, I engage in a reflexive turn. I first engage in a hermeneutical reduction and, near the end, evolve a possible explanation for the emergence of one of the proposed models: I have the (vague) image in my mind of the electrical field inside a cavity and the explanation one of my professors had provided then. Part of my notes pertain not merely to *what* I have done, the object of my concernful activity, but to the state itself. At this moment, the current moment and passage of chronological time literally frames and even reduces the event. The *experience* of flow now is constituted by a description, "I have spent the last three hours . . . I have not seen the time gone by," and by a sense that perhaps thirty minutes might have passed:

> It is 5 A.M. I find that I have spent the last three hours thinking through this problem rather than sleeping. I have not seen the time gone by and, if I had to say how much time I spent, would have given it at best thirty minutes. I have a sense of exhilaration. I want to see a physicist or several to talk more about the particle model and why it seems inappropriate. And ask them what they think about my alternatives. I want to know more about whether someone has already come up with an explanation, I think that the old timers like Faraday, who have been so consistent in their attention to the detail, would certainly have attended to something like this.
>
> When I look at what the tenth-grade students have done in their discovery work and what I have done one might say that I may have been more methodical. But then I also had more experience, and at least as many attempts at doing it. I have had the night in my favor, a longer period of thinking about it, and already have seen them do experiments with the material. I also have had a different motivation, orientation to a motive-setting object: seeking an explanation for this phenomenon. This is already the second long day and night session spent on this very problem.
>
> After writing these notes, I have gone back to write the stuff in the square parenthesis ((now in the preceding section)). Forty-five minutes have passed, and again I have not seen them passing. I am down on myself a bit because I seem to have rediscovered what someone already explained. But why would the three physicists at the university not have known about this? Why did they tell me that the particle model brakes down at this point? And why would they have tried and not come to a similar conclusion as I did?
>
> I remember now that there was something in my second year intro physics course about electrons arranging themselves such that, for example, around openings in a conductor there would be no fields inside. This is how the professor explained shielding. (Perhaps it was electrodynamics course—likely not.)

The early parts of this part of my notes express a sense of exhilaration, and this sense distinguishes this episode from everyday absorbed coping from flow. The notes talk about my orientation toward the physicists, who on the day before have been critical of the tests and the explanation that I advance. That is, the notes provide evidence for an other-orientation that has been underlying the activity as a whole and the observations in particular. I have not merely done these *for* myself but for someone else as well. And even if I had intended the results to be just for myself, the structure of the investigation, the ascertainment-seeking repetitions, the intended|non-intended variations in my procedure, all are such that I *could* defensibly present them to the other.

At this moment of reflection, I am also aware of the relation between what I am doing, as a form of human activity, and what others have done. I am beginning to appreciate "the old-timers," such as Michael Faraday, who have produced such an extensive corpus of notes that theses can be taken today as evidence for their experiments as these unfolded in time (e.g., Gooding, 1990). My attention then is focusing on the real purpose of my stay at the *Institute of Advanced Studies*, understanding how learners learn and seeing what I can learn by looking at their and my own process. The difference with students is recognized to lie in experiential differences that allow different hypotheses, forms of actions, and anticipations.

In the next paragraph, I then reflect on the note-taking episode itself, which, as a different form of absorbed coping, has seen forty-five minutes of chronological time passing without my awareness ("I have not seen them passing"). In absorbed coping of everyday activity, as in periods of *flow*, the *Moment*, the threefold nature of temporality is preserved. My anticipation, as my actions, are future oriented, because if I am not awaiting what is being taken care of from the very beginning, I will not be in the position to discover something as broken. And if everyday absorbed coping and flow are not oriented to the past, I will not be able to discover the broken *as* broken, a discovery inherently requiring memory. But this *making* present of the thing *as* broken necessarily *is happening in* the present.

At the same time, my notes show that during much of the investigation, prior to the reflexive turn, I have been absorbed, in fact, the "I" of the "I" no longer exists but has withdrawn itself. But this forgetting of self is not an effect of *flow* or absorbed coping. Rather, this forgetting is essential for the experience of temporality in the moments of coping and flow. "In order to 'really' get to work 'lost' in the world of tools and to handle them, the self must forget itself" (Heidegger, 1977/1996, p. 354 [324]). This form of forgetting arises neither just from work nor from transparent use of objects and tools, nor from the sum of the two, but from being part of a unit of relevance relations within which my taking care of things moves about with circumspection. For me, these relations are those to the material at hand and my quest for understanding the phenomenon of charging by induction in a defensible way.

A FINAL PUSH: NEW AND MODIFIED LENSES

After writing the reflexive note, after a long night of inquiry, I return to thinking about the physics problem that I have been in the process of tracking for a second night without sleep. The notes show that I continue to pursue the idea concerning the electrical potential and the field produced by charges, perhaps with the intent to track where these should be located and the question about whether the boundary should be counted to the material or the field, which is the center *part* of the three-part system. Although a new day has dawned, the notes still exhibit the sense of urgency for arriving at an understanding and absorbed flow. The solution now fo-

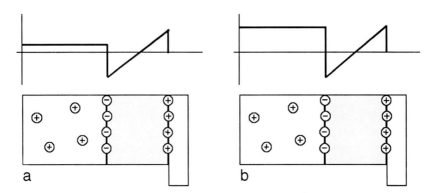

Figure 10.8. In these diagrams, I combined two forms of representation, which, in their vertical arrangement, constitute a layering of lenses or ontologies.

cuses not only on the electrical potential in the metal, where the charges have been induced, but in each part of the system.

> 6:06 A.M. I am making some coffee. I am thinking that even if there is no field, there is still a high concentration of the charges on the surface. But when the surface belongs to the metal then I should have some equilibration. But it could be such that, in terms of the potential, the charges "on the surface" already belong to the field on the outside. That is, I would get the following distribution of the potential: diagram 1 ((reproduced as Figure 10.8a)).
>
> As I make the drawing, I want to have the two triangles symmetric with respect to their areas (below and above the zero line) and measure them out, that is, I make the same height. I wonder how the height or area on the left-hand side has to compare to the other areas and/or heights. Because of the number of charges according to the atomic model on the surface of the charged object and the plate, I expect the potential to be the same. It's probably the same but opposite, for otherwise they do not add to zero on the surface and therefore there would be a field. Also, the number of charges is equal on the surface to the opposite in the material. I wonder how the charges are related to the electrical potential (voltage). I try dimensional analysis but do not get far because I do not remember them Q [As] = I/t. VI=J/s [W]. Actually, V=[J]/[As]Q,; V=E/Q. This is the energy of accelerated charge relation.
>
> I am thinking that perhaps because the charges are distributed in the plate, I can't have charge equilibrium on the boundary. So it could well be that the potential has to be the same leading to diagram 2 ((reproduced as Figure 10.8b)). Mereologically it would make sense then that the charges on the surface are no longer part, because they correspond to the second potential and to the grey area.
>
> It is 6:50 A.M. I am just not noticing the time passing.

Initially, my thinking is concerned with the way in which the changes in the electrical potential (voltage) within the system, which is now not just the metal where the charge separation is induced, but on the entire system including the charged nonconductor and the field between the two. The inquiry evidently is mediated by a different set of whole|parts relations, as the field between the two bodies also becomes a part. There are then two clear boundaries and the question arises whether these belong to the field or to the metal or charged object, respectively. Then, yet another idea is thrust into my consciousness: dimensional analysis. This form of analysis is often taught in high school science as a way of tracking the variables that appear in calculations. It is a form of checking whether the numbers "add up," for if the dimensions one ends up with after some calculation, the numbers themselves cannot be right.

In the final push, I revise the diagram that I have made (Figure 10.8a) so that the equal but opposite potential exists at the boundary between metal plate and field; that is, the tip of the triangle has to go as far below the line as the field in the metal plate goes above the field (Figure 10.8b). There is also a sense that the two triangular areas need to be the same—this seems to be a pattern in the field and at that moment is only a conjecture that requires further justification. However, the notes also articulate the presence of a sense that the solution is satisfactory, "makes sense," because in this latest model, the charges can be counted as part of the field, which goes from some negative to the equal but opposite voltage value.

The learning episode ends after a second night attempting to experimentally create and control some phenomenon, and then to create a model that allows me to understand what I have observed. The entire episode has been directed toward, motivated by, the apparent difficulties of the microphysical particle model to explain the absence of evidence for the induced charges at the surface of the metallic material (plate, electroscope). I do not push any further, perhaps because I am tired at that point, perhaps because I have had a sense of having gone as far as I could. My notes do not contain an entry about why the episode is ending; there is only one more set of entries, a set of descriptions of the history of the electroscope. Apparently this research does not yield an explanation of the phenomenon I have attempted to come to grips with in the course of the two nights.

FLOW

In these inquiries, I have not been aware of my Self, myself. A case of such nonthematic, non-self-referential awareness is the experience that is denoted by *flow*. During flow, a person is both keenly aware of what he or she is doing while not thematizing self, other, or Self-Other relations. The process is all there is— therefore the sense of flow. It is a form of being in the world singularly concerned with the things at hand rather than with understanding and theorizing oneself as doing something, especially as something different from the activity-defining object. There is only awareness of the process itself. In such cases I am so involved and absorbed in what I am doing that I am longer thinking of myself as separate from the immediate activity. I do not thematize a Self and therefore myself as a subject engaged in an activity as separate from what I am doing; because I do not thematize myself, I do not thematize the object as object apart from self (subject). In moments of flow, things are happening to me as much as I make things happen. These moments exhibit the intentional|non-intentional nature of learning, which requires both agency and passivity.

From my experiments in perception using a Maltese cross I know that fixing an image on the retina makes it disappear (Roth, 2005a). That is, as I achieve holding my eyeballs steady so that they no longer saccade, the cross I have been seeing so far dissolves. There is no more movement, I am not making time, and can no longer make difference. And with the object, the subject also disappears. I understand flow in this way. As I engage with the object, all my bearings to the surroundings become vague and fuzzy to the point that they are outside of my consciousness. In fact, consciousness requires the separation of subject and object. When the subject merges with the object, no consciousness is possible—it is a state of absorbed coping. As I engage with the object, time, related to my relationship to the world of people and things, also dissolves away. There is only process, even though the process still involves actions motivated by an *in-order-to*.

Interpreting the database from the tenth-grade physics course, which I have not established myself, has allowed me to go to the subject matter with a certain naiveté. It has allowed me to analyze learning independent of teacher intentions, which might have taken me to think in teleological or negative terms about the relation between planned curriculum and enacted curriculum outcomes. Although I have studied physics and obtained a masters degree in the subject, I have not considered the practical aspects of static electricity. If I have done these experiments at all, it must have been at the high school level, though I do no longer remember what I have done in physics at the high school. As I attempted to create the phenomena that are asked of the students, I frequently find myself in the same predicament that I observe the students to be in. This therefore has become an important lesson for me about learning in the high school laboratory. I experience these events although I already knew about the theoretical framework and knew what should be observed and how to explain the expected observations. I therefore have been at an advantage compared to the students. Furthermore, I have been at an advantage because I studied and therefore have been aware of learning from labs.

HANDS-ON: PREPARING LAYERING AND LEARNING

The learning episodes have occurred over two long, sleepless nights. These episodes not only constitute instances of absorption and flow, but also are instances of hands-on inquiry. The question someone may pose is this: How has engaging in the hands-on parts allowed me to learn anything that I would not have been able to learn otherwise? I am certain that I cannot provide an *ultimate* answer, but I do understand the event in a very different way than I have done previously.

The hands-on engagement has allowed me to gain a practical understanding of how the world works, or more, to set up a world and find out how it behaves when subjected to a variety of conditions. From this engagement, a first articulation of the world in observational terms arises. Most importantly, it is only in attempting to track the induced charges on the surface of the metal plate or electroscope that the ideas about the boundaries between parts of a hole emerged. Prior to these investigations, the question about the charges on the surface has not occurred to me. Perhaps because the particle model is so suggestive—the drawings featuring four negative charges in the material—and the corresponding positive charges near its surface is so imposing that neither students in the videotapes nor my physics colleagues at the university question it. That is, this model is a lens whose status of lens has withdrawn so that I take what I see as the natural (given) order of things. As lens, the model also is a tool (chapter 5); and the special character of tools is that I can discover its breakdown only in activity but not by simply looking.

Martin Heidegger suggested that no matter how intently, sharply, or keenly I just look at the outward appearance of things whatever form this takes, I cannot discover that which makes the thing the particular tool or equipment that it is; that is, I cannot discover anything available, the very condition that makes the thing handy. When I just look at things theoretically, I lack an understanding of their tool character. But when I am using equipment and tools, they have the tendency to withdraw. They do not seem to have any characteristics; or rather, any characteristic they may have is not salient to my consciousness. Their affordances and the practices that I have developed in dealing with them are in a relation of fittingness that has evolved from mutual constraints.

Just looking (staring) at something therefore does not provide me with the aspects of a thing because things are constructed through perception. Things are available to me not in terms of abstract representations but in terms of multiple views. These views and the motion of the individual together constitute the nature of the object-thing. My comment about the theoretical stare is not a rejection of scientific observation. In fact, at one level, my own engagement with the electroscope strictly is concerned with theory. Thus, scientific observation is in itself an activity that has its own primordial concerns and therefore its modes of seeing. Theoretical behavior is simply looking in a non-circumspect, thematizing way that therefore turns up characteristics that can be, because of their thematic and therefore objectified nature, shared among members of a community. But with all its quality, the theoretical look cannot properly articulate what makes praxis so special. And the theoretical look most frequently is not concerned with itself and the conditions that allow it to be theoretical.

My engagement with the investigation has allowed a new problematic issue to emerge: "How do I understand the charged object and its metal counterpart as a system?" This new lens emerges in the course of the investigation, itself, as my notes show, exhibiting an emergent quality. That is, although there is a wanting-to-know intention enacted, the resources for evolving a solution are outside my control, I cannot intend but only receive it. Because of the agency/sensibility dialectic, the having of ideas presupposes engagement. Here, this engagement is both intentional and unintentional, because that which is intended, a thing captured in knowledge that can be articulated, itself lies outside of the realm of thing I am able to consciously intend. All I can hope for is that opening myself to the world I am suf-

ficiently receptive for new realizations to emerge. That is, the hands-on involvement orients me such that I can also tune myself to become receptive.

But hands-on activity allows me to be receptive on condition that I do not have
to be afraid for the results. In my situation, this inherent fear to make myself a fool
mediates the repeated attempts in getting control over the phenomenon, to understand the circumstances that lead to specific observations. But it is not only the fear
to make myself a fool in the eyes of others; it is just as much a matter of making a
fool of myself in my own eyes. Why else would it make sense to engage in an extended inquiry, spending two nights without sleep, for something that might be
considered an unimportant issue?

For students, however, learning in and through inquiry in this way is more risky:
whatever they do is used as an occasion to evaluate. The marks they receive are a
form of threat, because these can negatively influence opportunities within the
school and in the future beyond. Students therefore may not be willing to engage in
extensive inquiries, because the payoff is not guaranteed as long as teachers take
some standard against which the outcome of their task involvement, observations
and explanations, are used as objects of the evaluation. One student once told me
about how much he liked open inquiry. But he also said that it was not a good way
of getting ready for university, as public examinations and high-stakes tests want
him to reproduce particular forms of knowledge and discourse rather than the kinds
of things that he might find out in open investigations. More so, he wanted direct
instruction in the topics that would appear on tests *precisely* because he subscribed
to the (individual, social) constructivist ideas of making sense. He, as other students, preferred to engage in a form of defensive learning, the intent of which is to
learn what it takes in order to avoid low grades as much as possible.

TOOLS AND THEIR EMERGENT PROPERTIES

This chapter is concerned with an interesting double movement in which students articulate their perception of new materials and thereby increase their possibilities for making different figure|ground and whole|parts configurations salient. In the process, tools, whose character during knowledgeable everyday activity it is to withdraw into and remain in the ground, emerge and become figure. That is, students learn *about* tools in a process that is opposite that of learning to use tools. Similarly, everyday activity has the character of concernful absorption in activity, a type of flow that has its own temporal characteristics, where much of the material world withdraws so not to encumber the work done by consciousness. The articulation of tools into whole|parts configurations involves taking them out of their connections in the here and now by abstracting and atemporalizing them. Coming to know a tool theoretically therefore is the result and outcome of a process, which requires the development of practical understanding prior to its articulation.

Manipulative and perceptual experience and the rather high-level categories that students learn are related. For example, the students in the German tenth-grade physics course learn about charging and discharging various substances, objects, and instruments. Thus, learning the use and function of electroscope as a whole and its parts is a major learning outcome stated in the curriculum of their unit. Yet a question imposes itself: How does what students do, for example, rubbing materials against each other, lead to the development of disciplinary maps and acquire, for example, the microphysical lens that allows them to understand phenomena in a particular way? The early chapters of this book show that teachers cannot assume that students perceive what they themselves experience; rather, it is more likely that they have *some* rather than *a* perceptual experience. At first, students' perceptions of the material elements at hand are more holistic, undifferentiated and coarse-grained. As they interact with these elements, fine structure develops both in perception and action. The material objects such as the electroscope are not given to students' consciousness once and for all, in detail, and put together from their parts. I use the notion *lifeworld* to refer to the complete world as constituted and available to the individual person, in all its parts and the actions it affords. The relationship between lifeworld and ontology (the nature of things that make the world) is dialectical: on the one hand, the lifeworld *constitutes* my basic ontology, a set of whole|parts configurations. On the other hand, the basic ontology constitutes the lifeworld; the things and opportunities for action I perceive makes the world of my experience, my lifeworld. This includes the types of entities that a person recognizes and acts towards and that otherwise mediate what she does.

WHOLE|PARTS CONFIGURATIONS OF TOOLS—IN THEORY

Philosophers have noted and remarked on the nature of the tool in practical human activity for quite some time. Rather than being present in and to consciousness, they withdraw so that the subject is aware of the action and activity rather than the material thing itself. Thus, for blind people, the cane is entirely transparent, has become so much part of themselves that their contact with the surrounding world occurs at the end of the stick; a competent carpenter is consciously aware of hammering rather than of the hammer and the nail; and those who wear glasses (as I do) know that these are not noticed most of the time. Bespectacled persons interact with the world as if the glasses were not standing between the eyes and what there is to see. That is, tools reveal themselves exactly then when they have disappeared—my glasses do their job when I attend to work rather than focusing on the glasses themselves, which happens, when dust interferes with my seeing. It is only in praxis that the conditions of the working of a tool can be discovered. Thus, the tool nature of glasses becomes evident in their use, not by theoretical inspection of their properties such as their focal length, the nature of the materials they are made from (glass, plastic), their mass and weight, and so on. The usefulness of glasses resides *precisely* in the fact that they withdraw from consciousness and are transparent to what I do. This usefulness does not become apparent in the theoretical stare. Thus, "even the most sharp and persistent 'perception' and 'representation' of things could never discover something like damage to a tool" (Heidegger, 1977/1996, p. 354 [325]).

In everyday praxis I encounter tools (and objects) as useful. Praxis therefore is not atheoretical or blind, but is associated with its own form of perception, *circumspection*. The term circumspection derives from Latin, *circumspicere*, to look around. I look around when I need something *in order to* achieve a goal. Thus, I encounter tools (instruments) in a particular way, namely to achieve something. Rather than perceiving it in the way a tool designer would, which reveals the whole|parts configuration of a tool and the way in which these parts are related, circumspect use encounters a tool as showing or doing something rather than as thing with properties. In knowledgeable, circumspect use, therefore, a tool withdraws into the ground—non-consciousness—leaving consciousness free to orient itself to other aspects of work; when hammering, I do not represent and track the hammer along its space-time coordinates but focus on hammering the nail.

The most fundamental way in which I encounter tools is as useful things. They allow me to do things and are approached as such. Their internal details are unimportant and unnoticed. I use a bicycle without knowing anything about the frame construction, I use hammers without knowing their dimensions, weight, material properties, and I use knifes without knowing anything about steel quality. In the same way, students encounter tools as such—i.e., as tools—rather than as objects with definite properties that are perceived at the instant eyes are laid on them. Thus, providing the drawing of an electroscope (Figure 11.1) falsely represents the nature of the things students encounter when they first use the instrument as a tool, because the diagram highlights features rather than usability. In this chapter I show

Figure 11.1. An electroscope is used to test for the presence of charges. If a charged object is brought near to or touches the top plate, the pointer deflects.

how a group of students "discovers" the electroscope as a useful thing and ends up using it *in order to* show the existence of charges, the relationship of voltage and distance of charged plates, etc.

To learn *about* tools requires more than theoretically looking, for example, as teachers expect this during demonstrations (chapter 1). Staring theoretically does not reveal the functioning of a tool specifically or any useful thing in general. Rather, the working of the tools recedes and hides *precisely* then when I take a theoretical look. But the theoretical look is not inherently bad. The theoretical look affords the development of theoretical understanding, which may in fact develop my practical understanding as I have found out in the study of hatchery personnel (Roth, 2005b).

There are particular issues of learning that arise when something is *used as* a tool but when teachers expect theoretical understanding *about* the tool to be developed at the same time. That is, what I encounter are useful things in relation with other useful things: My office is not an agglomeration of independent stand-alone entities but a workplace that allows me to do my research and writing. I do not encounter the chair as a Cartesian object, out there, independent of who I am, but as something that I can sit on. I encounter it in the same way that I encounter and presuppose my desk as a place where I can rest my arms, place books, or rest my coffee cup. While I write these sentences, I do not think or perceive the desk as an entity although I presuppose it in my concernful actions of writing sentences using a keyboard on my desk and watching the words appear on the monitor, itself resting on the desk. The association of useful things with other useful things genuinely shows itself in lived, practical experience. It is only when I discover that something is or has become unusable that it becomes conspicuous; but by becoming conspicuous, the thing also exhibits resistance to normal use.

While using tools in familiar and knowledgeable ways, when these are transparent to my actions, I enact a similar form of relation as when I am absorbed in activity. Learning *about* the tool therefore means that I need to break it out of its totality, that is, abstract it from its involvement in the temporal flow, make it an object of reflection, and make its whole|parts configuration thematic. Learning about the electroscope therefore consists of breaking it of its *in-order-to* relation, where knowledgeable agency puts it to use. It then begins to exist in an atemporal way, much like the two gigantic towers on the roadside begin to exist for me outside of the temporality of my experience and knowledgeability. Once I have perceived them, I begin thinking of them I can make attributions and find properties. In this mode of taking the object out of time, the object becomes objectively present.

While watching the videotapes from the beginning of the unit, I initially see students act as if: (a) the entire electroscope is electrically connected, pointer, suspension and outer ring, and as if what physicists known as insulation did not exist; (b) the base affords action of posing on the table without being thematized as such; (c) the ring affords carrying, holding; (d) the initial interactions are not with the plate at all, but the space between ring and suspension appears to be a much better place for getting an effect from the device; and (e) the laboratory table is transparent in and as equipment. It is from these actions that I-researcher can find the relation between students and tool—asking students would make thematic exactly what is not yet thematic. Thus, I know that the laboratory table, for example, functions as a tool that enables placing the materials for doing the investigations. The possibility that there is an effect of the table on the investigations emerges in lesson 5 where the metal plates are rested on Styrofoam plates to insulate them from the table. In being startled, the table becomes salient as a thing with electrical properties that students link to the electrical properties of the materials that they are working with.

Learning *about* the electroscope means that students accomplish tasks that are designed to allow them construct whole|parts relations that are more like that of the physicist, to participate in a shared ontology (minimally) with particular objects, events, causal relations. This ontology, or better, these ontologies constitute the things; mereology their whole|parts configurations. Learning scientists' science means using objects and instruments in ways that students draw on the same whole|parts configurations that scientists do. I show in chapter 5 how knowing science means being able to coordinate very different maps of the same territory, each of which has its own whole|parts relations. Knowing means knowledgeably coordinating these very different perspectives. Because even simple things may be rather complex—such as the example I use as illustration in chapter 5—when considered from the perspective of the multiple layers to be coordinated. Elsewhere, my collaborators and I exhibit the complexity of graphical displays in junior high school science textbooks that derives from the layering of multiple perspectives intended to facilitate learning (Roth, Pozzer, & Han, 2005). Whether confronting students with layered representations facilitates learning or whether students need to be assisted to become aware of the nature of the different layers still awaits an answer. To understand the electroscope actually means learning to coordinate different ways of perceiving the tool: through mechanical and electrical lenses.

Mechanically, there are two parts to the electroscope, the main circle with base and suspension, and the pointer rests by means of a needle-like axle on the central suspension so that it can move with respect to the main body (Figure 11.2). There is some other mechanical detail in the composition of the tool that students also discover, but which does not relate to the electrostatic phenomena at hand: (a) the top plate of the electroscope can be turned but it does not come to be unscrewed and (b) the ring can be removed from the base by loosen the screw in the side of

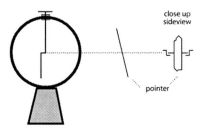

Figure 11.2. Mechanically, the electroscope consists of two parts, a body and a pointer, which is allowed to pivot freely as shown in the close-up side view.

the base and pulling the pin attached to the ring. These features, although they are aspects of the tool, are not relevant mechanical aspects of the phenomena to be explained. These features have to be kept in the ground as possible articulation, but articulations that are not relevant to the phenomena at hand. They are not part of the relevance relations that govern the electrostatic phenomena, though practical engagement with them is required to find out which aspects in fact are relevant.

Electrically, there are three parts to the instrument (Figure 11.3). At the center, there is the top plate-suspension-pointer configuration, which makes up the measuring part as such. The body supports the instrument proper; it consists of a stand and a ring of conducting material intended to electrically shield the central suspension and pointer. A piece of insulation separates the two other parts. The mechanical and electrical perspectives exhibit dissimilar whole|parts relations as the two maps clearly indicate (Figures 11.2 and 11.3). Thus, whereas from the electrical perspective, there are three parts there are only two parts from the mechanical perspective. The whole|parts configurations in the two perspectives are different such that the boundaries between parts on one map (Figure 11.2) do not coincide with the boundaries of the parts on the other map (Figure 11.3).

The scientifically legitimated and legitimate explanation of the electroscope requires the articulation and coordination of these two perspectives—charging affects the entire suspension-pointer part, but mechanically suspension and pointer

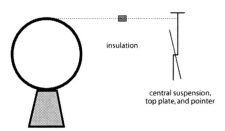

Figure 11.3. Electrically, there are three parts the electroscope: a central pointer-suspension-plate configuration (right), which is the core part of the instrument, the ring on a stand, which holds the measurement part up, and an insulating cylinder that electrically separates the two.

are different parts. These two ways of articulating (in words, in function) constitute two ontologies that have to be brought into alignment, much like the maps in a GIS representation (chapter 5). Most people using the device, including teachers and professors of physics, are aware only in implicit ways of these very different maps involved. Researchers may eventually find out that assisting students in articulating each map and then in the coordination of the two—or however many there may be in other instances—supports the learning process.

Initially the students do not attend to the different parts at all other than noting that the instrument works or that there are charges, as shown by the pointer deflection. But there is no evidence that the students *see* the pointer *as* pointer; rather, their action and talk are evidence that they use the instrument without attending to the particular whole|parts relations that my description highlights. They initially use the electroscope in the same way that they use the neon lamp initially, without attending to its fine structure (i.e., whole|parts relations). In these videotapes, the students do not attend to and perceive details of the pointer suspension and why it is "finicky": the pointer needs to suffice constraints for both ways of cutting the instrument, that is, its axle needs to touch the suspension so that the two constitute *one* electrical unit but needs to touch very slightly to allow any movement at all (Figure 11.2). The two conditions constrain the working of the instrument in opposing ways. The mechanically ideal case exists when the friction is zero, which can be achieved only in the limit where the two materials no longer touch; but in this limit, the electrical resistance becomes infinite. Electrically, the ideal case exists when there is zero resistance across the interface, which is achieved only in the limit when the two materials are perfectly in contact; but in this limit, the two materials have fused which means very high to infinite mechanical resistance. The two constraints lead to a fragile interface between pointer and suspension. It is not surprising, therefore, that the two teachers present in the classroom repeatedly reminded students to handle the instrument carefully so not to bend the suspension mechanism and therefore prevent the instrument from proper functioning.

WHOLE|PARTS CONFIGURATIONS—INITIAL STUDENT PRAXIS

One of the normal and most important tools in the teaching of static electricity is the electroscope. As any other tool, it is and has structure that affords actions. One can do things *to* it, which is not the normal mode, or use it to help doing things—establishing the presence and relative size of charges. When an object is used to assist in doing things rather than being itself the target of the action, it is a tool. The device allows students to enact numerous processes during their initial investigations:

- Touching: top, bottom of suspension, touching and moving back pointer, touching ring, placing styrofoam on plate, below central suspension;
- Carrying: on ring, base;
- Charged objects: Touching plate, pointer, central suspension, ring with object; bringing object close to pointer, plate; (sometimes not charging!); broad side, sticking through the ring; charging directly by rubbing plate with plastic bag;

- Discharging: touching plate, moving back pointer, touching central suspension;
- Moving, dismantling: turning and removing plate, pointer by hand;
- Verbally articulating parts: ring, plate, insulation, pointer, "shitty screw."

When the students in this course first use the electroscope, they put electrical stuff on and it works, it shows them how much there is. It is like a kitchen scale on which they place some cooking ingredients, foodstuff, and the pointer shows them how much there is, in ounces or grams. Here too, they do not ask themselves how the instrument works, what the mechanism is that shows them how much there is. They simply know from experience that ounces or grams are something that they weigh foodstuff with. The deflection, as indicated on the dial, is a linear function of the amount of weight; the weight marks are equidistant. In the present case, if they put electrical stuff on the "scale," the pointer shows them how much there is—there is a perceptual similarity between the electroscope and a traditional scale for weighing (e.g., in supermarkets). The pointer moves to a certain place and the deflection (linear, though not necessarily in the present case) bears a direct relationship to the amount placed; when they add more, the pointer deflects more. All of this is consistent with the understanding of a kitchen scale. In this sense, the electroscope is a piece of equipment that works like other devices that students are familiar with in their daily lives. Once students have found that electricity is put *onto* something—is like a liquid that can be taken from one material (container) by means of rubbing and put onto another, or simply rubbed off—electricity can be thought of as a liquid, as stuff that can be measured using the electroscope.

When Phil first encounters the electroscope, he is disconcerted. What is the nature of the instrument? In order for the instrument to show anything, he has to deal with it as if there was stuff in it. That is, in his actions the electroscope works like a food scale or graduated container such that he sees something when the electroscope is filled. The electroscope then is used consistent with an equipmental nature that resembles that of a container for measuring liquids. But this is inconsistent with the observation Phil is making at the moment he brings the transparency sheet close by without touching the instrument (see below). He exhibits surprise. This surprise makes available to the analyst that Phil has used the instrument consistent with a particular structure rather than consistent with some other structure. At the moment Phil exhibits being startled, he also exhibits a part of his lifeworld. From his actions, I conclude that he expects no electrical charges on the electroscope, and yet the instrument shows charges present. This is inconsistent with the way he anticipates this kind of equipment to work and when it does not, he is startled.

Early in the student investigations, the electroscope has tool character: students use it to prove the presence of charges, indicated by the movement of the pointer from its rest position. What makes learning about the instrument rather complex is that there are two ways in which it functions: (a) being held close to a charged body induces charges, which the instrument displays; and (b) charging the device by means of touching it with a previously charged body or using the induction-grounding method to move charges onto the device. In the first instance, charges are measured in a process similar to measuring the length of an object: the measurement process does not affect the quantity measured. In the second instance, charges are transferred to the instrument much like liquids are poured into a cylinder for measuring their amount. There is a different logic underlying the two measurement processes, which, in the present lessons, do not come to be articulated. Whether and how this failure to articulate the different forms of logic mediates learning remains to be researched.

Phil uses the electroscope like other instruments that are employed to measure *extensive* properties. He fills the instrument (container) and then has an indication that there is something and how much of it there is. But when the transparencies are approached (or other charged materials), the electroscope works like an instrument of an *intensive* property. It does not actually have to be filled to measure the property of stuff that is separate from the instrument itself. Intensive properties are qualitative in nature and do not change during the decomposition of the system. These include pressure, temperature, chemical and electrical potential, or concentration. *Extensive* properties are quantitative in nature, proportional to amount of material; they includes volume, mass, number of particles, magnetization, energy, and entropy. Therefore, to measure extensive properties, I have to have the entire sample filling the instrument. For intensive properties, I only need to measure a part. In the present situation, the electroscope sometimes works in the way an instrument for intensive properties, and sometimes it works as if it is an instrument for extensive properties. It can get even more confusing when the charging is done by induction. Then, an action that normally discharges an object actually brings additional charges to it and therefore changes the balance of charges so that, after hand and charged objects have been removed, the electroscope is charged. Here, an action that in other instances discharges the instrument actually does the reverse.

DISCOVERING A TOOL

One might assume that an instrument such as the electroscope is objectively available *as* instrument to all those present and that it is present in all its material details. These details might be expected to be perceptually and verbally articulated during a task that asks students to find out how the instrument works. In particular, it might be asked what possibilities there are for acting as students interact with the instrument. They have to act, as the working of the electroscope is not revealed to students when they initially stare at the instrument. It reveals itself *in* use. To (theoretically) understand its working, I already need to (practically) understand it to make the required hermeneutical reduction that yields observational descriptions and properties, which can then be logically reduced to variables that are combined and correlated to form causal explanations (see chapter 9, Figure 9.6). In the episodes that follow, I exhibit how different parts of the electroscope come to be articulated in and as a result of students' agency and sensibility.

Emergence of a Tool Function: Charging by Induction

This episode shows how a particular phenomenon, induction, and a particular feature of the electroscope emerge from intentional|non-intentional actions. The epi-

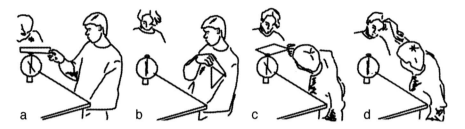

Figure 11.4. Chris, foreground and right, makes a discovery about the electroscope, here-to-fore only used as a tool; Marcel in the background watches and responds. a. The pointer is deflected while holding a charged transparency over the top. b. The deflection disappears when the transparency is pulled away. c. Christian checks that the transparency is not touching and yet deflection can be observed. d. Deflection disappears again.

sode is evidence for the non-intentional aspects of inquiry, as the student apparently randomly and without purpose brings a charged transparency near the electroscope in various ("unsystematic") ways (Figure 11.4). It is intentional in the sense that the student is in an accepting mode, ready to be "impressed" by something *notable* that emerges into his consciousness. The something discovered is notable, as it is something that can be noted, it is part of the material ground that lends itself to be structured. It is notable, in the (second) sense of having become a figure against the ground that he perceives, can point to, and can talk about. (Because Chris is not a high achieving student, teachers consider his behavior as *mere* play.)

In this episode, Chris finds out that the electroscope pointer deflects even if he does not touch the instrument similar to the way in which Phil has discovered this aspect. That is, prior to this discovery, he has treated the instrument as one that measures extensive properties, which here has meant that he has had to move the charges from the charged transparency or rod to the instrument. This is consistent with the way other students initially describe the functioning of the electroscope: electrons move between the charged material and the instrument even when there is a gap between the two (Episode 11.1, turn 04; see also Episode 11.4a below). Chris approaches the partially charged instrument in a *playful*, that is, *intentional|non-intentional* manner (see chapter 10), but then slows down the movement. The pointer begins to deflect more. Chris then removes the transparency rapidly (Episode 11.1, turn 02, Figure 11.4b), making the pointer return to its original state. He then shifts his body (Episode 11.1, turn 03, Figure 11.4c) and observes the pointer while bringing the transparency very close to the plate. He asks Marcel for an explication of the phenomenon he observes.

Episode 11.1

01 Chris: (8.0) ((Charges transparency, holds it over the top plate, Figure 10.4a.))

02   ((Rapidly pulls the transparency away.)) (2.0) ((Observes electroscope, Figure 11.4b)) ((Pointer returns to vertical.))

03		Hey, ((holds transparency above top plate, shifts his body to get a better look, Figure 11.4c)) why is it, when you only hold it above, then it also does it?
04	Marcel:	Yes, it's because it gives off electrons.
05	Chris:	Yes, and when I take it away ((Pulls transparency away, Figure 11.4d, returns it as in Figure 11.4c)), it is gone. And when I put them on again. ((Holds transparency above electroscope.))
06		(2.3)
07	Marcel:	Then it doesn't give them off. Then it can't give them off.

Chris rubs the transparency, thereby presumably charging it, and holds it above the electroscope (turn 01, Figure 11.4a). Any observer of the video clip can see that the pointer deflects. Chris gazes at it for a long while, then rapidly pulls the transparency away and toward himself (Figure 11.4b). I can see the pointer return to its vertical position. At this point, I cannot know what Chris has perceived. But the student rubs the transparency again, holds it above the plate, and then shifts his body so that he can see the electroscope and the transparency from the side (Figure 11.4c), as if he wanted to check that the latter does or does not touch the instrument. At this point, he articulates a problematic issue intended as a question to be answered by Marcel, the only other student currently at the table (turn 03). I now know what Chris has attended to and perceived: the pointer deflects even if the transparency does not touch it. In this sentence, Chris expresses something he notices and, simultaneously, that he is startled. He says what he says only because it articulates a noticing, which he would not have done (a) if he had not noticed it and (b) if he had expected the pointer to deflect. And because he does not understand, he asks Marcel for an explication. Let me articulate how Chris might have described the episode:

> I have used the electroscope to detect the presence of static electricity previously, and see that the pointer moves much like the pointer of the speedometer in the car. I do not observe its details and just notice when it deflects more or less. Now, playfully, I bring the transparency to the top of the electroscope without much intention. I watch. And all of a sudden it hits me. I observe something for the first time: The pointer deflects even if I do not touch. I check by looking from the side whether the transparency really does not touch *and* the pointer deflects when I bring the former close to the instrument. So far, have not noticed that the pointer deflects even when I do not touch it.

Much in the same way as I have not seen the two gigantic towers on the roadside, Chris has not attended to something that now becomes apparent to him in and through his actions. He could not have wanted to make this observation. He has made the observation because he has opened himself up to the world, which thereby could affect him, leave its mark through the material object that he has made his object of attention. In this instance, a chance variation leads him to perceive something correlated with his movement that brings the transparency in the vicinity of the instrument. There is no inherent necessity to make this or any other observation. The videotapes provide evidence that others and in different circumstances do not notice that the pointer actually deflects without touching the instrument or prior to touching it. But here, Chris articulates what he perceives in an observation sentence and thereby makes it available to others, his peer and any analyst watching the tapes. I do not have sufficient information from the videotape, so that it is not clear what Marcel is expressing here, but it is a contrast that correlates with the contrast Chris has made—only that it is in the opposite way a scientist would explain. Chris seems to anticipate a different response from the instrument.

In this episode, the inquiry shows features that are very similar to those that I describe in my own inquiry (chapter 10). Thus, Chris appears to notice something, and in noticing he is startled by the unexpected nature of what he sees (turns 01–03). He repeats the action several times, shifting his body and taking a closer look. He then articulates a question directed toward his peer, thereby seeking an explication for what he has observed. This question also provides explanatory resources for understanding the reason for his bodily shift: it allows him to ascertain that the pointer moves even if the charged transparency is merely held above the instrument without touching it. This clearly shows the structural similarity with my own actions that have led to ascertaining the reproducibility of preparation and observation. Chris needs to ascertain that the pointer moves *without* him touching the electroscope, and therefore controls the way in which he holds the transparency near the top part of the instrument.

In this instance, Chris states an observation categorical in the form of "If . . . then . . ." This statement is more than an observation categorical, it is the result of an inference about cause (his action) and effect (observation). This statement is clearly different from the observation Jenny makes at one point, "I saw [the lamp] glow." She utters a simple observation. This statement has the structure of a singular event, not that of a repeatable observation; though, framed in language, it is intelligible and therefore a possible observation. The difference between the two forms of statement is embodied in the grammar of the utterances. In Jenny's sentence, she is the subject that has perceived an event. As such, it may forever remain singular, though its possibility to be an event perceivable by others. Chris, however, produces a third-person construction. He is no longer the observing subject; any person can repeat his action ("When you only hold it . . .") and, as a consequence, anyone can observe the same outcome ("then it *also* does it"). Though his teachers may not think that he is capable of science, Chris here displays forms of behavior that are scientific, through and through.

Out of what appear to be random movements, Chris succeeds to isolate a consistent behavior of the electroscope. Not all their efforts are equally successful, especially during the early parts of their inquiry. For example, even though they repeatedly achieve the pointer staying in its position, the students in this group do not know how to get to that point. Initially, when they move the transparency inside the ring—similar to how I have investigated the instrument (Figure 10.7)—they inadvertently (i.e., likely without being aware) touch the pointer. As a result, the pointer stays deflected, something unanticipated because they fail to notice that they previously had touched. Later, when they have settled into charging the electroscope only from the top plate (by induction) they no longer achieve charging the electroscope permanently. Several students are openly frustrated at not being able to charge the instrument in the intended way, despite varying what they are doing. At one point Phil notices for the first time that the pointer stays deflected even when he removes the transparency, but he does not have an explanation for it. He later attempts to reproduce the phenomenon, but does not succeed despite many attempts. Here, students have charged an electroscope a number of times, through their "inadvertent" actions. At some point later, they (at least one of them) thematize it as something special, the pointer stays deflected leading to a charged electroscope. But they appear to wrestle with the question, "How do I reproduce the effect when I want to?" Although they have succeeded in achieving this state a number of times, when they now attempt to do it intentionally, they do not succeed in doing so. That is, at this point they do not yet understand the instrument, though they have discovered some essential elements of it.

Here, students are engaged in a way that exhibits structural similarity with what I have done. They are not satisfied with producing a phenomenon once, which means it would have been a singular event. From these repetition it becomes evident that a phenomenon is a phenomenon only when it can be reproduced, when it has the "If (when) . . . then" structure.

Emergence of Tool Parts

Tools are whole entities that are useful for something; and they do so by withdrawing into the ground. With the tool as a whole, its whole|parts configurations, too, withdraw into the ground, from which, if needed, they need to be recovered. An important aspect of the electroscope is the plastic material that insulates the outer ring and the central suspension connected to the pointer (Figure 11.3). Although this part of the electroscope is not hidden from view and therefore can be perceived easily, its presence in students' actions and consciousness should not be taken for granted. In fact, this, too, is an aspect that emerges in the course of students' investigations much like the inner structure of the neon glow lamp emerged in and through student involvement with the materials. That is, much like the structure of the glow lamp has been an achievement of the investigative work (chapter 4), the realization that the outer ring is insulated from the central part and top plate is a contingently achieved outcome of an active engagement with the world at hand and of a corresponding accepting attitude that overcomes the distance between subject and object of consciousness. Having access to a second set of tapes recorded in a German eleventh-grade physics class studying electrostatic phenomena, I have confirmed the same structure in the discovery of the insulating material *as* insulating material. This subsection is about how tool parts emerge in the consciousness of students generally and the plastic insulation in particular.

Whenever there are charges deposited on the electroscope, the pointer moves. As a result, the students develop a tool-type relation to the base and central suspen-

Figure 11.5. a. Tony asks Jenny (center) to charge the electroscope; Brita watches. b. He then wants her to touch the outer ring. c. When Jenny touches it, the pointer does not move. d. She then discovers the insulation between ring and pointer-suspension configuration.

sion, which do specific work; they do not relate to these aspects as objectified and articulated parts of the instrument that have functions crucial to its operation. Thus, the base has the function of holding the instrument, to place it on the table. The central suspension holds the pointer. It is not treated as something that is charged in the same way as the pointer and therefore that there is a repulsion between suspension and pointer. Students treat the central part as an indicator: differentiated no other than that the pointer moves. The remainder is simply there to hold the pointer in place and charge it.

As the students begin their investigations, they do not treat the protruding plate as something that allows them to do anything special—like the doorknob that affords turning rather than pushing down (as a handle) or pushing against the door (as in a swing door). They notice that the pointer can be moved sometimes by bringing a charged transparency broadside but not to the narrow side of the ring. Thus, there is a difference in their ways of using the electroscope that emerges in their interactions with the device. But these ways normally remain at the level of the non-conscious, though subsequent thematization may render the thinginess of these features. From the narrow side, there is simply nothing that happens—because of the shielding effects of the outer ring; but this is not (yet) available to the students. Approaching a charged object from the broad side (sometimes) moves the pointer. But it moves even better when the students bring the charged transparency inside the ring and close to the pointer or to the suspension from the other side—much in the way I have explored the instrument (Figure 10.5b). They find out that the tool works best when the charges are brought inside the ring, parallel to the normal axis of the plane spanned by the outer ring. The part designed to receive the charges, however, receives little attention at this point. Although the students have touched the top plate, they do not treat it as an important detail of the instrument. Concerned with what works, they find the largest pointer deflection when they bring the charged materials inside the ring; they use the instrument in this way consistently, though this is not standard physics practice.

There is a moment when Jenny and Clare argue about what they have to do to get the pointer discharged; but they come to agree that this can be done touching the suspension generally. At some point during the investigation, the four female students and Tom are hunkered around the electroscope (Figure 11.5), all apparently engaged in attempting to understand this device that is new and strange to the students. Jenny rubs the transparency hard, then touches with it the top of the electroscope, then rubs it again. Clare comments, "It stays." Tom asks students about what is happening, and Jenny suggests that something happens to the charges, following the outside of the instrument with her hand ("That the charges go over here . . ."). Tom exhibits surprise following the answer of the students and asks, "Here too?," while pointing to the circular outside. He is observably perplexed, not knowing what to say; he then suggests that they should touch the knob. Upon touching, the pointer returns to normal. Jenny loads the electroscope again, Tom asks them to touch the outer ring (Figure 11.5b), exemplifying what to do by touching the ring himself. He apparently intends students to describe what happens. When Jenny moves her hand up and down on the outer ring (Figure 11.5c), Clare notes, "Nothing at all." "Nothing at all," Tom repeats. Jenny then begins what becomes an explication for the behavior of the electroscope when someone touches the outer ring.

Episode 11.2

01 Jenny: There should be– Oh yea, because here it is insulated ((looks at the electroscope as in Figure 11.5d, touching the top plate)).

01 Tom: What can you say now?

02 Jenny: Yea, the charges can only be brought to this part. ((Touches the top plate of the electroscope.))

Here, Tom's presence allows students to learn about two aspects. Jenny realizes that a stable deflection can be achieved by touching the top plate with the materials. Jenny notices and articulates so that this becomes salient for all that there is a plastic piece that insulates the suspension from the outer ring. The two realizations are linked, because of the electrical properties of the central part, which is separated from the other metal parts of the electroscope. Tom achieves this by asking students to touch (discharge) the charged instrument on the knob and subsequently, in a second attempt, to touch the ring. It is *precisely* at that point that Jenny notes how the cylindrical piece of plastic near the top of the electroscope separates the ring and central suspension. Here, she perceives and verbally articulates the plastic part *as* insulation that electrically separates the central suspension-plate part and the outer ring.

If this had been a singular incident, some readers might be tempted to suggest that the women simply have not been interested sufficiently or that they are not the best students. However, I observe the same type of discovery not only in other groups in this course but also in the videotapes shot in another, eleventh-grade physics course studying static electricity. In one instance, an eleventh-grade student suggests that the electrons are spread over the entire electroscope. Although he and his group mates have developed an explanation that is scientifically correct in as far as the charging process goes, when the teacher asks them about the redistribution of the electrons, the student suggests that they are over the entire instrument (Figure 11.6). The student, however, has not noticed the insulation that sepa-

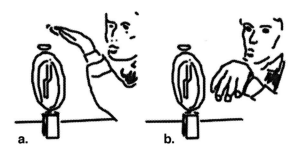

Figure 11.6. An eleventh-grade student shows where and how the electrons are distributed, using a gesture not unlike that used by a teacher in another class.

rates the outer ring from the central suspension-pointer configuration. That is, in his use, the electroscope is equipment first. When the teacher asks him to explain its particulars become apparent.

> When you hold the film above it, and then hold the finger to it, which means, there is an electron over-supply, somewhere in the device. And when I hold my finger to it, the moveable particles go into my body, this thing neutralizes somehow. And when I take it away, the film and the finger, then they sit somewhere on the thing here. And this is why the pointer deflects.

Here, the student uses the device itself as a background to his gestures to assist in his explanation of what has to be done (Figure 11.6). In the first slide, he shows how to approach the transparency in the initial part of the charging process. Then, his hands move down as he explains how the charges distribute over the instrument. However, it is only after repeated questioning by the teacher, and as part of the two students' unfolding explanation that one of them notices that there is a piece of insulating material that separates the outer ring from the central part. He points to the insulation. Another student then moves his hands up and pulls on the upper plate pulling it out of its seat as he suggests that they have to take the electroscope apart. This articulation thereby becomes a part of their world through the investigation, and through their own physical interaction with the materials. The equipment obtains a new aspect that it has not had before. It is now articulated into individual pieces, a composite thing rather than as an equipmental whole with the function of measuring charges and to be loaded with charges.

Parenthetically I note that this communicative effort constitutes one of the middle ground cases described in chapters 6 and 7, where students gesture in the presence of the materials. Part of the scene is present, and the hands do the remainder to bring the scene to life. That is, the hands are functioning as part of the scene and stand for and animate what the listener has to imagine. The hands do not have the same function as they have had in the experiment itself, for they are not re-doing what they had done before. Rather, they now have symbolic function, standing in for objects, and then get animated to tell parts of a story. They change as referents, too, and it is important to follow the story and check where the *coordination* between gesture and discourse is so that the story makes sense.

In the group of the four tenth-grade male students, the insulation also emerges as the result of a discovery. It is in responding to Tom's questions about discharging the electroscope by touching its outer ring that they learn that discharging is possible only by touching the central suspension or the top plate. Phil, for example, initially suggests that touching the outer ring discharges the electroscope. Thus far, no one has discharged in this manner; they always have touched the suspension to do it. They use the instrument, get it to work properly, and yet have not made thematic the instrument in terms of its whole|parts configurations and the functional relation between the different parts. When they touch the ring, no change is observed in the pointer position. At this instant, they first notice the plastic *as* insulator separating the central part from the outer ring (Figure 11.3). It is evident that they have not previously noticed that the ring is not connected or that it is conducting, although they have been talking about the conduction as occurring all along the central part from the plate down to the pointer. Thus, although students use the instrument appropriately, they do not understand it theoretically. They use it competently in an equipment sense because the ways they developed using it work for them without breakdown. They have a practical understanding of the instrument first. If they are to develop any theoretical understanding, it always has to be preceded, accompanied, and concluded by the practical understanding that arises from praxis. Because there is no reason to make salient any aspects of a working tool, especially when it is working rather than broken—in the way the female students think of the glow lamp (chapter 4)—they do not come to question whether in fact they can discharge the instrument by touching it other than they have been doing in the past.

In all recorded episodes, students begin to notice something for which they do not have an explanation: touching the outer ring does not discharge the electroscope. In being startled, the insulation comes to be figure, and students recognize that it electrically separates the inner and outer parts of the device. The result of the first touch contrasts does of another: touching the top plate or the central suspension returns the pointer to its zero position. In cognizing this difference, students make salient something that they then can reflect on. The students do not seem "to believe their eyes," and in one instance, the student repeats the charging-touching process four times before accepting what he has seen as a fact, something real, rather than an artifact. Here then, he engages in the action and systematic variation, repeated variation that brings about a consistent effect.

In the available videotapes, every single student "discovers" the existence of the insulation only in and through the interactions with teachers and specific questions that lead to situations of being startled and the awareness of some contradiction. Each time, these interactions concern the distribution of charges over the electroscope. In all groups, the students suggest that the charges are distributed throughout the instrument including the central suspension *and* the outer ring. That is, the students treat the electroscope as if it is electrically connected, that is, as if it is one piece rather than the three viewed through an electrical lens (Figure 11.3). This, of course, mitigates the kind of theoretical understanding about the device that students can develop.

A crucial aspect in each of the student–teacher interaction was the respective teacher's question: "What happens if you touch the outer ring of the charged electroscope?" The anticipated movement of the pointer and the lack of movement when they actually touch are sufficient to make them startled, and in being startled, the plastic piece becomes a being. In each case, at least one of the students in the group closely inspects the electroscope—similar to the way in which Chris inspects it (Figure 11.4)—then points to the cylindrical plastic part and suggests that it is insulating the central suspension from the ring. More poignantly, in one case, the insulation and the articulation of the instrument do not become salient to students even when Tara explicitly points to the different parts of the instrument. That is, much in the same way as I did not take my colleague's comment as pointing out a fact (chapter 3), the students have not taken Tara's pointing *as* pointing out something specifically. That is, even after the teacher had shown students the different parts of the electroscope, specifically pointing to the three electrically distinct parts, these parts do not become salient; but the discovery occurs when these same students later are asked about how to discharge the electroscope.

This episodes show that even if the teacher points out some articulation, it cannot be assumed that the students have attended to it, made it salient, articulated it, or have developed a relation to it that they can articulate in an observational sentence. Even if teachers intend to point out something, the effect of the action may differ, questioning the very theories of actions as individual (intentional) rather than as collective (interactional) phenomena. To me, this observation came as little surprise. Very early in my research while I was still teaching high school physics, I have found out from analyzing videotapes that students use what I have said in various ways to the point of supporting opposite points of view (Roth & Roychoudhury, 1992). At the time, I thought in terms of the theoretical concept of *interpretive flexibility*. Now I think about concept words in particular and language generally in terms of situated use. Thus, the students use utterances as resources, but include them in differently articulated significance relations.

FIRST DESCRIPTIONS OF HOW THE ELECTROSCOPE WORKS

The explications and theories students develop and the ways in which they arrive at them, bear a structural relationship with my own inquiries, though the particular resources that students and I have been using are different. Thus, insight comes sudden, though always after extended practice. It arrives "out of the blue" and therefore requires a welcoming subject. Therefore, not only must students be engaged and be doing something, but also they must be open to be affected by something they do not yet know. And in opening themselves to perception, they accept the responsibility for the things to be as they appear, even if the way in which they appear questions everything they have come to understand until that point. *Because* Chris is open, he can he notice the pointer movement when he does not touch the instrument with the charged transparency. The movement of the pointer is unex-

Figure 11.7. Marcel articulates a first explanation for how the tool works; Chris, to the right, is initially doing his own thing, then listens and watches. a. Marcel observes the pointer as he approaches and takes away the charged transparency. b. A sudden forward movement signals an insight. c. He turns the electroscope, first showing how the electrons move to the top plate. d. Pointing to suspension and holding the pointer with his right and left hand, respectively, he explains how the positive charges in each repel, leading the pointer to deflect.

pected, even though Chris never states what he expects to be seeing. But in and with his articulation of insight, he makes salient the difference between the new observation made over and against the previous state of affairs. With the perceived differences emerge new possibilities for verbally articulating the world, providing new possibilities for extracting variables that can be correlated in a subsequent logical reduction.

Descriptions of how the electroscope works constitute hermeneutical reductions that are made possible because students have had biographical experiences. Descriptions constitute articulations, which themselves (verbally) articulate the (perceptual) articulations in and of the material world that are salient to the subject. Before any explication can be produced, (conceptual, verbal) articulations are required, which themselves presuppose (perceptual) articulation of the object. That is, any theoretical understanding articulated in an explanation presupposes a practical understanding, which has isolated the object perceptually and descriptively from its relevance hole.

In the push for an explication, students may stop the manipulations themselves but reproduce (some of) the movements involved in the preceding investigation (see also chapters 6 and 7). These movements therefore re-present the events—contrasting the actual repetitions, which make them present again in some form. In the present situation, Marcel slowly moves the transparency towards and away from the top plate of the electroscope. As his hand moves back and forth, he intently looks at the instrument (Figure 11.7a). He stops for four seconds, staring at the instrument (Figure 11.7b). Then, all of a sudden, he utters:

This is clearly logical. Look, all of this is connected together, and that ((gestures along suspension to top plate)). When these here, the whole, when all this gives off electrons, here, to this here, and all this is positive ((points to pointer)), and it is logical that if this is positive ((points to suspension)) and that is positive ((points to pointer)) that these must repel.

The episode begins with Marcel gazing intently at the instrument and the charged transparency, slowly moving the latter up and down. He signals a sudden insight: He jerks his body forward and says, "This is clearly logical." By bursting out and by jerking his body, Marcel unmistakably announces to bystanders something that has emerged in his consciousness with considerable force. He has become aware of something *as* something. Here, in what is recognizable as a moment of insight, Marcel articulates perceiving the central part of the instrument as being connected, "all of this is connected." This sentence does not have a personal pronoun or the "If . . . then . . ." structure. Yet, Marcel's perceptual articulation no longer is *merely* singular. The fact that it is articulated in an observation statement inherently presupposes the intelligibility of its content and structure. Being intelligible also means that the singular observation is a *possible* form of observation, and in this way, an observation that every other human being can make. Here, then, the very articulation of the fact, which is a highly individual event, already embodies its cultural (historical) nature in that it immediately transcends singularity toward plurality.

Using his right hand Marcel then shows how electrons move from the lower part of the central section to the top plate—his fingers curl around the central part, one finger moving up the pointer, another along the suspension (Figure 11.7c). This movement suggests that the electrons come from two parts. As a result of this movement, the lower part is positive according to his explanation. He points to the suspension with his right hand and moves the pointer with his left, articulating both as charged positively and therefore as repelling each other.

In this explanation, Marcel articulates the coordination of two properties, the electrical and the mechanical. From the former, the entire central part is a unit: all parts are connected so that the electrons flow freely. He enacts the flow by a movement of his hand. Marcel then articulates the mechanical properties through gestures and manipulations. Using his right and left hands to point to the suspension and move the pointer, he actually makes salient the mechanical properties of the system: the pointer moves relative to the suspension, which itself is attached to the top plate. Thus, mechanically the suspension and pointer are separated and articulated (having a joint and being different), but electrically they form one as shown in his previous gesture. Even the fact that the pointer is made from one piece is not something given to the students the moment they laid eyes on the instrument. Thus, as Matt discovers that the two parts of the pointer really constitute one and the same piece so that when it deflects on the bottom it deflects at the top and to the same degree; that is, the symmetry of the pointer above and below its axle has been an (intellectual, perceptual) achievement rather than being given to him when he looked at the device.

Students sometimes do something in a patterned way practice without being consciously aware of it; realizing what they do *as* a particular practice, too, is an achievement. The two different forms of relating to the instrument—discharging the electroscope and talking *about* discharging—are neither inherently related nor is the necessity to relate them for evolving an explanatory discourse given by the device itself. For example, the four young women do not "discharge" the electro-

Figure 11.8. Matt, Phil, and Marcel (from left to right) sit around the electroscope attempting to explain how it works just after Phil has done the experiment charging by influence.

scope during the initial part of their inquiry. The pointer deflects, returns to zero; but the students do not make salient that a particular action brings the pointer back. In one case, Jenny forces the pointer back to the zero position, apparently in an instance of a mechanical action—not knowing that touching itself discharges the pointer, which now would move back to the zero position by itself. The young men find out about the discharging by accidental touching the suspension. In other groups in this and another class, students bring the pointer back to the zero position in a mechanical way rather than simply touching the top of the instrument. Discharging by mechanically moving the pointer back to the zero position has developed into a pervasive practice prior to the events descript in the next section. The practice is so prevalent that Tara feels compelled at one point to tell students not to touch the pointers to prevent damaging them. Students also discharge through touching the suspension, for example the plate or the lower tip, but without thematizing this touching *as* discharging. It is a practice—a patterned action—that they have not articulated. And when they articulate it, it turns out that they do not theoretically understand what they have been doing.

How does the practice of discharging the electroscope from the top come about? In the case of the male group, this emerges accidentally. Initially Phil mechanically returns the pointer to the zero position. A little later, Marcel who, like Matt, has repeatedly touched the top plate in a playful manner, has done so when the electroscope was charged. The deflection disappears and Phil notes, "Now you discharged it again." A little later, Matt discharges the electroscope while touching the pointer with his finger. When less than two minutes later one of the two teachers comes and asks them about charging and discharging the electroscope, Phil and Matt answer that they have to touch on the top plate. However, Phil then also proposes that they could really touch anywhere along on the instrument.

As students interact with each other, their verbal articulation of the device emerges and slowly evolves. Matt, Phil, and Marcel are sitting around the electroscope (Figure 11.8). They are fully absorbed in the task of constructing an explanation of how the electroscope works. While Matt engages in articulating an explanation, Phil reproduces the experiment: he brings the transparency close to the top plate, which makes the pointer deflect. He briefly touches the bottom part of the suspension, which is followed by a return of the pointer to the zero position. He then removes the transparency, which is followed by the deflection of the pointer.

Episode 11.3

01 Matt: It is like with the Styrofoam that is being pulled. It then therefore deflects and wants to go up. And that then we charge it with electrons from the ground. ((Gestures a movement from the right shoulder to the finger and pointer suspension.)) Understand?

02 Phil: ((Looks at Matt, expressing astonishment, shakes head.))

03 Matt: For example, all the electrons from here ((points to bottom of suspension [Figure 11.8], moves along suspension to top)) go up. Watch. In here are electrons, yea? Up here you have a charged body, then the electrons want to go up there, yea. All go up there, because it is made of metal.

04 Phil: Yea, everything is made of metal.

05 Matt: At this time you get there on the bottom, with the electrons from your finger, you push them in here, and then you move your body back, and then there are a few more electrons in it. You understand? And therefore . . .

Matt explains the system in terms of a metaphor in which electrons move like water, accumulating in one end, and thereby giving room for more electrons to come from electrical ground to the lower part of the electroscope. The central suspension is like a water basin, a swimming pool where the water can accumulate on one end through some mechanism, and then there is room on the other for more to come in. In this episode, there is no evidence that they see the apparatus as consisting of *different* electrical parts (as articulated in Figure 11.3). The electroscope is but a device that shows the presence of charges. Both Phil and Matt talk about the metallic nature, without noting that the frame is electrically separated from the suspension. Importantly, Matt frames the electrical property of the suspension including the pointer as metallic, allowing electrons to move freely from the bottom to the top plate. Phil, on the other hand, points out the metallic nature of "everything," without explicitly excluding the piece that insulates the central suspension from the outer ring and stand. Here, then, the different whole|parts configurations can be seen at work. From Phil's perspective, everything is made of "metal," a perspective that actively interferes with a scientific description of the instrument. Without the insulation, the instrument does not work in the way it does.

TEACHING: REVEALING AND DEVELOPING THE DOMAIN ONTOLOGY

My teaching career began just after I completed a masters of science degree in physics. The aspect I loved most in all of my schooling and training to that point, if anything, were the open-ended laboratory investigations that completed my degree requirement. When I started teaching, I believed that the laws and theories could be seen and discovered through investigations. However, I realized early on that students do not see events in the way I do, even, when they produce the phenomena in the way I intended them to. I have found that students generally do no rediscover in the phenomena those aspects that it took scientists often generations to articulate and theorize. At the time, I realized how important it is to let students conduct investigations in groups and the importance of interacting with these groups to allow them to perceive the events in ways that support the theories they are to learn. Interactions between teachers and students are important for bringing about the preconditions for articulating appropriate explanations of phenomena—perceiving what they are supposed to perceive and isolating factors in a process of logical reduction, which they have to relate to one another subsequently. That is, teachers can mediate the processes articulated in Figure 9.6 from biographical experience through hermeneutic reduction to logical reduction by, in the first instance, assisting students to perceive, then interpretively articulate relevant aspects, which only subsequently come to be related externally as variables.

In the extended episode that follows, the teacher coaxes and guides students into articulating the instrument in terms of its electrical properties, which, combined with the mechanical properties of the suspension-pointer configuration, leads to a deflection of the pointer. While reading through it, readers should keep in mind that the conversation is unfolding, that the participants do not know at the time of turn 01 what they will have said and done after the following turn 02 or any further turn in their conversation. Because they do not know what others will say, they cannot have a prepared script of what to say when it is their turn or even at what time they will have a turn. Rather, each turn has to be understood as both preparing an orientation and moving the interaction ahead without any individual having control over where the conversation is going.

Tara has joined the four students, all oriented toward the electroscope, the functioning of which they attempt to explain (Figure 11.9). Matt begins this episode, articulating part of the investigation where they have brought the transparency to the top part of the electroscope. He then suggests that—as they have articulated

Figure 11.9. Matt, Phil, Marcel, Tara (teacher), and Christian (from left to right) in a conversation about the electroscope, which reveals different ontologies. (Line 25 in transcript.)

previously—the electrons in the central suspension "want to go there," that is, to the top plate (turn 01). As Tara acknowledges to be listening, Matt continues uttering "electron exchange," but Tara again only acknowledges listening to him (turn 04). Matt then articulates a conclusion ("and therefore"), which turns his earlier utterances into instances of antecedents.

Episode 11.4a

01	Matt:	So up here comes the charged body, electrons, or so, um, want to go up there touch the body, want to go there
02	Tara:	Um.
03	Matt:	electron exchange, or something, isn't it?
04	Tara:	Um, um.
05	Matt:	And therefore we get a deflection of the ele– elecs– electroscope, or what's its name.

Until now, Tara has allowed Matt to articulate a first explication. Now, however, she becomes a more active interlocutor. She first ascertains what she has heard Matt saying (turn 06), and, when the student confirms her framing, then follows up with a question that asks him to explain why he describes electrons as moving upward toward the top plate (turn 08). Both Marcel and Matt respond that "they" move, thereby responding to the first part of Tara's utterance, "What do they do?" But this is apparently not what Tara wants to elicit, as she both acknowledges the appropriateness of the description ("they move") but also emphasizes that the transparency has to be charged positively for this movement to occur ("And lack of electrons means?" [turn 21]).

Episode 11.4b

06	Tara:	You said that they want to go up there?
07	Matt:	Yea, exactly.
08	Tara:	What do they do there, that they want to do so?
09	Marcel:	They move.
10	Matt:	Yea, they all move.
11	Tara:	Yea, it is in this part, that is, when the transparency is charged positively, will be.
12	Matt:	And perhaps it will be.
13	Tara:	The electrons are negative, attracted.
14	Matt:	Exactly.
15	Tara:	So they pull themselves up here and what is down here, what state? ((Points to bottom part of suspension.))
16	Matt:	It's, um, it's less heavy, less heavy there.
17	Phil:	Lack of electrons.
18	Matt:	Lack of electrons.
19	Tara:	Lack of electrons. No, it's not less heavy.
20	Matt:	Yea, evidently.

CHAPTER 11

21 Tara: Lack of electrons. And lack of electrons means? How is this part
               charged?
22 Phil: Positive.

In his turn, Matt does not articulate anything about the electrical state, which
Tara articulates in her next turn, "Electrons are negative," and she adds, as a consequence, these are "attracted" (turn 13). In uttering "exactly," Matt not only acknowledges having heard what Tara has said but also that this is just what he
thinks to be happening. He expresses that there is no difference in what Tara makes
salient and what he has been saying so far. Tara then reiterates the statement Matt
has begun with (turn 01) in saying that the electrons "pull themselves up here"
(turn 15). But this is not her real point. Rather, Tara's utterances provide evidence
for her intention to assist students in making salient the state of the bottom part of
the suspension, which the students successively articulate as and in terms of "less
heavy," "lack of electrons," and, after one more teacher intervention, "positive"
(turn 22).
    Theories require particular ontologies that allow the articulation and causal rela-
tions. Here, what is to be explained is how the electroscope can be charged using
the macroscopic process visible to everyone. But for the explanation, there needs
to exist a set of things somewhat different than that available in front of them. Matt
describes the situation as one where something is less heavy (turn 16), that is,
something less heavy is pulled upwards in the central suspension and something
else, by implication, is heavier and therefore not attracted as much. This presents
the central suspension as something like a set of communicating tubes. What is the
case in one part is exactly the case in another. But a different image here is a basin
that has been rocked such that a lot of the liquid has moved to one side and therefore made place for more to come in. It is like pushing down on one of the communicating tubes to let even more water in.

Episode 11.4c
23 Tara: Positively. Isn't it? And what is charged positively? This part and?
24 Chris: Yes, only that part. ((Points to pointer-suspension.))
25 Tara: This part and?
26 Chris: And the cup.
27 Tara: No, there these are, they are all negative.
28 Phil: And the–
29 Tara: And the pointer, isn't it?
30 Chris: Okay, clear.

Tara wants students to understand that the lower part of the electroscope is
charged positively when there is a positively charged material held above the top
plate of the device (turns 23, 25, 27, 29); when students do not utter the right words
and descriptions, Tara rejects them and provides others (e.g., "No . . . they are all
negative" [turn 27]; "pointer" [turn 29]). For Chris, the charges are distributed
equally in the entire pointer-suspension-plate configuration, which is reasonable

*Figure 11.10. Tara moves her hand in a semicircle, which begins at the central suspension,
moves down and then up along the outer ring. (Line 23 in transcript.)*

because metals are conductors (turns 24 and 26). Tara contradicts him, suggesting
that the "cup" (i.e., top plate) contains the electrons and therefore is negative. What
she apparently wants to hear is that the pointer and lower part of suspension are
positive. As Chris does not come forth with the expected answer, she eventually
supplies it (turn 29). Episode 11.4c ends with Chris' acknowledgment that he has
understood what Tara wants him to understand (turn 30).

In this case, it becomes quite clear that the students perceive a different
whole|parts configuration—i.e., have a different ontology—than their teacher. To
her, there are different parts to the central suspension, one that is closer to the top
and which is charged negatively, and the part that is farther away, which is charged
positively. To the students, all parts are connected and electrically conducting. Although Matthias earlier has had his own theory articulating exactly the same
whole|parts configuration, he is silent as the teacher tells him that he cannot con-
nect the two explanations.

But Tara, too, articulates with her gestures—and likely without her conscious
awareness—a particular whole|parts configuration that upon reflection, she may
well reject. In turn 23, while asking how the bottom part of the central suspension
is charged, she moves her hand in a semicircle down the suspension and then up at
the outer ring (Figure 11.10). The movement of her hand therefore suggests that
the charges are not only present in the central suspension but also in the outer ring.
Her gesture shows the whole|parts relation that students enacted prior to their dis-
covery of the insulation. I am not suggesting that Tara is aware of this. She is totally absorbed in the teaching, attempting to assist the four students to understand
the functioning of the electroscope, and here, the deflection of the pointer when a
presumably charged body is brought close to the upper plate. Yet her actions imply
the electrical unity of the instrument as a whole. But the actions are all that students can perceive—rather than what she might have in her mind or the sense of
what she has or might want to say. These actions (gestures) lend themselves to
being perceived, understood, and interpreted as pertaining to the instrument as a
whole and therefore provide students with sense-making resources that Tara herself would not want to articulate. And yet, she does articulate them.

In the final part of this episode, Tara then provides a full verbal articulation of
the phenomena in the electroscope through a microphysical lens.

Figure 11.11. Tara holds her hand above the electroscope, simulating the charged trans-parency, then gestures how electrons would move if attracted to the top plate. (Line 33 in transcript.)

Episode 11.4d

31 Tara: And what happens when all of this is charged in the same way?
             [((Looks at Phil)) (0.5)]
32 Phil: [((Nods.))   ]
33 Tara: Then there are repulsive forces, right? Then this will be deflected
             ((Points to pointer)). So there is nothing else happening than that
             up here ((holds flat hand above top plate, Figure 11.11)) a charged
             body will attract the electrons upward ((Gesture with flat hand up-
             ward, Figure 11.11)) or repel them downward ((Hand turns, moves
             from up toward table, in reverse of previous movement)), which
             ever, right? And these sides are thereby charged ((Points to bottom
             part of pointer-suspension configuration)) we call this influence,
             and this works only with metals.

In this situation, while Tara provides her explanation, the hand moves, sometimes embodying experimental aspects—such as when she holds it above the top
plate, palm downward, suggesting, because simultaneous with uttering "a charged
body" the charged transparency—sometimes the explanatory aspects, such as when
the hand moves, palm upward, parallel to the instrument, from the bottom to the
top where the hand previously gestured the placement of a transparency sheet. In
this explanation, the electrons are treated somewhat like a fluid, which moves
within the pointer-suspension configuration, toward or away from a previously
rubbed transparency. The electroscope is an instrument, and what matters is the
pointer movement. It is, according to the explanation, brought about as the same
charges are both in the pointer suspension and in the pointer itself. The interplay of
mechanical and electrical properties, however, is not invoked.

DISCOVERY, LEARNING, AND TEMPORALITY

As a whole, the episodes exhibit how the electroscope initially is a tool in the
hands of the students, who develop particular practices. They learn to use it to

prove the presence of electrical charges. I show that the students frequently are not conscious of *what* they are doing in the sense that they have developed ways of using the instrument that work; but they do not explore if there are other ways of using the tool that yield the same results. As a tool, the electroscope is encountered in the inconspicuous way: It shows what it is intended to show, and it does so obviously and objectively. In these episodes, the electroscope does not reveal its inner workings or even its inner structure and the relation between parts and between parts and the whole. However, in a moment of being startled, the tool becomes an object of objectifying consciousness. In a process of hermeneutic reduction, the tool takes on not only object character but allows properties to emerge. For example, students discover the cylindrical plastic piece *as* insulation, which electrically separates the outer ring from the central suspension; students also discover that the top plate and the central suspension are one piece from an electrical perspective, whereas they consist of two (or three, if one counts the removable top plate as separable) pieces from a mechanical perspective.

Before being startled, which consisted in realizing that the electroscope cannot be discharged by touching the outer ring, the "true nature" of the tool could not have been discovered by thematizing and thematic, theoretical perception. To see the insulating plastic *as* insulating plastic, the observer already has to know the electroscope and its functions, that is, its tool properties, which are inherently linked to knowing the tool practically. However, I can become aware of a breakdown only because it is already in a relevance relation to the future and past; breakdown is experienced *precisely* because I already understand the tool practically. I can become conscious of a breakdown only when my anticipation, which is oriented to the future but grounded in past experiences, is not realized. That is, when my tool has not done (past) what I have anticipated (future), I experience a contradiction that corresponds to the material resistance that the tool offers to my action; this contradiction, as the term implies, is a contradiction in consciousness. The contradiction is associated with a resistance that arises from the materiality of the things with which I interact. Here, the situation does not exhibit itself in the way I expected—i.e., the pointer does not return when I touch the outer ring. But to perceive the contradiction, I need to be open, allowing the counterpart of my agency to occur for sensibility to reveal the world to me: "If circumspect letting things be relevant were not *awaiting* what is taken care of 'from the very beginning,' and if awaiting did not temporalize itself in the *unity with* a making present, Dasein could never 'find out' that something is missing" (Heidegger, 1977/1996, p. 355 [325]).

Coming to know, learning, a thing such as the electroscope means this: Knowing through experience how it behaves if I push it or hit it, bend it or break it, when I subject it to hot and cold, that is, when I find out how it behaves and responds *in the context of relevance* that constitute causal connections, by which states it passes, how it stays invariant across all the variations that I subject it to. Theoretically knowing a tool means breaking it out of its normal relevance relation, its usefulness, its reality, the very condition that allows it to be tool and withdraw from conscious attention. Reality, or, which is the same thing, the materiality of objects and the causal relations my agency|sensibility discloses them to be in, inseparably belong to each other; they mutually presuppose and constitute each other.

The possibility of discovering something new therefore is founded in sensibility in a mode that I might characterize by acceptance or hospitality. To learn, I have to open myself to be affected by, to be accepting to, whatever it is that I do not know but will come to know through my engagement. The temporal structure of accepting, therefore, is an awaiting and making present of something that is not yet part of retention, and therefore something that is not inherently recognizable *as* something. Both awaiting and making present are temporal modes that cannot be theorized by drawing on chronological time. The fact that the students in the present episodes have been able to find out anything at all is due to the fact that they have remained in an accepting state. Individuals who are no longer in an accepting stage have closed themselves to learning; they see the world in the ways that they have always seen it. They see the social and material world always through their existing lenses, which have formed in the past, and which they are no longer in the mood of changing. The world becomes static and atemporal. Older people and individuals who have been thoroughly enculturated into a discipline appear to be less inclined and perhaps have no penchant for placing themselves into an accepting mode and its inherent demand for possible change in my ways of doing because I have encountered something new.

Throughout the episodes in this chapter, the temporal nature of engagement and learning is quite evident. Movement—mind, body—makes time as much as it is subject to time. The temporality characteristic of learning cannot be measured by chronological time. I do not and cannot know when Chris will have the insight that Tara wants him to have; and even telling him does not help, as the episode between Tara and the female students showed, who do not articulate the whole|parts configuration although she intends to point it out to the students. To get from what might be denoted as knowledgeability at some point (e.g., "A") to the knowledgeability at some other point (e.g., "B"), students move along trajectories. Models, such as conceptual change, which describe learning in terms of some initial and final states, are non-viable, as they do not allow an understanding of how whatever is learned changes and or how whatever has changed has occurred in time. That is, even if the models correctly depicted initial and end state of learning, I know very little if I do not know how anyone can go from A to B. But this kind of knowledge is exactly what teachers need to assist their students in moving in particular directions given what students currently know and perceive. In the epilogue that follows, I articulate why I am not or no longer a constructivist of the radical, social, or conceptual change brands.

LEARNING—AFTER CONSTRUCTIVISM AND CONCEPTUAL CHANGE

Constructivism (Piagetian, radical, social) and its incarnation as conceptual change theory have been the reigning theories in science education for the past forty years. They continue to be used as theoretical referents, though there is mounting evidence of the aporia they face in explaining learning as it emerges in real time and how human beings experience it (e.g., Roth & Duit, 2003). Constructivism has not provided descriptions that explain why students specifically and all human beings generally say what they say and do what they do. The fundamental shortcoming of constructivism lies in the fact that it does not account for the reasons human beings have for their actions, and these reasons sublate the individual–collective divide that underlies much of constructivist theories. Constructivism is also, and thoroughly so, wedded to the Kantian and Cartesian programs, which detach knowing from the material world including the body, considering knowledge structures to be abstractions from experience, including the long-term and momentaneous emotional states that not merely impinge on but are integral to what I do and how I do it. Before briefly articulating and critiquing the main tenants of constructivist theory, I revisit a series of investigations involving the balance beam that shed light on the aporia constructivism faces. It clearly exhibits the problems with some of the presuppositions that underlie the treatment of perceptual experience in research on perception, learning, and development.

PERCEPTION, LEARNING, AND DEVELOPMENT

Throughout this book I show how the world appears to individuals is under continuous change; my lifeworld, the world I perceive and towards which I act is under continuous transformation. I continually see new phenomena even in familiar surroundings and get better at seeing how things are from the way they look. These observations fly into the face of the assumptions underlying educational theory and practice. As a science teacher uses demonstrations, do I not assume that students see relevant events? As a theorist, do I not assume that children interact with (the structures in) a stable world that is, through experience, assimilated into an appropriately adapting (accommodating), autopoietic mind? As the following example shows, there exists some research that can be reinterpreted in support of the present observations.

Jean Piaget and his followers described the development of reasoning on the balance beam (e.g., Inhelder & Piaget, 1958) in terms of the progressive evaluation of weight and distance. Whereas the child initially focuses on weight or distance

323

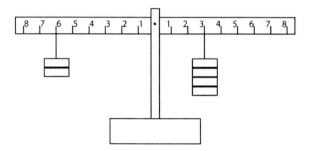

Figure e.1. Balance beams such as depicted here, both as equipment and in the form of drawings, have been used as a paradigmatic case for investigating proportional and multiplicative reasoning. What do students perceive and therefore what do they respond to in their answers?

only, it will (in the concrete operational stage) develop and use an addition schema to make judgments about the behavior of a lever given the weights and distances on either side. The child begins (in the formal operational stage) to relate weights and distances by means of the proportionality scheme. In this approach, it is assumed that children perceive weight and distance in the way adults or scientists take these features. Do children look at a balance beam such as that depicted in Figure e.1 and perceive the weights *as* weights and distances *as* distances in the way a scientist sees them? This is an important question, for this theory is valid only when the assumption that children perceive the weights and distances as measured and explained by scientists is justified. Or do children perceive the material configuration in some other way? That is, does their perception structure the field in ways that differ from scientists and therefore, do children act toward and with very different resources than Piaget had assumed?

Research studying children of different ages raises serious doubts about what students seen when asked about balancing the scale: the children in this research do not at all act upon the properties of weight and distance (Metz, 1993; Roth, 1998). Rather, if these properties are salient at all, then it is because they are the *outcome* of extended perceptual and motor experiences with the materials at hand. For example, during a test that preceded an empirical classroom study of learning science while designing machines, the seventh-grade students in my research have been presented with balance beams such as depicted in Figures e.1 and e.2. Consistent with the episodes featured throughout this book, it turns out that the seventh-graders' responses are very different when the distance markers and numbers are present versus when they are absent. In the former situation, students generally add, divide, and multiply *numbers*. That is, rather than using weights and distances as resources for describing and explaining the balance beam they use numbers.

In the second case where there are no numbers and markers, many students first count the number of weights (metal nuts) in a situation such as depicted in Figure e.2, and then reason: "On this side (left) there is half as much weight, so I have to go twice as far out to balance the beam." In this explanation, the student clearly

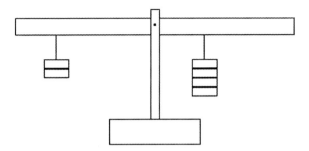

Figure e.2. In one empirical investigation, I used a balance beam without markings and numbers. I wanted to know how students would reason about making it balance given unequal weights on the two sides. Would students' answers be the same or similar to those provided in other cases such as in the one depicted in Figure e.1?

uses weight *as* weight and distance *as* distance, as can be seen from the comparison. He talks about going out "twice as far" to balance the beam, where the distance is articulated in terms of an action. The same student, on the other hand, reasons about the same problem in the presence of numbers and marks in a very different way: "I have two less [nuts] on the left [than on the right], so I have to go two [units] more." Here, the students conducts a simple addition of numbers, some being used to compare the number of metal nuts, the other to count lines on the arms of the device. The central point therefore is that the children often do not perceive *weight* and *distance* but *numbers* or number of things. The conflation of these different structures has led researchers to inappropriate conclusions concerning children's reasoning. During the subsequent experimental unit, students have repeated opportunities to explore the equal arm balance and other types of levers. This experimental unit, too, provides evidence for the emergent nature of devices.

When they use the lever systems during their own investigations, the students initially attend to the *position* of the weights along the beam followed by attention to *change of location*, *size of change in location*, and *relative distance*. Only when the relative distance has been indexed to the fulcrum do these students perceptually attend to "distance" as conceived in the developmental literature. That is, the children do not perceive and act in a world as Piaget and others understood; rather, the perception of this world in these terms has been the *outcome* of interactions of a behavioral environment perceived in very different ways. The world available to these children has changed as my world has changed with appearance of the gigantic twin towers, or the "Landwehr" and distance posts, and as it has changed for the tenth-grade physics students when an increasing number of features characterized their glow lamps or electroscopes. There furthermore is a progression from what appears to be the case on the balance beam and what they subsequently know as how things really are.

The results of that study, as the present book in its entirety, suggest that science educators ought to take individuals' perceptions and their perceptually available worlds as changing. Such an approach offers a genealogy of experience, crises, and

325

regressions that are not orientated primarily toward the development of a scientific rationality. It offers a lived reorientation of the field of experience that includes the perceptive field and its changes in a constitutive way. This allows me to emphasize the autopoietic (self-organizing) character of concrete sensorimotor actions that are always situated in and always transform the embedding situation. The developing individual (student or scientist) is imbued with his or her own rationality; this rationality is not to be measured using a known developmental endpoint as teleological referent. Researchers can then see development as a double reorganization including both the perceptual articulation of things in the world and the transformation of the (perceptual) object world. I do not encounter an autonomous, unique world, characterized by object permanence and invariant structures. Rather, the very world I—developing individual—encounter is a function of the genealogy of my experience. If the aim of science educators is to understand development, they need to understand what the individual perceives, which is to be thought of as an order that is neither chaotic nor rational in the Western scientific sense of the word. In my ethnographic studies, even those involving highly trained and very experienced scientists, I have begun taking a genetic perspective to phenomenological inquiry, which allows me to uncover how new structures emerge in and through their activities (Roth, 2005b). This allows me to think about and explain the emergent character of the perceptual field and thereby arrive at forms of understanding that do not over-hastily attribute divergent task performances to the absence of cognitive ability.

As a result of my research concerning learning in science laboratories, I have abandoned the constructivist paradigm as a useful theory for articulating and explaining knowledgeability and changes in observable behaviors. In the mid-1980s, I conducted my dissertation within a neo-Piagetian framework, which integrates developmental perspective and information processing. I subsequently used radical constructivism as a lens to study learning only to substitute social constructivism for it when my close inspection of videotapes exhibited the irremediably social nature of learning not captured by radical constructivism. However, I eventually abandoned the latter theory, too, because it turned out to be plagued with considerable contradictions.

CONSTRUCTIVISM AND CONCEPTUAL CHANGE

In science education, the dominant learning theory in the 1960s, when it replaced behaviorism, became Jean Piaget's stage theory. Its interest to science education may have arisen from the emphasis it placed on the interaction of the child with the world. These interactions came to characterize the thought forms of the child, which are based on the sensorimotor, pre-operational, concrete-operational, and formal characteristics exhibited in executing certain tasks. Whereas this theory pays close attention to the patterns of actions in the concrete world and the patterns that thought appears to exhibit, especially in the earlier stages that are explicitly modeled on bodily actions, science educators lost interest in the theory, including even those researchers who favored students' engagement in laboratory tasks as an important mode of learning science. It may be that the lack of a theoretical articulation between bodily engagement with the world and forms of thought provided science educators with an aporia. Whereas the parallel nature between material action and form of thought—e.g., in the operational stage—was intelligible, plausible, and appealing there is no explicit mechanism that shows how the bodily actions are transformed into thought. That is, even in the concrete operational stage, the thought forms, which constitute "internalized operations," were independent of actions and operations, inherently directed toward external objects. The integrative and transformative changes Piaget wrote about in essence disconnect the child, experiencing in and through its body, from its mental structures, said to have been abstracted and internalized. The essence of his thought has been formulated in a book written in the later stages of his life:

> Knowing reality means constructing systems of transformations that correspond, more or less adequately, to reality. They are more or less isomorphic to transformations of reality. The transformational structures of which knowledge consists are not copies of the transformations in reality; they are simply possible isomorphic models among which experience can enable us to choose. Knowledge then becomes a system of transformations that become progressively adequate. (Piaget, 1970, p. 15)

For Piaget, therefore, (scientific) knowledge bears an *isomorphic* relation to reality. The isomorphism expresses itself in the logico-mathematical structures that underlie the material world and therefore, as commonly held among philosophical physicists at the time, the human mind—in part because it is made of the same matter as the world science describes. Piaget was not so much interested in the empirical knowledge that can be derived from the object itself—which is the point of view of empiricism, which Piaget describes as being "valid in the case of experimental or empirical knowledge" (p. 16). In this case, abstraction is abstraction *from* the objects: a child who takes two objects in his hands may realize that they have different weight. All of this Piaget finds noteworthy, but he really is interested in a second form of knowledge, which is abstracted from something more ephemeral than objects: actions. A child counting a set of pebbles placed in different configurations and arriving each time at the same number is his quintessential example of how the mathematical concept of commutativity comes to be discovered.

This theory of (simple, reflective) abstraction from experience, still of interest to mathematics educators, fails to provide a reasonable mechanism for articulating the process of abstraction itself. The notion also emphasizes knowledge as something that operates separate and somehow transcends practical engagement with the world. Although Piaget realizes that knowledge is active, he has detached knowledge from the practical activity that preceded it. This may very well be the remnant of his penchant for a metaphysical realism.

Another problem of Piagetian theory becomes important especially with the rise of *social* constructivism. Although Piaget recognizes that there not only are psychological aspects in the emergence of scientific knowledge but also sociological

327

ones, he does not articulate the relationship between the two. Piaget appears to be exclusively preoccupied with the psychological factors that the social and societal aspects of knowledge and knowledgeability are left unattended. Not surprisingly, the father of the sociocultural and cultural-historical schools of (social) psychology, Lev Vygotsky (1986), held him accountable for these theoretical shortcomings characterizing Piaget's theory as idealist. (Social constructivism has the opposite problem in that it focuses on the construction of knowledge in communities, leaving unattended the corresponding problem of the relation between collective and individual knowledge.) The demise of Piagetian theory parallels the emergence of two theories, which for the past twenty years have had a stronghold on theorizing knowing and learning in science education: (radical, social) constructivism and conceptual change.

Radical constructivism affirms that humans are *entirely* responsible for the world in which they think to be living: they *construct* it on the basis of their experiences (Glasersfeld, 2004a). Whereas much of the construction is said to occur non-consciously, outside of awareness, humans are said to yield knowledge interpretatively by the subject who experiences something. The key claim in this epistemology is the independence of knowledge from the world: it does not reflect the structures of the world but rather its structures are imposed on the world. Thus, whereas Piaget thought of an isomorphism between the structures of the world and the structure of thought, radical constructivists think of knowledge in terms of how well it allows human beings to adapt and be adapted independently of any claims about the relationship between knowledge and material structures.

Perhaps the most fundamental point radical constructivists make is that there is nothing like truth. Ernst von Glasersfeld is thoroughly Kantian (as Piaget) in the sense that he maintains all human knowledge—apart from space and time, which are given a priori—to be constructed in response to interactions with a world that does not have inherent structure, that is, there are no specified things out there though there is a material world that allows experience in the first place. Glasersfeld differs from Kant in the sense that the latter arrives at a transcendental world, whereas the former insists that knowledge structures are entirely human, constructed by the individual. Where both are wrong is in failing to recognize that the world is not an unstructured primal soup. There are boundaries in the world and these boundaries are available to me in my experience—all I have to do is jump and I will notice quickly when I confront a medium different than air, such as the water in pool or the walls enclosing my office. Both are right, again, in that these boundaries do not *define* a thing *as* a thing.

Likely because of its extreme centering on the individual human—whereof the *radical* in radical constructivism—radical constructivism has trouble when it comes to articulating the role of society and the social environment. As everything else human beings experience, society and social environment, too, are constructed by the individual person. Thus, it does not reject the social in human experience but it rejects society as something given (Glasersfeld, 2005b). A radical constructivist, according to the author, cannot accept society as something given, preceding consciousness—though this is exactly what happens when children are born, they always and already come to a world structured by the habitual ways in which people go about their merry ways in it. Accordingly, society and social facts first have to be analyzed as conceptual constructions if one wants to explicate and evaluate their role in the ultimate construction of concepts.

In this position, Glasersfeld clearly articulates the two opposing forms of reduction: radical constructivism reduces knowing to the individual and its experience in the world, whereas social constructivism reduces knowing to the collective. This collective entity, society or community of knowing, is said to produce knowledge in and through collective activity. Drawing on a famous aphorism stated by the Russian social psychologist Lev Vygotsky, social constructivists attempt to overcome their divide with radical constructivism by having every action, thought, conception, and so forth appears twice: first on an interpersonal then on an intrapersonal plane. In my view, neither reductionism can work. More so, the individual, collective, and material aspects of knowing need to be thought together, in terms of units that do no reduce knowing to any one of the three poles.

A variant of constructivism is better known under the banner it flies: conceptions and conceptual change (e.g., Duit & Treagust, 1998). Rather than focusing on the abstraction of processes, which have shown to be of interest especially to mathematics educators, science educators are more interested in the construction of scientific concepts. These concepts reflect structures in mind that determine human actions in particular situations, including their talk about concepts. In the conceptual change literature, the role of experience remains underthematized and undertheorized and a greater role is given to the possible temporal and temporalizing processes in which students replace their naïve conceptions for more appropriate scientific ones. What are the temporal dynamics that lead from one conception or conceptual framework to another, as, for example, expressed in Figure 9.1? Early work in the field pursued the possibility that students could be coaxed into abandoning their conceptions, in part through the cognitive conflict that was expected to arise between two different conceptions relative to the same situation to be explained.

Conceptual change inherently concerns the breaking of structure and the construction of new ones. What theorists have failed to consider are the contextual aspects of knowing, both from psychological and from sociological and materialist perspectives. Thus, on the one hand, knowing is theorized independently of the body and its movements and emotions; and on the other hand, knowing somehow existed independent of the situation in which it was produced and reproduced. The theory, then and now, emphasizes the individual human being as a rational actor *constructing* and *reconstructing* his or her knowledge as a function to satisfy the four basic conditions for change to occur: dissatisfaction with existing conceptions, and intelligibility, initial plausibility, and fruitfulness of the new conception.

It turns out that students specifically and human beings generally do not necessarily abandon their ways of going and talking about things in the face of evidence that appears to exhibit the viability of a conception. In a paradigmatic example, a twelve-year-old girl does not abandon saying that ice melts faster when wrapped in wool than in aluminum foil despite being confronted with the corresponding material situations. More recent improvements of the theory include the social context, motivation, and emotion—but these are epicycles added to planetary circles than a radical reframing of theory in the face of evidence exhibiting its non-viability.

A key problem of constructivist thought lies in its failure to articulate how human beings experience what they experience and how patterned actions (practices) emerge in the continuity of their engagement with the material world, which includes themselves and other human beings. The constructivist literature presupposes the givenness of worldly things—for example, constructivists do not question whether the twelve-year-old girl actually perceives what they perceive, and therefore acts in a world that is at least perceptually equivalent. The experience generally is taken to be the same, but is separated from the way in which students are said to interpret it and construct (knowledge about) it. This key problem therefore also can be framed in terms of its focus on knowledge in the head.

A second major problem lies in the inability of constructivist theory in general but conceptual change in particular to provide a mechanism for the changes in the structures it presupposes to exist prior and post instruction. This failure, as Lev Vygotsky has pointed out, is also apparent in Piaget's work: "there is no self-development, there can be no development in a strict sense of this term, only a dislodging of one form by another" (Vygotsky, 1986, p. 54). That is, constructivism does not provide a way of explaining how the structural relations of one to all other concepts are broken and reassembled in new ways; and most importantly, it fails to provide a description of the between state where the first structure is broken and the next one is assembled. A third, related problem lies in the failure to appreciate that a comparison between two concepts as competing frameworks for understanding some phenomenon actually requires that the individual *understands* the second, replacement concept: But this, by definition, is the very object of learning. How is the individual to compare his or her existing concept with a new one, which it only knows after it has learned it?

A fourth and perhaps the most serious of all problems constructivism has is its positing of the subject, which constructs itself in an autopoietic process, as it adapts its knowledge so that it fits with its experience. Beginning epistemology with the subject and time, however, leads to the failure of both Kant and Hegel, who, as Edmund Husserl already articulates at the beginning of the twentieth century, fail to show how subject and time themselves are constituted. That is, the subject and time presuppose their own existence. No human knowledge, individual or collective, can be constituted on this basis. A fifth and related problem pertains to constructivists' failure to theorize learning itself as a temporal phenomenon.

TOWARD A VIABLE THEORY OF LEARNING

Throughout this book I describe and theorize phenomena that have not been addressed in the constructivist literature other than in the most general and abstract terms. For example in chapters 1 and 2, I show how students not merely *interpret* the (given) world differently but in fact *perceive* a different world. That is, the condition for establishing the greater usefulness of a new conception over a given one is not fulfilled: the thing in perception to be explained is very (and even radically) different. This problem arises in addition to the previously stated one in which students are to *evaluate* a conception prior to having learned it, which is the outcome of the learning episode.

In the second part of this book, I describe very different perceptual experiences and the emergence of new things and aspects in the world of students, as these become apparent in their talk and material actions, and in my own world. Thus, the evidence provided shows how the things that I come to perceive and be knowledgeable about are not given to me once and for all when I first lay my eyes on them or when light rays from them fall onto my retina because of the way in which I am located and oriented. Rather, these things emerge into my consciousness and begin to be articulated into whole|parts schemas in and through experience and in time, especially in the states of being startled and of experiencing breakdown. Radical constructivists in particular might say that their theory predicts this, but I am not confident about their ability to justify this claim. Constructivism says nothing about sensory experience and how it relates to the knowledge I am supposed to have; and it says especially little about the relationship between sensory experiences in the world, which *presupposes* the world, and something that does impinge upon me (touch of the object, smell, light rays and objects these bounce off, etc.). That is, without a material world that embodies something to be structured, there is nothing that could be structured, and there is nothing in particular that would allow a structured structuring individual to construct any knowledge about.

Finally, constructivism tells us little to nothing about the passivity that underlies all of cognition, as the very condition for sensibility is the underlying passivity of the body to receive something that comes from the other. Even though there is a transitive element in sensibility, whereby I can actively open myself to the possibility to sense (see, feel, hear, smell) something, the possibility of being inescapably subject to the experience of pain originating in my body leads me to the passivity of passivity.

Throughout this book I provide examples that show how perception articulates the world; but implicated in (practical) articulation is the possibility to articulate in words. Any articulation therefore presupposes the other, which means that any description of individual experience inherently presupposes collective experience. Saying whatever is said presupposes intelligibility both of the process of saying and the said (content of the saying). In exploring individual experience, I therefore always explore the possibility of experiencing at all, and therefore experience as a collective phenomenon.

When students are asked to "explore" the (electroscope) thing without having been demonstrated some way in which it might be used, they have to disclose what one can possibly do *with* and find out *about* the instrument. Their actions in part are grounded in their past experiences, sedimented in the routine operations that their goal-directed actions draw on. Yet they are, metaphorically speaking, in the dark about what it is they are to learn, and therefore lack knowledge of the motive for doing what they are to do. That is, in addition to finding out about facts they have to find out about the motive underlying what they do. In this, they discover, for example, that the pointer of the electroscope moves (in some situations) when a transparency that has been pulled through the clamped knees is brought close to the instrument. Students essentially live in, perceive, and act toward a lifeworld in which this instrument comes to have relevance relations with other things. My lifeworld *constitutes* the objective world environment in which I move and toward which my actions are directed, and to which I adapt. Learning means expanding and articulating this lifeworld, as new things that heretofore lay outside of my horizon are included or things within it are perceived in new whole|parts configurations.

In chapter 5, I use the layering of maps—exemplified by the geographers' practice of GIS mapping—as metaphor to rethink knowing and learning in science. This analogy is consistent with the idea that the world is interpretively flexible. But it makes evident in a much better way than other metaphors that even my primary perception constitutes a map, the relation to the structures in the material world I know very little about. This map is layered with other maps, and in fact may be reconfigured by its interactions with other, disciplinary maps. In the second through fourth parts of the book, I provide many examples of how the idea of layering makes differences in an otherwise continuous flux of communicative expressions.

Contrasting constructivist articulations, my own descriptions of knowing and learning emphasize the non-verbal components that always already accompany what it means to knowledgeably do something—including talking about stuff. I may use a tool without knowing anything *about* the theoretical structure that its designers have built on and that they have built into it. I know nothing or little about the theoretical structure much in the same way that a tennis player has to have no theoretical knowledge of physics whatsoever and still play world-class tennis. I may not even be aware of any structure at all as long as the tool (instrument) does what it is intended to do: be part of the relevance relations between the (social, material) setting and myself, even in moments of flow, that is, when there is no sense of self involved.

Radical and social constructivists, including conceptual change researchers and philosophers, have little space or time for my body and its emotive states that are integral to my actions. By focusing on the rationality of the supposed construction, the constitutive role of emotions in rationality essentially is covered up and unavailable to analysis. Emotions, though I repeatedly touch on them here, and though they are an emergent aspect of my research agenda, are not (yet) central to the present work and will have to await treatment in the future. I provide some space, however, to another issue totally excluded in the constructivist literature, time and temporality in and of experience.

In true Kantian tradition, constructivists presuppose time and temporality in and of experience as external to human activity: time is a condition for having experiences at all. It is true that Piaget had some interest in *notions* of time, which he suggests are the result of psychological constructions derivative from experiences of motion. But this does not touch on time as a precondition for *experiencing* motion phenomena in the first place, which requires the notion of difference, itself grounded in an underlying understanding of time across which difference occurs. Piaget is only interested in how children come to understand chronological time, not in the experience of time as such. Time is at the source of spatial difference, too, as even the recognition of an object as object requires the eye to saccade (which Piaget does not realize when he says that humans "perceive a whole line as simultaneous" [1970, p. 61]), that is, move in time to produce the difference that underlies the (re-) cognition of an object. Piaget and radical constructivists are not at all concerned with the experience of time but rather with an understanding of time as it is used in the sciences. Piaget was interested how children come to develop an understanding of chronological time rather than in the temporality of their experience and therefore their learning. And conceptual change researchers do not consider time other than as what has passed between pre- and post-instruction structures.

In the present book, I place time at the center of experience, describing knowing and learning as essentially temporal phenomena, including the perceptual ground. Chronological time is very different from the experience of flow, the pulsations of activity, actions, and operations; it is very different from my experience of time as something that may stand still, slow down, and speed up. Thus, both knowing and learning require work, they are in time, and they make time. Throughout this book I articulate the various forms of work involved and how these forms change in the course of working. Each act of knowing is an act, and as act, it changes the actor. Already the Greek knew that a person cannot step into the same river twice, but the continuity of human experience and changes therein are absent in received theories of knowing and learning, most notably (radical, social) constructivism and its conceptual change incarnation.

Both chapter 10 and 11 exemplify what an orientation to temporality reveals to the researcher. There are moments that are characterized in terms of *flow*, both with normal everyday involvement in the world and when there are special forms of emotionality involved arising from the fact that something may be done for its own sake. But the engagement is non-intentional in the sense that the learner cannot make thematic that which knowing is going to be, though I-learner may frame what I do in descriptive terms: In chapter 10 I show how I, a trained scientist, pursue an understanding about the extent to which the particle model holds up in explaining the tests following a charging-by-induction procedure. This framing does *not* give me the object of what I want, and it therefore remains open exactly *what* I have to do to get where I will eventually end up finding myself. The fact that I may be on a wild-goose chase or what I later deem to have been cul-de-sacs makes evident that my learning has this non-intentional aspect so that what it is directed at is not and cannot be given.

These non-intentional aspects have a special importance in my way of thinking about learning today, because it allows me to understand why, viewed from the third-person, outsider perspective, students (sometimes, often) appear to be engaged in random, irrational, and trial-and-error variations of what they do and articulate. From the inside, I engage in rational behavior generally being able to articulate why I do what I do. I do what I do and say what I say because perceptual

experience comes onto me without being specifically called upon, because it happens to me rather than being rationally selected from alternatives, and because being ready to learn means that I have to open myself and be vulnerable to the foreign and strange. The notion of trial and error frequently is used in a depreciative
way—to indicate that there is not much preparatory thinking involved. I suggest a
more positive framing: it is exploring and thereby creating a field that is partially
structured in and through exploration and that can subsequently be structured further by means of hermeneutical reduction followed by a logical reduction. These
successive reductions lead to knowledgeability that has some likeness with the
science teachers want and are asked to teach.

Opening myself to the foreign and strange during explorations of foreign territory, making a commitment to be changed and therefore to learning, also means
that I am taking and have to take risks. Prior to talking to the physics professors, I
really made sure that what I am observing would hold up to their scrutiny; and I do
not want to make a fool of myself. I do not know whether that which I come to
perceive and the way I articulate it in my communicative actions is in any way
compatible with what science and science teachers perceive and know. This risk is
also inherent in my own, a physicist's actions, when I attempt to *consistently* reproduce the investigation that charges a metal plate by induction (chapter 10) and
then allow new forms of thinking to emerge into my consciousness, which I subsequently test as to their viability.

Prior to knowing what some learning episode is to teach me, I cannot know
what actions I have to produce and reproduce to make the observation consistent;
and I cannot know whether what I perceive and do reproduce the actions and
perceptions that science and science teachers want me to reproduce. The latter is a
condition to learn science as it is rather than developing my own (naïve and not so
naïve) lenses that allow me to understand and anticipate the observations following
my actions. This risk I take during the learning episode is associated with emotional valences that mediate my engagement at the limit of my knowledgeability,
and, as a result, lead to the experience of *flow*. In flow, the subject of activity no
longer experiences itself as subject that is different from its object, which provides
the intentional impetus (motive) of the actions. That is, flow experiences are based
on an intentional|non-intentional dialectic, because without motives and goals, I
would not do what I do, but in the absence of the subject, there cannot be an intention. That is, the experiences of being absorbed in everyday coping or in flow-
yielding activity transcends the intentionality that is at the core of both constructiv-
ism and cultural theories build on the agency|structure dialectic.

Constructivists inherently cannot say much about these forms of experience,
that is, passivity and passivity of passivity, because the central characterizing verb
of constructivism, *to construct*, is transitive, and therefore has a specific object.
There cannot be a transitive verb when the object is not given; subject, transitive
verb, and object *presuppose* each other—as this is embodied in the various forms
of cultural-historical activity theory. A construction is always a construction of
something, and this something is setting the motive of activity or goal of action.
Inherently, the verb "to construct" therefore highlights the *intentional* aspects of

what learners do at the expense of sensibility, which is the prerequisite for being affected by something or somebody, that is, for having an experience, period. This lack of attention to sensibility is also a problem of the dialectical materialist worldview. I repeatedly show how researchers fail to theorize human learning appropriately when they only focus on actions and agency, which are also integral aspects of constructivist approaches. If agency is all there is, how can human beings sense anything at all? This sensing and the sensibility it presupposes have to be central features of a theory of knowing and learning.

In the third part of this book, *World and Language*, I articulate the relations between engagement in the material world and language, and (in chapters 6, 7) show how communication emerges in and from particular orientations to the world. In particular, I show how perceptual, manipulative, and gestural modes of knowing constitute the ground for verbal discourse to emerge and evolve. These modes initially constitute a unit that does not distinguish between the material body of language and the sense it conveys. But verbal discourse, though it becomes the dominant articulated mode, does not *replace* other modes of knowing but rather accompanies them; it also is the one mode that is able to do what the other modes have done before language reaches a mature form of development. In chapter 8, I then show the reverse trajectory: how I move from reading instructions to doing and creating something in the material world. My doing in the material world presupposes my understanding of what the text describes, which in turn presupposes an understanding of what it denotes. That is, the movement from text to action is evidence for the fact that the bodily modes of understanding have not disappeared but are present, although language may be the only mode overtly articulated at some point in time. But the name of the action in a recipe presupposes my practical understanding of it, which means that the understanding underlying naming includes the action itself. This, too, remains a feature totally obliterated in constructivist and conceptual change work—an expression of their exclusive focus on knowledge as something located underneath the skull and between the ears.

A viable theory of knowledge allows me to understand what I do when I learn. It necessarily accounts for my experience of the world, my perception, and my reasons for acting this rather than that way. What I do and how I do it also is mediated by my emotions, both long-term orientations that I consider in rational cost-benefit ways and present emotional states that are grounded entirely in my body. But reasons for acting and cost-benefit considerations are processes that are inherently social in nature. Even though my own investigations in chapter 10—of the charging-by-induction phenomenon and the particle model supposedly explaining it—involved nobody else, and although the experience of flow was entirely limited to my bodily self, its orientation was inherently social both in terms of its object as object and its orientation toward my being able to account for what I have done. This social orientation lies at the very origin of repeating without apparent reason what others see as having been done already.

Only a stable world can be lifeworld; only a stable world is articulated and can be articulated. Only a stable world orients what I do, because I have evolved practices in which future states are anticipated—implicitly (non-thematized) or explicitly (thematized). This entire book is dedicated to the attempt of articulating knowledgeability and the experience of the learner through the learner's eyes. To know what I do, even if this means knowing that I do not know what I do, researchers trying to understand my cognition need to theorize me acting and perceiving in my lifeworld and at its limits. Without it, researchers fail to understand that the two gigantic twin towers by my wayside do not exist for me and instead attribute my failure to engage in particular learning actions because I "misinterpret," "misconstrue," or "alternatively construct" what is at hand. My purpose therefore is to give reason back to learners, understanding what they do and why they do what they do, and thereby allowing them to both reproduce as well as produce in new ways the actions, events, and objects that surround them in their sociomaterial worlds. Giving learning back to me-learner and my experience—and giving it back to me as something that involves my emotions and bodily states, my anxieties and states of flow—lies at the very heart of what I have been working at in the writing of this book.

CHANGING EDUCATIONAL PRACTICE

The theoretical perspective on the relationship between perception, on the one hand, and learning and development, on the other, has profound implications for education. I do not have the space for elaborating on these implications and therefore limit myself to the following comments.

Science demonstrations and science museums are based on the (implicit) assumption that perception extracts something from visual stimuli (by looking, starring, observing, etc.) and that this something supports understanding science. Likewise, the use of hands-on activities is based on the presupposition that students can extract something from their perceptual experience that leads to or supports the development of abstract scientific knowledge. How this is supposed to happen is seldom if ever discussed in the literature on learning from hands-on activities. If lifeworlds (and their objects) are brought forth through active exploration and if perception differs inherently then we need to begin research on knowing and learning by investigating what students actually rather than what they possibly perceive or ought to perceive. Students react to and change because of the things *they* perceive, which they integrate in their thoughts and action-guidance, rather than because of the (theoretical) structures that researchers, teachers, or physicists describe. Science educators generally forget that our worlds are not pre-given but that what is perceptually available to me had, at one point, emerged into my conscious thought during exploration. This amnesia impedes the understanding of students' difficulties in learning from a simple observation such as this occurs in demonstrations. Perhaps a critical and reflective investigation of their own learning difficulties would allow teachers to improve addressing the learning difficulties of their students.

I can assume that students' perceptions (in laboratory activities, demonstrations) provide them with a fundamental experience; these orient what students do and perceive as real. But, looking at something once or twice usually does not allow students perceive—that is, to know how things are from how they look. Thus, I have had to cross the same intersection many times from different directions and under different light conditions before it was an object for me in its own right, which I could know and know about. This form of perceiving requires extended exploration. Yet, to provide another example, many textbooks provide just one photograph to illustrate a concept. Clearly, one sample image is insufficient for learning to make a perceptual distinction between instances and non-instances of a concept; that is, one image does not allow the perceiver to distinguish invariant features to those that are incidental with respect to the object to be known.

A dialectical phenomenology of perception is therefore foundational to further reflection on the relation between conscious observers and their worlds. However, the present investigation shows that I have no conscious control over what is perceptually revealed to me in the next moment. I do not construct our perception or observations; this image of someone constructing perceptions and knowledge is akin to the Cartesian homunculus extracting information from the screen. Rather, I show how new objects and events are thrust into my (singular plural) awareness and therefore become furniture for my lifeworld. At best, then, I can prepare for perceiving in new ways by putting myself into a state of readiness, allowing myself to be open toward disclosure of the unknown. (This is the same disposition required of the researcher, who attempts to make sense of videotapes, transcripts, or interviews. It is through extended exploration of my materials [databases] that I come to see new social psychological phenomena.)

The value of conscious reflection in the evolution of perception does not lie in some capacity to overcome perception but rather in its capacity to remain faithful to the sensorial sources from which it sprang. It is when the things I perceptually track emerge as new figure|ground configurations and are then integrated into my capacities for thought and action-guidance that I change from merely looking at to *seeing*. To become salient at all, a phenomenon (to be discriminated as this or that event within a dynamic situation as a whole) must have underlying invariant structure that changes only insignificantly in the course of repeating exploration. Perception presupposes—and includes as its inextricable feature—the exploration of the world. The resulting invariants are hierarchically organized and concern the whole|parts structure of the event; that is, some elements are suppressed whereas others are essential.

In sum, I show in this book that to perceive is, in some ways, to encounter and give sense to the world by actively exploring and orienting within it. Perception is a changing process that continually constitutes new phenomena. Each time I perceive something new, I also reconstitute my world by taking what is salient and giving it sense and forget in a process of amnesia how the world has been before. This has considerable implications for educational research and praxis. If developing and learning individuals always and already act in and toward a subjective world, I have to ask, "How is it possible that they eventually come to by-and-large agree on perceiving the world in the same way?" (There are exceptions, which are treated under such labels as schizophrenia, hallucinations, etc.) "How is it possible that some individuals become scientists, learn to perceive the world in a particular way, although their early perceptions are rather distinct from those of scientists?" "How do individuals become scientists when they cannot derive structures by interacting with a fixed world?" Teachers and researchers must remain aware that they act in a polythetic world, that is, in a world where entities and concepts share many common characteristics without that any one of them has to be essential for being in the same group. The world simply is not monothetic, that is, structured uniquely so that merely looking would give me *the* single possible way of seeing things, and therefore the things themselves. And this can lead to an understanding that being inherently is being singular plural. It is this double nature, linking singularity and plurality, which is fundamental to the individual and collective nature of human experience and knowledgeability in general and language in particular.

Ultimately, this book is about position, which inherently is dis-position, a different position, which comes with a different disposition and perspective. I am articulating and arguing for a different position than the one that science educators have taken heretofore. Changing position allows science educators to see their work in a different way, but they have to develop the disposition of seeing in new ways similar to students asked to see physical phenomena in new ways. This book therefore also constitutes the description of a new form of map, a new set of lenses to be donned. As any set of lenses, any position, the one I propose comes with presuppositions (really, pre-sup-positions), not all of which can be articulated simultaneously with the position *precisely* because this requires taking a different position. But I wrote this book in the hope that it might assist other science educators to develop a better understanding of the fundamental aporias involved in perceiving the world in a particular (scientific) way and learning to navigate (with) the maps that are particular to science. Being singular plural inherently means that any learning is my-learning, a first-person experience, which therefore requires a first-person perspective to be understood. But being singular plural also means that all experience is inherently intelligible, realizes a singularity the possibility of which already inheres in the plurality of the world. A singular plural (first-person) perspective on learning therefore does not lead to solipsism. In fact, the opposite is the case. Taking a singular plural perspective leads science educators immediately to culture and the possibilities for understanding phenomena and their explications generally. Taking a singular plural perspective also implies re-introducing time and temporality into theories of learning, accounting for my experience of being in the world, perceiving what I perceive, making the decisions I make under the constraints I am conscious off. It means allowing learning to be the learning of human beings, aspirations, emotionality, and temporality included.

REFERENCES

Amerine, R., & Bilmes, J. (1990). Following instructions. In M. Lynch & S. Woolgar (Eds.), *Representation in scientific practice* (pp. 323–335). Cambridge, MA: MIT Press.

Bateson, G. (1972). *Steps to an ecology of mind*. New York: Ballantine.

Bateson, G. (1980). *Mind and nature: A necessary unity*. Toronto: Bantam Books.

Bergson, H. (1969). *L'évolution créatrice*. Paris: Presses Universitaires de France.

Bourdieu, P. (1980). *Le sens pratique*. Paris: Les Éditions de Minuit. (English translation, R. Nice, *The logic of practice*, Cambridge, UK: Polity Press, 1990.)

Bourdieu, P. (1997). *Méditations pascaliennes*. Paris: Seuil. (English translation, R. Nice, Pascalian meditations, Stanford: Stanford University Press, 2000.)

Bucciarelli, L. L. (1994). *Designing engineers*. Cambridge, MA: MIT Press.

Butterworth, B., & Hadar, U. (1989). Gesture, speech, and computational stages: A reply to McNeill. *Psychological Review, 96*, 168–174.

Csikszentmihaly, M. (1997). *Creativity: Flow and the psychology of discovery and invention*. New York: Perennial.

Cole, M., & Levitin, K. (2000). A cultural-historical view of human nature. In N. Roughley (Ed.), *Being humans: Anthropological universality and particularity in transdisciplinary perspectives* (pp. 64–80). New York: deGruyter.

Collins, H. (2001). Tacit knowledge, trust and the Q of sapphire. *Social Studies of Science, 31*, 71–85.

Davidson, D. (1986). A nice derangement of epitaphs. In E. Lepore (Ed.), *Truth and interpretation* (pp. 433–446). Oxford: Blackwell.

Deleuze, G. (1994). *Repetition and difference* (P. Patton, Trans.). New York: Columbia University Press. (First published in 1968)

Depraz, N., Varela, F. & Vermersch, P. (2002). *On becoming aware: Steps to a phenomenological pragmatics*. Amsterdam: Benjamins.

Derrida, J. (1981). *Dissemination*. Chicago: University of Chicago Press.

Derrida, J. (1999). *Adieu to Emmanuel Levinas*. Stanford, CA: Stanford University Press:

Derrida, J. (2005). *On touching—Jean-Luc Nancy*. Stanford, CA: Stanford University Press.

Désautels, J., & Roth, W.-M. (1999). Demystifying epistemology. *Cybernetics & Human Knowing, 6*(1), 33–45.

Dreyfus, H. L. (1991). *Being-in-the-world: A commentary on Heidegger's 'Being and Time,' division I*. Cambridge, MA: MIT Press.

Duit, R., & Treagust, D. (1998). Learning in science—From behaviorism toward social constructivism and beyond. In B. J. Fraser & K. G.. Tobin (Eds.), *International handbook of science education* (pp. 3–25). Dordrecht, The Netherlands: Kluwer Academic Publishers.

Franck, D. (2001). *Dramatique des phénomènes*. Paris: Presses Universitaires de France

Garfinkel, H. (1967). *Studies in ethnomethodology*. Englewood Cliffs, NJ: Prentice-Hall.

Garfinkel, H. (2002). *Ethnomethodology's program: Working out Durkheim's aphorism*. Lanham, NY: Rowman & Littlefield.

Gibson, J. J. (1986). *The ecological approach to visual perception*. Hillsdale, NJ: Lawrence Erlbaum Associates.

Glasersfeld, E. von (2004a). Questions et réponses au sujet du constructivisme radical. In P. Jonnaert & D. Masciotra (dir.), *Constructivisme—choix contemporains: hommage à Ernst von Glasersfeld* (pp. 291–317). Québec: Presses de l'Université du Québec.

REFERENCES

Glasersfeld, E. von (2004b). Introduction à un constructivisme radical. In P. Jonnaert & D. Masciotra (dir.), *Constructivisme—choix contemporains: hommage à Ernst von Glasersfeld* (pp. 11–36). Québec: Presses de l'Université du Québec.

Gooding, D. (1990). *Experiment and the making of meaning: Human agency in scientific observation and experiment.* Dordrecht, The Netherlands: Kluwer Academic Publishers.

Hegel, G.W.F. (1977). *Phenomenology of spirit* (A. V. Miller, Trans.). Oxford: Oxford University Press.

Heidegger, M. (1977). *Sein und Zeit.* Tübingen: Niemeyer. (English version: *Being and time,* J. Stambaugh, Trans. Albany: State University of New York Press, 1996.)

Held, R., & Hein, A. (1963). Movement-produced stimulation in the development of visually guided behavior. *Journal of Comparative and Physiological Psychology, 56,* 872–876.

Holzkamp, K. (1983). *Grundlegung der Psychologie.* Frankfurt/M.: Campus.

Holzkamp, K. (1993). *Lernen: Subjektwissenschaftliche Grundlegung.* Frankfurt/M.: Campus.

Husserl, E. (1952). *Ideen. Husserliana IV* (Hrsg. M. Biemel). Den Haag: Martinus Nijhoff.

Husserl, E. (1969). Formal and transcendental logic (D. Cairns, Trans.). The Hague: Martinus Nijhoff. (First published in 1929)

Inhelder, B., & Piaget, J. (1958). *The growth of logical thinking from childhood to adolescence.* New York: Basic.

Kant, I. (1968). *Werke III: Kritik der reinen Vernunft 1.* Frankfurt a/M.: Suhrkamp.

Kirsh, D. (1995). The intelligent use of space. *Artificial Intelligence, 73,* 31–68.

Lakoff, G. (1987). *Women, fire, and dangerous things: What categories reveal about the mind.* Chicago: University of Chicago Press.

Latour, B. (1983). Give me a laboratory and I will raise the world. In K. D. Knorr-Cetina & M. Mulkay (Eds.), *Science observed: Perspectives on the social study of science* (pp. 141–170). London: Sage.

Law, J., & Lynch, M. (1990). Lists, field guides, and the descriptive organization of seeing: Birdwatching as an exemplary observational activity. In M. Lynch & S. Woolgar (Eds.), *Representation in scientific practice* (pp. 267–299). Cambridge, MA: MIT Press.

Leont'ev, A. N. (1978). *Activity, consciousness and personality.* Englewood Cliffs, NJ: Prentice Hall.

Levinas, E. (1969). *Totality and infinity* (A. Lingis, Trans.). Pittsburgh, PA: Duquesne University Press.

Levinas, E. (1978a). *Autrement qu'être ou au-delà de l'essence.* La Haye : Martinus Nijhoff. (English version : *Otherwise than being or Beyond essence,* A. Lingis, Trans. Pittsburgh, PA: Duquesne University Press, 1998.)

Levinas, E. (1978b). Existence and existants (A. Lingis, Trans.). The Hague: Nijhoff.

Levinas, E. (1987). *Time and the other* (R. A. Cohen, Trans.). Pittsburgh, PA: Duquesne University Press.

Lynch, M., Livingston, E., & Garfinkel, H. (1983). Temporal order in laboratory work. In K. D. Knorr-Cetina & M. Mulkay (Eds.), *Science observed: Perspectives on the social study of science* (pp. 205–238). London: Sage.

McNeill, D. (1992). *Hand and mind: What gestures reveal about thought.* Chicago: University of Chicago Press.

Merleau-Ponty, M. (1945). *Phénoménologie de la perception.* Paris: Gallimard. (English version: *Phenomenology of perception,* C. Smith, Trans. London: Routledge, 1962.)

Merleau-Ponty, M. (1964). *L'œil et l'esprit.* Paris: Gallimard.

Metz, K. E. (1993). Preschoolers' developing knowledge of the pan balance: From new representation to transformed problem solving. *Cognition and Instruction, 11,* 31–93.

Mikhailov, F. (1980). *The riddle of self.* Moscow: Progress.

Müller, A.M.K. (1972). Die präparierte Zeit: Der Mensch in der Krise seiner eigenen Zielsetzung. Stuttgart, Germany: Radius.

Nancy, J.-L. (1992). *Corpus.* Paris: Métailé.

Nancy, J.-L. (2000). *Being singular plural.* Stanford, CA: Stanford University Press.

Pessoa, L., Thompson, E., & Noë, A. (1998). Finding out about filling in: A guide to perceptual completion for visual science and the philosophy of perception. *Behavioral and Brain Sciences, 21*, 723–802.

Piaget, J. (1970). *Genetic epistemology*. New York: Norton.

Pickering, A. (1995). *The mangle of practice*. Chicago: University of Chicago Press.

Quine, W. V. (1995). *From stimulus to science*. Cambridge, MA: Harvard University Press.

Ricœur, P. (1984). *Time and narrative Vol. 1*. Chicago: University of Chicago Press.

Ricœur, P. (1985). *Time and narrative Vol. 2*. Chicago: University of Chicago Press.

Ricœur, P. (1988). *Time and narrative Vol. 3*. Chicago: University of Chicago Press.

Ricœur, P. (1991). *From text to action: Essays in hermeneutics, II*. Evanston, IL: Northwestern University Press.

Roth, W.-M. (1995). *Authentic school science: Knowing and learning in open-inquiry science laboratories*. Dordrecht, The Netherlands: Kluwer Academic Publishing.

Roth, W.-M. (1998). Starting small and with uncertainty: Toward a neurocomputational account of knowing and learning in science. *International Journal of Science Education, 20*, 1089–1105.

Roth, W.-M. (2000). From gesture to scientific language. *Journal of Pragmatics, 32*, 1683–1714.

Roth, W.-M. (2002). Gestures: Their role in teaching and learning. *Review of Educational Research, 71*, 365–392.

Roth, W.-M. (2003). Competent workplace mathematics: How signs become transparent in use. *International Journal of Computers for Mathematical Learning, 8*, 161–189.

Roth, W.-M. (2004a). Emergence of graphing practices in scientific research. *Journal of Cognition and Culture, 4*, 595–627.

Roth, W.-M. (2004b). Perceptual gestalts in workplace communication. *Journal of Pragmatics, 36*, 1037–1069.

Roth, W.-M. (2005a). *Doing qualitative research: Praxis of method*. Rotterdam: Sense.

Roth, W.-M. (2005b). Making classifications (at) work: Ordering practices in science. *Social Studies of Science, 35*, 581–621.

Roth, W.-M. (2005c). Mathematical inscriptions and the reflexive elaboration of understanding: An ethnography of graphing and numeracy in a fish hatchery. *Mathematical Thinking and Learning, 7*, 75–109.

Roth, W.-M. (2005d). *Talking science: Language and learning in science*. Lanham, MD: Rowman & Littlefield.

Roth, W.-M., & Duit, R. (2003). Emergence, flexibility, and stabilization of language in a physics classroom. *Journal for Research in Science Teaching, 40*, 869–897.

Roth, W.-M., Hwang, S., Lee, Y-J., & Goulart, M. (2005). *Participation, learning, and identity: Dialectical perspectives*. Berlin: Lehmanns Media.

Roth, W.-M., McRobbie, C., Lucas, K. B., & Boutonné, S. (1997a). The local production of order in traditional science laboratories: A phenomenological analysis. *Learning and Instruction, 7*, 107–136.

Roth, W.-M., McRobbie, C., Lucas, K. B., & Boutonné, S. (1997b). Why do students fail to learn from demonstrations? A social practice perspective on learning in physics. *Journal of Research in Science Teaching, 34*, 509–533.

Roth, W.-M., & Pozzer-Ardenghi, L. (2006). Tracking situated, distributed, and embodied communication in real time. In M. A. Vanchevsky (Ed.), *Focus on cognitive psychology research*. Hauppauge, NY: Nova Science.

Roth, W.-M., Pozzer-Ardenghi, L., & Han, J. (2005). *Critical graphicacy: Understanding visual representation practices in school science*. Dordrecht, The Netherlands: Springer.

Roth, W.-M., & Roychoudhury, A. (1992). The social construction of scientific concepts or The concept map as conscription device and tool for social thinking in high school science. *Science Education, 76*, 531–557.

Sewell, W. H. (1992). A theory of structure: duality, agency and transformation. *American Journal of Sociology, 98*, 1–29.

341

REFERENCES

Smith, D. E. (1987). *The everyday world as problematic: A feminist sociology.* Toronto: University of Toronto Press.

Smith, B. (1997). Boundaries: An essay in mereotopology. In L. E. Hahn (Ed.), *The philosophy of Roderick Chisholm* (pp. 534–561). La Salle, IL: Open Court.

Smith, B. (2001). Objects and their environments: From Aristotle to ecological psychology. In A. Frank, J. Raper, & J.-P. Cheylan (Eds.), *The life and motion of socio-economic units* (pp. 79–97). London: Taylor and Francis.

Smith, B., & Casati, R. (1994). Naïve physics: An essay in ontology. *Philosophical Psychology, 7,* 225–244.

Suchman, L. A. (1987). *Plans and situated actions: The problem of human-machine communication.* Cambridge: Cambridge University Press.

Suchman, L. A., & Trigg, R. H. (1993). Artificial intelligence as craftwork. In S. Chaiklin & J. Lave (Eds.), *Understanding practice: Perspectives on activity and context* (pp. 144–178). Cambridge: Cambridge University Press.

Tweney, R. D., & Chitwood, S. C. (1995). Scientific reasoning. In S. Newstead & J.S.B.T. Evans (Eds.), *Perspectives on thinking and reasoning: Essays in honour of Peter Wason* (pp. 241–260). Hove, East Sussex: Lawrence Erlbaum Associates.

Uexküll, J. von (1973). *Theoretische Biologie.* Frankfurt a/M.: Suhrkamp. (First published in 1928)

van Gelder, T. (1998). The dynamical hypothesis in cognitive science. *Behavioral and Brain Sciences, 21,* 616–665.

van Gelder, T. J., & Port, R. (1995) It's about time: An overview of the dynamical approach to cognition. In R. Port & T. van Gelder (Eds.), *Mind as motion: Explorations in the dynamics of cognition* (pp. 1–43). Cambridge MA: MIT Press.

Vygotsky, L. S. (1986). *Thought and language.* Cambridge, MA: MIT Press.

Vygotsky, L. S. (1989). Concrete human psychology. *Soviet Psychology, 27*(2), 53–77.

Wartofsky, M. (1979). *Models: Representations and scientific understanding.* Dordrecht, The Netherlands: Reidel.

Widlok, T. (1997). Orientation in the wild: The shared cognition of Hai‖om bushpeople. *Journal of the Royal Anthropological Institute, 3,* 317–332.

INDEX

T

U

V

W

ABOUT THE AUTHOR

Wolff-Michael Roth is Lansdowne Professor of Applied Cognitive Science at the University of Victoria, British Columbia, Canada. For most of the 1980–1992 period, he taught science, mathematics, and computer science at the middle and high school levels. From 1992 on, already working at the university, he taught science in British Columbia elementary schools at the fourth- through seventh-grade levels always associated with research on knowing and learning. More recently, he has conducted several ethnographic studies of scientific research, a variety of workplaces, and environmental activist movements. His research focuses on cultural-historical, linguistic, and embodied aspects of scientific and mathematical cognition and communication from elementary school to professional practice, including, among others, studies of scientists, technicians, and environmentalists at their work sites.

In 1999, the author followed an invitation to spend three months as fellow in the cognitive neuroscience section of the *Hanse Institute of Advanced Studies* located in Delmenhorst, a town in northern Germany not far from Bremen. At the University of Bremen, he was associated with the physics education department, most notably with Manuela Welzel and Stefan von Aufschnaiter and their research group. This book is to a large extent the outcome of the work conducted during this stay, which afforded him to engage in research unfettered by the normal demands of his professorial life. The particular investigations evolved from the attempt to construct evidence that was inconsistent with the (radical) constructivist and conceptual change positions that the physics educators represented.

Wolff-Michael Roth publishes widely and in different disciplines, including linguistics, social studies of science, and different subfields in education (curriculum, mathematics education, science education). His recent books include *Toward an Anthropology of Science: Semiotic and Activity Theoretic Perspectives* (2003), *Rethinking Scientific Literacy* (2004, with A. C. Barton), *Talking Science: Language and Learning in Science Classrooms* (2005), *Participation, Learning, and Identity: Dialectical Perspectives* (with S. Hwang, Y. J. Lee, and M.I.M. Goulart, 2005). He most recently completed *Doing Qualitative Research: Praxis of Method* (2005) and edited *Auto/biography and Auto/ethnography: Praxis of Research Method* (2005), both published by SensePublisher. He has received many awards for specific research articles, books, and his research programs from organizations both within and outside education.

Printed in the United States
84442LV00002B/103/A